© Jeffrey MacMillan

TODD S. PURDUM is the author of *An Idea Whose Time Has Come* and *A Time of Our Choosing*. He is a staff writer for *The Atlantic*, having previously worked for more than twenty years at *The New York Times*, where he covered beats from city hall to the White House and served as Los Angeles bureau chief. He has also been a contributing editor at *Vanity Fair* and a senior writer at *Politico*. A native of Macomb, Illinois, and a graduate of Princeton University, he lives in Los Angeles with his wife, Dee Dee Myers, and their two children.

Additional Praise for *Something Wonderful*

"[A] delightful new book . . . [Their impact is] Broadway magic if anything is, and Todd Purdum has given readers the most elaborate and entertaining exploration of that magic they're ever likely to read."
—*The Christian Science Monitor*

"Remind[s] us of the bold breadth of the business—in the broadest sense—of the Rodgers and Hammerstein partnership, [whose] melodies . . . ventured sprawlingly across the planet, all day and deep into the night."
—*The Wall Street Journal*

"A fresh and revelatory look at the personalities of these legendary figures, their relationship with each other, their creative process, and their groundbreaking innovations . . . Full of illuminating anecdotes about the biggest stars of the day . . . A celebration of the lives and legacy of one of the most iconic partnerships in artistic history, sure to please anyone who loves musical theater."
—*Broadway World*

"A beautifully balanced accounting of two complicated men, the theater artists who surrounded them, and the quite astounding works they created. Purdum writes with grace and care about the creation of their best and their least achievements, and he subtly points to their differences and difficulties as human beings . . . Like the R&H catalog itself, he takes on his subject with taste, relish, fairness, and a clear sense of the importance of the subject matter. A wonderful read."
—Jack Viertel, author of *The Secret Life of the American Musical*

"*Something Wonderful* is above all a marvelous book about the arts and the artistic process. Todd S. Purdum provides a more than satisfying biography of Rodgers and Hammerstein, their successes and failures, their marriages, their money. But he's just as comfortable, and very acute, writing about their craft . . . On top of everything else, *Something Wonderful* has soul . . . I'm happy to have read this book, and I was also extremely happy while I was reading it. It's a very happy book, and you can't say that about everything we read." —Nick Hornby, *The Believer*

"Come backstage . . . It's all here in Purdum's book. From describing the real-life moment that inspired 'Some Enchanted Evening' to detailing the drafts for 'Edelweiss,' Purdum has produced something wonderful indeed." —*BookPage*

"This brisk and lively biography of the greatest team in musical-theater history remains happily focused on what matters most: the shows . . . A solid, affectionate description of artists who look more important today than at any time since, oh, 1945." —*Broadway Direct*

"Readers will learn the stories behind the music and how this most successful of writing duos crafted some of the finest musicals to grace the American stage . . . Something wonderful, indeed." —*Booklist* (starred review)

"Purdum's anecdote-filled account is a sterling primer on the influential duo, both for newcomers to their work and to those looking to rekindle an old flame." —*Publishers Weekly*

"Joyous, brisk, and gossipy . . . An exuberant celebration of musical genius." —*Kirkus Reviews*

"Scrupulously researched and infinitely fascinating . . . An impressive addition to the literature celebrating the American musical theater." —Harold Prince

"Rodgers and Hammerstein drew pictures, made lists. They understood and rewrote the longings of the heart . . . I love the intimacy of the stories Todd Purdum tells—he shows himself to be especially sensitive to Oscar Hammerstein's special connection with Richard Rodgers." —Carly Simon

"Clear, precise, and passionate, this is a necessary book, and even better, one that is a joy to read." —James Kaplan, author of *Frank: The Voice* and *Sinatra: The Chairman*

Something Wonderful

Something Wonderful

RODGERS AND HAMMERSTEIN'S BROADWAY REVOLUTION

TODD S. PURDUM

PICADOR   HENRY HOLT AND COMPANY   NEW YORK

picadorusa.com • instagram.com/picador
twitter.com/picadorusa • facebook.com/picadorusa

Picador® is a U.S. registered trademark and is used by Macmillan Publishing Group, LLC, under license from Pan Books Limited.

For book club information, please visit facebook.com/picadorbookclub or email marketing@picadorusa.com.

Designed by Kelly S. Too

The Library of Congress has cataloged the Henry Holt edition as follows:

Names: Purdum, Todd S., author.
Title: Something wonderful : Rodgers and Hammerstein's Broadway revolution / Todd S. Purdum.
Description: First edition | New York : Henry Holt & Company, 2018. | Includes bibliographical references and index.
Identifiers: LCCN 2017044836 (print) | LCCN 2018025112 (ebook) | ISBN 9781627798358 (ebook) | ISBN 9781627798341 (hardcover)
Subjects: LCSH: Rodgers, Richard, 1902–1979. | Hammerstein, Oscar, II, 1895–1960. | Composers—United States—Biography. | Lyricists—United States—Biography. | Musicals—United States—20th century—History and criticism.
Classification: LCC ML410.R6315 (ebook) | LCC ML410.R6315 P87 2018 (print) | DDC 782.1'40922 [B] —dc23
LC record available at https://lccn.loc.gov/2017044836

Picador Paperback ISBN 978-1-250-21486-7

Our books may be purchased in bulk for promotional, educational, or business use. Please contact your local bookseller or the Macmillan Corporate and Premium Sales Department at 1-800-221-7945, extension 5442, or by email at MacmillanSpecialMarkets@macmillan.com.

First published by Henry Holt and Company, LLC

First Picador Edition: May 2019

10 9 8 7 6 5 4 3 2 1

For my parents,
who taught me these songs

And for Dee Dee, Kate, and Stephen,
who make my heart sing them

CONTENTS

Prologue: All They Cared About Was the Show   1

1. The Sentimentalist   15

2. A Quality of Yearning   39

3. Away We Go   65

4. Bustin' Out   96

5. So Far   121

6. Enchanted Evening   146

7. Parallel Wives   177

8. Catastrophic Success   204

9. Beyond Broadway   235

10. Auf Wiedersehen   267

11. Walking Alone   296

Epilogue: Bloom and Grow Forever   314

Notes	321
Bibliography	347
Acknowledgments	353
Permissions Acknowledgments	359
Index	365

Something Wonderful

Prologue

ALL THEY CARED ABOUT WAS THE SHOW

At the stroke of 8:00 p.m. on the rainy Sunday evening of March 31, 1957, in a converted vaudeville house on Upper Broadway in Manhattan, timpani rolled, herald trumpets blared a fanfare, and soon a chorus sang out, "The prince is giving a ball!" The crowded old theater at the corner of West 81st Street was the CBS Television Network's smallest color studio, No. 72, but the program beaming live from its transmitters was being broadcast over the largest network ever assembled—245 local stations from coast to coast, including twenty-nine in Canada. The network had bigger, better studios in Hollywood, but this one had been chosen for its proximity to New York's theater scene. For the real hosts of the evening were no mere princes, but the kings of Broadway themselves: Richard Rodgers and Oscar Hammerstein II, the reigning creators and impresarios of the modern musical theater, and two of the most influential producers of mass popular entertainment in Eisenhower-era America.

This evening's production was *Cinderella*, a ninety-minute original musical play created especially for television, and it found Rodgers and Hammerstein at the very height of their powers. With a budget of $385,000, a live orchestra of thirty-three pieces, and an all-star cast,

Cinderella preempted *The Ed Sullivan Show* and *General Electric Theater*, two of the most popular programs of the day. Sponsored by Pepsi-Cola and the Shulton Company, makers of Old Spice toiletries, the special broadcast was ballyhooed in full-page newspaper advertisements across the country and promoted in more than a hundred announcements over CBS stations alone. Shulton had offered a portable television set, two clock radios, and ten recordings for those station managers who did the most to promote the show. Letters were sent to the principals of public schools, urging them to encourage their students to watch the program, and Kenyon & Eckhardt, Pepsi's advertising agency, sponsored prizes for a letter-writing contest in which people were asked to nominate "the nicest person I know" or to suggest "my wish for my town." Five million four-page color *Cinderella* comic books were printed for insertion into cartons of Pepsi, and a long-playing album of the show's score would be on sale from Columbia Records first thing Monday morning.

By now, this level of interest, attention, and dominance was par for the course for Rodgers and Hammerstein. After all, this was the team that had revolutionized the American musical theater, integrating song, story, and dance as never before with their blockbuster *Oklahoma!* in 1943, and then gone on to create the beloved and enduring hits *Carousel*, *South Pacific*, and *The King and I*—a new show every other year for fourteen years and counting. Their songs, a bursting catalogue written for specific characters and dramatic situations in individual plays, had nevertheless produced a powerhouse lineup of popular hits, from "People Will Say We're in Love," to "You'll Never Walk Alone," to "Getting to Know You," that had become part of the soundtrack, the background music, the very vernacular of America. The titles themselves—"There Is Nothin' Like a Dame," "Oh, What a Beautiful Mornin'," "I Whistle a Happy Tune"—evoked the infectious, ebullient, can-do optimism of the era.

What is more, Rodgers and Hammerstein were also universally regarded by even their envious peers and competitors as perhaps the best (and richest) pair of businessmen in show business—with their own music publishing house, sole ownership of their dramatic properties, and a casting and producing organization that held open auditions every Thursday morning to spot new talent and fill out long-running and touring productions of their shows. They had pioneered the practice of recording original cast albums of Broadway musicals and were the first to exploit lucrative merchandising tie-ins for their shows, with themed pajamas, dolls, and tropical fashions from *South Pacific*. Just three years earlier, in 1954, the General Foods Corporation had chosen to celebrate its twenty-fifth anniversary with an all-star tribute to Rodgers and Hammerstein, a program carried on all four extant television networks.

Now the boys were aiming even higher, bringing *Cinderella* to CBS in an effort to top NBC's highly successful live productions of a musical version of *Peter Pan*, starring Mary Martin, in 1955 and 1956. Their package deal with the network called for them to bear the "above the board" costs of the show—that is, talent, costumes, scenery, and so on—while the network would pay for cameras, lights, sound, and technical equipment. Rodgers and Hammerstein would own the finished show outright, with an option for a single rebroadcast by CBS. And they had scored a casting coup: Julie Andrews, then the hottest star on Broadway, moonlighting from her role as Eliza Doolittle in *My Fair Lady*, to play Cinderella.

Rodgers and Hammerstein had first met Andrews two years earlier, when she auditioned for a role in what turned out to be their biggest commercial and critical flop, *Pipe Dream*, a musical set among the raffish characters of John Steinbeck's Cannery Row. Rodgers had sarcastically pronounced her singing "absolutely adequate," and asked if she was up for other parts. She had replied that Frederick Loewe and Alan Jay Lerner had approached her about a musical version of George Bernard Shaw's *Pygmalion*, which they would in fact transform into *My Fair Lady*. So now a happy reunion was possible, and Andrews managed to squeeze rehearsals for *Cinderella* into her days and afternoons off. The creative team rounded out the cast with a roster of some of Broadway's most reliable names: Howard Lindsay, the co-author and co-star of *Life with Father* (to this day the longest-running nonmusical play in Broadway history) and his wife, Dorothy Stickney, as the king and queen; Edie Adams, fresh from her triumph as Daisy Mae in *Li'l Abner*, as the fairy godmother; the comediennes Kaye Ballard and Alice

Ghostley as the stepsisters; Ilka Chase as the stepmother; and an unknown newcomer named Jon Cypher as the prince. (The production floor manager was also just getting his start in show business, but he would go on to big things: Joseph Papp, founder of the New York Shakespeare Festival and the Public Theater.)

Hammerstein, who wrote the libretto, had kept the *Cinderella* story simple and sweet: no modern touches, no anachronistic interpolations, no wised-up twentieth-century idioms. But the logistical demands of the production were daunting. Studio 72, a former Keith-Albee-Orpheum vaudeville house and later a movie theater, was a cramped space of just forty-two hundred square feet whose orchestra seats had been removed and filled in with concrete to make a level playing surface with the stage. Into this shoe box would have to be fit at least seven sets (of necessity, vertical ones) in tones of lavender and chartreuse, bulky color cameras, dressing areas for men and women, and a walled-off echo chamber for an orchestra that included violins, various woodwinds, horns, and a harp. "I just thought it was going to be the greatest train wreck in the history of show business," Adams would recall.

To guard against that possibility, a rigorous rehearsal schedule was laid out, including two full-scale dress run-throughs that the producers referred to as the New Haven and Boston out-of-town tryouts that were then standard practice for Broadway-bound musicals. At one rehearsal Rodgers himself, always a stickler for having his music performed exactly as written, interrupted the director, a television veteran named Ralph Nelson. "Yes, Mr. Rodgers, what is it?" Nelson asked. "That boy in the second row in the back, you're singing an E-flat instead of an E-natural," Rodgers replied.

The special effects were crude by modern standards—a shot of a burning sparkler superimposed over a shot of the fairy godmother to herald her arrival; a comparable effect for the pumpkin-turned-carriage; and a system to administer a small shock to the four white mice who were about ready to be transformed into horses but had a tendency to grow somnolent in their cage under the hot studio lights. And because of the technical limitations of the time, viewers on the West Coast would not see the full-color production at all, only a kinescope—a black-and-white film version shot off a television monitor, which is the record of the evening that survives today.

The final run-through ended at 4:30 p.m. on the afternoon of the broadcast, and a few minutes later, Ralph Nelson assembled the cast for a pep talk. "I love television," he told them. "The trouble is, it's the closing night. I want it to be your best performance.... I'm worried about people being nervous.... It's there in the control room also.... I want this performance for myself.... Do exactly what I'm expecting you to do.... I love you all.... If I said anything more, I'd cry."

Nelson needn't have worried. There were a few glitches, yes. At one point, Cypher, who would go on to fame as Chief of Police Fletcher Daniels in *Hill Street Blues*, sang over some lines that were supposed to be Dorothy Stickney's. Critical reception would prove to be somewhat mixed, with Jack Gould of the *New York Times* complaining that "the warmth of ageless make-believe sometimes was submerged in the efficiency of the modern touch." But the audience? The audience was stupendous. More people watched *Cinderella* together than had ever collectively watched any event in the history of the planet to that point. At least 107 million people saw part of the program, in a country whose population at the time was roughly 172 million. Even today, only the Super Bowl draws an audience close to comparable. The viewers on that single Sunday evening would have filled a typical Broadway theater seven nights a week—for 165 years.

"I walked outside the theater Sunday night ... and the streets were absolutely—it was raining—the streets were absolutely deserted," Jon Cypher would recall. "Absolutely deserted. There were no cars, there were no people. It was almost as though they had dropped a neutron bomb, that the buildings had been preserved but all the people had died. It was a very, very peculiar feeling. Everybody was inside watching the show."

THE DATE OF *Cinderella*'s broadcast was no coincidence for Richard Rodgers and Oscar Hammerstein. Everybody had been inside watching their shows since another March 31, exactly fourteen years earlier, when their first collaboration, *Oklahoma!*, had opened at the St. James Theatre in the middle of World War II and turned the American musical theater upside down. From the distance of three-quarters of a century, it is difficult to fathom just how revolutionary *Oklahoma!* was in its day. It was not, as is so often said, the first musical play to integrate dance into its drama. (Rodgers's *On Your Toes* had done that.) Nor was it the first to eschew typical musical comedy conventions, such as an opening chorus. (Rodgers's *Pal Joey* had done that, too.) Nor was it the first to deal with serious themes and personalities in its story line. (Hammerstein's *Show Boat* had broken that ground.)

But *Oklahoma!* was the first to do all three at once, with the smashing success that it did, and all in the service of realistic character development. The play's plot turned on nothing more substantial than which of two men—a sunny cowboy or a brooding farmhand—would take a pretty young farm girl to a box social, and it opened with a lone woman churning butter on an empty stage and the cowboy singing in the wings about "a bright, golden haze on the meadow." Yet *Oklahoma!* was as radical in its way as Lin-Manuel Miranda's hip-hop, genre-bending *Hamilton* would be more than seventy years later. The reason was simple: Rodgers and Hammerstein's combined lifetimes of consummate theatrical knowledge, taste, and skill.

Between them, Rodgers and Hammerstein knew virtually everything there was to know about the theater. As a child, Oscar Hammerstein had thrilled to Broadway spectacles and Buffalo Bill's touring Wild West show at the turn of the twentieth century. He went on to write books and lyrics for operettas with the likes of Sigmund Romberg and Rudolf Friml, and then pioneered the creation of the serious modern musical play with *Show Boat* in collaboration with Jerome Kern in 1927. Dick Rodgers, seven years younger, had had his first big hit, the *Garrick Gaieties*, in 1925, the same year *The Great Gatsby* was published, and had enjoyed a successful, and exclusive, twenty-year collaboration with the brilliant lyricist Lorenz Hart, fizzy with the joys of the Jazz Age and 1930s escapism. The collaboration with Hart finally foundered over the lyricist's severe alcoholism, which left him unable to function, and Rodgers turned to Hammerstein, who was ready for a new partner himself, after a long and disappointing string of commercial and critical flops. By the time the two men finally teamed up, Hammerstein would recall years later, they didn't "want anything that 'looks like a good musical comedy.' "

They wanted something else.

And they would find it, each broadening and deepening his art, not just with *Oklahoma!* but with a succession of unconventional works, including *Carousel*, in which the ne'er-do-well antihero kills himself near the top of the second act; *South Pacific*, in which an American navy nurse and marine lieutenant grapple with interracial romance and prejudice during World War II; and *The King and I*, a sublimated love story of cross-cultural conflict in which the principal characters never so much as kiss but share the sexiest polka ever danced. Rodgers and Hammerstein worked with some of the biggest stars on Broadway, and made or boosted the careers of many others—including Shirley Jones, Florence Henderson, Shirley MacLaine, Celeste Holm, Alfred Drake, Sean Connery, John Raitt, Marlon Brando, Shelley Winters, Sal Mineo, Larry Hagman, and Yul Brynner—but some of their most important works featured unknowns. They preferred singers who could act to actors who could sing, and they developed a reliable stock company of behind-the-scenes collaborators—directors, stage managers, arrangers, conductors, scenic designers, and rehearsal accompanists—who would stick with them through the years, sometimes to their own financial detriment. One of their co-producers, Richard Halliday, the husband of Mary Martin, the original star of *South Pacific* and *The Sound of Music*, once complained, when Rodgers and Hammerstein had rejected some silly bit of stage business for the star, "All *you* care about is the *show*!" and it was true.

At the height of the partners' success, Leonard Bernstein would say of Rodgers, "He is, perhaps, the most imitated songwriter of our time. He has established new levels of taste, distinction, simplicity in the best sense, and inventiveness." David Ewen, Rodgers's biographer of the same era, would judge that "nobody in the past forty years has written as many good songs for the stage over such a sustained period as he; nobody writing music for the popular theater has been heard and loved by so many people in so many different parts of the civilized world." As for Hammerstein, the *New Yorker*'s Philip Hamburger concluded,

"His songs are distinguished by such lucid wording, such unabashed sentimentality, such a gentle, even noble, view of life, and such an attachment to love, home, small children, his native country, nature and dreams come true that he has been called the Bobby Burns of the American musical stage."

In their prime, the partners seemed to stand for the best of America: forward-looking, liberal, innovative, internationalist—progressive both artistically and ideologically. One need take only the briefest glances at the conventional Broadway fare that surrounded them at the beginning of their collaboration—and the flock of imitators that sprang up after their success—to recognize the radical nature of their innovations and the reach of their influence. As the decades wore on, and the tumult of the 1960s upended American society, it was a paradox of Rodgers and Hammerstein's success that the musicals that had once been hailed as pioneering and daring would come to be seen in some critics' eyes as conventional, conformist, patronizing, paternalistic, retrograde. Yet even as a new generation of composers, lyricists, and directors explicitly rejected and moved beyond the well-made formula that Rodgers and Hammerstein had perfected, in favor of "concept" musicals in which plot and character were often secondary to style and theme, such innovations would have been impossible if Richard Rodgers and Oscar Hammerstein II had not first blazed the trail.

As COLLABORATORS, THEY were a conundrum. They had much in common. Both had been born in the same swath of what was then upper-middle-class Harlem. Both attended Columbia University, where they were members of the Pi Lambda Phi fraternity, and fell under the spell of the college's musical comedy troupe, the Varsity Show. Both had had unhappy, even miserable, experiences working in Hollywood, both grappled with bouts of depression (though Rodgers's problems were far more severe and enduring), and both preferred New York. Both were married to women named Dorothy, who were both interior decorators, though with wildly different tastes and styles. Both were the keenest of businessmen—though both tended to downplay their interest in the nuts and bolts for public consumption—and both could be chary with collaborators, stingy with credit, and notoriously tight with a buck.

"Dick loved money more than anybody I've ever seen, except Oscar," the costume designer Lucinda Ballard would recall. "But I think it was different with Oscar. I think part of Oscar's nature was that he couldn't bear for people to spend money, and also he was very stingy— really stingy. And yet, Oscar was the most lovable person I almost ever knew, and Dick really was not."

Neither particularly fancied nightlife. Hammerstein perfected the art of backing out of cocktail receptions so discreetly (Jerome Kern called it "the Hammerstein glide") that no one would realize he had gone, and on once running into Rodgers at a party, had inquired, "Fancy meeting you here—who's minding the score?" Indeed, in their sober suits, they could have passed for bankers or lawyers or, as Groucho Marx once put it, "a couple of chiropractors." For eighteen years, through ups and through downs, they maintained an unbroken public front of unity, harmony, and calm. "In our collaboration, Mr. Rodgers and I have no definite policy except one of complete flexibility," as Hammerstein would write in the preface to his collected lyrics.

The truth was far more complex. The two men only rarely worked in the same room, with Rodgers preferring to compose at his Manhattan apartment or Connecticut country house, and Hammerstein writing at his farm in Bucks County, Pennsylvania, or in his Manhattan town house. Rodgers was prolific and lightning fast—Noël Coward once said he could pee melody—while Hammerstein might labor for days or weeks over a single lyric before sending it off for Rodgers to write the tune. (Both had generally worked in just the opposite way with previous partners—music first, lyrics second—a remarkable reflection of their shared versatility.) Hammerstein once complained that Rodgers's facility so irked him that he could have "thrown a brick through the phone," when informed how quickly his partner had found a melody, while Rodgers confessed that his reputation as a speed demon "used to make me a little angry, you know, as if I perspired these tunes." Hammerstein was a passionate political advocate for liberal and left-wing causes, while Rodgers was a conventional, middle-of-the-road liberal who steered clear of controversies. To the ends of their days, each maintained that he'd never been sure whether the other really liked him.

A GLIMPSE OF the careful, starchy formality of their professional relationship—even after long years of working together—can be seen in the only written record of their collaborative method that survives: an exchange of letters during the creation of *Cinderella*, as it happens. Hammerstein had gone to Australia to attend the 1956 Olympics, and he and Rodgers sparred delicately from afar over a ballad called "Do I Love You Because You're Beautiful?," which would become the prince's love song to Cinderella. It bears noting, as a sign of their symbiosis, that Hammerstein's principal qualms involved the music and Rodgers's the words.

Writing on November 10, 1956, from the Hotel Windsor in Melbourne, Hammerstein said he was uncomfortable with one of his lyrics for the prince: "Am I making believe I see in you, a girl too lovely to be really true?" partly because he thought it uncomfortably echoed his own famous song, "Make Believe," from *Show Boat*. He suggested, "Am I telling my heart I see in you . . ." as a more emotionally revealing alternative. But his main suggestion involved the melody.

"Would it not be more exciting and psychologically sounder," he asked, "to finish the refrain in major, even though you have started in minor. It is my conception that although the last line is a question the lover really believes she is 'as beautiful as she seems.' So after starting with doubt, the major finish would imply: 'Oh, hell, I love you and I really think in my heart of hearts you *are* as beautiful as you seem.' This is based, of course, on the assumption that it is not musically ungrammatical to start with minor and finish with major."

Nine days later, Rodgers replied, with a touch of the schoolmaster's asperity, that he had no objection to the phrase "making believe," since it was simply common parlance (and by implication nothing special that anyone might attribute to Hammerstein), but added, "I am not devoted to the line 'A Girl Too Lovely to Be Really True,' for the simple reason I am not devoted to splitting infinitives." Then, raising the temperature just a notch, Rodgers added, "Apparently you don't remember that you gave me a pretty good briefing on the subject of going into a climax" at the end of the refrain. "At that time I agreed that you were absolutely right and I changed the tune to subscribe to your suggestion. . . . There is absolutely nothing ungrammatical about ending in major when you start in minor. It is quite conventional and extraordinarily effective. I think you will find that you have the lift at the finish that you expected."

On November 28, Hammerstein answered, wounded that Rodgers had not noted his concern about making believe. "I think 'Telling my heart' has more emotional importance," he wrote defensively. "You, apparently, don't because you didn't even mention it. Let us wait until we get together which will be in two weeks." Hammerstein added that he had tried to avoid the split infinitive, and had even considered asking Rodgers to change his melody to aid in the effort, but thought the result would be less musically interesting.

Five days later, Rodgers had the final word. "As I said in my last communication, once you and I sit down in a room and discuss these matters of syllables and notes, there isn't the remotest possibility of disagreement."

In an interview, Rodgers once explained that when he and Hammerstein had a divergence of opinion, they resolved it with Gallic politesse in the manner of Alphonse and Gaston: "We'll do it your way." In this case, as in so many others, they apparently did: Hammerstein's original words, which he doubted but Rodgers approved of, remained as written, and Rodgers's melody, which Hammerstein proposed to alter, was, in fact, changed to end in a satisfyingly uplifting major key.

"I guess like Gilbert and Sullivan or any of the geniuses, they were wary of each other," recalled the actor George S. Irving, who had parts in both *Oklahoma!* and the last musical Rodgers ever wrote, *I Remember Mama*, shortly before his death. "But when it came to the crunch . . ."

WHEN IT CAME to the crunch, they delivered—time and time again. But the results often hid the enormous effort and emotional toll involved.

Barley three months after *Cinderella*'s debut, Rodgers would sink into a depression—fueled partly by alcohol—that was so deep and severe as to require months of hospitalization at New York's Payne Whitney psychiatric clinic. Years after his death, Rodgers's daughters publicly revealed a secret that had been well kept in his lifetime: for much of his career, he was an alcoholic, albeit a high-functioning one, and an incorrigible womanizer with a girlfriend in almost every show he produced and a hideaway love nest in a Times Square hotel. When a chorus girl once slapped her hips in turn, saying that one side represented weight gained in New Haven and the other one extra pounds put on in Boston, Rodgers rejoined that he himself preferred Providence.

For his part, Hammerstein's reputation as a "cockeyed optimist," to borrow one of his most famous lines from *South Pacific*, belied a sometimes sardonic character, who could be surly and hypercompetitive with his own children, and cutting in debate with adversaries or supplicants when they crossed him. He was every bit as hard-driving a businessman as Rodgers. Even while relishing (and deserving) his sentimental reputation as a devoted family man, he apparently conducted at least one discreet affair of his own with a statuesque showgirl.

And yet. And yet the songs these two men made together. They are woven as seamlessly into the fabric of American life as "The Star-Spangled Banner" or "Home on the Range." In Rodgers and Hammerstein's prime, only the music of Gilbert and Sullivan and Stephen Foster enjoyed a foothold in popular taste that had endured as long as their own songs have today. When a gravely wounded army lieutenant named Bob Dole struggled to recuperate after World War II, the only song that gave him comfort was Jane Froman's recording of "You'll Never Walk Alone," from *Carousel*. More than sixty years later, when Barack Obama became the nation's first African American president, the opera star Renée Fleming sang the same song at his inaugural concert, and it has become the favorite game-day anthem of soccer fans worldwide. As a young basketball standout at Princeton, Bill Bradley psyched himself up for every big game in the early 1960s by playing "Climb Ev'ry Mountain," from *The Sound of Music*. When grieving White House staffers arrived for Richard Nixon's resignation on the morning of August 9, 1974, they heard the Marine Band in the Grand Foyer playing songs from *South Pacific*. For a state visit by the Austrian president, Ronald Reagan's staff ordered the marines to play "Edelweiss," because someone thought it was the Austrian national anthem. When the broadcaster and Kennedy heiress Maria Shriver married the actor-bodybuilder Arnold Schwarzenegger, she called the Rodgers and Hammerstein office for permission to march down the aisle to the strains of "How Do You Solve a Problem Like Maria." Even today, visitors to Disneyland's Main Street U.S.A. hear "The Surrey with the Fringe on Top" from *Oklahoma!* blaring from hidden stereo speakers in the park.

Collectively, the team's musicals won thirty-four Tony Awards, fifteen Academy Awards, two Pulitzer Prizes, two Grammys, and two Emmys, a record unmatched by any other songwriting team. Later in life, Dick and Oscar liked to play a game in which they imagined that *Oklahoma!* had been a failure, "and then we tell each other why it was a failure, and how ridiculous we were to do what we did," as Rodgers once explained. Indeed, nothing about their collaboration's success was foreordained. If they had never so much as met, Rodgers and Hammerstein each would be remembered as signal figures in theatrical history. Together, they achieved immortality. But no one could have known that on the long-ago March evening when a handsome young cowhand loped onto a stage, singing about the dawn.

CHAPTER 1

The Sentimentalist

The sophisticate is a man who thinks he can swim better than he can and sometimes drowns himself. He thinks he can drive better than he really can and sometimes causes great smashups. So, in my book, there's nothing wrong with sentiment because the things we're sentimental about are the fundamental things in life, the birth of a child, the death of a child or of anybody, falling in love. I couldn't be anything but sentimental about these basic things. I think to be anything but sentimental is being a "poseur."

Oscar Hammerstein II

There is some dispute about whether he saw his first play at the age of three or four or five—or even eight—but there is no dispute that Oscar Hammerstein II was born into the theater. He never had a chance to escape it—and he tried. His paternal grandfather and namesake, the first Oscar Hammerstein, was the most famous theatrical producer in America, if not the world, when his grandson was born in Harlem on July 12, 1895. The elder Hammerstein was the son of German Jewish parents from Stettin, Prussia, and he showed an early talent on the flute, piano, and violin. But his father wanted him to pursue more practical subjects. Hammerstein resisted, and one day after his father beat him for going skating in a park, the son sold his violin and lit out first for Liverpool and then New York, arriving in America at the age of eighteen.

He found work in a cigar factory on Pearl Street in Lower Manhattan, and eventually became a cigar manufacturer himself, ultimately owning patents for some eighty devices used in production. He used the proceeds to pursue his passion: the theater, where he made his money in vaudeville and lost several fortunes in pursuit of opera, his first love. At one point, his Manhattan Opera House rivaled the mighty Metropolitan Opera itself, which bought him out on the proviso that he not produce any opera in America for ten years. He fled to Europe, went broke, came home, and went broke again, saved only by his son Willie, the younger Oscar's father, who managed the family's legitimate theaters and, later, its variety houses. The old man was a romantic, but also a realist. One of his favorite maxims: "There is no limit to the number of people who will stay away from a bad show."

Oscar II had hardly any contact with his famous forebear while growing up (his own father wanted his offspring to avoid a theatrical career at all costs), but he would inherit his namesake's pragmatism: The composer Johnny Green called Oscar II "a businessman-poet," and his future partner Richard Rodgers would describe him as "a dreamer, but a very careful dreamer." The younger Oscar first met his grandfather, a gruff and forbidding figure in a black silk top hat, in the lobby of Hammerstein's Victoria Theatre, a vaudeville house at 42nd Street and Seventh Avenue in Times Square. Later, alone in the darkened theater, young Oscar watched transfixed as a bevy of women, costumed as water maidens, sought to untangle a large fishing net and sang a beguiling siren song. At intermission, his father took him backstage, where he promptly came face-to-face with a large lion in a cage. Suddenly, the cage started to roll toward him, and he feared he might be sick to his stomach. By one later account, he went home, slept fourteen hours, and "when he awoke, he announced that the theater would be his life work."

At the age of four, for reasons he himself would later be unable to explain, Oscar was sent to an apartment one flight below his own family's to live with his maternal grandparents, who were of Scots-Presbyterian stock, while his younger brother, Reginald, remained upstairs with their parents, Willie and Allie. Young Oscar started each day sharing a milk punch spiked with scotch with his grandfather, James Nimmo, and at bedtime they would split a bottle of Guinness stout. Every morning, the pair would troop to nearby Mount Morris Park shortly before seven, in time to see an attendant climb the winding staircase to a bell tower and sound the hour. His grandfather told him that it was the devil who rang the bell, a little old man whose heart was filled with kindness and his pockets with sourballs of the kind that Grandfather Nimmo himself dispensed. Oscar would later attribute his love of the theater to his Grandfather Hammerstein and his sunny, upbeat view of life to Grandfather Nimmo.

If Oscar and Reggie thrilled to all aspects of the theater (a special favorite was the Wild West show of "Buffalo Bill" Cody, which they managed to see over and over for free by volunteering to be two of the children in a stage coach chased by a tribe of wild Indians), Oscar's father fulfilled his role as the theatrical businessman of the family with more duty than joy. He didn't like the theater, didn't see plays except his own, and didn't even audition promising acts he'd heard about, on the theory that if they were good enough, they'd come to him. He trudged to the theater each morning, returning home for an early dinner before trooping back downtown again to count the nightly box-office receipts. Oscar would later recall, "Kissing him goodbye in the morning and hello in the evening was nearly the whole story of my experience with my father during my early youth. I didn't really get to know him. He didn't really become a force of any kind in my life until my mother died. I was fifteen then. Up until that time I had respect and affection for him merely because he was my father. He seldom scolded me and never punished me, I think the extent of his rebukes would be asking: 'Is that nice?' if he disapproved of something I had done or said."

By his own reckoning, "Ockie," as he would be known to his family and intimates for the rest of his life, was a cossetted mother's boy. "She was my friend, my confidante, obviously my worshipful admirer and also the firmest and strongest person I knew," he would remember late in life. "Without ever punishing me, and without ever seeming stern, she had a way of letting me know when she meant a thing to be done or not to be done." Allie's death from a botched abortion and the resulting peritonitis (she was an early advocate of birth control, but methods were unreliable then) affected him deeply. During her illness, he would recall, "I didn't believe she was going to die for the simple reason that I couldn't visualize a world without her, couldn't imagine living without her." After she died, he found he was able to carry on with his life, and noted that this early trauma "crystallized an attitude" he had had toward death ever since. "I never feel shaken by death, as I would have been if this had not happened to me when I was fifteen. I received the shock and took it, and sort of resisted as an enemy the grief that comes after death rather than giving way to it. I get stubborn about it and say it is not going to lick me, because it didn't then."

More than forty years after his mother's death, Oscar would write to his own eldest son, Bill, that "whatever order or form I have got out of life has been extracted from chaos," adding, "my strange disorderly unsystematic family may have developed in me a tolerance for disorder which makes it possible for me to live in a disorderly world, even though I crave another kind." Indeed, Stephen Sondheim, his protégé and surrogate son, would judge that "Oscar's point of view . . . was both more hard-headed and more quirky than people who think of him as a naïve and dreamy idealist might expect."

AFTER ALLIE'S DEATH, Willie Hammerstein remarried—to his wife's maiden sister, Anna, who was known as Mousie. She was a buxom, tattooed, somewhat blowsy woman, whose favorite greeting was "Hiya, Tootsie," but she became a loving stepmother, encouraging a warmer relationship between Willie and his sons. By their teenage years, both Oscar and Reggie were spending their summers at the Weingart Institute, a pioneering and renowned summer camp in Highmount, New York, where Oscar made enduring friendships with his fellow campers, including Harold Hyman, who became his longtime physician, Leighton Brill, who would work as his assistant for two decades (and would for a time run the Hollywood office of Rodgers and Hammerstein, with mixed results), and Myron and David O. Selznick, the brothers who would win fame as Hollywood's first talent agent and one of its legendary producers.

In 1912, at the age of seventeen, Oscar entered Columbia University, where his contemporaries included the future publisher Bennett Cerf, the future screenwriter Herman Mankiewicz, the future lyricist and Metro-Goldwyn-Mayer publicist Howard Dietz, and an antic, elfin personality named Lorenz Hart, whose future would be interwoven with Hammerstein's own in ways he could scarcely have fathomed. In part to please his father, Oscar enrolled in a pre-law curriculum. But Willie Hammerstein died of kidney disease at age thirty-nine in 1914, and with him died any last obstacle to Oscar's pursuit of a theatrical career. From the beginning, the allure of Columbia lay less in its classrooms than in the Varsity Show, a musical comedy extravaganza staged each spring in the grand ballroom of the Hotel Astor in Times Square. Though the shows were amateur—performed by undergraduates and typically produced by recent alumni—they approached professional caliber and were routinely reviewed by the major New York newspapers. Hammerstein joined the University Players as both a performer and writer, and his first appearance was as a "consumptive poet" in the 1915 show, *On Your Way*. The critic of the New York *Evening World* wrote of his performance, "Oscar is a comedian and as a fun-maker he was a la carte, meaning all to the mustard."

The following year's show, *The Peace Pirates*, witnessed a bigger milestone for Oscar, who had written a few of the sketches for his friend Herman Mankiewicz and had made an impression as a blackface comedian. After one Saturday matinee he met a dark-eyed teenage boy, the younger brother of Oscar's fraternity brother Morty Rodgers. In later years, there would be lighthearted disagreements over whether young Dick Rodgers was wearing short pants or long, but the result of their first meeting is clear: that very afternoon, Richard Rodgers resolved to go to Columbia and write Varsity Shows himself.

For his part, Hammerstein transferred to the Columbia Law School after his junior year and continued to write for the Varsity Shows, but his work was juvenile, betraying few traces of the craft he would later hone so painstakingly. The 1917 show, written in partnership with Herman Axelrod, was called *Home, James*, and it featured an ethnic comedy number, of the sort typical at the time, called "Annie McGinnis Pavlova," about a shanty Irish girl who tries to pass as "the pride of the Ballet Russe." Another effort included this inelegant rhyme:

> *I want to be a star in moving pictures*
> *Like Chaplin, Pickford, Fairbanks and the other fixtures.*

Oscar spent time as a $5-a-week process server for a law firm called Blumenstiel and Blumenstiel, but he was a miserable failure and the job didn't last. So in the summer of 1917, he approached his uncle Arthur, who had taken over the family theatrical business from Willie, and begged for work in one of his shows. Arthur had promised his brother that he'd keep Oscar out of show business, but his nephew was adamant. "It's in my blood," Oscar insisted, "and furthermore I need the money."

Oscar needed the money, in part, because he had fallen in love with Myra Finn (as it happened, a distant cousin of Richard and Morty Rodgers), whom he had known for years but had recently reencountered at a weekend party at the New Jersey shore. Petite at four feet eleven inches, and two years younger than Oscar, she was known to her friends and family as "Mike" and had a quicksilver personality that was by turns attractive and off-putting. Her parents opposed the match, skeptical of Oscar's prospects, but the couple persisted, and they were married in the Finns' apartment on August 22, 1917.

Uncle Arthur had also finally relented, hiring Hammerstein as assistant stage manager for his long-running show *You're in Love*, at the princely salary of $20 a week. (Oscar was lucky: the chorus girls of the era earned $18 a week and had to supply their own shoes and stockings after the first pair wore out.) When the show closed that summer, Arthur rewarded Oscar with the permanent staff job of production stage manager, and the younger man quickly set about learning every facet of the trade, working as an office boy and play reader in the daytime and stage manager at night, and looking for any chance to contribute during the rehearsals of new shows. Though Arthur had made him promise not to try to write anything for at least a year, an opportunity arose that fall when the latest Hammerstein show, a bit of fluff called *Furs and Frills*, ran into trouble out of town. The overworked authors assigned Oscar to write lyrics for the second-act opening. In the end, he wrote only the opening chorus, intended to help the audience returning from intermission get seated as dancers hoofed across the stage at a house party:

Make yourselves at home,
'Neath our spacious dome.

Do just as you please
In twos or threes if you'd rather—
But rest assured you'll be no bother.

"In those days, it was more of a free-for-all, slapdash kind of thing—the musical comedy," Hammerstein would recall. "Someone would find a theater un-booked, and someone else would try to whip up a book and music and lyrics and fill the theater if they could." There were rigid rules of composition: an opening chorus number to let late-arriving audience members be seated, followed by the "ice breaker," a not very important second number to get the show on its way. The second act of any show was usually written during rehearsals. In time, Hammerstein himself would break and rewrite all of these rules, but for now he was simply soaking up all he could.

"I don't think I had any high-minded notions that I was going to revolutionize the theater," he would say. "I think I just did my best with each play. Sometimes it was all right, and sometimes it wasn't any good at all."

The newly minted man of the theater stood six feet one and a half inches, quite tall for his day, and, weighing just under two hundred pounds, was slim enough that spring to have been turned down for army service in World War I for being underweight. He was built, as one writer put it, like a football coach, with a face deeply pockmarked and a small gold signet ring on his left little finger. In his prime, he favored English shoes from Peal & Co., and shirts from Turnbull & Asser, and when white dinner jackets were in vogue, he dared to wear a salmon pink one to a Hollywood party. But his principal touch of sartorial flash was a weakness for brightly colored bow ties, "not that he was a dandy," as his protégé Stephen Sondheim would put it, "he just always looked perfect, patrolling that delicate territory between the casual and the formal." He spoke in an accent that, to the modern ear, sounds almost dese, dems, and dosey (pronouncing "board" as "bawd," "working" as "woiking," and "fast" as "fay-ast"), but that was typical of his social class. He also had a slight speech impediment that tended to blur *l*'s and *r*'s.

By the spring of 1919, Oscar was at last at work on a play of his own. Uncle Arthur had read a melodramatic story about a young woman whose efforts to escape her tyrannical family and a drunken lover led her to an engagement to a man she didn't like and a job in a gambling house before an eventual happy ending with her now-sober true love. Titled *The Light*, it opened on May 19, 1919, in Springfield, Massachusetts, where the headline in the local paper proclaimed it was "not destined to shine very brilliantly," before moving on to New Haven, where it winked out altogether after just seven performances. But Oscar was undaunted. "When I went into the Saturday matinee, I knew I had a big flop," he would recall. "There must have been about twenty people in the Shubert Theatre that day. When the ingénue came on, one of her lines was, 'Everything is falling down around me . . .' and at that precise moment her petticoat started falling down. I didn't wait for the yell that followed. I just ran out of the theater, went into the park, and sat on a bench. While I was sitting there, an idea came to me for a new show, so I started writing it." Oscar's determination proved fateful. Barely two months later, Oscar Hammerstein I died of complications from kidney problems at age seventy-three. Soon enough, the grandson's fame would rival the old man's.

THE SHOW THAT Oscar started writing on the park bench was a World War I romance about a veteran of the American Expeditionary Force torn between his love for a woman he'd met in France and his hometown sweetheart. Hammerstein was prepared to write the book and the lyrics, but he needed a composer. He found one in Herbert Stothart, Uncle Arthur's staff music director. A veteran of the University of Wisconsin music faculty, Stothart was ten years older than Oscar and would go on to acclaim as a Hollywood composer and orchestrator. But the new team's first task was to persuade Arthur that their show, tentatively titled *Joan of Arkansaw*, was bankable. They did so by having Oscar read the script aloud, while Herb laughed uproariously on cue at the jokes. The gambit worked, and the pair was off and running, working in the standard method of the day, with the music coming first and the words following. This practice was partly a carryover from the widespread American importation of European operettas, in which

English words had to be fitted to preexisting tunes, and Hammerstein would follow the pattern through all his collaborations over the next quarter century, until reversing the order with Rodgers.

The show, by now retitled *Always You*, opened in New York on January 5, 1920, and the results were pleasing enough to produce sixty-six performances and a ten-city national tour that summer. The music was "catchy and a pretty chorus of girls help to put 'pep' into it," the *New York Times* declared, adding, "Also, the lyrics are more clever than those of the average musical comedy."

Always You also taught Oscar a hard-won early lesson. The plots of most musical comedies of this era were paper-thin and often nonsensical, and while the writer of a show's libretto was typically blamed for its failure, he was given no credit for its success. Yet even the slenderest story lines had to be artfully constructed to make a show work. At the opening night performance of *Always You*, Oscar was annoyed that some of his favorite jokes prompted only feeble laughter, whereas a joke he'd expect to cause little reaction made a big stir—because the punch line depended on a careful setup in the previous scene. This discovery gave birth to a lifelong conviction: that an audience follows the plot, and is gratified only when the story is well wrought. This was a skill Oscar began honing in earnest with his next collaborator, who would become one of his most important teachers.

Otto Harbach, twenty-two years Oscar's senior, was the son of Danish immigrant farmers and a graduate of Knox College in Galesburg, Illinois, where he was a friend of the prairie poet Carl Sandburg. A onetime aspiring English professor, Harbach had kicked around various jobs in newspapers and advertising before teaming up with the composer Karl Hoschna to contribute songs to Broadway shows. Their notable successes included "Cuddle Up a Little Closer" and "Every Little Movement Has a Meaning All Its Own." After Hoschna's premature death in 1911, Arthur Hammerstein hired Harbach to write the book and lyrics for *The Firefly*, a project intended for the composer Victor Herbert, who walked out on the job, to be replaced by Rudolf Friml. As *Always You* embarked on its national tour in the summer of 1920, Arthur was already planning his next show, *Tickle Me*, a vehicle for Frank Tinney, a famous vaudevillian of the day. Oscar wanted to write it, but his uncle decided to team him up with the more experienced Harbach, who was an advocate of integrating songs into the plot of a show, and of elevating the role of lyricist, who had tended to be subordinate to composers, stars, and spectacle.

It was a fateful collaboration. Harbach, a kind and generous mentor, insisted that Oscar, whose instinct was to write quickly, slow down and think seriously about his goals before putting words on paper. He likened the construction of a musical play to building a fire, in which all the elements—logs, kindling, matches, a good flue—had to come together. Harbach would not only impress upon Hammerstein the importance of strong dramatic values but would also stamp his lyrical diction with the floridity then common in operetta—a litany of dreams, moons, stars, and dew that would resurface in Oscar's later work, long after he had otherwise moved on to more modern forms of expression.

Together with a third collaborator, Frank Mandel, and with music again by Stothart, Hammerstein and Harbach cooked up a plot in which Tinney, playing himself, accompanied a movie company to Tibet, which provided a backdrop for elaborate production numbers, including one of a giant horseshoe waterfall of glistening soap bubbles, from which a chorus of beautiful girls emerged in the first-act finale. The show opened in New York on August 17, and while the reviews were mixed, they were good enough to sustain a run of 207 performances, no mean feat when the Broadway competition included W. C. Fields and Fanny Brice in the *Ziegfeld Follies* and Eugene O'Neill's *The Emperor Jones*.

The next four years of Oscar's career read like an old-fashioned movie montage, in which calendar pages flip by or front-page newspaper headlines spin around with dizzying speed to denote the passage of time: show after show at the pace of one, two, or even three a year, sometimes written in collaboration with Harbach, sometimes with others. There was *Jimmie* (1920) about a missing heiress; *Pop* (1921), a straight comedy about an elderly husband and his thrifty wife; *Daffy Dill* (1922), a Cinderella story about a poor girl and a rich boy; *Queen O' Hearts* (1922), a musical vehicle for Nora Bayes, the vaudeville star who had introduced "Shine On, Harvest Moon"; *Wildflower* (1923), about a capricious Italian heiress who must control her temper if she wants to inherit her father's millions; *Mary Jane McKane* (1923), a musical about a pretty country girl who poses as a plain Jane to get a job in the big city; *Gypsy Jim* (1924), a drama about a failing attorney and his hypochondriac wife who are saved by an eccentric millionaire; and *New Toys* (1924), a comedy about a marriage that turns unhappy with the arrival of children.

In this last work, there was more than an element of autobiography, since by now Oscar's marriage to Myra was on the rocks. They had begun their life together in a small apartment on West End Avenue in Manhattan and their first child, William, named for Oscar's father, was born in 1918. A daughter, Alice, followed in 1921. (Both children were delivered by Richard Rodgers's father, a leading Manhattan obstetrician.) By 1923, the Hammerstein family had decamped to Long Island's north shore, first to Douglaston in Queens, and the following year to Great Neck, a leafy enclave on the west shore of Manhasset Bay. Oscar did not yet know it, but Mike had already begun a string of infidelities, including an affair with one of his own collaborators, the British librettist Guy Bolton. Their son William, who was known as Billy, would recall the simultaneous pleasure and discomfort at waking up to find Oscar beside him in the other twin bed in his childhood bedroom instead of the master suite. Many years later, Oscar himself would sum up his feelings in a terse autobiographical jotting. "False values—My fault as well as hers. I am an idiot, but work hard."

Oscar was later frank to confess that much of his work in this period was none too good. "A Long Island commuter, I prided myself that I could often write the refrain on one trip into New York and the verse on the way back that night," he would recall. "Not many of these were good songs. I was too easily satisfied with my work. I was too often trying to emulate older and better lyric writers, saying things similar to the things they were saying. It would have been all right if I had been content to imitate the forms of their songs, but the substance should have been mine and it was not. I know that insincerity held me back for several years, and I know that even after I'd had a period of success, it again handicapped me and caused me to have failures."

As early as *Always You*, Oscar had diagnosed the shallowness of much of current Broadway fare—the appetite for comely maidens and high-C tenors, jokes and hokum—in a song called "The Tired Businessman." But he had long aspired to something higher. Oscar admired works like *The Merry Widow*, Franz Lehár's 1905 operetta, because of its then-daring plot. Its heroine was a widow (and thus not a virgin) who married to save her fictional principality's fortunes, not for love. Such a story may seem quaint and creaky in the twenty-first century, but it was what passed for realistic in its day. In 1924, Oscar would at last have a crack at such a story himself.

As USUAL, THE inspiration came from Uncle Arthur, who had heard tales of an annual winter carnival in Montreal, featuring a spectacular ice castle on the outskirts of town that, at the end of a week's festivities, was melted by citizens carrying torches. Oscar and Otto Harbach entrained for a Canadian field trip and promptly learned that the story was fiction, but they proceeded to gather local color all the same. Rudolf Friml and Stothart were engaged to write the music, while Oscar and Otto devised a plot that proceeded to break with any number of musical comedy conventions. For one thing, it features a murder. For another, it ends with just two people left standing onstage instead of the usual chorus in full array. The show centers on Rose-Marie, the house singer at Lady Jane's Hotel in Saskatchewan, who is the darling of the Royal Canadian Mounted Police and the itinerant fur trappers who frequent the lodge. Though she pines only for the trapper Jim Kenyon, a wealthy rival named Edward Hawley fancies her. He witnesses a murder and scapegoats Jim, but promises to spare him if Rose-Marie will consent to his proposal of marriage. She does, but in the end, the real murderer is revealed and the true lovers reunited.

When *Rose-Marie* opened at the Imperial Theatre on September 2, the playbill contained an unusual note of aspiration: "The musical numbers of this play are such an integral part of the action that we do not think we should list them as separate episodes." The critics liked the results. The *New York Herald Tribune* was rapturous: "A beautiful and highly colored composite photograph of a three-ring circus and shown to the accompaniment of the most entrancing music it has long been our privilege to hear." The *Evening World* singled out Oscar's contributions: "The fertile brain of Oscar Hammerstein has lent valuable aid to the more experienced Harbach and the collaboration has spelled Efficiency with a capital E." The show clocked 557 performances, a record-breaking run for the time.

Four months later, in January 1925, Oscar, Myra, Billy, and Alice sailed for England, where Oscar would supervise the London production of *Rose-Marie* before taking a solo six-week holiday in Paris, cementing a love for that city that would stay with him forever. Returning to New York, he asked Harbach to collaborate on a new show he had in mind. Otto was amenable but asked Oscar first to collaborate on an assignment he had already accepted: a new musical with Jerome Kern, at age forty already the dean and most admired of American popular composers, whose soulful ballads like "They Didn't Believe Me" and "Look for the Silver Lining" broke away from the European waltz tradition to incorporate contemporary dance rhythms. Classically trained in New York and Heidelberg, Kern was known for lush and soaring melodies that still managed to have a peculiarly American sound. He and Hammerstein had met only once or twice, but at the start of his career Kern had been a piano accompanist for Oscar's father, Willie. Kern and Oscar hit it off immediately, united by a shared work ethic and love of dramatic storytelling. Their new project was *Sunny*, a vehicle for Broadway's reigning musical star, Marilyn Miller, and it told the story of the tangled love life of an English circus performer who comes to America.

Even after all Oscar had already done to buck established conventions, the show gave him a lasting lesson in the perquisites of performers, who demanded their turn regardless of the exigencies of the plot. Years later, he would describe working with Miller. "I told her everything— gave her the dialogue, acted out scenes, ran through tentative lyrics," he remembered, "—and when I was through, she looked at me and said, 'Mr. Hammerstein, when do I do my tap specialty?'" Needless to say, a tap dance was written into the script. Another challenge came when Kern played a bouncy, repetitive melody for Miller that began with a long, sustained high note, a B-natural held for nine beats. What word could be easily sung at such length? Oscar's answer was "Who," and the song became a highlight of the first act.

The show had a raft of troubles in its out-of-town tryout in Philadelphia, but by the time it opened at the New Amsterdam Theatre in New York on September 22, 1925, the kinks had been ironed out and it settled in for a fifteen-month run. Hammerstein plunged into new shows in quick succession, including *Song of the Flame* (1925), in collaboration with Harbach and with music by Stothart and a hot young composer named George Gershwin; *The Wild Rose* (1926), with Harbach and Friml; and, most successfully, *The Desert Song* (1926), with Harbach and Sigmund Romberg. Romberg, a Hungarian Jewish émigré whose *Student Prince* had been a hit in 1924, had contributed to Broadway revues during the World War I years and would remain a frequent collaborator and lifelong friend to Oscar. *The Desert Song* was a swashbuckling tale of intrigue in French Morocco, owing more than a little to the Rudolph Valentino "Sheik" craze of the day. It ran for 471 performances and was a critical success but was yet another frivolous and fanciful operetta with a plot that bore only the slightest passing resemblance to real life. Oscar's next project would be on an altogether different plane and would change the American musical theater forever.

EDNA FERBER'S NOVEL *Show Boat* had been a sensation upon its publication in 1926, remaining on the bestseller lists for three months. Kern loved the book, and one day in the fall of that year he telephoned Oscar, saying that while he had only finished half the story, he thought it would make an ideal show for them. After working separately to make outlines of the plot, they found that each had chosen the same basic scenes as the spine of the drama, and they set about acquiring the rights from Ferber. Because of the success of *Sunny*, Broadway's reigning impresario, Florenz Ziegfeld himself, was willing to take a chance by producing a show that departed dramatically from his usual frothy displays of female pulchritude. That said, Ferber's book in no way seemed a natural source for a musical play.

Show Boat is a sprawling, episodic novel, chronicling three generations in the life of a Mississippi River family, from the 1870s to the 1920s. The ebullient leader of the clan is Andy Hawks, captain and owner of the *Cotton Blossom*, a floating show palace, and his comic foil is his doughty battle-ax of a wife, Parthy Ann. When their leading lady, Julie LaVerne, is revealed to be of mixed-race ancestry and forced off the boat for being married to her white leading man, the Hawkses' virginal daughter, Magnolia, steps into the spotlight and falls in love with Gaylord Ravenal, a ne'er-do-well riverboat gambler who becomes her own co-star, before abandoning her and their child when his fortunes fall. Working with Kern over many months, Oscar proved a master of artful adaptation, condensation, and plotting. "It isn't just the controversial subject matter," Stephen Sondheim would recall. "It's the fact that he was trying to do something based on reality, instead of some fairy tale."

Oscar was delighted to be working with such rich and rewarding material, and he dug into the libretto and lyrics. In one small but typically telling example, Hammerstein turned one of Ferber's almost throwaway asides into a revealing scene that helped propel the story. In the novel, Magnolia loves to sing Negro spirituals in the kitchen with Queenie and Jo, the showboat's black servants. Catching them all singing one day, Mrs. Hawks is appalled, declaring, "I don't know where you get your low ways from! White people aren't good enough for you, I suppose, that you've got to run with blacks in the kitchen." In his libretto, Oscar heightened this moment by having Julie sing to Magnolia an old folk song she loves, only to have Queenie interrupt, demanding to know why Julie is so familiar with a song that she herself has never heard anybody but black folk sing. This not only has the effect of foreshadowing the dramatic confrontation to come, but "Can't Help Lovin' Dat Man" is a song of marvelous power and economy.

In this helpless lament of a lover who knows all too well the pain she's in for, Oscar also employed a device he would use over and again in his career: repetition to heighten the impact of a sentiment. The first two renderings of the phrase "Can't help lovin' dat man of mine" do not rhyme with anything that comes before them, and thus stand out. Only at the very end of the refrain does Hammerstein rhyme "mine" with "fine" and "shine" in a final resolution.

Seeking to tie the story of *Show Boat* together with the geographical feature that runs through it, Oscar devised a hymn to the Mississippi itself—a notion that appeared nowhere in Ferber's book, and one that he made powerful by an even more sparing use of rhyme. The opening lines of the song, "Ol' Man River," written in dialect that may fall heavily on today's ears but was intended to be a sympathetic hymn of weary resignation and "implied protest," prove the point. The first rhyme comes ten lines—and forty words—into the song. Hammerstein himself explained his aim: "If a listener is made rhyme-conscious, his interest may be diverted from the story of the song. If, on the other hand, you keep him waiting for a rhyme, he is more likely to listen to the meaning of the words."

For her part, Ferber would never forget the first time she heard Kern play and sing the song, in his true but reedy voice. "The music mounted, mounted, mounted, and I give you my word my hair stood on end, the tears came to my eyes, I breathed like a heroine in a melodrama," she would recall. "This was great music. This was music that would outlast Jerome Kern's day and mine." They were great lyrics, too. Once, a perhaps apocryphal story goes, someone within earshot of Hammerstein's second wife mentioned "Jerome Kern's 'Ol' Man River.'" She was quick to retort, "Oscar wrote 'Ol' Man River.' What Mr. Kern wrote was *la-la-dum-dum, la-la-dum-dum*."

Oscar himself was ambivalent about whether lyrics could properly be considered poetry. Though written in verse, a lyric's words are not meant to be read silently or recited aloud, but sung—and their cumulative power is inextricably linked to the music that accompanies them, and that inevitably heightens their effect (or exposes their weaknesses). In his best work, Hammerstein seemed to understand this instinctively, keeping the words as simple and conversational as possible, allowing the music to do the work. In this, he was the polar opposite of the most pyrotechnic wordsmiths among his peers (Cole Porter, Lorenz Hart, E. Y. Harburg), who called attention to their work in ways that he did not. Richard Rodgers, attempting to contrast the work of Hammerstein and Hart, whose lyrics could express both joy and heartbreak through complex and coruscating internal rhyme schemes, once said, "I think the basic difference between the two men was that Oscar was interested in the what. And I think Larry was interested, even more, in the how. How do you say it. Oscar was interested in what do you say. Larry had a peculiar, exciting way of saying things. Oscar said them with a great deal more purity."

That purity went hand in hand with a simplicity that Stephen Sondheim would call "naked plain-spokenness," a quality that has left Hammerstein's lyrics vulnerable to the barbs of sophisticates over the decades. "Hammerstein's work is full of life, but not liveliness," Sondheim once wrote. "He is easy to make fun of because he's so earnest." Hammerstein himself once explained his success as a lyricist by saying that his own vocabulary was not enormous, and that a bigger one might well have hampered him, or persuaded him, as Philip Hamburger wrote in the *New Yorker* at the height of his success, "to substitute 'fantasy,' 'reverie,' 'nothingness,' 'chimera,' 'figment,' or even 'air-drawn dagger,' for the simple word 'dream.' "

Show Boat opened on December 27, 1927, to rave reviews. John Byram in the *New York Times* declared that the show had "about every ingredient that the perfect song and dance concoction should have." The *Herald Tribune* pronounced it "a beautiful, colorful and tasteful production." But the *New York American*'s reviewer may have been the most perceptive: "Here at last we have a story that was not submerged in the trough of musical molasses; here we had a 'book' the humor of which emerged naturally and the unusual quality of which struck one as something peculiarly different. . . . *Show Boat* is going to have a wonderful sail—no storms—no adverse winds—nothing to keep it from making port—goodness knows when. I don't."

Broadway would never again be quite the same. Neither would Oscar Hammerstein.

MONTHS EARLIER, HAMMERSTEIN'S personal life had taken a tumultuous turn. An unexpected delay in the opening of *Show Boat* (Ziegfeld had initially wanted it to christen his new Ziegfeld Theatre, but when a show called *Rio Rita* was finished first and proved a solid hit, he changed his mind) had left Oscar at liberty. On March 2, 1927, his marriage to Mike increasingly strained, he headed alone to London on the SS *Olympic* to supervise production of *The Desert Song* at the Drury Lane. His boyhood friend Howard Reinheimer, who was now also his lawyer, had come to see him off. As they boarded, Reinheimer introduced Oscar to Henry Jacobson, a diamond merchant, and his wife, Dorothy, a tall, red-haired, blue-eyed former showgirl who didn't pay much attention and hoped she'd not be stuck with an unattached stranger on the crossing. But the next morning, when she saw Oscar again on deck and got a good look at him, she would recall, "it was like the rivers rushing down to the sea." "He looked at me and I looked at him, then I really saw him, and he said, 'If I was a little boy at school and you were a little girl at school, I'd carry your books home for you.'" It was love at first sight, a love of the sort Oscar would later describe so powerfully in the song "Some Enchanted Evening."

Dorothy Marian Kiaora Blanchard had been born in Tasmania, an island off the coast of Australia, the daughter of a ship's pilot who would ply his trade in Melbourne's Port Phillip Bay. When she and Oscar met, she was just shy of twenty-seven, four years younger than he. She had had a brief early marriage to an Australian infantry officer whom she divorced for desertion in 1922, before heading to New York where she joined the cast of *André Charlot's Revue of 1924*, an English musical starring Gertrude Lawrence and Beatrice Lillie. She toured for a year as Lillie's understudy, then met Jacobson, with whom she now had a young son, Henry Jr.

On the ship, Oscar and Dorothy compared notes on their marriages, neither of which was particularly happy, and in London they met often, realizing that the bond between them was no mere fling. When Myra herself later arrived in London, Dorothy was shocked to hear her privately confess that she'd just left a lover in New York. Once the two couples were back in America, Oscar and Dorothy saw each other when they could, and Henry Jacobson, who knew about the affair, even proposed renting a house near the Hammersteins in Great Neck, in the apparent hope that Dorothy would get Oscar out of her system. Late that summer, she asked Henry for a divorce, but he refused, still certain that the infatuation would pass. That is how things stood as rehearsals for *Show Boat* began in September, with all parties miserable and unable to resolve the situation. To complicate matters even further, by the end of the year Dorothy was pregnant with a second child, willing to give Henry and her marriage another chance, and told Oscar she couldn't see him again. Months of agony followed. Dorothy's daughter, Susan, was born in March 1928, and still Dorothy refused to see Oscar, who could not bring himself to ask Myra for a divorce. Finally, that summer, Dorothy began seeing Oscar again, and in September sympathetic friends felt compelled to tell him of Myra's long string of affairs.

"Oscar snapped," wrote Hugh Fordin, Hammerstein's biographer. "He couldn't eat or sleep. He worked all night after working all day in the theater. A few days after his confrontation with Myra, he voluntarily entered Leroy Sanitarium, a small private hospital on Manhattan's Upper East Side. Wrapped in sheets, he was given cold baths to calm him and wheeled back to his room, shaking, crying, muttering the names of baseball players. He cried himself to sleep, repeating, 'It's not going to lick me,' over and over to himself. He had no psychiatric treatment, discussed his problems with no one. Within two weeks, he was functioning again, leaving the hospital on occasion in white tie and tails to dance with Dorothy."

The next week he checked out of the hospital, and soon after, Myra at last agreed to a divorce. Two months later, Dorothy told Oscar she herself had resolved to divorce Henry and would leave for Nevada, then famous as the capital of the quick divorce, as soon as possible. Her period of required residency in Reno was hellish for Oscar. He wrote fervent love letters, referring to her as a goddess and his "dear, dear, dear darling prize," and pining for her "dear, lovely breasts." In another letter he complained that the average cost of a long-distance phone call was running $30 to $100. (Their bill would exceed $3,000, about $42,000 in 2017 dollars.) Two weeks later, he expressed his feelings after a minor spat on one of those calls. "I've plunged everything on one horse—shot the works on one roll—and of course I watch it anxiously," he wrote, adding that he longed to hold her in his arms in "silent, contented hours of understanding."

His union with Dorothy would provide the stable domestic foundation that anchored the rest of Oscar's creative life. Writing to her from Jerome Kern's yacht *Show Boat* in Palm Beach on April 29, 1929, he all but ached. "My dear little baby, the strain is getting harder and I can hardly wait until next Monday to kiss you and hold you and realize that I shall never live away from you again," he told her. They were married in Baltimore two weeks later (the legal complications surrounding Oscar's own divorce from Myra made a wedding outside New York advisable), and over the Fourth of July weekend, aboard the *Show Boat* anchored off Connecticut, Oscar distilled his emotions into a love song written for his and Kern's new show, *Sweet Adeline*. The title said it all: "Don't Ever Leave Me."

To the end of her life, Dorothy would save the little cards that came with flowers or jewelry, in which Ockie would sometimes address her in a kind of baby talk, signing, "I lud you."

OSCAR'S HAPPY REMARRIAGE laid the foundation for a loving home environment and cemented his reputation as a friendly paterfamilias, a reputation that he himself would echo in sentimental songs about domestic bliss. Hammerstein's friend the songwriter and producer Billy Rose once explained, "Asking me what I think of Oscar is like asking me what I think of the Yankees, Man o' War and strawberry sundaes." But for those closest to him, especially his children, he was not always so easy to be around. At the end of his life, when he won an award as Father of the Year, he confessed that such an honor might "be a big surprise to our children." He was hopeless with tools or routine household chores. If his water glass was empty at the dining table, he expected someone else to fill it and it never occurred to him to fetch the pitcher himself. He engaged in verbal and physical teasing with his children that could edge into taunting. James, the son he had with Dorothy in 1931, allowed that Oscar was "a wonderful father to everyone except his children," and once described him as "a ferocious, mean-spirited, but funny, competitor," not above stooping to any bit of strategic psychological warfare to win a chess game or tennis match.

And after his marriage to Dorothy, Oscar was also a frequently

absentee father to his two older children, Billy and Alice, who spent
time in boarding schools or living with their mother as she shuttled
between New York and Europe, while Oscar and Dorothy lived with
Jimmy and Susan, her daughter from her first marriage. (Henry Jacobson Jr. lived with his father.) His letters to Myra in this period paint a
painful portrait of the practical realities of a broken home. In one notable case, he quarreled with his former wife's wish that Billy and Alice
spend the summer together. "They are not companionable to each
other," Oscar wrote. "They have a brotherly and sisterly affection that
is sufficiently fed by the several visits a year they have been having
together. They have not the same interests. They are always picking at
each other. Why be theoretical about these things? It is hard enough to
figure out how each of them can divide time between you and me without adding a third and unessential consideration."

The Kern-Hammerstein partnership had continued profitably,
though not exclusively, in the wake of *Show Boat*, and Oscar also kept
writing shows with Romberg—notably *The New Moon* in 1928, which
featured such hit songs as "Lover Come Back to Me," "Stouthearted
Men," and "Softly, as in a Morning Sunrise." But the advent of talking
motion pictures with *The Jazz Singer* in 1927 had created a fresh—and
highly lucrative—market for musical movies in Hollywood, and by the
end of 1929 Oscar had joined the parade of Broadway songwriters and
actors who headed west, lured by the promise of easy money and a
relaxed lifestyle. He signed a contract with Warner Bros. in which he
would write four operettas over two years at $100,000 per picture
against 25 percent of the profits, with final approval of each film. But
his first effort, *Viennese Nights* (written with Sigmund Romberg), was
a box-office bust, a casualty of Hollywood's sudden flood of musical
offerings. Another film, *Children of Dreams*, was already in the works
and would be released in 1931, but soon after *Viennese Nights'* release
in November 1930, Jack Warner offered Hammerstein and Romberg
$100,000 to buy out the remaining two films on their contracts. Public
tastes had changed, and studios now took to advertising movies by
promising that they contained *no* music. Hammerstein found himself
on the eastbound Santa Fe *Super Chief* headed back to New York.

"Pretty soon we were all shipped back on the Chief, with settlements in our pockets, but having lost not only several years on Broadway but having lost our touch, it was hard for us to get back," he would recall. "Many of us took several years before we could really get back in the swing of the success we'd enjoyed before."

That was an understatement. Hammerstein and Kern would have one more success, *Music in the Air*, a 1932 backstage romance about the music publishing business, but after that, Oscar hit a dry patch that would last for eleven years. He tried a move to London, where his and Kern's *Three Sisters* lasted just forty-five performances in 1934. After its failure, Oscar asked Jerry, "What next?" and the answer was "Hollywood. For good." So the Hammersteins returned to California with high hopes and a contract at Metro-Goldwyn-Mayer.

"Their chief interest is developing me as a producer," an optimistic Oscar wrote to Myra, explaining, "A producer guides a production from its inception, chooses a story, casts it, confers with the writers and director and supervises their work. He is regarded as much more important than a writer. The money I'm getting now is very nearly the maximum for a writer, but if I make good as a producer I can command more. . . . Since it is usual to call in several writers on a picture (and I am beginning to see virtues in the idea) it is hard for a writer to build up an individual reputation as he does in the theater. Hence the producer, as the captain of the team, runs off with the honors. For some reason or other I have made a big hit with Louis B. Mayer. He looks upon me as a kind of protégé and keeps talking about grooming me as a producer, telling me to take my time and learn the business at his expense."

The reality was more discouraging—and, in the end, much more depressing. "The saddest word I know is 'but,'" Oscar once told an inquiring journalist, and throughout the 1930s his career was one long disappointing but. Hammerstein would work for MGM, Paramount, Columbia, and RKO Radio Pictures, contributing to a half dozen not especially distinguished original films (and some good adaptations, among them a first-rate *Show Boat* for Universal in 1936), while shuttling back and forth to Broadway to work on a like number of flop musicals with Kern and others. On contract to one studio or another, he was paid by the week, churning out lyrics and treatments, whether they were good or bad, and whether a film ever got produced. "I was selling words instead of gambling with them, speculating with them," he would say years later. "That wasn't good for me." As his successes dwindled, and he felt deepening financial pressure to support two households and a demanding, perpetually restless ex-wife, Oscar's mood darkened. He complained bitterly to Myra about the cost of keeping up appearances. "In Hollywood above all other places," he wrote, "their psychology is to think a man unimportant and undeserving of big money if he lives at a modest level and does no entertaining, though God knows I do as little as possible either to give or go to parties." Later that year, in a letter to his lawyer Howard Reinheimer, Oscar sounded a frankly self-pitying note. "When you come out here," he wrote, "will you bring my insurance policies and my will, so that we can have a survey of that situation? Also bring the document that I keep asking for, telling me what, if anything, I am worth."

With his creative energies stymied, Hammerstein channeled his efforts into political activity, helping to found the Hollywood Anti-Nazi League to fight the rise of Hitler, and lending his support, writing skills, and money to a raft of other liberal or left-wing efforts. But he would never forget this fallow period, and correspondence from the time shows him to be hypersensitive about credit, quibbling with a writer for the *New Yorker* who had failed to give him credit for *Show Boat* and who answered Oscar's second letter of complaint by noting his surprise "that you have the interest or the leisure to pursue a matter such as this."

As failure piled on top of failure, Hammerstein grew more depressed but did not lose his sense of humor. In November 1938 he wrote to his old friend the playwright and producer Hy Kraft, "Forgive me for not writing sooner. I have been so busy producing flops that I haven't had time for anything else." And a month later, he told Lester Jacobs of *Variety*, that "three flops in a row have knocked me out as a possible advertiser" in the trade bible's forthcoming commemorative edition. In 1939, his and Kern's *Very Warm for May* closed on Broadway after only eleven weeks, though it did produce one hit song, "All the Things You Are." Royalty checks from past successes kept coming in, and Oscar's muse had not deserted him altogether. After Paris fell to the Nazis in June 1940, Oscar was moved to write a hymn to the city he loved. Kern set the lyrics to music and "The Last Time I Saw Paris" won the Academy Award for Best Original Song in 1941 after being sung by Ann Sothern in *Lady Be Good*.

But a hit song here and there could not compensate for a decade's worth of failed plays. The last straw was *Sunny River*, a nineteenth-century New Orleans love triangle written with Romberg, which opened three days before Pearl Harbor in December 1941 and lasted just thirty-six performances. Wolcott Gibbs in the *New Yorker* pronounced it "a majestic bore," while Burns Mantle of the *Daily News* called it "one of the worst books with which musical comedy has been burdened in recent years."

Oscar was forty-six years old, and his career in musical theater seemed at an end. In 1940 he and Dorothy had bought a seventy-two-acre cattle farm in Doylestown, Pennsylvania, two hours by car from Manhattan, where Broadway figures like George S. Kaufman and Moss Hart already had country homes. "I was pretty blue," he would recall. "I just wanted to come down here to the farm and sit around and be alone and think. It's not easy to hear people say the parade has passed you by."

On January 2, 1942, a day before *Sunny River* closed, the show's producer, Oscar's friend Max Gordon, wrote to him from Hollywood. "I want you to keep your courage because you and I will still do great things in the theater together but they won't be musical comedies," Gordon said. "It is just silly to risk a hundred thousand dollars on what six men are going to say about it in the paper the next day. . . . I would like you to try to find a play for next season, or to write one. If I have any plays that need an excellent director, you certainly will have a crack at that and, if you set your mind down to write a play, I know you can do it. You cannot afford to waste your time any more with musical shows and I cannot afford to produce them."

Gordon had no way of knowing just how wrong he was. Only a few weeks earlier, Hammerstein had welcomed a visitor to Highland Farm, an old acquaintance from his Varsity Show days. It was Richard Rodgers, with an intriguing proposal, and Oscar's luck was about to change.

CHAPTER 2

A Quality of Yearning

> There's a common misconception that you can stand on the top
> of a mountain and look at a sunset and sit down and write some-
> thing beautiful. I don't think it goes that way. I think the sunset,
> the mountain, the experience all go inside and may not come out
> for fifty years. But they become part of your knowledge, part of
> your personality . . . part of your education, part of your technique . . .
> and, eventually, you express yourself.
>
> Richard Rodgers

Richard Rodgers was once asked what he had done before he became a composer. His answer: "I was a baby." If that is an exaggeration, it is only the slightest one. From his earliest consciousness, he was surrounded by the sound of music, in a "passionately musical family," and he was, in fact, something of a prodigy.

He was born on June 28, 1902, to William Rodgers, a stolid, respectable upper-middle-class physician, and his wife, Mamie, in the summer bungalow colony of Arverne, on the Rockaway Peninsula in Queens. Like Oscar Hammerstein, he spent his early childhood in Harlem, a prosperous Jewish neighborhood that, he would recall, was then "quite rural," in the shadow of the same Mount Morris Park where Hammerstein watched the old man climb the bell tower each morning. And like Oscar, he was raised in the household of his maternal grandparents, Jacob and Rachel Levy, who had prospered in the silk trade. That arrangement was an everlasting sore point for Dick's proud father, who had struggled to achieve his professional status as his family's first doctor—indeed, its first educated man—and who chafed at living with his in-laws.

Will Rodgers was the son of a Russian Jewish immigrant—the family's original name was Rogozinsky—who first settled in Missouri, then made his way to New York where he worked as a barber at Delmonico's, the most elegant Manhattan restaurant of its day. His father died when Will, the firstborn of eight children, was only eighteen, leaving him as the family's provider. He worked variously as a cloak-and-suiter and a customs inspector on the New York City docks before putting himself through college and medical school, changing his name along the way to William Abraham Rodgers and hanging out his doctor's shingle in 1893. Three years later, he met and married Mamie Levy and, upon returning from a European honeymoon, set up housekeeping with her strong-willed, frequently feuding parents in a tense ménage, dominated by Dr. Rodgers's long stretches of hostile silence.

But around the piano, where Dick and his older brother, Morty, gathered with their parents each evening before and after dinner, "there was music every day, every day, every day," Dick would recall, adding that his mother was the best sight reader he ever knew. "And, curiously, it was show music," not heavy classical pieces, but the latest piano and vocal arrangements from the popular operettas of the day: *The Chocolate Soldier* and *The Merry Widow*, whose lilting waltz score Dick had memorized by age five without ever having seen the show. By age six, he was fiddling around with "Chopsticks," adding improvised chords and rhythms. His first teacher was his father's sister Tily, but soon enough he had exceeded her skills and was playing tunes by ear. Around the same time, he saw his first live theater, a children's production of *The Pied Piper*, and he was hooked. For the rest of his life, he would equate being in a theater with being in a good mood. "If I'm unhappy," he would say, "it takes my unhappiness away. If I'm happy, I get happier."

Dick's piano playing came to an abrupt halt early in 1910, when he was not yet eight. He awoke one night in agonizing pain, his right index finger swollen to nearly the size of his wrist. When his parents returned home from the theater, his father plucked a scalpel from his office and made "one terrifying slash in the finger to allow the pus to escape." The cause was osteomyelitis, an infection of the bone marrow, and in those days before antibiotics, there was a real risk of amputation if the wound did not heal and drain properly. For months, Dick's right arm was in a sling, the wound kept open to drain, until finally a specialist was able to extract a quarter-inch-square piece of pitted bone fragment, and—a year later—reconstruct a new fingertip so that Dick was once again able to play the piano. Decades later, he would wonder if his lifelong tendency to hypochondria was born of the night when a "loving father" suddenly appeared to "cut me savagely with a knife."

As DICK RODGERS matured, so did his musical tastes. His unquestioned idol was Jerome Kern, already considered the quintessential American composer of popular music, whose melodies had an insinuating simplicity that made the filigree of European operettas sound antique. "The Kern scores had the freshness, and I think even as a child I knew that, and it did something for me and to me," Rodgers would recall. "I think he was a father to a lot of us." With his collaborators Guy Bolton and P. G. Wodehouse, Kern had written a pioneering series of intimate, modern musicals—with titles like *Very Good Eddie*, *Leave It to Jane*, and *Oh, Boy*—staged at the tiny Princess Theatre. Dick first saw *Very Good Eddie* on its tour of the then-prevalent "subway circuit," in which recent shows toured New York City's boroughs after the end of their Broadway runs. He went back half a dozen times. It is difficult to describe the inner mathematical and melodic workings of music in mere words, but Rodgers summed up his feeling for Kern this way: "The sound of a Jerome Kern tune was not ragtime; nor did it have any of the Middle European inflections of Victor Herbert. It was all his own—the first truly American theatre music—and it pointed the way I wanted to be led."

Dick was an indifferent student. Like Oscar Hammerstein, he spent a summer at the Weingart Institute camp. But the academic institution that fired his imagination was Columbia University, where his older brother, Morty, was a student and fraternity brother of Hammerstein's. After a matinee of the 1917 spring Varsity Show, Morty took Dick backstage where he met "a very tall, skinny fellow with a sweet smile, clear blue eyes and an unfortunately mottled complexion," who accepted "my awkward praise with unaffected graciousness and made me feel that my approval was the greatest compliment he could receive." Dick resolved then and there to go to Columbia, too, and he started out by promptly writing his very first copyrighted song, "The Auto Show Girl," commemorating Manhattan's annual automotive exhibition.

The song went nowhere, but Dick was on his way, and by the end of 1917 he had written his first complete musical show, *One Minute, Please*, for the Akron Club, a social-athletic group to which Morty Rodgers belonged. In his autobiography nearly sixty years later, Rodgers would confess that he really had no idea whether the show was any good or not, "but I thought it glorious." And so began a long and often disappointing apprenticeship of one amateur production after another, including *Up Stage and Down*, a 1919 benefit for a charity known as the Infants Relief Society, which played for one night in the ballroom of the old Waldorf-Astoria hotel at Fifth Avenue and 34th Street. The lyrics for three of Rodgers's songs (including one called "There's Always Room for One More") were written by that same tall, skinny fellow who had inspired Rodgers two years earlier: Oscar Hammerstein himself. So twenty-four years before their collaboration revolutionized Broadway, they had already taken each other's measure and worked successfully together.

Rodgers now knew that his unswerving ambition was to write songs for the theater, but he lacked one essential: a collaborator to write the words. He found one on a Sunday afternoon in the spring of 1919, shortly before *Up Stage and Down* opened, when Phillip Leavitt, another classmate of Morty's, introduced him to a twenty-three-year-old Columbia graduate named Lorenz Hart, who was looking for a composer. Dick's vivid first impressions, recorded decades later, are worth quoting in detail. "The total man was hardly more than five feet tall," he would remember. "He wore frayed carpet slippers, a pair of Tuxedo trousers, an undershirt and a nondescript jacket. His hair was unbrushed and he obviously hadn't had a shave for a couple of days. All he needed was a tin cup and some pencils. But that first look was misleading, for it missed the soft brown eyes, the straight nose, the good mouth, the even teeth and the strong chin. Feature for feature he had a handsome face, but it was set in a head that was a bit too large for his body and gave him a slightly gnomelike appearance."

But what really dazzled the sixteen-year-old Dick was Larry's talk, which was animated, opinionated, and seemingly endless. Leavitt recalled that when he and Dick arrived, Hart was at work on a lyric called "Venus," with a first line that went something like, "Venus, there's no difference between us!" and was "always rubbing his hands together, piston-like." Hart already had firm ideas about what was missing in the Broadway lyrics of the day, having not only written and performed in Varsity Shows himself but having translated the lyrics of German operettas for the Shubert brothers, among the Great White Way's leading producers. Hart told Rodgers that most contemporary lyrics were childish and witless, poorly rhymed if not actually illiterate, and that the theatergoing public deserved something better. The younger man sat rapt, instantly captivated; then he played a few of his own melodies, at which Hart immediately brightened. As Dick would famously recall years later, "I left Hart's house having acquired in a single afternoon a career, a partner, a best friend and a source of permanent irritation."

Lorenz Hart was born in 1895, the elder son of Jewish immigrants from Hamburg who liked to say they were descended from the poet Heinrich Heine. His father, Max, was a Tammany ward heeler who was no taller than his son, and almost as wide as he was tall. He claimed to be in the real estate business but had actually been convicted for both grand larceny and fraudulent use of the mails, and Larry would genially describe him as "a crook." Max Hart was variously flush or flat broke, but when in the money spent generously on Larry; his kindhearted wife, Frieda; and their second son, Theodore Van Wyck, named in part for a mayor of New York whom Max had helped to elect, and always known as Teddy. To all of Larry's friends, the Hart household was a warm and welcoming place, full of food, drink, good fun, and conversation—the polar opposite of Dick Rodgers's staid and silent bourgeois family. Years later, Rodgers would fondly recall the Harts as "unstable, sweet, lovely people."

Max Hart's friends included theatrical luminaries like Lillian Russell, and Larry had begun going to the theater and vaudeville when he was six. Like Dick Rodgers (and Oscar Hammerstein), he immersed himself in the world of show business, seeing every show he could, reading hungrily, learning foreign languages, and falling in love with Kern's Princess Theatre shows. He was already mastering the intricacies of interior rhymes (in which the matching sound falls in the middle of a phrase, not the end) and feminine endings (in which the rhyme comes on the penultimate syllable of a word, not the last). "I think of him always as skipping and bouncing," Oscar Hammerstein would recall. "In all the time I knew him, I never saw him walk slowly. I never saw his face in repose. I never heard him chuckle quietly. He laughed loudly and easily at other people's jokes, and at his own, too. His large eyes danced and his head would wag. He was alert and dynamic." But he was already falling prey to the curse that would cripple him and cut his life short: an inability to control his consumption of alcohol that left him unable to work in the morning, capable of short bursts of productivity after his first drink before lunch, and by late afternoon unable to function. After Larry left the Rodgers family apartment one day, Dick's mother declared, "That boy will never see twenty-five." And at a time when homosexual acts were still a crime, Larry Hart was also privately, painfully, and guiltily gay—a secret that he believed would kill his mother if she ever found out.

Hart's demons would torture him and strain his collaboration with Rodgers as the years went on. But the immediate challenge was whether the new duo's songs would ever see the light of day. They spent that spring and summer of 1919 trying to get some presentable enough to audition, and by August, once more through Phil Leavitt's intercession, they felt ready enough to try some on another Leavitt acquaintance: the former vaudevillian Lew Fields, who now had a second career as a successful actor and producer. Dick trekked alone to Fields's beach house in Far Rockaway (Larry begged off, claiming a headache), where Fields allowed that he would not simply buy one of the team's songs, "Any Old Place with You," but would interpolate it into his current musical, *A Lonely Romeo*. ("I'd go to hell for ya, or Philadelphia," went one line in Hart's lyric.) So it was that on August 26, 1919, at a Wednesday matinee at the Casino Theatre, Rodgers and Hart made their Broadway debut. "It wasn't much of a splash," Rodgers would recall decades later, "but to Larry and me Niagara Falls never made such a roar as the sound of those nice matinee ladies putting their gloved hands together as the song ended."

Splash or no splash, the boys from Columbia would have a long drought before they made it back to the big time again.

FOR THE NEXT six years, as Dick continued his formal education, first at Columbia and then at the Institute of Musical Art (now the Juilliard School of Music), Rodgers and Hart honed their craft in one amateur or benefit musical show after another. In his autobiography, Rodgers would list a string of their frivolous titles, as if totting up the price of a painful apprenticeship: *You'd Be Surprised, Fly with Me, Say Mama!, You'll Never Know, Say It with Jazz, The Chinese Lantern, Jazz à la Carte, If I Were King, A Danish Yankee at King Tut's Court, Temple Bells*. By the spring of 1925, Dick was almost twenty-three and still living at home. He would later recall that the hellish silences of his childhood had been replaced by his own hellish sense of guilt at not having more to show for himself. He was desperate enough that when a friend mentioned that an acquaintance who owned a wholesale babies' underwear business was looking for someone to take over his operation—at the rich sum of $50 a week—he was intrigued. He met the man, who made him a firm offer, and was puzzled when Dick asked to think about it overnight. At dinner that very evening, Dick received a telephone call that would change his life. The Theatre Guild, Broadway's most prestigious producing organization, was staging a musical benefit to raise money to buy decorative tapestries for its new theater, and a friend of Dick's had recommended him as just the guy to write the songs. "By the time I got to sleep that night, I was sure of one thing," he would recall years later. "The world was going to have to get along with one less tycoon in the babies'-underwear business."

The new job would not pay anything—and for that reason, Larry was at first reluctant to take it. But this would be more than just another amateur show. The Guild had brought Shaw and Strindberg and Ibsen to modern American audiences, and to do a show—even a benefit show—under its auspices was an opportunity too good to pass up. The

Guild was the brainchild of Lawrence Langner, by trade a successful patent lawyer, and Theresa Helburn, a theater-loving Bryn Mawr alumna, and since 1918 its business model enlisted a subscription audience to support noncommercial productions of prestige plays. The benefit performance was envisioned as a musical revue, with songs and sketches lampooning topical events, the Guild's own high-art pretensions, and its current production, Ferenc Molnár's *The Guardsman*, starring the American theater's reigning royal couple, Alfred Lunt and Lynn Fontanne. There were to be two performances on Sunday, May 17, 1925, at the Garrick Theatre on West 35th Street, where *The Guardsman* was playing but was dark that day. After a frantic rehearsal schedule, on a shoestring budget of less than $3,000, the matinee performance of *The Garrick Gaieties* got under way, with Rodgers himself conducting the eleven-member orchestra.

All went routinely until midway through the second act, when June Cochrane, the ingénue, and Sterling Holloway, a gangly red-haired song and dance man (who would become famous to later generations as the voice of Walt Disney's animated Winnie the Pooh), stood in front of the curtain without a speck of scenery and sang a bouncy, infectious fox-trot that Dick and Larry had written for an unproduced show called *Winkle Town*, and which now took flight. The song was called "Manhattan," and it was a joyous ode to urban living, rhyming "what street" with "Mott Street."

The number stopped the show, and the actors sang two encores until they exhausted all of Larry's available words. "This show's gonna run a year!" Hart cried out when the curtain rang down. In fact, there was just one more scheduled performance—that very night. What to do? The reviews were raves. "All of it is fresh, spirited and engaging," Alexander Woollcott wrote in the *New York Sun*. "Some of it is bright with the brightness of something new minted." Rodgers begged Terry Helburn for permission to use the theater for matinees the following week. She agreed, and the show promptly played to standing-room-only houses despite a heat wave, emboldening Rodgers to propose that the *Gaieties* be allowed to take over the theater for a regular run. When Helburn demanded, "And what do you suggest we do with *The Guardsman*?" Rodgers would recall, "Giving her the benefit of my many years of success in the theatre, I said simply, 'Close it.' " She did, and the *Gaieties* ran for 211 performances, with Rodgers and Hart each taking home $50 a week in royalties (and Rodgers another $83 a week for conducting). Within a year, Rodgers and Hart would have three shows running on Broadway at once. And years later, when the team arrived at an opening at the Guild Theatre on West 52nd Street, Hart pointed proudly to the tapestries and said, "We're responsible for them."

"No, Larry," Dick replied. "They're responsible for us."

How did these two men—so unlike in personality, temperament, and almost everything but talent—manage to work together so well? There exists an old film clip—from *Masters of Melody*, a 1929 quasi-documentary short—depicting Dick and Larry reenacting the creation of their 1925 song, "Here in My Arms." The clip is fanciful, but it offers an uncomfortably intimate window into the imbalance of their partnership. As Larry sits in checkerboard pajamas and slippers in an easy chair—looking a bit like a jailbird—Dick is perched at the piano, pencil between his teeth, picking out notes, and then jotting down lyrics.

"Here in my arms, I think it's adorable," Hart says.

"Too long, Larry!" Rodgers replies. "Too long!"

"All right," Hart rejoins. "Here in my arms, it's adorable!"

In fact, their collaboration was almost as cinematic, in the sense that they really did usually work in the same room, creating music and lyrics together, if not actually simultaneously (though in later years, Larry would have to have at least some lines of melody from Dick before he could even get started). While Rodgers did not need a piano to compose, he usually had one nearby, while Hart would scribble words on whatever scraps of paper he might have at hand: the margins of magazines or newspapers, old playbills, the backs of letters, or discarded toilet-paper rolls.

Though Rodgers was the younger partner, he was the dominant one almost from the start. In a joint profile of them at the height of their fame, the *New Yorker* would describe Larry as "small, tumultuous," and Dick as "poised, immaculate," adding that while Rodgers was under five feet seven inches, he nevertheless seemed tall by comparison with

Hart. In their early years together, Hart referred to his partner as the General. Later he would call him Teacher, or the Professor. If Hart began to look disheveled, Rodgers liked to say, he would take him off to the nearest children's department to shop for new clothes. If Dick's default expression when pondering a note, or reproving his errant partner, was a sour-looking scowl, his satisfied smile when he resolved a problem, or made one of the puns he loved, was wide and beatific, and his brown eyes would dance with a mischief and joie de vivre that matched Larry's brio.

There was never a written contract between them, but their contributions were complementary from the beginning, as Hart once explained to a journalist: "We map out the plot. Then Dick may have a catchy tune idea. He picks it out on the piano—I listen and suddenly an idea for a lyric comes. That happens often. On the other hand, I may think of a couple of verses that will fit into the show. I write them out and say them over to Dick. He sits down at the piano and improvises. I stick my oar in sometimes and before we know it, we have the tune to hang the verses on. It's like that—simple!"

It wasn't that simple, of course, and often Rodgers's first order of business was simply to find Hart so the two could get to work, a problem that steadily worsened over the years as Hart's drinking increased and his tolerance for alcohol diminished. But mutual affection and respect got them through a lot. Rodgers would recall how Hart hated to change a lyric once it was committed to paper. "When the immovable object of his unwillingness to change came up against the irresistible force of my own drive for perfection, the noise could be heard all over the city," he said. "Our fights over words were furious, blasphemous and frequent, but even in their hottest moments we both knew that we were arguing academically and not personally. I think I am quite safe in saying that Larry and I never had a single personal argument with each other."

What made a Rodgers song? The composer and music scholar Alec Wilder studied the likes of Jerome Kern, Irving Berlin, George Gershwin, Cole Porter, and Harold Arlen and concluded that, of all the bunch, Rodgers's songs "show the highest degree of consistent excellence, inventiveness and sophistication." Rodgers, like his contemporaries, generally worked within the conventional thirty-two-measure confines of the American popular song, a form that in its essence is as rigid and unyielding as a sonnet, yet susceptible to almost as many infinite variations as a snowflake. The most common format is the so-called A-A-B-A pattern, in which the main melody (and often the title) is stated in the first eight bars of music. The same melody is repeated for another eight measures. Then there is typically an eight-measure middle section—called a "bridge" or "release"—which introduces a new melodic notion. (Think of the part of Lennon and McCartney's "Yesterday" that begins, "Why she had to go, I don't know, she wouldn't say.") Finally, the melody is restated one last time, often with a slight variation leading to a climax at the end. There are alternatives to this basic scheme, but they, too, generally share a second characteristic typical of the twentieth-century popular song: a cyclical journey through successive musical keys or moods. The trip usually ends up satisfyingly back where it began, on the tonic chord—the musical foundation, the "do" note of the key in which the song is written. The result is that thousands of songs have been written in this standard format, yet hardly any sound the same. "The great composers," the critic and writer William Zinsser once explained, "never run out of ways to put the notes together in a pattern that makes us say, 'Isn't that wonderful! I've never heard anything like that before.' "

Singers and musicians often cite a seeming paradox in Rodgers's melodies: They turn and twist in surprising ways—with, say, a shift to a minor key when major would have been more expected. Having taken their unexpected path, no alternative seems half as logical or appealing, as if the tunes had been formed in air, only to be plucked down and put on paper by the composer. But Rodgers had his bag of tricks, as he suggested in his own description of the way music works on Western ears. "It was a revelation to learn," he once wrote, "that by some curious kind of musical magnetics, the fourth step of the scale was pulled down to the third, and that the seventh was pulled up to the eighth. Nobody has ever explained it scientifically, but if you take the simple phrase of music that goes with 'Shave and a haircut, two bits,' you'll find that the note that goes with 'two' is carried, whether it wants to or not, to the note that goes with 'bits.' It's almost impossible for it to go anywhere else."

The note that goes with "two" is the seventh tone of the major scale, known as the "leading tone," the "ti" that wants by its nature to be brought back to "do." In a musical phrase, the seventh tone lands with a pang, a note of unresolved longing, and Rodgers exploited this reality to the fullest. "We'll have Man-HAT-tan" is a case in point, with the syllable "hat" lingering on the seventh tone in a way that sweeps the listener along. "There's a sigh in the music that's emotional," says Bruce Pomahac, the longtime director of music for the Rodgers and Hammerstein organization. "Without wanting to rip away the magic of what he did, there are things that he did again and again. This is why, in a brand-new song, he's still Richard Rodgers to us." By his own account, Rodgers himself was not always conscious of the technical underpinnings of his composition, but he sensed instinctively where a song should go. "What Rodgers's facility was, was how many ways he could take you away from 'do' and then bring you back to it," Pomahac explains. Moving in and out of keys, alternating between irresolution and release, he adds, Rodgers is "having sex with you, and you're not aware of what he's doing. It just feels really good."

The music critic Winthrop Sargeant once wrote of Rodgers that "any attempt to reduce his style to a formula is doomed," noting that his melodic invention may have been greater than that of any other Broadway composer. "Time and again, you think you can guess what Rodgers is going to do next," Sargeant wrote, "only to find him doing something else entirely."

Rodgers once told an interviewer that art could be defined "as the expression of an emotion by means of a technique." That is an elegantly clinical way of describing a process that is at least partly chemical. If he could not quite define the secret of his success, he knew it when he saw it. "I knew exactly what was happening to me," he would remember. "I loved every minute of it. . . . I roll success around in my mouth like a piece of candy and get the last bit out of it." Decades later, he would insist that he had never been complacent about success. "Never, never," he said. "There are certain elemental things that are always gratifying: eating, a warm bath, making love, and having a successful show."

As if to make up for lost time, after the success of the *Garrick Gaieties*, Rodgers and Hart embarked on a burst of frantic productivity: seven new shows in New York and London in 1925 and 1926 alone, most often with books written by their friend Herbert Fields, Lew Fields's son. Then, as today, there was constant cross-pollination between Broadway and the West End, as British producers commissioned works by American composers and American impresarios imported popular British shows. The plots of Rodgers and Hart's shows were mostly forgettable fluff: a Revolutionary War romance in *Dearest Enemy*; a marathon bicycle race in *The Girl Friend*; a second edition of *The Garrick Gaieties*; quasi-Freudian psychological fantasy in *Peggy-Ann*; a Lower East Side girl's search for love in *Betsy*.

"Larry and I used to thrash around an awful lot trying to find ideas that had not been done, trying to break through the walls," Rodgers would recall. "We didn't always do it, but we did try."

The songs in these shows bore the unmistakable stamp of the Jazz Age, capturing the insouciance and energy of flaming youth, and going on nearly a century later, they are still staples of the jazz and cabaret repertoire: "Blue Room," "Mountain Greenery," "A Tree in the Park." Only *Betsy* was a disappointment, lasting just thirty-nine performances and delivering an unexpected indignity: its star, Belle Baker, had secretly commissioned a new song from her friend Irving Berlin, and when the opening night audience heard "Blue Skies" in the second act, no one was more stunned than Dick and Larry, who were doubly chagrined when Berlin stood up and took a bow for what would become a smash hit song.

In January 1927, Rodgers and Hart left for London, to oversee English productions of their New York shows. On a side trip to Paris, in a taxicab with some New York friends, they avoided a bad collision by mere inches. "Oh, my heart stood still!" someone said. "Hey, Dick, that's a title for a song!" Larry exclaimed, from the floor of the cab, where he had landed with his hat jammed over his eyes. Soon enough "My Heart Stood Still" made its way into a British revue produced by

Charles Cochran: *One Dam Thing After Another*, where it quickly became the favorite song of the Prince of Wales and the hottest song in England. It would make an equal impression back in New York that fall, when it became part of the score for Rodgers and Hart's adaptation of Mark Twain's *A Connecticut Yankee in King Arthur's Court*, though to use it, Dick and Larry had to buy the rights back from Cochran, for a reported $10,000 (or about $137,000 in current dollars). It was worth the price: eleven years later, it had earned Rodgers and Hart some $50,000 in royalties.

Between January 1928 and February 1930, Rodgers and Hart would turn out six more musicals on Broadway, virtually every one of them producing at least one new song that has lasted all the intervening years. Some of their efforts were more ambitious than others. *Chee-Chee* (1928) was a most unusual tale: the story of the son of a Chinese court eunuch who is desperate to avoid promotion to his father's job (and to escape his emasculating fate). Only one song, "Moon of My Delight," has survived from a score that Dick and Larry had sought to integrate so seamlessly with the plot that they put a note in the program, taking a page from Hammerstein's approach in *Rose-Marie*, explaining, "The musical numbers, some of them very short, are so interwoven with the story that it would be confusing for the audience to peruse a complete list." Asked why he wanted to grapple with such an unusual story, Hart waggishly said, "It's got balls!" The veteran Broadway music director Buster Davis would later sum up the effort as "Rodgers and Hart invade the Orient. The Orient wins." The play lasted only thirty-one performances, the shortest run of any Rodgers and Hart show to date. But among the New York critics, the show in fact won five pans, two mixed reviews, and six raves, and Dick and Larry showed their continued willingness to experiment with unusual story lines and songs that served and developed the plot. And for Rodgers, the foray to the Far East foreshadowed territory he would be drawn to explore with Oscar Hammerstein two decades later.

A more conventional effort was *Simple Simon* (1930), co-written by and starring the great vaudeville clown Ed Wynn, who played a newsstand operator in Coney Island who dreams of Cinderella and her fantastical adventures in two fairy-tale kingdoms. One song from the score, "Ten Cents a Dance," became a huge hit for the star who sang it, Ruth Etting, and perhaps the grittiest evocation ever written about the life of any working girl.

In the summer of 1929, Dick had at last moved out of his parents' home, to a penthouse apartment of his own, with a large wrap-around terrace on the eighteenth floor of the Lombardy Hotel on East 56th Street between Park and Lexington Avenues. His only neighbor on the floor was Edna Ferber. Charles Cochran was beckoning about a new show in London. So was Hollywood, where the demand for talking pictures was still red-hot. And so, too, was someone even more alluring—and much closer to home.

BY HIS OWN account, Rodgers had always had an eye for pretty girls. When he was barely ten, his grandfather took him to a production of *Snow White and the Seven Dwarfs* starring Marguerite Clark, a fetching, doe-eyed stage and screen ingénue of the day. "My prepubescent fantasies were restricted by my innocence," he would recall decades later, "but as I look back on them I realize I was doing very well mentally for a ten-year-old and was clearly heading in the right direction." From his teenage years on, Dick had dated plenty of girls, including, discreetly (and by his later remembrance, chastely), an older married woman named Helen, with whom he took long walks in Central Park and spent hours listening to Brahms. But nothing had quite prepared him for the feeling he experienced in the fall of 1925 when he went to pick up his friend Ben Feiner to see King Vidor's sweeping World War I film *The Big Parade* and noticed Ben's sixteen-year-old sister, Dorothy, who suddenly seemed all grown up, and was waiting for her own date with an heir to the Bergdorf Goodman department store fortune. "Although I had seen her at the theatre only a short time before, she no longer looked like just a young kid," Dick would remember. "In fact, she looked like the prettiest girl I had ever seen." Indeed, years later, nothing would please Dick more about *Words and Music*, MGM's otherwise fanciful and often laughable 1948 biopic about Larry and him, than the actress who played the role of the young Dorothy: it was Janet Leigh, at her dewiest and fresh-faced best, and she bore an uncanny resemblance to the young Dorothy Belle Feiner. Dick made up his mind to wait a year—sixteen seemed too young for the twenty-three-year-old composer—to ask Dorothy out.

By coincidence, that is just what happened. In September 1926, the White Star liner RMS *Majestic*, bearing Rodgers back from England, where he and Hart had written a show called *Lido Lady*, stopped across the English Channel in Cherbourg to pick up passengers from France. Among them was Dorothy Feiner, who was on her way home from an extravagant Parisian shopping trip with her parents, to acquire the wardrobe she would soon take with her to Wellesley College. Dorothy and Dick had many mutual friends on the boat, she would recall years later, "but as far as Dick and I were concerned, we were alone on that vast ship." When the *Majestic* docked in New York, Rodgers tore off the corner of a magazine page and gave her his phone number. (More than fifty years later, she would still have that scrap of paper.)

Dorothy went off to Wellesley that fall while Dick remained a bachelor about town in Manhattan, and they began a sometimes tempestuous and not-always-exclusive courtship that would last three and a half years. That December, Dick took Dorothy to the first night of his and Larry's new show, *Peggy-Ann*, her first Broadway opening. Some of her other beaux talked of marriage, but Dick did not. She broke off the relationship for a time, hoping she wouldn't miss him, but she did. In February 1928, bored at college and pining for Dick, she left Wellesley and went to Europe with her parents to soothe her sorrow. Her ship passed Dick's in the North Atlantic, and he sent her a radio message, "Hullo." Not realizing he'd intended to start a conversation via wireless, she was hurt, and wired him back, "Goodbye." But they could not make a break, and as 1928 turned into 1929, and Rodgers and Hart kept up a tremendous burst of productivity as the toast of Broadway, Dick and Dorothy's relationship deepened.

From the beginning, Dorothy seems to have known that she would always have competition. When the notion of marriage first came up, probably sometime in late 1929, her father warned her: "Look, I like him very much, but I think you must realize that he is going to be surrounded by the most attractive women and they'll be coming along new every year, younger and younger. And as you get older, they'll still be coming." So "if this is going to worry you, you shouldn't marry him." Dick himself made no secret of the fact that he was highly sexed. His letters to Dorothy when they were apart in the early years of their marriage are full of painfully passionate declarations of ardor, protestations of fidelity, and gently dirty jokes, like the one about an "absent-minded commuter who kissed the train good-bye, jumped on his wife and went to town."

"There is in Rodgers's music a quality of yearning," says Timothy Crouse, the writer and the son of the playwright Russel Crouse, who knew Rodgers in later years. "The yearning may be for many things, but to my mind it has to do above all with the longing for a woman; it's erotic at its source. Even as a boy, I could see that Dick was slightly different when talking to a woman than when talking to a man—more vibrant, more vivacious. I think that he needed the electricity of contact with attractive, talented women—they sparked his creativity. In the sanctum of his imagination, they may have been his target audience. Part of what drew him to the musical theater may have been that it always contained the tantalizing possibility of romance; it was a world of license that you didn't find in other parts of the society."

The couple were married on March 5, 1930, in "a bower of flowers" in Dorothy's parents' living room on Park Avenue, two weeks after the Broadway opening of *Simple Simon*. They headed to Europe for a six-week honeymoon, which culminated in London, where Rodgers and Hart had been commissioned to write a new show, *Evergreen*, about an actress who poses as a woman of sixty to further her stage career. When she falls in love with a younger man concerned about her age, the truth eventually comes out. The show provided an opportunity for Rodgers and Hart to recycle a song that had been dropped from *Simple Simon*, "Dancing on the Ceiling."

Dancing on the ceiling is also what the new Mrs. Richard Rodgers must have sometimes felt she was being forced to do, as she set up housekeeping not only with her husband but with his writing partner as well. The three of them moved into a large rental house on York Terrace in Regent's Park, and though Dorothy was very fond of Larry, "it was a lot to take on a ménage à trois when I hadn't yet managed the ménage à deux." To compound matters, Dorothy soon enough realized she was pregnant, and each morning, a disheveled, unshaven Larry would interrupt their breakfast with the queasy-making smell of a fat black cigar. Dorothy would flee upstairs, Dick would yell, Larry would apologize profusely and then "repeat the whole performance absent-mindedly the next morning."

The newlyweds had barely gotten used to their London routine before they uprooted themselves again, first back to Manhattan, and then to Hollywood, where Warner Bros. had offered Rodgers and Hart a three-picture deal.

THE VOGUE FOR film musicals that *The Jazz Singer* had sparked was still in full swing, and in June 1930 Richard Rodgers arrived in Southern California. His finances had taken a hit in the 1929 crash, and Broadway productions were being curtailed, so the lucrative offer from Los Angeles was especially appealing. But just as Oscar Hammerstein had, Richard Rodgers would find his years in Hollywood personally and professionally unsatisfying. The problems started with the first movie he and Hart were assigned to work on, a confection called *The Hot Heiress*, about a riveter in love with a socialite. The stars were Ben Lyon, a popular matinee idol who had made a splash in Howard Hughes's 1930 World War I aviation epic, *Hell's Angels*, and Ona Munson, who had appeared on Broadway in *No, No, Nanette*. The only rub: Lyon could not sing, and Munson's range was so limited that her songs had to be as uncomplicated as possible. By August, Dick and Dorothy were headed back to New York, where she endured a rocky pregnancy and several times came close to miscarrying, while Dick returned to London to finish work on *Evergreen*. Their daughter Mary was born in January 1931, and the following month, Rodgers and Hart had a new show on Broadway, *America's Sweetheart*, about a couple who move from Minnesota to Hollywood determined to make it in the movies but wind up struggling instead. Its subject matter must have cut uncomfortably close to the bone, because *The Hot Heiress* opened in March and was a fat bomb. With the craze for musical movies suddenly over, Jack Warner bought out the rest of Dick and Larry's contract. Their next move was uncertain.

But that fall, Hollywood came calling again—with a more appealing proposition. Paramount Publix (as it was then known) was the most cosmopolitan and continental of the Hollywood studios at the time, with a stable of European émigré directors and performers, and it came up with a vehicle for the French music hall performer Maurice Chevalier. *Love Me Tonight* is based on a play called *Tailor in the Chateau* and tells the story of a romantic Parisian tailor who falls in love with a lonely princess and masquerades as a baron to win her hand, before being discovered by the servants in her castle. In the end, love conquers all. Once again, the plot was as weightless as a French meringue, but Rodgers and Hart had a crucial ally in the innovative director, Rouben Mamoulian. An Armenian émigré, Mamoulian was himself a recent recruit to Hollywood from Broadway, where he had staged the original production of DuBose and Dorothy Heyward's play *Porgy* for the Theatre Guild in 1927.

Owlish, bespectacled, and temperamental, Mamoulian was possessed of an extraordinary visual sense and an instinctive feel for storytelling in song. Together with Dick and Larry, he devised a singular method of staging a musical film using a previously underutilized tool: the camera itself. In his memoir, Rodgers would recall the basic premise. "What we had in mind was not only moving the camera and the performers, but having the entire scene move," he would say. "There was no reason why a musical sequence could not be used like dialogue and be performed uninterrupted while the action took the story to whatever locations the director wanted." Mamoulian was not only the film's director but its producer, and he agreed completely. Just as he had with the opening scene of *Porgy* on stage, Mamoulian began the film with a steadily growing symphony of everyday sounds as Paris awakens.

Minutes later, as Chevalier fits a bridegroom for a new suit in his tailor shop, he launches into one of Rodgers and Hart's all-time great ballads, "Isn't It Romantic?" Seamlessly, without a break, the scene shifts (as does the song) from the tailor, to the customer, to a passing taxi driver and his fare, to soldiers on a troop train, to a gypsy boy who overhears them, to a campfire where the music swells to the strain of gypsy violins, to the bedchamber of Princess Jeanette (played by Jeanette MacDonald), who expresses her longing for a lover she has yet to meet. The lyrics—really snatches of rhyming sung dialogue—are so perfectly suited to the action that Hart had to write a more generic alternative for the published sheet music version of the song. And Mamoulian's narrative camera technique, pathbreaking at the time, was so successful that it became the template that has been used ever since, with appropriate technical refinements and enhancements, to film complicated song and dance sequences. His innovations can still be seen in movie musicals like *La La Land*.

If only the rest of Dick and Larry's sojourn in Southern California had produced any project even remotely as satisfying. But it did not. From 1931 through 1934 came one disappointing experience after another. Hollywood was where the money was, so that is where Rodgers and Hart stayed, in a succession of rented houses in Beverly Hills. (Larry eventually took his own place after one too many late nights took its toll on Dorothy Rodgers.) Dick summed up their entire output for the year 1933, when they worked variously for MGM and the producers Samuel Goldwyn and David O. Selznick, this way: "One score for a film that wasn't made; one score, mostly unused, for a film no one can recall; one song for Goldwyn; one song for Selznick."

Like Oscar Hammerstein in the same period, Dick chafed at being a studio worker for hire, subject to the whims of directors, producers, and executives, when he'd grown used to having creative control of his own projects on Broadway. To make matters worse, Dorothy was frequently away, in New York, or on vacation by herself, sometimes taking young Mary with her, sometimes leaving her in Dick's care. In the summer of 1933, she went to New York for a minor operation, while Dick remained in Hollywood. He was miserable, and told her so in no uncertain terms. "I've been hideously faithful to you, my pet, and not through a sense of duty!" he wrote on June 13, paraphrasing a Hart lyric. Three weeks later, he was if anything even more frank. "As a matter of clinical fact, sleeping in your bed has had a salutary effect on my morale," he wrote on July 4. "It gives me a sense of contact that I can't get in any other way. I *could* go to your closet and bury my head in your clothes, but the honest hysteria I could achieve by doing that would be lost in the fact that it's been done on the screen. . . . Angel, darling, don't pay too much attention to this. It's just your lover, a little nuts with all this longing, trying to tell you he adores you and wants to be with you. If you think I'm drunk, tant mieux. That's when the real stuff comes out. I love you. One Richard."

Around the same time, he confided to her his frustrations with Hollywood in general. "Some Thursday night, when the servants are all out and there's a great crowd in the Vendome"—a popular restaurant on Hollywood Boulevard—"I'm going to walk in and yell, 'Fake!' at the top of my lungs and walk out again."

It was in these dark days that Dick happened upon a question printed in the syndicated "New York Day by Day" column: "Whatever happened to Rodgers and Hart?" Rodgers's hands shook as he held the newspaper. "I called Larry up and said, 'We gotta get out of here.'" And they did.

From the moment they returned to New York, things started looking up, and no one would ever again have to wonder what had happened to Rodgers and Hart. Indeed, from 1935 through 1942 they would enjoy an almost unbroken run of success: ten shows, all but one of them hits. In these years, they also produced a bumper crop of songs that were among the best they ever wrote. Their efforts ranged from the spectacular—*Jumbo*, a circus vaudeville featuring acrobats, live elephants, and Jimmy Durante, for the producer Billy Rose in 1935— to the satirical—*I'd Rather Be Right*, their 1937 lampoon of Franklin D. Roosevelt starring the great George M. Cohan himself, with a book by Broadway's leading comedy playwrights, George S. Kaufman and Moss Hart. That same year, Dick and Larry wrote the book, music, and lyrics for *Babes in Arms*, a let's-put-on-a-show story about the children of old vaudeville troupers who stage a musical revue to keep from being sent to a work farm. The cast featured a crop of young unknowns singing some of the most adult, sophisticated songs that Dick and Larry ever wrote, among them "Where or When," "I Wish I Were in Love Again," "My Funny Valentine," and "The Lady Is a

Tramp." In 1938 and 1939, the team wrote two shows: *I Married an Angel*, which paired them with a hotshot young director named Joshua Logan; and *Too Many Girls*, which introduced a young Cuban band leader named Desiderio Alberto Arnaz y de Acha, who would soon be known simply as Desi Arnaz.

Two other Rodgers and Hart projects from this period deserve special attention for the pioneering strides they made. The first is *On Your Toes* (1936), which they had begun in frustration during their last year in Hollywood as a potential vehicle for Fred Astaire. The plot was conventional Broadway hooey. Junior Dolan, the son of vaudeville hoofers, gives up the family business for life as a serious student of music at Knickerbocker University, where he falls in love with a coed, Frankie Frayne, and becomes friends with Sidney Cohn, who is writing a jazz ballet called *Slaughter on Tenth Avenue*. They try to sell the idea to a Russian ballet company, whose prima ballerina is interested not only in the dance but in Junior himself. Complications ensue when another dancer, a rival for the ballerina's affections, puts a mob contract on Junior, who must keep dancing as fast as he can until the cops arrive to save him in the nick of time.

The ballet was Larry's idea, and from the start it had been seen as integral to the plot. Ballets had been used in Broadway musicals before, but invariably as one-offs in a loose revue format, not as storytelling devices. To choreograph the show, Rodgers and Hart turned to George Balanchine, a Russian émigré who was already energizing the American ballet scene and had been signed as the resident dance master of the Metropolitan Opera. Dick and Larry had seen his work and knew he was the man they wanted, but Rodgers was hesitant about just how to proceed, as he would recall years later. "I didn't know a thing about choreography and told Balanchine that I was unsure how we should go about it," he remembered. "Did he devise his steps first and expect me to alter the tempos wherever necessary, or did he fit his steps to the music as written? Balanchine smiled and with that wonderful Russian accent of his said simply, 'You write. I put on.' And that was the way we worked."

The ballet made *On Your Toes* electrifying, and its star, Ray Bolger, wowed Broadway audiences with his style of rubber-legged, "skin-and-boneless" dancing that suggested he was dangling from a puppeteer's string, his feet never touching the floor. (He would later play the Scarecrow in *The Wizard of Oz*.) Rodgers's insistent, syncopated melody, with its signature brassy main theme, was his most extended musical undertaking to date, and for many years the sheet music for the ballet outsold all other Rodgers compositions. On the Broadway of 1936, the ballet "caused an uproar," according to the *New York Herald Tribune*.

The other notable Rodgers and Hart show of this era is *Pal Joey* (1940), based on a series of John O'Hara's stories in the *New Yorker* about a louche emcee in cheap nightclubs and the rich woman who keeps him and builds him his own club. It was O'Hara's idea, and the notion came as a complete surprise to Rodgers, but it instantly appealed to him as "something really special." "The 'hero' was a conniver and a braggart who would do anything and sleep anywhere to get ahead," Rodgers would recall. "The idea of doing a musical without a conventional clean-cut juvenile in the romantic lead opened up enormous possibilities for a more realistic view of life than theatregoers were accustomed to." Hart was just as enthusiastic, having spent "thousands of hours in exactly the kind of atmosphere depicted in the stories," and "thoroughly familiar with the Pal Joeys of this world," as Rodgers would put it. With a book by O'Hara, the best-selling author of the novels *Appointment in Samarra* and *BUtterfield 8* and a withering observer of class and status in American life, the show promised something new in musical comedy, and its creation was perhaps predictably rocky from the start. O'Hara himself was often unreachable for weeks at a time during the writing. George Abbott, who was both the director and producer, haggled with Rodgers about royalties and doubted the show's commercial prospects.

But as personified by a young dancer from Pittsburgh named Gene Kelly, whom Dick and Dorothy Rodgers had spotted in William Saroyan's *The Time of Your Life* the year before, Joey is an unregenerate heel from the start. He spurns a dewy-eyed ingénue, Linda English, for a prowling cougar, Vera Simpson (played with relish by Vivienne Segal, one of Larry Hart's favorite actresses), and when Joey's behavior is too much even for Vera and she dumps him, the young lovers are not hap-pily reunited but walk offstage in opposite directions at story's end. Rodgers would later sum up the action by saying there wasn't one decent character in the whole play, "except the girl, and she was stupid." The setting brought out Hart at his wickedest. He could write not only pastiche production numbers for the nightclub scenes—their titles tell all: "That Terrific Rainbow," "The Flower Garden of My Heart"—but cynical solos for Joey and Vera that plumbed their characters in ways barely heard of in run-of-the-mill musical comedies. Even the most ten-der ballad in the show—"I Could Write a Book"—is sung by Joey to Linda as a blatant con and come-on.

"Bewitched," the most enduring song in the play, with its unforget-table alliteration ("Bewitched, bothered, and bewildered"), combines a flowing, romantic melody by Dick with short, self-mocking lyrics by Larry, so full of double entendres they had to be bowdlerized for radio play. When Joey and Vera sing of their illicit love nest—their "Den of Iniquity"—Hart deploys French to add another hint of sophistication, and when Vera finally gives up on Joey, she sings a stinging reprise of "Bewitched" to his face.

The show opened on Christmas night 1940 and shocked audiences and critics alike. The most famous first-night review was Brooks Atkin-son's judgment in the *New York Times*, which began, "If it is possible to make an entertaining musical comedy out of an odious story, Pal Joey is it," and ended, "Although it is expertly done, can you draw sweet water from a foul well?" Gene Kelly would recall waiting in Larry Hart's apartment for the reviews, and when Atkinson's was read aloud, "Larry didn't say anything to us; he just started to cry" and walked out of the room. Kelly would also remember the stark difference between the icy reception the show received from theater party matrons from the suburbs on Wednesday matinees and the apprecia-tive laughs it got from more "swinging" audiences on Friday and Sat-urday nights. Still, the show ran for eleven months, followed by a three-month tour, and Wolcott Gibbs's review in the *New Yorker* proved prescient. "I am not optimistic by nature," Gibbs wrote, "but it seems to me just possible that the idea of equipping a song and dance production with a few living, three-dimensional figures, talking and behaving like human beings, may no longer strike the boys in the business as merely fantastic."

As THE NEW Year dawned, Rodgers and Hart had reached the peak of artistic and creative achievement. Each had an income of well over $100,000 a year, which Dick managed carefully and which Larry spent as fast as he could. But their partnership was in trouble, and 1941 would be the first year in six years without a fresh Rodgers and Hart show on Broadway. Indeed, it was unclear whether there would ever be another one again.

The trouble was Larry. He had loved Hollywood as much as Dick had hated it, seduced by the soft weather, the easy lifestyle, and the swimming pools where he would practice the one form of physical exercise he had ever deigned to engage in. He was also increasingly seduced by alcohol, late nights, and pursuits that he and Dick never talked about. More and more, those pursuits involved his close friend Milton Bender, a onetime dentist who had given up his practice to become a theatrical agent, hanger-on, relentless pursuer of handsome young chorus boys, and, perhaps, a procurer of willing men for Larry. The Broadway publicist Gary Stevens described Bender as "a very devious, nefarious, strange man," who preyed on gay men, and dubbed him "Assputin."

Indeed, Bender was cordially despised by virtually everyone else in Hart's orbit, though it was universally assumed by everyone except Larry's mother that whatever Hart's actual sexual activities, they did not involve women. Years later, the actress Diahann Carroll reported, Dick dismissively referred to Hart as "that drunken little fag." But the emotion that shines through in all of Rodgers's public and private recollections of Hart is deep and abiding, even indulgent, affection— coupled with unconcealed irritation. There are fleeting references in Rodgers's surviving letters to Hart's nocturnal ramblings. "Had dinner with the shrimp last night and hit the hay while he went about his nefarious (get it?) business," Rodgers wrote to Dorothy from Hollywood in 1937. Five days later, after she had apparently pressed him on his meaning, Rodgers wrote again, "My crack about Larry was just for fun. I have no idea what he does with himself after I leave him, but according to his morning reticence, I have to draw my own conclusions. However, he seems to be functioning quite well and that's my major concern unless he manages to get into trouble."

But by 1941, Hart was barely functioning at all. "He no longer seemed to give a damn about anything," Rodgers would recall. Rodgers was approaching forty, more confident than ever of his abilities, and more determined than ever to remain productive. He was growing increasingly frustrated.

Suddenly that summer, there was a ray of light. In June, Rodgers began talking with his former neighbor Edna Ferber about adapting her new novel, *Saratoga Trunk*, into a musical. What if they could get Ferber's old *Show Boat* collaborator Oscar Hammerstein to write the book? "Larry and I sit with everything crossed hoping that you will do Saratoga Trunk with us," Rodgers wired Hammerstein on June 29. But by the following month, complications had arisen. Warner Bros. already owned the film rights and was balking. Ferber was acting up. Still Rodgers wrote Hammerstein, "Even if nothing further comes of this difficult matter it will at least have allowed us to approach each other professionally. Specifically, you feel that I should have a book with 'substance' to write to. Will you think seriously about doing such a book?"

Two months later, with Hart still disinclined to work, Rodgers found himself in Philadelphia for the out-of-town tryouts of a new musical, *Best Foot Forward*, written by Hugh Martin and Ralph Blane and directed by George Abbott, for which Dick had agreed to become a silent producer. Rodgers was getting nowhere with Hart on a proposed musical adaptation of Ludwig Bemelmans's autobiographical essays, *Hotel Splendide*. On a chance, he picked up the phone and invited himself to Hammerstein's farm in Doylestown, an hour away. Over lunch, Dick poured out his worries about Larry, while Oscar said not a word. When Rodgers finally finished, Hammerstein thought for a couple of minutes and then replied slowly, "I think you ought to keep working with Larry just as long as he is able to keep working with you. It would kill him if you walked away while he was able to still function. But if the time ever comes when he cannot function, call me. I'll be there."

CHAPTER 3

Away We Go

There's a bright, golden haze on the meadow. . . .

Oscar Hammerstein II

For a play that would come to epitomize the essence of the American experience, it took shape a long way from home, first at Les Deux Magots in Paris and then in a $2-a-day rented room in Cagnes-sur-Mer, France, in the autumn of 1928. Rollie Lynn Riggs, a twenty-nine-year-old gay cowboy turned poet and playwright, had come to Europe on a Guggenheim Fellowship to pursue his art. Born on a farm outside Claremore, Oklahoma, to a mother who was one-eighth Cherokee, Riggs had worked as a day laborer, a movie cowboy, a proofreader at the *Wall Street Journal*, and a schoolteacher in Chicago, and he had spent time in the writers' colonies of Provincetown, Massachusetts, and Yaddo, in Saratoga Springs, New York. Now like other members of the Lost Generation, he had arrived in France—to write a play that he hoped would preserve the memory of his childhood in Indian Territory, before Oklahoma became a state. The plot would revolve around a courtship at a "play-party"—a house party with music, singing, and square dancing—and it would feature the cowboy songs he and his cousins had sung in their youth.

"Indeed, the subtitle might almost be 'An Old Song,'" Riggs wrote to a friend, "for, like the old songs of its period, it tries to reproduce a gone age in the Middle West—its quaintness, its absurdity, its sentimentality, its pathetic and childish melodrama, its rude vigor, its touching sweetness." He would call his drama *Green Grow the Lilacs*, after a popular nineteenth-century folk song about a spurned lover, and he would write in the published preface to the play that his aim was to "recapture in a kind of nostalgic glow" a past that was fast disappearing from memory, by throwing away ordinary theatrical conventions—swift action, a complex plot—and instead trying "to exhibit luminously, in the simplest of stories, a wide area of mood and feeling."

Green Grow the Lilacs was first presented by the Theatre Guild on January 26, 1931. It featured Franchot Tone, a young actor just making his name on Broadway, as Curly McClain, a cocky young cowhand who is courting a comely farm girl, Laurey Williams, and it opened with his singing "Git Along, You Little Dogies!" offstage. The cowboy's rival for Laurey's affections is Jeeter Fry, her surly farmhand, and a traveling peddler adds spice to the mix. (The peddler was played by Lee Strasberg, who would go on to fame as perhaps the leading teacher of method acting in America.) The cast was rounded out by a troupe of real cowboys from a rodeo that had just closed at Madison Square Garden. As it happens, the farmhand is killed in the second act, but the basic plot involves no surface conflict more riveting than which of the two men will take the girl to the party. Brooks Atkinson of the *New York Times* pronounced the effort "less a play than a hale and hearty narrative of loves, jamborees and neighborly skirmishes," though he did praise the "warming relish of its characters," adding, "How alive they are!"

Obliged to go on the road to fulfill commitments to Guild-affiliated theaters around the country, the company closed the show after just sixty-four performances. But Theresa Helburn, the doughty co-director of the Guild, never gave up on the property, and in July 1940 she was pleased to see a revival of it at the Westport Country Playhouse, a summer stock theater in Connecticut that was owned by her Guild partner, Lawrence Langner. By evening's end, the audience's obvious appreciation of the gentle tale made Helburn believe there was life in the old chestnut yet. "After the show, Terry came backstage to see everybody," the assistant stage manager, Elaine Anderson, would recall years later. "No matter what anybody tells you today, I was there when it happened, and I remember it was strictly *her* idea. She said to us all, 'This would make a good musical!'"

Helburn's notion was more than an idle thought. After years as Broadway's most prestigious producer of quality drama, the Theatre Guild was on the ropes. A run of flops and a flock of unhappy subscribers had left the group's finances in shambles and it was far from clear just how long it could sustain itself. There were "prospects of utter disaster," Lawrence Langner would recall. At the beginning of 1942, the Guild had only about $30,000 in the bank, and Helburn decided the answer might just be "a totally new kind of play with music, not a musical comedy in the familiar sense, but a play in which the music and dancing would be aids to and adjuncts of the plot itself in telling the story." Years later she would confess that she was not sure when she had become convinced that *Green Grow the Lilacs* was such a vehicle. "What I do remember is trying to make other people share my conviction," she would recall. "When you're trying to raise a lot of money, people reminded me, you ought to offer them a sure-fire success, not a play that hadn't done so well in the past. Musicals, they said in disgust, don't have murders in the second act."

But Helburn thought at once of a composer who was in search of a strong second act for himself—the same bright fellow whose musical genius had helped her buy a new set of tapestries for the Guild Theatre seventeen years earlier: Richard Rodgers.

IN THE SPRING of 1942, Rodgers had managed to wrest one more show out of Larry Hart: *By Jupiter*, another comic vehicle for Ray Bolger, based on the play *The Warrior's Husband*, about the Amazon women's war with the men of Greece. But he had only been able to do so after checking Hart into Doctors Hospital in Manhattan to dry out, then taking a room there himself and ordering a piano to be delivered from Steinway & Sons so he could force Larry to finish the score. The moment the show got to Boston for its tryout, Hart disappeared for three days. *By Jupiter* was a hit—it would have the longest original run of all the Rodgers and Hart shows—but it took its toll on Rodgers. When Terry Helburn asked him to read the script of *Green Grow the*

Lilacs, he was more than willing to entertain new directions. Helburn assumed, of course, that she would be commissioning a Rodgers and Hart show, but Larry was having none of it. He told Dick he was going off to Mexico for a much-needed rest. Rodgers called his bluff, insisting, "The only reason you're going to Mexico is to drink. When you come back, you'll be in worse shape than ever."

Dick made one last offer in the offices of Chappell & Co., their music publisher: If Larry would check into a sanitarium for alcohol treatment, he would go with him, and they could work together there. But that idea had no appeal for Hart, so Rodgers, with blood rushing to his head, delivered his ultimatum: "If you walk out on me now, I'm going to do it with someone else."

"Anyone in mind?" Hart asked, looking at the floor.

"Yes, Oscar Hammerstein," Rodgers replied.

"Well, you couldn't pick a better man," the sheepish Hart replied. When he left, Rodgers found himself suddenly alone—and in tears.

Hart went off to Mexico, and when he returned a month later, "he had to be carried off the train on a stretcher," Rodgers would recall. Meantime, backstage at the Shubert Theatre one day, Rodgers approached some young cast members of *By Jupiter* with a question: "Hey, kids, have any of you ever been to Oklahoma?"

By sheer coincidence, Hammerstein himself had recently rediscovered *Green Grow the Lilacs* and believed it would make a fine new musical. On a visit to Hollywood in May, he had read the play aloud to Jerome Kern, but Kern did not warm to the subject. Hammerstein wasn't ready to give up, and on his return to New York, he reached out to the Theatre Guild about acquiring the rights. He was told the play was already spoken for, by Rodgers and Hart. At this point, two developments occurred almost simultaneously: one incontrovertible, one slightly curious.

One development was that Dick Rodgers called Oscar Hammerstein, invited him to lunch in the Barberry Room of the Berkshire Hotel on East 52nd Street, and asked him to read *Green Grow the Lilacs*. "I don't have to read it," Oscar replied. "I know it and I'm crazy about it. I'd love to do it with you."

The other development was a brief dispatch in the *New York Times* on July 23: "The Theatre Guild announces that Richard Rodgers will write the music, Lorenz Hart the lyrics and Oscar Hammerstein the book for its adaptation of the play *Green Grow the Lilacs* by Lynn Riggs. The authors will commence work shortly."

It is possible that the Theatre Guild's announcement as rendered by the *Times* was a mistake, though that seems unlikely, since the Guild itself was quoted as making the statement. It's more probable that Rodgers or the Guild still held out hope that Hart could be brought along. In any case, as Rodgers would recall, in the space of that single lunch and without anything more than a handshake agreement, "Rodgers and Hart became Rodgers and Hammerstein," fifty-fifty partners in a brand-new enterprise. Neither man's life would ever be the same.

THE NEW TEAM'S first story conference took place at Dick's country home, a fifteen-room, five-bath Colonial house on six acres off Black Rock Turnpike in Fairfield County, Connecticut. He and Dorothy had bought it in the summer of 1941, and except for periodic hotel stays in Manhattan when work called them to town, they would live there with their daughters Mary and Linda for the duration of World War II. In Dick's view, the most attractive feature of the place was a massive old oak tree with a ninety-foot canopy that towered over the front yard, and it was under the shade of this tree that he and Oscar set to work on the new show.

Their first and most basic problem was that nothing much happens in *Green Grow the Lilacs*, certainly nothing that would lend itself to the traditional storytelling techniques of musical comedy. Rodgers and Hammerstein did not set out to break the usual Broadway conventions so much as they decided that it would be all but impossible to adhere to them and still do justice to the spirit of their tale. How, for instance, could they introduce the typical singing and dancing ensemble that opened a musical comedy? Strawberry festivals, sewing parties, quilting bees were all considered and eliminated as "corny devices," Hammerstein would recall. After much back and forth—discussions lasting weeks—they decided to open their musical the same way Lynn Riggs had opened his play, with Aunt Eller sitting alone on the stage churning

butter, and Curly the cowboy heard singing offstage. But singing what?
Back home in Doylestown, Hammerstein turned for inspiration to
Lynn Riggs's opening stage directions: "It is a radiant summer morning
several years ago, the kind of morning which, enveloping the shapes of
earth—men, cattle in a meadow, blades of the young corn, streams—
makes them seem to exist now for the first time, their images giving off
a visible golden emanation that is partly true and partly a trick of the
imagination focusing to keep alive a loveliness that may pass away."

Oscar admired this ripe prose passage, and in a painstaking effort
that took three weeks, he fashioned the first words of poetry that his
new partner would set to music:

> *There's a bright, golden haze on the meadow.*
> *There's a bright, golden haze on the meadow.*
> *The corn is as high as an elephant's eye*
> *An' it looks like it's climbin' clear up to the sky.*
>
> *Oh, what a beautiful mornin',*
> *Oh, what a beautiful day.*
> *I got a beautiful feelin'*
> *Ev'erythin's goin' my way.*
>
> *All the cattle are standin' like statues,*
> *All the cattle are standin' like statues.*
> *They don't turn their heads as they see me ride by,*
> *But a little brown mav'rick is winkin' her eye.*
>
> *Oh, what a beautiful mornin' . . .*
>
> *All the sounds of the earth are like music—*
> *All the sounds of the earth are like music.*
> *The breeze is so busy it don't miss a tree*
> *And a ol' weepin' willer is laughin' at me!*
>
> *Oh, what a beautiful mornin' . . .*

"Well," Rodgers would recall years later of the moment that he received the finished lyric from Oscar, "you'd really have to be made of cement not to spark to that," and he wrote the accompanying melody in about ten minutes.

In fact, Dick and Oscar's first song set the tone for the whole of their collaboration, combining fidelity to the source material with a novelty, simplicity, and directness of expression that seemed so fresh as to be shocking. It was as if their separate careers had ideally prepared them for a sudden and unexpected collision that brought out the best in both men, with Rodgers's unadorned melody perfectly matching Hammerstein's artless words.

As his collaboration with Hart wound down, Rodgers had decided that his piano playing was not what it ought to be, and he commenced a course of study with Herman Wasserman, a virtuoso teacher whose students had included George Gershwin. Rodgers explored the rich Romantic melodies and harmonies of Brahms and Schumann, and in the process, his daughter Mary believed, his own musicality deepened and darkened. The fizziness and vitality of his work with Larry Hart did not disappear, but it was now undergirded by a new richness and seriousness.

For his part, Hammerstein summoned all the theatrical craft he had learned over the past twenty-five years, his lyrics distilling the character, personality, and perceptiveness of his protagonist. This would be a realistic, plain-spoken cowboy, but one with a poet's eye. He would not sing in the standard thirty-two-bar format of a popular song but in the form of a folk ballad, with a repeating chorus, and verses in which the first two lines are each sung twice—in the manner of the turn-of-the century "field hollers" of farmworkers that gave rise to the blues. And in writing this single song, Hammerstein set the pattern that prevailed for 90 percent of his collaboration with Rodgers: he would write the words first, as he had always wanted to. And he would write them—almost always—from afar, not in the same room with Dick, but standing at a tall captain's desk at the southeast-facing window of the second-floor study of his Pennsylvania farm.

Oscar's rural surroundings made their mark on his work; what

Lynn Riggs's words didn't supply by way of imagery, his own observations would. For instance, on a hot summer morning some years before, he had noticed a herd of cows standing motionless on a hillside a half mile away, and composed a short stanza in his head, which he memorized:

> *The breeze steps aside*
> *To let the day pass.*
> *The cows on the hill*
> *Are as still as the grass.*

Now those old lines, slightly altered, found a new home. Firsthand evidence influenced the song in other ways. Hammerstein had originally written, "the corn is as high as a cow pony's eye," only to find on one of his frequent long walks that the midsummer corn on a neighbor's farm was much taller than that. Rodgers was similarly open to revision and adaptation. His original pencil sketch for "Oh, What a Beautiful Mornin'" shows that he initially set the first six syllables of the opening phrase of the chorus to a descending melody that repeated the same three tones down the scale. But he erased the original notes in favor of the sinuous, four-tone, descending *and* ascending melody the world now knows.

Oscar was instantly proud of his effort. In a letter to his son Bill, who seemed to question the song's sixteen bars of verse and sixteen bars of chorus, he defiantly noted that "Dixie," "Home Sweet Home," and "Old Black Joe" all used the same form. "I don't compare it to 'Old Man River,'" he wrote. "I say it may have a longer life. It is a sure standard, and so simple that it will be adopted as the thing to sing every time the sun shines bright. School children will start the morning exercises with it and so will camps start their days with it."

With the tone of the show now set, the next task was to work on the plot. Some decisions were minor. Oscar changed the name of the menacing farmhand from Jeeter to Jud, presumably to avoid any association in an audience's mind with Jeeter Lester, the Georgia sharecropper who was the lead character in Erskine Caldwell's best-selling 1932 novel *Tobacco Road*, the dramatic version of which had recently concluded an eight-year run on Broadway. Borrowing a page from the operetta tradition—indeed from grand opera as well—Hammerstein devised a comic subplot involving another pair of lovers, by expanding the bit part of Laurey's friend Ado Annie Carnes (changed from a pudgy wallflower to a buxom mantrap), and giving her a partner in a rope-twirling cowboy named Will Parker, who is mentioned only in passing and never so much as seen in *Green Grow the Lilacs*. He named the peddler Ali Hakim (changing him in the process from Syrian to Persian) and set him up as Will's rival for Annie's affections, creating a parallel trio with Laurey, Curly, and Jud. Having already turned Lynn Riggs's opening stage directions into a song, Oscar would keep large chunks of his dialogue, and its period dialect, while trimming the flab and sharpening the jokes. He built up the dramatic tension between Curly and Jud by having them bid for Laurey's picnic hamper at a box social.

But it was in revising and condensing the play's flaccid ending that Hammerstein displayed his masterly skills as an adapter and editor. In Riggs's script, Curly and a knife-wielding Jeeter struggle during the raucous celebration of Curly and Laurey's wedding night, and Jeeter falls on his knife and is killed. After this climactic moment, the scene shifts to Aunt Eller's farmhouse several days later. Curly has been hauled off to jail pending trial, but he breaks out and sneaks back for one stolen night with his bride, before agreeing to return and face his fate the next morning. The curtain falls with the sound of Curly's voice singing to Laurey offstage, his future ambiguous. Laboring through repeated drafts over the summer, Oscar shortened the action into a summary trial in which Curly is found not guilty of Jud's death the very same night, and the newlyweds ride happily off on their honeymoon. "What was the third act of this play is all covered in about five minutes in our second act," Hammerstein would recall years later. Riggs's version takes thirty pages of dialogue. Hammerstein's takes three.

OSCAR HAMMERSTEIN'S WORK habits were as disciplined as Larry Hart's had been chaotic. He would rise at seven and have a long rubdown from his tenant farmer, Peter Moen, who doubled as his masseur.

After a shower and breakfast with Dorothy, he would repair to his study. The cozy room, with flowered curtains and Venetian blinds at the windows, was equipped not only with the stand-up captain's desk but also a comfy armchair and ottoman, where Oscar sometimes worked with a yellow pad propped up on his knees, along with a typewriter, a dictionary stand, and a complete multivolume set of the *Oxford English Dictionary*. Hammerstein would work until late morning, when he dispatched correspondence and dealt with pending business matters. After lunch at one, he would return to the study, where he worked until five, before emerging for a game of tennis or other relaxation. The routine was much the same day in and day out.

Generally working with a soft black pencil, sometimes typing badly, Oscar sketched out ideas, snippets of lyrics, strings of rhyming words— bits of a mosaic that would eventually find their way into finished songs. As if to ground himself in the story, he drew a map of Claremore, Oklahoma's environs, showing the imagined location of Laurey's farmhouse, the Verdigris River, the Santa Fe Railroad line, and so on. He catalogued simple prairie food items, like sourdough bread, bacon, dried apples, beans, flapjacks. He jotted down stray phrases: "Clear as the wind that blows behind the rain," "June bugs zooming round the roses." He listed possible rhymes appropriate to the period or the region: "Table d'hote—coyote," "Bloomers—rumors," "Alkali—Apple pie."

One challenge was how to let the audience know that Curly and Laurey, who spend most of the first half of the play sparring and fussing, are really falling in love. An early effort expanded on a line of dialogue. After Laurey denounces Curly as a "braggin', bow-legged, wisht-he-had-a-sweetheart bum!" Aunt Eller explains: "She likes you— quite a lot." "If she acts like she wants to shoot you," a draft song lyric ran, "she likes you quite a lot." A second stab was a duet between Curly and Laurey called, "Someone Will Teach You," in which they each hope the other will find the right partner someday. One chorus went like this:

Someone will teach you
And clearly explain

How really important you are.
Someone will teach you
To walk down a lane
As if you were ridin' a star.

Only after these false starts did Hammerstein light on the mutual pro-
testation that became "People Will Say We're in Love." In this case
Rodgers had written the music first. Dick and Oscar then hit upon the
notion of "having the lovers warn each other against any show of tenderness lest other people think they were in love," and Hammerstein
came up with a raft of possible injunctions:

Don't tie my ties for me,
Don't tell pretty lies for me . . .
Don't buy a hat for me,
Don't turn Democrat for me—

For the bridge of the song, Rodgers unconsciously made the musical
interval between the first two notes the precise opposite of the interval
he had used for the opening of the chorus—descending the scale, for
emphasis, instead of rising up, as he had at the start. Meantime, Hammerstein tried out these lyrics to accompany Rodgers's release:

Don't start collecting things,
Handkerchief, dance card or glove.
Kind friends are suspecting things—
People will say we're in love.

Line by line, revision after revision, Oscar kept at the song. Finally, this
opening quatrain emerged, sparkling with clarity and simplicity:

Don't throw bouquets at me—
Don't please my folks too much,
Don't laugh at my jokes too much—
People will say we're in love!

And Hammerstein polished the lyrics for the bridge into even greater specificity and directness, with a knowing glimpse—in the not-so-sardonic word "sweetheart"—of the infatuation his words pretend to conceal:

> *Don't start collecting things*
> *Give me my rose and my glove;*
> *Sweetheart, they're suspecting things—*
> *People will say we're in love!*

In a similar bit of alchemy, Hammerstein turned the slightest passage in the opening scene of Riggs's play—Curly's invitation to Laurey to go with him to the dance—"in a bran' new surrey with fringe on the top four inches long—and *yeller*"—into a song of such shimmering loveliness that Oscar would later confess that hearing it always made him cry. On his trusty yellow pad, he sketched out a long list of words that, when pronounced with an Oklahoma twang, might rhyme with "surrey," including curry, hurry, flurry, blurry, worry, arbitrury, sanitury, millinury, stationury, and vury vury. Rodgers provided a rhythmic, repetitious melody that mimics the sound of horses' clopping hooves, until, for the final chorus, the tempo slows to a whisper:

> *I can see the stars gittin' blurry*
> *When we ride back home in the surrey,*
> *Ridin' slowly home in the surrey with the fringe on top.*
> *I can feel the day gittin' older,*
> *Feel a sleepy head near my shoulder,*
> *Noddin', droopin' close to my shoulder till it falls, kerplop!*

Rodgers's own preferred work time was the morning, at the piano; his daughters would recall that the happiest sound of their childhoods was of their father picking out tunes. He would leave the living room door open, and the notes would drift out. But there were rules: no distractions, like whistling or humming, that might disturb his concentration. Years later, someone would ask Rodgers how long it had taken him to compose the entire score of the show. "Do you mean 'flying time' or 'elapsed time'?" he asked. "Counting everything," he would estimate, "the most I could make it come to was about five hours. But the total 'elapsed time' covered months of discussion and planning."

EVEN AS OSCAR began collaborating with his new partner, another newcomer—a twelve-year-old boy—entered the Hammerstein family's life, destined to become Oscar's lifelong friend, surrogate son, and favorite pupil—and his greatest lasting legacy to the American musical theater beyond his own work. The boy's name was Stephen Joshua Sondheim.

Sondheim's mother, the former Janet Fox, and known all too tellingly as "Foxy," was a Manhattan dress designer and a friend of Dorothy Hammerstein's. In June 1942, after her divorce from Herbert Sondheim, a maker of women's ready-to-wear clothing, her only son, Stephen, came to Doylestown to visit. He wound up skipping his planned trip to summer camp and stayed all summer instead at Highland Farm, joining a growing wartime ménage of strays and displaced persons that included the children of two other friends of Dorothy's who had fraught relationships with their own mothers. "He was the boy who came to dinner," James Hammerstein would recall. Soon enough, Foxy Sondheim bought a farm of her own on the opposite side of Doylestown and young Stevie became an honorary member of the Hammerstein clan, often riding his bike to Highland Farm and spending the weekends there to avoid his unhappy home life. Stevie—precocious, a skilled pianist, frighteningly good at wordplay, puzzles, and strategic games—quickly became a favorite of Oscar's, earning the uncritical affection that Hammerstein so often found it difficult to bestow upon his own children, and sometimes seeming to displace them in their own home. "I loved him as a brother, but Steve was not warm," James Hammerstein would recall years later. For his part, Sondheim would acknowledge that Oscar, like his own father, was not good with children until they reached a rational age, "and the trouble with that is, by the time you are at a rational age, a number of wounds have been inflicted and scars have formed."

Stevie taught Oscar how to play chess, but soon enough the competitive older student beat the young instructor. Sondheim had set a complicated, multi-move trap, which Hammerstein eluded at the last moment. "Gosh, you're getting good," Sondheim told him. "You saw what I was setting up."

"No," Oscar replied. "I heard your heart beating."

IF THE THEATRE Guild was banking on Rodgers and Hammerstein to save the day, rounding out the rest of the creative team was equally important. A crucial decision was the hiring of Rouben Mamoulian—the same innovative director who had teamed with Rodgers and Hart for the film *Love Me Tonight*—to take control of the new show. Mamoulian had returned to Broadway, winning critical acclaim for his direction of George Gershwin's *Porgy and Bess* for the Guild in 1935, just as he had for the original play. But like Hammerstein, he had lately suffered a fallow period.

With a projected budget of $90,000—lean even by the standards of Broadway's constricted wartime economics—the new show would be far from lavish in its mounting. The scenic designer Lemuel Ayers would make extensive use of the simplest and least expensive form of stagecraft: painted backdrops, albeit in clean strokes and bold colors that evoked Grant Wood. The costumer Miles White designed authentic period clothing in candy-colored tones that would have to be toned down.

There was no budget for big-name stars. The Guild was initially interested in Shirley Temple for Laurey, but her parents didn't think she was right for the part. Terry Helburn offered Groucho Marx the role of the peddler, but he turned her down. For their part, Rodgers and Hammerstein were intrigued by Mary Martin, who had made her debut in Cole Porter's *Leave It to Me* in 1938, but she was skeptical of the idea.

Though Dick and Oscar had worked with the top names in their business, and though they would help create any number of new stars, they preferred to let their shows take the spotlight. And while they would prove terrific at spotting new talent, they also preferred to work with known commodities. So the part of Laurey went to Joan Roberts, who had been in *Sunny River* for Oscar, and Curly would be played by

Alfred Drake, a veteran of Dick's *Babes in Arms*. Rodgers and Hammerstein wanted the gangly Charlotte Greenwood, who had been a Broadway star since the teens but was now busy as a character actress in Hollywood, as Aunt Eller, but she was unavailable, so they settled for Betty Garde, a well-known radio performer. Lee Dixon, a veteran song and dance man, was cast as Will Parker; the Yiddish actor Joseph Buloff as the peddler; and Howard Da Silva, a onetime steelworker from Cleveland, as Jud Fry, who lives in a filthy smokehouse with a collection of dirty postcards and an even bigger collection of resentments. The solo that Dick and Oscar would write for Jud, "Lonely Room," is a brooding soliloquy of angry despair unlike anything ever heard before in a Broadway musical:

> *The floor creaks,*
> *The door squeaks,*
> *There's a field mouse a-nibblin' on a broom,*
> *And I set by myself*
> *Like a cobweb on a shelf,*
> *By myself in my lonely room.*

(It would become Mary Rodgers's favorite of her father's songs.)

Celeste Holm, a twenty-five-year-old actress and singer who had appeared in the Theatre Guild's production of William Saroyan's *The Time of Your Life* that also featured Gene Kelly, auditioned for the soubrette role of Ado Annie. Oscar had conceived the character as a girl who simply "cain't say no" to any would-be suitor. Holm had been warned not to sing a Rodgers song, since he was known to be finicky about how his own music was performed, but was told not to sing a song by another popular composer, either. So she chose a Schubert art song, "Who Is Sylvia?" and as she headed to the stage, she fell down a short flight of steps, music flying. "That was funny," Rodgers told her. "Could you do it again?" But he was concerned. "You have a trained voice," he said. "I'd like you to sing it as if you'd never had a lesson in your life—a bold, unedited farm girl voice."

In response, Holm blurted out, "I can call a hog."

"I dare you," Rodgers countered.

"So I did," Holm would recall. "None came. But that's how it happened."

The other auditions, conducted before potential backers to raise the needed money for the show, were painful exercises. Rodgers and Hammerstein trooped to penthouses and town houses, wooing wealthy angels, with the help of Drake and Roberts singing the main songs. At one elaborate session held in the home of the socialite Natalie Spencer, a residence so grand that it had its own ballroom, they pulled out all the stops and still raised not a penny. The show was "too clean," Lawrence Langner would recall. "It did not have the suggestive jokes, the spicy situations, the strip-teasers and the other indecencies which too often went with a successful musical of those days."

Indeed, perhaps the best way to understand just what this new show would *not* be is to cast a glance at another then in the works, one that passed for the epitome of sophisticated Broadway fare: Cole Porter's *Something for the Boys*, produced by Michael Todd and starring Ethel Merman. It was a smart-alecky, wised-up romp about three cousins who inherit a ranch next to a military base outside San Antonio. They decide to turn it into a hotel for servicemen's wives, but the local commander mistakes it for a brothel and complications ensue. The score featured Porter's trademark risqué topical songs and a torchy ballad for Merman. It made jokes about Admiral Nimitz and General Eisenhower and the meatless days imposed by wartime rationing. The climax came when Merman intercepts radio transmissions through the fillings in her teeth, saves a distressed plane, and ends the military brass's boycott of her hotel. "The entire show was a bald contrivance," one theater historian would write, but *Life* magazine called it "gay and glittering," and it would last for 422 performances, a phenomenal run for its day. *Something for the Boys* was a musical comedy, all right. Whatever the Theatre Guild was cooking up was something else altogether.

AS THE FALL of 1942 dragged on into winter, the project was getting to be known up and down Broadway as "Helburn's Folly," and on the way to yet one more backers' audition, she had a suggestion for Hammerstein. "Terry said to me, 'I wish you and Dick would write a song about the earth,'" Oscar would recall. "Coming out of a clear blue sky, the suggestion shocked me . . . I forget what I said. I remember what I thought. I thought it was one of the silliest and vaguest ideas I had ever heard. Now the strange fact is that two days later, I had written a lyric which I never intended to write." The lyric Oscar wrote was indeed a hymn to the land, to the possibilities of statehood and a new life together for Laurey and Curly. Aunt Eller would start the verse, joined by Laurey and Curly, who would then sing the rousing chorus:

> They couldn't pick a better time to start in life!
> It ain't too early and it ain't too late.
> Startin' as a farmer with a brand-new wife—
> Soon be livin' in a brand-new state!
> Brand-new state
> Gonna treat you great!
> Gonna give you barley,
> Carrots and pertaters—
> Pasture for the cattle—
> Spinach and termayters!
> Flowers on the prairie where the June bugs zoom—
> Plen'y of air and plen'y of room—
> Plen'y of room to swing a rope!
> Plen'y of heart and plen'y of hope. . . .
>
> Oklahoma,
> Where the wind comes sweepin' down the plain
> And the wavin' wheat
> Can sure smell sweet
> When the wind comes right behind the rain . . .

There had been no such notion, no such sentiment, anywhere in *Green Grow the Lilacs*. The new song envisioned a bigger and better future for the protagonists. As it turned out, it spelled a bigger and better future for the show itself.

If Terry Helburn sparked Oscar's creativity, Hammerstein could also be his own muse. He took a single line of Aunt Eller's dialogue from *Green Grow the Lilacs*—about how territory folks "orter hang together"—to create a stirring second-act opening number about the civic obligations of incipient statehood, "The Farmer and the Cowman."

> *And when this territory is a state,*
> *And jines the union jist like all the others,*
> *The farmer and the cowman and the merchant*
> *Must all behave theirsel's and act like brothers.*

The Guild had decided to invest $25,000 of its own capital (leaving it with just $15,000 in emergency reserves), and a private pool of regular backers (including the producer Lee Shubert) put in another $15,000. But that still left Langner and Helburn less than halfway to their goal of $90,000. MGM already owned the film rights to *Green Grow the Lilacs*, so Helburn asked the studio for a direct investment in the musical, but it wasn't interested. Helburn persisted: If MGM owned the film rights, how could the Guild attract other investors, who would rightly worry that the new musical's film prospects would be encumbered? So MGM granted the Guild an option to buy the rights to Riggs's original play within thirty days of the opening.

Then the Guild approached Harry Cohn, the head of Columbia Pictures, a scrappy, second-tier studio, arranging a private audition just for him. He liked the show, but his board of directors resisted. So Cohn agreed to invest $15,000 of his own money, provided that Max Gordon, who then had a production deal at the studio and had told Oscar that he was done with Broadway musicals for good, anted up an equal sum—which Gordon reluctantly did.

FROM THE BEGINNING, dance was envisioned as a vital part of the show, and Helburn and Langner had a particular inspiration, a struggling young choreographer named Agnes de Mille. The daughter of the film director William de Mille (and the niece of his more famous brother, Cecil B. DeMille, who capitalized his "d"), she had been kicking around Hollywood and New York for more than a decade. She had recently been commissioned by the Ballet Russe de Monte Carlo to choreograph *Rodeo*, a suite of western dance music by Aaron Copland. Langner and Helburn invited Rodgers and Hammerstein to join them on opening night, October 16, and the next day, Helburn sent de Mille a telegram: WE THINK YOUR WORK IS ENCHANTING. COME TALK TO US MONDAY.

But Dick and Oscar had their doubts. Was this untested talent up to the task of choreographing a Broadway show, and one on which so much was already riding? After de Mille met up with Hammerstein in a drugstore on 57th Street and pleaded her case, the partners relented, and de Mille laid down her own strict rules in her first working meeting with Hammerstein.

"First, I informed him, I must insist that there be no one in the chorus I didn't approve," she would recall. "I sat up quite straight; as I spoke I looked very severe. 'Oh, pshaw,' he murmured. He was sorry to hear I was going to take that attitude—there was his regular girl, and Lawrence Langner had two, and Dick Rodgers always counted on some. For one beat, I took him literally, there being no trace of anything except earnestness in his face, and then I relaxed on that score for the rest of my life." (In fact, Rodgers did usually have a regular girl in his shows.)

De Mille would wind up fighting bitterly at times with Dick and Oscar, and especially with Rouben Mamoulian, to get her way. She would be paid a flat $1,500 for her work on the show—supplemented with a $50-a-week bonus after the opening—and eventually with a one-half percent royalty for all New York and major touring productions. But to the end of her life, she would remain bitter about what she viewed as Rodgers and Hammerstein's greed. And in interviews and oral histories in her later years, she appeared to mischaracterize Hammerstein's ideas about the show's signature dance: a ballet at the end of the first act titled "Laurey Makes Up Her Mind." De Mille would insist that Hammerstein originally envisioned a circus-themed piece, whereas she injected the themes of dark sexuality and danger as Laurey is torn between the sunny Curly and the brooding Jud.

But before de Mille was even hired, Hammerstein had sketched out a fairly detailed scenario for the ballet. Oscar did envision having Aunt

Eller appear as a circus rider in pink tights, with Curly driving a golden surrey. But after Laurey takes the "elixir of Egypt" that the peddler has sold her, Hammerstein imagined, she would fall into a trance and "a ballet is started which states, in terms of fantasy, the problems that beset Laurey. The treatment will be bizarre, imaginative and amusing, and never heavy." His initial thought was that the dream figures could either be played by the actors who portrayed them in the rest of the show, or by separate dancers (de Mille would choose the second option).

In a later draft titled simply, "Prelude to Ballet," a group of girls sing to Laurey as she repeats their chant: "I am a girl who knows what she wants and I can choose . . ." Then, Hammerstein wrote, "The wispy figure of a bride glides on from the shadows." Laurey gazes ahead of her, entranced in her daydream, murmuring, "Yes, yes." This is followed by a terse typewritten note: "Take it, Agnes!"

Take it de Mille did, devising a dream-turned-nightmare in which Laurey is attracted to Curly but irked at his cockiness, and is both repelled and intrigued by Jud. Curly and Laurey's wedding is inter- rupted by a menacing Jud, who chases her into a saloon where the girls of his dirty postcards come to life, dancing a can-can and taunting her to a jangling rendition of "I Cain't Say No." Jud and Curly fight to the eerie strains of "The Surrey with the Fringe on Top" transposed into a minor key, and Curly is killed. Jud carries Laurey off in his arms, just as she awakens from the dream to find him standing over her, waiting to take her to the party as the first-act curtain falls.

In twelve or thirteen minutes, the ballet elaborates on the story and the characters in ways that would take pages of awkward exposition in dialogue. Here, too, de Mille was in charge. She repeatedly asked Rodgers for a score for the dances, and he replied, "You have the song tune, what more do you want?" So de Mille improvised, choosing themes from the score, which the rehearsal pianist would improvise, with Rodgers's later approval. Years later, friends of Rodgers's would explain that this was because the composer didn't have the patience to sit in the rehearsal room with de Mille for hours at a clip. But at least in the beginning, he watched her closely.

"The first three days were absolutely crucial and Dick Rodgers sat right beside me," she would recall decades later. "Right by the piano, watching every move. I couldn't say, 'Put your shoes on' or 'Button your shoes' or 'Turn your back,' he was there watching. And the girls were so nervous, the dancing girls, that they really almost had fits, they were almost sick with nerves, and they said, 'He's watching us, he's watching us.' And I said, 'My dears, he's not watching you; he's watching me. He'll get around to you later.' Well, at the end of the third day, we had done the postcard section and he came up to me and put his arms around me and said, 'Where have you been all my life, Agnes?' And I was in. I was accepted."

Hammerstein was equally impressed.

"The ballets in *Oklahoma!* deal with the inner longings of the characters, with their roots, their environment, their reasons for being what they are," he would explain years later in an essay for *Dance* magazine. "Here indeed the choreographer becomes the collaborator of the author and composer, not merely for the enhancement of one or two moments in the play but in helping to build the very bone and muscle of the story."

REHEARSALS BEGAN ON February 8, 1943, in the Guild Theatre. The show's working title was *Away We Go*, from an old square dance call. Decades later, George S. Irving, a young actor in the ensemble, would recall Rouben Mamoulian's opening pep talk to the cast. "On the first day of rehearsal he pointed to the radiators attached to the wall and he made a very elaborate speech about how this was like a temple, beaming down at our efforts," Irving remembered. "I was twenty years old. I didn't know from nothing. I was so happy to be working."

Mamoulian and Hammerstein generally worked with the actors on the main stage, while Rodgers, de Mille, and the conductor Jay Blackton drilled the singers and dancers in a downstairs lobby lounge. "It was like being in a cement mixer," de Mille would recall. Tensions between her and Mamoulian were "shatteringly bad." The rehearsal setbacks may have been typical, but it was already becoming clear that the new show was not. "You know, we had no real chorus kids," Betty Garde would recall. "They were all from Juilliard. The singers were from Curtis in Philadelphia and Agnes de Mille's dancers and other ballet schools.

They were fresh." At one point, the stage manager, Jerry Whyte, was thinking of quitting. Betty Garde urged him to stay with it. "This is going to run five years on Broadway," she insisted.

In those days, it was standard procedure for Broadway-bound plays to go on the road for out-of-town tryout performances, where live (and perhaps less jaded) audiences could provide a test of what worked and what didn't—and where scenes could be rewritten or restaged to address problems. The Shubert Theatre in New Haven, Connecticut, was a favorite first stop, and the new show's opening there was set for Thursday, March 11, a "split-week" run of just three performances. The cast had finished its final dress rehearsal at five o'clock that morning without ever making it through the second act. That night, Betty Garde would remember, "We had to go on cold with the second act and just grope our way around stage. It was unbelievable."

In her dressing room at the Shubert, Celeste Holm was besieged with last-minute instructions from the producers. First was Lawrence Langner. "Just remember the Chaplinesque quality of the part," he said. "The fact that she can't say no is, to her, a tragedy." Then came Terry Helburn, exhorting, "Up, up, up! We're counting on you for the comedy so lift every scene you're in!" And finally Armina Marshall, Langner's wife and also a Theatre Guild official, with these words of encouragement: "I suppose I shouldn't say this, but I think you're absolutely wrong for the part, but good luck." "Thus fortified," Holm recalled, "I went upstairs and realized it was going to be between me and the audience."

She needn't have worried. Her comic solo, in which Ado Annie laments

> When a person tries to kiss a girl
> I know she orta give his face a smack.
> But as soon as someone kisses me
> I somehow sorta wanta kiss him back!

stopped the show cold. Days later, as the company decamped for Boston, Oscar devised new lines for the needed encore.

Over the years, the canard has grown up that the show was in serious trouble at this point. It is true that the Broadway producer Mike

Todd told anyone who would listen at the New Haven opening that he
didn't see how the play could succeed, and he left at intermission—but,
he later explained, only because he had to bail a friend out of jail. Still,
the Guild's backers were skeptical. Max Gordon, for one, was nervous
enough to off-load $2,500 of his $15,000 share to Al Greenstone, who
for years had printed the souvenir programs for the Guild and loved
the show. Greenstone would not only reap many times his investment;
he was so grateful that he sent checks back to the Guild in thanks for
the privilege of being in on the ground floor.

There were rumors that Mamoulian might be sacked. On Saturday, two days after the opening, Alfred Drake spotted George Abbott
in the theater in New Haven and asked if he'd come to take over. *Why?*
Abbott wondered. *The show was fine.* What's more, audiences liked it
from the start—and so, contrary to legend, did the critics. The *New
Haven Register* pronounced it "a rollicking musical . . . jammed to the
hilt with tuneful melodies . . . ideal escapist entertainment." At one
midnight postshow story conference, Richard Rodgers interrupted his
fretting colleagues. "Do you know what I think is wrong?" he asked.
"Almost nothing. Now, why don't you all quiet down."

Still, Mamoulian would remember that when the show pulled into
Boston for a two-week run, the producers were hardly on speaking
terms with their director, regarding him as an obstinate obstacle. The
Boston opening was Monday, March 15, and one scenic change ordered
by Mamoulian backfired: he'd commissioned a flock of pigeons to
lend outdoorsy verisimilitude, but they flew straight to the rafters,
where they stayed for the rest of the run. There would be other, more
important changes over the next two weeks. "Boys and Girls Like You
and Me," a tender but slow-paced second-act duet for Laurey and
Curly, was dropped in favor of an exuberant reprise of "People Will
Say We're in Love," with the lovers declaring, "*Let* people say we're
in love."

"Oklahoma," in the big eleven o'clock slot near the end of the show,
had been conceived as a solo for Curly (after Aunt Eller's introduction),
but Mamoulian thought it was falling flat. Then a member of the
ensemble, Faye Elizabeth Smith, had a suggestion for Rodgers: What if
the whole chorus joined in? Dick liked the idea, and to carry it out

he turned to the show's incomparable orchestrator, Robert Russell Bennett.

An orchestration is to a melody line what a finished oil painting is to an artist's first charcoal or watercolor sketch, the polished composition that fleshes out the subtle harmonies of color and sound that surround and expand and enhance the painter's flash of inspiration. Leonard Bernstein once described the cadre of top-flight Broadway orchestrators as a corps of "subcomposers who turn a series of songs into a unified score." Even a symphonically trained composer like Bernstein did not generally arrange his own music for the theater, and while Rodgers theoretically possessed the technical knowledge to have done so himself, he much preferred to focus on the thousand and one tasks that creating an original musical play required, instead of deciding what the oboe part should sound like. "Arrange me a hit!" Rodgers liked to say, quoting an apocryphal songwriter who threw down a blank piece of manuscript paper to his orchestrator. The assertion was true enough, as Bennett himself was the first to acknowledge, noting that no orchestrator could work his magic "when the tunes are not good tunes and the poor desperate souls look up to you with big eyes and say they know you will make it all sound wonderful."

But Bennett, a musical polymath who grew up playing piano, trumpet, trombone, violin, and organ in dance bands and silent movie houses before establishing longtime collaborations with the likes of Jerome Kern and Cole Porter (and a close friendship with Hammerstein), knew that the reverse was just as true. He had been born in Kansas City in 1894 and by age ten was playing cornet in his father's band. He went on to study composition in Paris and remained a lifelong musical snob. He once wrote that "twenty-seven bars of Beethoven's Opus 84" was "worth the whole output of musical comedy since I started working on it." He explained modestly that his trade secret was to approach a Broadway composer's music "with the least possible embellishment," but he was also under no illusions about the ultimate importance of his work to the success of a show. "Mother brings a beautiful baby into the world, nourishes it, brings it up into a radiant, enchanting young girl," he wrote of a typical Broadway composer.

"But she suffers because she never learned to design her daughter's clothes."

On this show, Bennett's contributions were palpable and essential. Working with de Mille and using Rodgers's basic tunes, he wrote the score of the ballet, including its ominous, funereal finale, and he was still frantically orchestrating the piece on the eve of the New Haven opening. An orchestrator's pay was good—perhaps $100 for a typical ballad, more for a complicated dance number—in an era when $100 a week was a more than respectable salary even in Manhattan. But not until the mid-1950s would orchestrators receive royalties on even the longest-running or most successful shows, from which a composer might make millions, so the work was grueling and often thankless. "Either write fast or do without much sleep, or both," was one of Bennett's rules for success in his trade.

When Rodgers summoned him to rework the "Oklahoma" number, Bennett had already returned to Manhattan from the tryout run. So he hopped a train for Boston on Sunday morning, March 21, and by the time he reached Old Saybrook, Connecticut, he had worked out the basic eight-part vocal arrangement of the song—including an inspirational ending all of his own devising, in which the chorus undertook a driving, rhythmic spelling lesson—chanting "O-K-L-A-H-O-M-A" before singing a final, glorious, "Oh-klah-HOHHHH-mah!"

When Bennett arrived at the Colonial Theatre in Boston, he handed his chart to the conductor, Jay Blackton, who taught the harmonies to the chorus as quickly as possible, while de Mille staged the song with the entire cast moving down to the footlights in a kind of flying wedge. When the revised number went into the show on Monday night, the effect was electrifying. Blackton, conducting in the pit, couldn't see the reaction of the audience behind him. "But I certainly could hear it!" he remembered. "Amazing!"

MEANTIME, DE MILLE and a big chunk of the cast fell ill with German measles, while Dorothy Hammerstein was hospitalized with a raging fever of unknown origin. Still, Oscar was cautiously optimistic, writing to his son Bill, "I think I have something this time." A few days later, on March 25, Hammerstein elaborated, saying that the show had suddenly taken on "the aura of a hit" and would be a worthy heir to *Show Boat.* "I don't believe it has as sound a story or that it will be as great a success. But it is comparable in quality and may have a very long life. All this is said in the hope that a handful of beer-stupefied critics may not decide that we have tried to write a musical comedy and failed. If they see that this is different and higher in its intent, they should rave. I know this is a good show. I cannot believe it will not find a substantial public. There! My neck is out!"

There was one last change to come. Before leaving New Haven, the producers had already decided that *Away We Go* was the wrong title for the show, but there was no time to alter the playbills and posters for the Boston run, so an alternative would have to await the New York opening. Among the options floated by Langner and Helburn: *Swing Your Honey, One Two Three, Party Tonight,* and *Singin' Pretty.* It is not clear who came up with the idea of calling the show *Oklahoma.* Betty Garde would insist she had been the first one to broach it, over dinner at Gallaghers Steakhouse while the show was still in rehearsal in Manhattan. By the middle of the New Haven run, everyone was on board with the idea. But now there was another fillip: Late one night, Helburn called from Boston to tell Joe Heidt and Helene Hanff of the Guild's publicity department, who were working in unheated offices to save money, to say that the decision had been made to add an exclamation point, to make the title *Oklahoma!* The word had already been reproduced three times on each of the ten thousand press releases that had been prepared for mailing to Guild subscribers, so Hanff set about inking in thirty thousand exclamation points by hand, while Heidt called printing firms and sign painters all over town to get them to change the copy.

A lot was riding on that single burst of punctuation. Would Broadway audiences be carried along?

On Wednesday, March 31, Oscar and Dorothy Hammerstein went for a walk around the farm in Doylestown before heading into Manhattan for the opening that night. "I don't know what to do if they don't like this," he told her. "I don't know what to do because this is the only kind of show I can write."

In New York that morning, it had begun to snow, and it continued to snow all day, turning into a cold, wet drizzle as night fell. The fourteen hundred–odd seats of the St. James Theatre were far from full. Cast members were urged to invite their friends to see the show for free, to fill the house. Agnes de Mille had bought ten front-row balcony seats and couldn't figure out how to get rid of them all. Servicemen headed for the nearby Stage Door Canteen on West 44th Street were dragged in off the pavement, and some young dancers roped in three of their friends—Betty Comden, Adolph Green, and Judy Tuvim (soon to be Judy Holliday), who performed in a comedy troupe called The Revuers—and bundled them into the theater under a marquee blacked out by wartime regulations. The management had given strict instructions that no one was to be seated during the opening number. De Mille, who was standing at the back of the house holding Rodgers's hand, would recall that "Oh, What a Beautiful Mornin' " "produced a sigh from the entire house that I don't think I've ever heard in a theater; it was as though people hadn't seen their homeland, it was perfectly lovely and deeply felt." "The Surrey with the Fringe on Top" drew comparable appreciation, but it wasn't until "The Farmer and the Cowman" at the top of the second act that the house went wild, "and the audience just screamed and hollered and Dick and I were there hugging each other, and somebody rapped me on the back and said, 'Stop making love to Rodgers and look what's happening to the theater.' And they were just whooping and hollering."

From there, the excitement only built until Russell Bennett's rousing choral version of the title song, and the curtain rang down around eleven twenty, and the audience floated out into the night. The cast and creators repaired down the block to Sardi's to await the reviews, but even before they arrived, a little man wedged his way through the crowd and flung his arms around Rodgers. It was Larry Hart, and he was exultant. "Dick!" he exclaimed. "I've never had a better evening in my life! This show will still be around twenty years from now." He was only wrong by at least half a century.

The critics were just as effusive. "*Wonderful* is the nearest adjective, for this excursion," wrote the *New York Times*. The *Herald Tribune* declared, "Songs, dances and a story have been triumphantly blended . . . a jubilant and enchanting musical," while the *Daily News* called the show "the most thoroughly and attractively American musical comedy since *Show Boat*. It has color and rhythm, and harmony plus."

Jules Glaenzer, a Cartier executive who had played host at some of the early backers' auditions, gave an opening night party in his apartment after the gathering at Sardi's. When Rodgers arrived, Glaenzer offered him a drink. "No, thanks, Jules," the composer said. "I'm not going to touch a drop. I want to remember every second of this night." He stuck to ginger ale.

The next morning, Mary and Linda Rodgers would recall, newspapers were spread all over their parents' bedroom at the Volney Hotel on East 74th Street. Though it was a school day, their mother took them horseback riding and to the Central Park Zoo to celebrate with a lunch of frankfurters. Dick and Oscar met at the St. James around noon, and there was pandemonium, with a line of ticket buyers stretching down the block and a policeman struggling to keep order at the box office.

"Shall we sneak off to someplace quiet where we can talk," Dick asked, "or shall we go to Sardi's and show off?"

"Hell," Oscar answered. "Let's go to Sardi's and show off."

THE SHOW WAS a sensation, and the seemingly endless demand for tickets quickly became the stuff of legend. For years, the story circulated that Rose Bigman, the secretary of the Broadway columnist Walter Winchell, had seen the show in New Haven and wired him with the discouraging verdict: "No legs, no jokes, no chance." Winchell did circulate that line in his column, but his secretary was not his source. In fact, as Winchell and Rodgers would confirm in an exchange of letters years later, it was Rodgers himself who, after the New York opening, told Winchell that some unnamed wag had dismissed the show in New Haven with a racier putdown, "No legs, no tits, no chance!" to which Rodgers had added, "And now no tickets!"

But the cold facts alone were more than impressive enough. A somber black-and-white placard in the St. James lobby told the tale: "We have no tickets for *Oklahoma!*" There were a few vacant seats for the first weekday matinee, Terry Helburn would recall, but "that night the house sold out for the next four years." The first five shows alone had 151 standees. When Oscar's tenant farmer, Peter Moen, asked for a pair of tickets for his son's forthcoming wedding, Hammerstein asked, "When's the wedding?" Moen's answer: "The day you can get the tickets." At one point in the run, Armina Marshall of the Theatre Guild lost her Tibetan terrier, Chang. She let the newspapers know she was offering a reward of two seats to *Oklahoma!* to anyone who found him, and he was returned the following day. By May, Helburn and Langner were writing Dick and Oscar, asking them to set aside each Thursday lunch for the foreseeable future, to discuss *Oklahoma!* business matters.

The show won a special honorary Pulitzer Prize and would run for a record-breaking 2,212 performances—five years and nine weeks—in an era when no musical had ever run longer than 1,400 performances, much of the time with a touring national company playing to packed houses in major cities all across the country. The road company began in New Haven in October 1943 and closed nine and a half years later in Philadelphia. By 1949, a year after the Broadway run ended, Hammerstein estimated that the producers and backers had collectively earned more than $4 million, presumably not counting his and Rodgers's authors' royalties. The producers had exercised their option to buy the film rights back from MGM in virtually the first hours after the Broadway opening, and they resolutely refused all early offers for the movie rights, confident that demand would only grow. Press reports noted that the creators had set an asking price of $500,000 for a seven-year movie option, simply in an effort to deter any would-be buyers.

But *Oklahoma!* was much more than a Broadway hit; it was a

huge cultural phenomenon, and much of that had to do with World War II. When Celeste Holm was cast in the show, her grandmother, the chairman of the drama committee of the New York State Federation of Women's Clubs, told her that it would be "the most wonderful musical for right now, when people are going out to fight for this country, and may die for it, to be reminded of the kind of courage, the unselfconscious courage, that settled this country."

And indeed, at every performance, there were rows of men in uniform, sitting in reserved seats or taking standing room. Sometimes, the New York City Fire Department would bend the rules and let a couple of them stand in the wings backstage. The theater historian Ethan Mordden would recall that his parents "showed up at the St. James box office, hoping against hope that there might be something—a cancellation, perhaps? Nothing." Mordden's father "was in uniform, and he mentioned that he was shipping out for Europe the next day. The ticket seller silently pushed over a pair, fifth row center."

Just as Irving Berlin's "White Christmas," from the 1942 film *Holiday Inn*, spoke to GIs stationed in distant battlegrounds, *Oklahoma!* became a symbol of home and hearth and the values that the Allies were fighting for. A "brand new state"—indeed, a brave new world, one with "plen'y of heart and plen'y of hope." A grand land that was standing firm against dark threats from Germany and Japan. A parliament of man where folks might all behave theirsel's and act like brothers. In the succinct summation of the theater historian Max Wilk, the show presented wartime audiences with "a lovely two-hour promissory note set to music that we could take back home."

In a letter to Richard Rodgers in December 1979, after the opening of a smash-hit revival of *Oklahoma!*, thirty-six years after its debut, the writer John Hersey would recall a morning on the battlefront in Sicily in 1943.

"I'd had a pretty crummy night," Hersey wrote, "sleeping on the ground, muddy and damp, nothing to look forward to but cold C-rations for breakfast. A G.I. who might perfectly well get killed that day (because though the Italians were retreating there were some nasty skirmishes) got up and stripped to the waist and poured some cold water in his helmet and began to shave. The sun hit us. Everyone was grumbling as usual. Suddenly the soldier stood up and began singing, 'Oh, what a beautiful morning.' A pretty good voice. There was a fair amount of irony in his singing, and his pals laughed. All the same, it *was* a beautiful morning, and all of a sudden there was an almost unbearable intensity in the way the men looked around at the view."

CHAPTER 4

Bustin' Out

I have a story. I see a stage. I know what my settings are going to be. I know in most cases who will be the performer. I am standing in the orchestra pit. The lights are beginning to dim, the curtain is going up. I must have a song here with the proper music. I sit down and write that music.

Richard Rodgers

The immediate and overwhelming success of *Oklahoma!* changed everything overnight for Rodgers and Hammerstein, especially for Oscar, whose long unlucky streak had ended with the biggest possible bang. "I am suddenly a much cleverer man than the dope who wrote *Sunny River* and *Very Warm for May*," he wrote his son Bill on April 12, 1943. Offers from Hollywood came pouring in. "Of course the red carpet was rolled out at the entrance of all studios and I could have made enough deals to keep me very busy for five years—and keep me very rich, too," Hammerstein wrote again later that summer. "But I didn't make any, for which I am very proud of myself." Having endured so much disappointment and failure, Oscar was determined not only to savor his success, but also to think carefully and strategically about his next steps. In yet another letter to Bill around this same time, he explained his thinking. "Dick and I don't want to start on another show unless we see the chance in it for writing another blooming masterpiece," he wrote. "This may require some time to find."

For his part, Rodgers would recall, "Since *Oklahoma!* was still playing to packed houses, we didn't want to step on our heels by writing a new musical." And he, too, felt the same pressure to deliver another smash. Shortly after *Oklahoma!* opened, Rodgers got a call from the producer Sam Goldwyn, who had just seen the first act of the show and asked Rodgers to meet him after the performance for a drink. When they met, Goldwyn "drooled to Dick for an hour, about every detail and department of the show," Oscar would recall. "Then he got on the music and said it was wonderful, finishing with a question: 'Do you know what you ought to do next? . . . Shoot yourself!' "

So what did the new partners do next? They split up—at least temporarily—to pursue projects of their own. For Dick, this meant one last attempt to save Larry Hart from total self-destruction. His idea was a revival of their 1927 hit, *A Connecticut Yankee*—not just a reproduction, but a re-imagination of the original show, with an updated book and a half dozen new songs. Rodgers and Herb Fields, the author of the original book, hit upon this approach as one that Larry might find manageable, and even appealing—especially since they proposed to cast Vivienne Segal, his favorite actress, in the expanded role of Morgan Le Fay.

Hart joined Rodgers in Fairfield, staying sober, working at reasonable hours, and producing some of the best lyrics he ever wrote, including "To Keep My Love Alive," a sparkling comic catalogue in which Morgan Le Fay lists the many ways in which she has dispatched all her husbands to an untimely demise. But the moment rehearsals were over and Hart's work was done, he fell apart once more. The night of the Philadelphia opening, October 28, he went on a bender from which he never recovered. The New York critics liked the show, but it's not clear that Larry Hart ever got to read the reviews. The night of the New York opening, Hart arrived at the Martin Beck Theatre already drunk, standing, as was his usual custom, at the back of the house, jangling coins in his pocket, at one point even singing along with Vivienne Segal. At intermission, not bothering to retrieve his checked overcoat, he ducked out into the rainy night for a drink or three at a nearby bar, returning for the second act singing still louder. Acting on orders left

by Rodgers, who had feared just such a scene, two men escorted Hart
out to the lobby, and his brother Teddy's wife, Dorothy, took him back
to her apartment, where he eventually fell into a sweaty, troubled sleep.
But when Dorothy and Teddy Hart woke the next morning, Larry was
nowhere to be found.

A search of all the usual haunts turned up nothing, until finally the
composer Frederick Loewe found him sitting in the gutter outside a bar
on Eighth Avenue. The next day, he was admitted to Doctors Hospital,
his face flushed, laboring to breathe, with a temperature of 102 degrees.
By Sunday, his white blood count had plummeted, and mutual friends
intervened with Eleanor Roosevelt, who arranged for the War Production Board to have a supply of the still scarce new wonder drug, peni-
cillin, flown in. But it was too late. On the night of November 22, Dick
and Dorothy Rodgers and other friends and family members were
gathered in the hospital corridor outside Hart's room when an air-raid
drill suddenly blacked out all the lights in the building except for
shaded emergency bulbs. The doctor had just emerged from Larry's
room to say that he was dead when the all-clear siren sounded and
all the lights came back on at once. "To those of us in the hospital
that night, the lights going on again at that moment was some sort of
cosmic assurance that the darkness which had always surrounded
Larry had suddenly disappeared," Rodgers would recall. "That in death
he could at last enjoy the warmth and brightness that had eluded him
all his life."

OSCAR'S OWN PET project was an idea he had been toying with for
years. In 1934 he had seen a concert version of Georges Bizet's opera
Carmen at the Hollywood Bowl, and he was certain that such a grip-
ping story—the tale of a straight-arrow Spanish soldier, Don Jose, who
is seduced by a sultry gypsy—and such stunning music could find a
modern mass audience much wider than that for traditional opera,
especially if it was written in English and updated to a contemporary
setting. Sitting alone at Highland Farm one day in January 1942, just
after the abysmal failure of *Sunny River*, he listened to a recording of

the opera by Milan's La Scala company, playing it over and over, while studying the libretto along with an English translation and the complete piano score. Without confiding his plans to anyone, he began working on an adaptation.

Oscar seized on the idea of transferring the gypsy setting in southern Spain to the black American South; instead of being a cigarette factory worker in Seville, Carmen would be Carmen Jones, a parachute factory worker in South Carolina in a contemporary setting, while Don Jose would become Joe, an army corporal. His rival for Carmen's affections, the bullfighter Escamillo, would become Husky Miller, a heavyweight prizefighter.

Oscar hewed closely to the original score, dropping some arias that did not fit his condensed two-act libretto, but his new lyrics brought a thrilling intensity to what had been the stiff and stilted English translation that then prevailed. Consider just these few lines from Carmen's signature "Habanera" (in the original French, "L'amour est un oiseau rebelle," or "Love is a rebellious bird"). The standard English translation of the aria began:

> *Ah! Love thou art a willful wild bird,*
> *And none may hope thy wings to tame,*
> *If it please thee to be a rebel,*
> *Say, who can try and thee reclaim?*

Oscar's version, in conversational black dialect, remade the song:

> *Love's a baby dat grows up wild*
> *An' he don' do what you want him to,*
> *Love ain' nobody's angel child*
> *An' he won't pay any mind to you . . .*

Hammerstein finished the libretto in July 1942, just about the time he met Dick Rodgers for lunch at the Barberry Room and agreed to work on *Green Grow the Lilacs*. Despite his recently expressed aversion to producing any more Broadway musicals, Max Gordon took an option on *Carmen*. But he could not initially raise the needed money, and Oscar was busy with the Theatre Guild project in any case. Finally, that November, even as Rodgers and Hammerstein were deep in the midst of work on what would become *Oklahoma!*, an unlikely backer emerged: Billy Rose, the blustery songwriter and producer responsible for Rodgers and Hart's *Jumbo*. Rose had been raised by an opera-loving mother, and when Hammerstein sent him the libretto for *Carmen Jones*, he was entranced. Rose was committed, but production would have to await completion of the Rodgers and Hammerstein show.

By July 1943, with *Oklahoma!* selling out every night, Hammerstein was at last immersed in rewrites of *Carmen Jones*—he thought he could improve it about 25 percent after not having looked at it for a while. He wrote to his son Bill with excitement about the creative team being assembled to mount the show. The director would be Hassard Short, a British veteran considered a master of stylish stagecraft, and Bizet's orchestrations would be adapted by Robert Russell Bennett. Hammerstein also reported that the show's public relations team had turned up a critique of *Carmen* by the philosopher Friedrich Nietzsche, who had "said that the music was neither French nor German but African!" so Hammerstein added, "I am not as original as I thought and Nietsche was ahead of his time. Furthermore, I am pretty sure I am misspelling his name." (He had.)

John Hammond, a Columbia records executive who was a jazz and blues aficionado (and would one day sign a young Bruce Springsteen), agreed to help recruit the needed cast of a hundred black actors, no mean feat in that segregated era, especially since—in the usual manner of opera casting—two singers would be needed for each of the principal roles, to avoid voice strain. Luther Saxon, who was working in a naval yard, was cast as one of the Joes, while Glenn Bryant, a six-foot-three-inch New York City police officer, took the role of the boxer Husky Miller. Muriel Smith, who would play one of the Carmens, worked as a film scraper in a photographic lab.

Oscar gave his copyright in the show to Dorothy as a present, and after tryouts in Philadelphia and Boston, the New York opening was set for December 2 at the Broadway Theatre. Hammerstein was worried—especially about the verdict of the classical music critics—but Broadway's most hardened reviewers reached over each other for superlatives. "Bravo!" wrote the *Herald Tribune*. "The theatre and music have had a memorable wedding . . . as wonderfully exciting as it is audacious. . . . The libretto has been brilliantly translated . . . something more than a major theatrical event." The show would run for just over five hundred performances.

"It looks as if I will make more in 1944 than in any other year of my career," Oscar wrote to Bill. "You understand, naturally, that only a small part of this remains mine—80 to 85% will go to build planes, destroyers, etc. and help repair boats that recline on reefs. But, God knows, I don't kick. I'm in favor of these taxes, for the good of the nation and the good of my own soul. Furthermore, I am luckier than most lucky earners, for beyond what I am making now, I have created, this year, two catalogue properties which will bear fruits every year for the balance of my life—and a good part of yours and Alice's and Jimmie's. Also, after the big Broadway grosses start to fade, these properties are natural record-breaking picture sales. All in all, your old man is sitting pretty, at last—after some struggles and not a few disappointments."

That Christmas, Oscar took out an ad in *Variety* that would become one of the most famous in the trade paper's history:

Holiday Greetings

OSCAR HAMMERSTEIN, II

author of

SUNNY RIVER
(Six Weeks at the St. James Theatre, New York)

VERY WARM FOR MAY
(Seven Weeks at the Alvin Theatre, New York)

THREE SISTERS
(Six Weeks at the Drury Lane, London)

BALL AT THE SAVOY
(Five Weeks at the Drury Lane, London)

FREE FOR ALL
(Three Weeks at the Manhattan Theatre, New York)

* * * * * * *

I'VE DONE IT BEFORE AND
I CAN DO IT AGAIN

The notice was seen as a sign of Hammerstein's endearing humility, a great joke, and the talk of the town. But years later he confessed that he hadn't meant it that way at all. "I thought it was quite the opposite and I didn't mean it as a modest gesture," he would say. "I really meant it as a rebuke to all the people who had concluded I was through and who were now concluding that I was a genius. Neither was true. I wasn't through because I had had a succession of flops, and I wasn't suddenly a different man or a better writer because I was on a wave of successes now. I wanted to remind everybody in the theater that success or failure is always just around the corner."

OSCAR'S POST-*OKLAHOMA!* boast that his head had not been turned by Hollywood notwithstanding, he and Dick had in fact accepted one irresistible offer from the movies in the summer of 1943: to write a musical remake of 20th Century Fox's warmhearted 1933 family comedy *State Fair*, which had starred the beloved Will Rogers as the patriarch of an Iowa farm clan, Janet Gaynor as his daughter, and Lew Ayres as the newspaper reporter who woos her at the annual Iowa State Fair. Given their mutual loathing of Hollywood, the partners extracted just one condition from the studio chief Darryl Zanuck: they must be allowed to write the picture in the East, without taking up residence in Hollywood. Zanuck agreed, with the result, as Rodgers would put it, that a story about Iowa would be filmed in Southern California and written in Connecticut and Pennsylvania. The team would be paid handsomely for its efforts: $50,000 each. But the larger import of the deal was that it established a happy working relationship with Fox, a collaboration that would result in that studio's making the film adaptations of all but one of Rodgers and Hammerstein's shows.

Oscar began writing the screenplay in January 1944, after taking a Christmas break to luxuriate in the success of *Carmen Jones*. The job was no great challenge but a pleasant diversion. Charles Winninger, *Show Boat*'s original Cap'n Andy, took the Will Rogers part as Abel Frake, the proud owner of a champion Hampshire boar, while Jeanne Crain, a Fox contract ingénue, played his daughter, Margy. The band singer Dick Haymes, who had replaced Frank Sinatra as Tommy Dorsey's vocalist, was cast as Margy's brother, Wayne, and Dana Andrews as Pat Gilbert, the reporter. Fay Bainter rounded out the cast as Mrs. Frake, maker of prizewinning mincemeat (into which she and her husband have each surreptitiously spirited a snifter of good brandy).

Zanuck's one condition, when the score was done, was that the authors make a weeklong visit to Los Angeles, to review screen tests and help with casting, and the studio footed the bill for first-class travel and hotel for Dick and Oscar and their Dorothys. Once they arrived, Zanuck ignored them for days, until the eve of their departure, when he summoned them to his office on the Fox lot to regale them with stories of his wartime experiences in the Army Signal Corps in North Africa. "He had paid us a lot of money and had acceded to our working conditions," Rodgers would recall, "but wanted the satisfaction of being able to make us do as he wished. It was one more example of the kind of ego-satisfying extravagance that eventually helped contribute to the downfall of the Hollywood studio system."

Rodgers's score included a batch of carefree, winning tunes, some invoking the spirit of Larry Hart, including "That's for Me," "Isn't It Kinda Fun," and "A Grand Night for Singing," together with a couple of appropriately corny numbers, including the title song whose opening lines

Our state fair is a great state fair,
Don't miss it, don't even be late!

It's dollars to doughnuts that our state fair
Is the best state fair in our state!

ranked as subpar Hammerstein wordplay. The standout song, the score's most enduring hit, was the wistful, lovelorn ballad "It Might As Well Be Spring." The song was a resourceful nod to the reality that while the character of Margy was agitated as if she had spring fever, state fairs are routinely held in late summer and early fall. It is also the only Rodgers and Hammerstein song for which a complete alternate melody, different from the final version, is known to exist. Rodgers's initial take was a legato musical line, but as he pondered Hammerstein's words

I'm as restless as a willow in a windstorm,
I'm as jumpy as a puppet on a string!
I'd say that I had spring fever
But I know it isn't spring . . .

he thought better of his first idea, and instead substituted a syncopated melody that jumped from interval to interval, as if the notes themselves were puppets on strings. It won the Academy Award for Best Original Song of the year. The film, directed by Walter Lang, opened in August 1945, just as the war was ending, and was a solid hit, grossing $4 million. It remains an eminently watchable example of workmanlike skill, but it was not a pioneering piece of art. Oscar himself was under no illusions about it; after seeing an early screening he wrote to its producer, William Perlberg, "My overall disappointment was the fact that the story and the characters were presented with less realism than I had anticipated and that the picture emerges as more of a 'musical comedy' than I hoped it would be." John McCarten's verdict in the *New Yorker* was succinct. "Nice, I believe, would be the word for it," he wrote. "I don't think you could use anything stronger."

EVEN AS DICK and Oscar were writing *State Fair*, Terry Helburn and the Theatre Guild began digging into their trunk yet again, to find a project that could follow *Oklahoma!* Helburn's new idea was a musical adaptation of *Liliom*, the well-loved 1909 drama by the Hungarian playwright Ferenc Molnár, which at first had confused European audiences because its hero dies ignobly halfway through the action. But after the mass loss of life in World War I, theatergoers began to take the play to heart, and the Guild had first produced it on Broadway in 1921. It ran just sixty-five performances but left an impression, becoming a staple of amateur theater companies and a 1934 film directed by Fritz Lang and starring Charles Boyer.

Billed as "a legend in seven scenes and prologue," the play tells the story of the title character—in Hungarian, Liliom means "lily" and is an ironic slang term for "tough"—a ne'er-do-well Budapest carnival barker, and Julie, the unlucky servant girl who loves him unconditionally, even though he abuses her. Within minutes of meeting, they fall in love, and Liliom loses his job because Mrs. Muskat, the carnival boss who has been keeping him, is jealous of Julie. With no prospects, the young lovers marry, and Julie promptly becomes pregnant. Desperate for money, Liliom agrees to commit a robbery, but he bungles it, killing himself to avoid arrest. He arrives in a night court version of purgatory and is given one last chance to set things right on earth—a chance he also bungles, by striking his teenage daughter, Louise, just as he had struck her mother. The play ends with one of the most famous curtain lines in theater history, with Louise asking, "Is it possible for someone to hit you—hard like that—real loud and hard—and not hurt you at all?" and Julie replying, "It is possible, dear—that someone may beat you and beat you and beat you—and not hurt you at all."

To modern ears, such a misty, sentimentalized depiction of spousal abuse is so off-putting as to be revolting—and indeed changing attitudes have made modern productions of *Liliom* problematic, at best. But a generation of twentieth-century audiences viewed the story differently, and the critic John Mason Brown summed up the property's hold: "Few plays to have come out of the modern theater have equaled Molnár's fantasy in imagination or pathos, in charm or universality, in tenderness or timelessness." As it happened, no small part of that tenderness and charm was attributable to Larry Hart. Though he received no public credit, the multilingual Hart had translated the play into English.

And just as with *Green Grow the Lilacs*, there had been a recent revival of *Liliom*—in this case on Broadway in 1940, with Burgess Meredith and Ingrid Bergman as the doomed lovers and Elia Kazan as the villain, Fiscur, who cons Liliom into the robbery. The production ran just two months, but Helburn believed it demonstrated the play's enduring appeal.

So now, in November 1943, at one of their weekly "gloat lunches" to discuss *Oklahoma!* business and future projects, Terry asked Dick and Oscar what they thought of her idea. The answer, at first, was not much, in part because the play's Hungarian setting seemed anything but timeless in 1943, with World War II raging across Europe and events unpredictable. But Helburn persisted. *How about changing the setting to New Orleans?* she proposed. *Liliom could be a Creole.* "And I studied that and then I gave that up because I did some reading and that dialogue gave me a pain," Oscar would recall. "Zis and zat and all those z's seemed a little corny." Discussions went on for some weeks. Finally Rodgers lit upon the idea of setting the story in New England in the late nineteenth century, which everyone agreed might work. Liliom, the title character, would become the euphonious Billy Bigelow, still a carnival barker. Julie would be a millworker instead of a housemaid.

"I began to see an attractive ensemble," Hammerstein would recall. "Sailors, whalers, girls who worked in the mills up the river, clambakes on near-by islands, an amusement park on the seaboard, things people could do in crowds, people who were strong and alive and lusty, people who had always been depicted on the stage as thin-lipped puritans—a libel I was anxious to refute." As for the two main characters, he said, "Julie, with her courage and inner strength and outward simplicity, seemed more indigenous to Maine than to Budapest. Liliom is, of course, an international character, indigenous to nowhere."

But even before this crucial decision on locale was made, Helburn and her colleagues had had to grapple with more fundamental concerns about the dark nature of the plot, and the all too unsympathetic central character. After a meeting with Dick and Oscar in December, Helburn summarized her own informal survey, which found that people liked Liliom, despite his flaws. "When I say, 'Why? He was such a bastard,'" she reported, "their replies vary, but it's usually, 'Yes, but he was so human,' or 'such a cute bastard' or 'such an insolent and charming devil.'" She added, "I'm sure he gets over much closer to Clark Gable than to Pal Joey." By the next month, Helburn was advising the partners that the mood and tone could be halfway between *Carmen Jones* and *Oklahoma!* "with great audience appeal," and after another meeting with Dick and Oscar she allowed that "the general feeling at the end of the conference seemed to be that while the play was a challenge, it would be an inspiring one to meet."

There was one other obstacle: Ferenc Molnár had resolutely refused to allow a musical adaptation of *Liliom*, turning down Puccini himself on the grounds that he wanted the property to remain his play, not someone else's opera. But nothing was too good for the authors of *Oklahoma!*, and the playwright, who had emigrated to New York to escape the Nazi persecution of Hungarian Jews, relented the very day after seeing that show. Now the challenge was how to transform his dark and delicate drama into a compelling piece of musical theater.

As USUAL, DICK and Oscar began at the beginning. The play had started with a silent prologue, set in the amusement park, which introduced the principal characters. Hammerstein went further, devising a detailed pantomime that swiftly sketched out Billy's magnetism; his complex relationship with the carousel owner, Mrs. Mullin (Mrs. Muskat in the original); Julie's fumbling, intense attraction to Billy; Mrs. Mullin's jealousy of Julie; and Billy's studied nonchalance toward both of them. In eight minutes, the central dynamic of the plot is laid bare, to the accompaniment of a sweeping set of waltzes by Rodgers. Dick had long felt overtures were wasted on Broadway audiences, with an auditorium full of distracted, rustling latecomers still taking their seats, and was eager to try something new. So the curtain would rise as the first notes of music sounded, and though Rodgers liked to insist that he didn't employ the standard songwriter's trunk of stored-up tunes that could be plucked at will to suit a new purpose on short notice, in this case he did seize on a bubbling suite of waltzes he had first written more than a decade earlier, for the film *Hallelujah, I'm a Bum*. "There will be no dialogue or lyric," Oscar wrote to Bill in August 1944, "only pantomimic action set to a waltz suite which Dick wrote."

And just as he had done with *Green Grow the Lilacs*, Oscar hewed closely to the original playwright's scheme, while deftly turning spoken dialogue into sung lyrics. By the time of the producers' story conferences in December 1943, Terry Helburn wrote that Hammerstein had regarded the crucial early scene in which Liliom and Julie meet on a park bench and tentatively explore their mutual attraction "as almost too beautiful and too tight to tamper with in any way, but he did feel that the curtain with the falling acacias might lend itself to a beautiful number." This number would become perhaps the greatest "conditional love song" of any Broadway score, and once again, Hammerstein found his inspiration directly in Molnár's words, in which Liliom queries Julie: "But you wouldn't marry a rough guy like me—that is,—eh—if you loved me—"

"Yes, I would," Julie replies. "If I loved you, Mister Liliom."

Oscar's first stab at a lyric was as halting as the would-be lovers' exchanges:

> If I loved you
> I would tremble ev'ry time you'd say my name,
> But I'd long to hear you say it just the same.
> I dunno jest how I know, but I ken see
> How everythin' would be
> If I loved you . . .
> If I loved you
> I'd be too a-skeered t'say what's in my heart
> I'd be too a-skeered to even make a start
> And my golden chance to speak would come and go
> And you would never know
> How I loved you—
> If I loved you.

Through his usual painstaking process of condensation, sharpening, and refinement, Hammerstein eventually produced the far more powerful final result:

If I loved you,
Time and again I would try to say
All I'd want you to know.
If I loved you,
Words wouldn't come in an easy way—
Round in circles I'd go!
Longin' to tell you, but afraid and shy,
I'd let my golden chances pass me by.
Soon you'd leave me,
Off you would go in the mist of day,
Never, never to know
How I loved you—
If I loved you.

The scene continues at length, with sung dialogue in the manner of opera—not in the typical singsong of recitative, but with a natural conversational tunefulness. Rodgers once boasted that "what Kurt Weill calls recitative, I call melody," and the claim was not misplaced in the case of "If I Loved You." Stephen Sondheim would call "The Bench Scene" "probably the singular most important moment in the evolution of contemporary musicals" as Billy sings of the lovers' cosmic insignificance:

There's a helluva lot o' stars in the sky,
And the sky's so big the sea looks small,
And two little people—
You and I—
We don't count at all.

The scene ends as it did in Molnár's original, with acacia blossoms softly falling. But Hammerstein one-ups Molnár's suggestion that "the wind brings them down" by having Billy point out that there is no wind, and having Julie acknowledge that they are "jest coming down by theirselves—Jest their time to, I reckon." For better—and for worse—it is Julie and Billy's time, too.

———

A TOUGHER CHALLENGE for Oscar was what to do about what he called the central "tunnel" of the play, the grim depiction of Julie and Liliom's early married life, as they sponge off Julie's aunt Hollunder, who runs a decrepit photography studio, and bustles in and out complaining of Liliom's shiftlessness. Hammerstein kept the thrust of this section—Billy's sullen unwillingness to learn any other trade besides that of barker, and his refusal to take his old job (and his old protectress, Mrs. Mullin) back. Yet Oscar lightened the mood by making the newlyweds the guests of Julie's cousin Nettie Fowler, who operates a seaside spa where local sailors, fishermen, and mill girls gather for recreation. This provided a logical setting for ensemble numbers. And as in *Oklahoma!*, Hammerstein created a secondary pair of comic lovers, beefing up Molnár's original characters so that Julie's friend Marie becomes a fellow millworker, Carrie Pipperidge, and her suitor, Wolf the porter, becomes a self-satisfied fisherman, Enoch Snow, whose stolid bourgeois respectability stands in contrast to Julie and Billy's dangerous passion.

Oscar's portrait of Victorian New England was greatly aided by a raft of period details dug up by his new research assistant, his twenty-three-year-old daughter, Alice. Since Hammerstein couldn't envision Victorian New England by looking out his window at the grazing cattle in Doylestown, Alice uncovered information on all manner of Yankee customs, mores, and history, drawing up long lists of local flora (gooseberries, raspberries, blackberries, blueberries) and fauna (moose, caribou, wolf, fox, beaver), figures of speech ("Fixin' to make a quick getaway"), and dialect ("blesh" for "blush," "bespoke" for "engaged"); explaining the difference between sloops and yawls; and cataloguing actual names of the era that would make their way into the script: Bascome, Pipperidge, Bigelow. She compiled summaries of the spread of cigarette smoking after the Civil War, the manufacture of revolvers, the working hours and conditions in cotton mills. So exhaustive were her labors that at one point Oscar rebuked her: "I don't need all that. You have research poisoning."

But consider her careful précis of the loose-limbed collection of recipes-cum-travelogues in *Mainstays of Maine*, by the Pulitzer Prize–

winning New England poet Robert P. T. Coffin, describing the ingredients necessary for a seaside island clambake:

> A good New England cook uses no book. "Put in what you think is right.". . . CODSHEAD CHOWDER . . . Catch the cod and cook them, still flapping, in an iron kettle. Onions, salt pork. Cook till the fish begin to flake apart. . . . Split sticks or bayberry and clamp them on clamshells, and these are the only proper spoons for this chowder. . . . After this come the LOBSTERS. They have been broiling on the coals. Rake them out, split them down the back, pour in the butter, salt and pepper. After the lobsters come the CLAMS. Cook these in rockweed thrown over coals of driftwood. . . .

And consider how Oscar transformed that descriptive litany into an ebullient ode to gluttony in "A Real Nice Clambake":

> *Fust come codfish chowder,*
> *Cooked in iron kettles,*
> *Onions floatin' on the top,*
> *Curlin' up in petals!*
> *Throwed in ribbons of salted pork—*
> *An old New England trick—*
> *And lapped it all up with a clamshell,*
> *Tied onto a bayberry stick!*
> *Oh-h-h*
> *This was a real nice clambake . . .*
>
> *Remember when we raked*
> *Them red-hot lobsters*
> *Out of the driftwood fire?*
> *They sizzled and crackled*
> *And sputtered a song*
> *Fitten fer an angels choir . . .*
>
> *We slit 'em down the back*
> *And peppered 'em good,*

And doused 'em in melted butter—
Then we tore away the claws
And cracked 'em with our teeth
'Cause we weren't in the mood to putter! . . .

Then at last come the clams—
Steamed under rockweed
And poppin' from their shells—
Jest how many of 'em
Galloped down our gullets—
We couldn't say oursel's!

For yet another song, a big choral celebration of New England spring to be sung by the ensemble in the middle of the first act, Oscar proved himself utterly heedless of not only research—but of some immutable biological realities. In "June Is Bustin' Out All Over," he catalogued the effects of warming temperatures on the amatory activity of humans and animals alike, at one point declaring:

June is bustin' out all over!
The sheep aren't sleeping any more.
All the rams that chase the ewe sheep
Are determined there'll be new sheep,
And the ewe sheep aren't even keepin' score!

After a backers' audition at Jules Glaenzer's apartment in February 1945, Hammerstein received a letter from one prospective investor: Gerald M. Loeb, a founding partner of E. F. Hutton. Loeb noted that he himself had been raising sheep at his country house in rural Connecticut, "and seemingly the females are in heat just once a year—autumn—and lambs are born only in late winter. By Easter they are in the language of the market place 'spring baby lambs.'" A sheepish Oscar replied: "I was delighted with the parts of your letter praising my work and thrown into consternation by the unwelcome news about the eccentrically frigid behavior of ewes in June. I have since checked your statement and found it to be true. It looks very much as if in the interest of scientific honesty I shall have to abandon the verse dealing with sheep."

In fact, Peter Moen, Oscar's tenant farmer in Doylestown, had told him the same thing, but in the end, he didn't change the line, explaining to someone else who inquired, "What you say about sheep may all be very true for most years, sir, but not in 1873. 1873 is my year and that year, curiously enough, the sheep mated in the spring."

WITH THIS NEW show, the Guild had no trouble raising money, and the $180,000 budget was quickly secured. Most of the creative team responsible for *Oklahoma!* was also reassembled, looking now not like a risky bet but a sure thing. Jo Mielziner, already one of Broadway's most prolific scenic designers, replaced Lemuel Ayers to do the settings, and Robert Russell Bennett had to beg off completing the orchestrations because of the demands of a radio contract, so the work was finished by Don Walker and an important new talent found by Agnes de Mille: Trude Rittmann, a German-born, classically trained composer and arranger, who would work with de Mille to create the dance music and perhaps also the dramatic underscoring played beneath some of the dialogue.

Rouben Mamoulian balked at first when asked to direct the show— perhaps still smarting from his bitter wrangles with de Mille, or from an equally bitter quarrel with Dick and Oscar in the aftermath of *Oklahoma!*'s success, in which he arranged a series of press interviews that, in the partners' eyes, took too much credit for the show. He held out for a percentage of the new production, but it was already sold out. Eventually, Dick, Oscar, and the Guild gave him a cut of their own shares, and he signed on.

Rodgers and Hammerstein themselves tangled with Langner and Helburn over the financial terms of their deal. So eager was the Guild to re-sign their winning team that they offered to pay the partners 7.5 percent of the show's weekly gross, in an era when the standard was 2 percent each for composer and lyricist, and 1 percent for the book writer—plus 50 percent of the producers' profits after repayment of investors. Sometime later, in October 1944, Helburn sent Rodgers and Hammerstein a letter attempting to renege on part of this generous deal, arguing that it would shortchange the Guild. Oscar's reply was a brisk dismissal. "This was not a deal we extracted from you by any grim bargaining," he wrote. "It was your own proposition made to us by people experienced in producing and familiar with the mathematical contingencies of all kinds of shows."

Though by this point Dick and Oscar could have had their pick of Broadway's biggest stars, they once again chose to cast the show they now called *Carousel* largely with unknowns. For Julie, they recruited Jan Clayton, a young singer and actress from New Mexico who had been knocking around in minor movie roles after being discovered by an MGM talent scout. She auditioned for Terry Helburn in Los Angeles and then flew to New York for a session with Rodgers and Hammerstein in which she sang "The Trolley Song" from *Meet Me in St. Louis*—which did not go well. Mamoulian agreed to work with her for a couple of days, while Rodgers taught her "What's the Use of Wondrin'?," a rueful solo in which Julie acknowledges the helplessness of her love for Billy:

> Common sense may tell you
> That the endin' will be sad
> And now's the time to break and run away.
> But what's the use of wond'rin'
> If the endin' will be sad?
> He's your feller and you love him—
> There's nothin' more to say.

At the end of Clayton's next audition, Oscar said simply, "Well, shall we all go over to Sardi's and have a little glass of champagne to celebrate our new Julie?"

For the role of Billy, Rodgers and Hammerstein and the Guild turned to one of their own discoveries: John Raitt, a former track star at the University of Southern California who had been singing at schools and YMCAs around Los Angeles and had won a radio contest on which Armina Marshall's niece had heard him perform. He was promptly hired as Curly in the national company of *Oklahoma!* for ten months, and auditioned for *Carousel* singing Figaro's entrance aria from *The Barber of Seville*. "There is our Liliom!" Dick Rodgers told Langner on the spot.

From the outset, *Carousel*'s creators envisioned Billy's big moment as the scene at the end of the first act when he realizes he is going to be a father, and it was Rodgers—the father of two daughters—who imagined that Billy sings "first with pride of the growth of a boy, and then suddenly realizes it might be a girl, and changes completely with that thought." The song would show how the burdens of impending fatherhood impel Billy to find a way to get the money to care for his child—to "go out and make it, or steal it, or take it, or die!" as Oscar would write—and at the same time would demonstrate to the audience how Julie could ever have fallen in love with such a seeming loser to begin with. The "Soliloquy" Rodgers composed would be a tour de force, nearly eight solid minutes of soaring music tailor-made for Raitt's iron-clad baritone. Raitt would never forget the first time he saw the piece, written on a long stretch of music manuscript paper, folded accordion-style, and thought it must have been fifteen minutes long.

Well into January and February 1945, as casting proceeded, Oscar worked on revisions of the book. From the start, he and Dick had been determined to provide a more uplifting ending than Molnár's fatalistic conclusion, in which Liliom returns to earth with a stolen star, only to make a hash of things once more by striking his teenage daughter. The play ends with his life unredeemed. "It was not the anxiety to have a happy ending that made me shy away from that original ending," Hammerstein would recall. "But because I can't conceive of an unregener-ate soul, I can't conceive of a dead-end to any kind of existence. And to indulge myself, I changed the ending." In Oscar's version, Billy still strikes Louise when she rejects his proffered gift of the star, but this is immediately followed by a scene at her high school graduation, in which Billy reappears—invisible to her and Julie but seen by the audience—and whispers, "I loved you Julie. Know that I loved you!" Louise's classmate puts her arm around the girl, and we sense that her life will be all right.

This action unfolds with a stirring reprise of the song first sung to Julie by her cousin Nettie after Billy's death, a tune so authentic-sounding that it might be mistaken for the old New England hymn that the plot explains it is:

> When you walk through a storm
> Keep your chin up high
> And don't be afraid of the dark.
> At the end of the storm
> Is a golden sky
> And the sweet silver song of the lark.
> Walk on through the wind,
> Walk on through the rain,
> Though your dreams be tossed and blown.
> Walk on, walk on, with hope in your heart,
> And you'll never walk alone!
> You'll never walk alone.

Christine Johnson, a Metropolitan Opera mezzo soprano, was cast as Nettie, and she never forgot the first time she sang "You'll Never Walk Alone" in Rodgers's office. "I tell you," she remembered years later, "when I finished, there was something almost spiritual about it—in the silence, we all just felt it, we knew that this wasn't just an ordinary little hymn-like song. This was some kind of classic."

When Ferenc Molnár showed up to watch the first run-through of the show, Dick and Oscar dreaded his reaction. They knew that the new ending, in Rodgers's words, "so completely changed the spirit of the original that we awaited a humiliating dressing down from the playwright." Instead, a delighted Molnár, his monocle popping out of his eye, exclaimed, "What you have done is so beautiful. And you know what I like best? The ending!" Irving Berlin would later compare the emotional power of "You'll Never Walk Alone" to the Twenty-third Psalm. When the singer Mel Tormé, standing at the back of the theater one night, told Rodgers that the song made him cry, the composer just nodded impatiently and replied, "It's supposed to."

CAROUSEL OPENED OUT of town for a four-day run in New Haven on March 22, 1945, and young Stevie Sondheim, on a break from boarding school, sat next to Dorothy Hammerstein. The story of marital discord and parental regret overwhelmed him, and he wept copious tears into Dorothy's fur wrap. "Apparently, certain kinds of fur will stain from tears," he would recall years later, "and I stained hers irrevocably."

When the curtain at last rang down, tears were in order for another reason: the show had run four hours—thirty to forty-five minutes too long. "This was, as Jo Mielziner remarked, the best musical-comedy script he'd ever read, and it had been beautifully directed, but almost none of it came off as we had expected," Agnes de Mille would recall. "The staff repaired to a hotel room where sacrifice and a cold supper awaited." Drastic cuts were in order. In a two-hour conference, the creative team conducted major surgery on the second act, discarding five scenes, about half of a de Mille ballet in which Billy sees what has happened on earth since his death, a couple of complete songs, and several choruses of others. "Now I see why these people have hits," the stage manager, John Fearnley, would recall. "I never witnessed anything so brisk and brave in my life."

The Boston opening was set for March 27, and writing in the *Boston Post* two days before, Oscar sounded a wary note. "We veterans are the most cautious people in the theater," he confessed. "We have marks of old bruises to remind us not to count the grosses till the ticket-racks are empty." Hammerstein was right to worry. In the second act, he had discarded the magistrate's court to which Molnár had consigned Liliom in favor of a New England parlor, where Billy finds himself face-to-face with a pair of heavenly characters known only as "He" and "She," a kind of Mr. and Mrs. God, Oscar had called them in an early draft. It was a lovely, delicate scene, with a charming proto-feminist sensibility, and a sly wit.

"Who's the lady?" Billy asks He at one point.

"I suppose you are like all the others. You thought, when you arrived here, you'd have to deal only with a man," He answers.

"Yes, sir," Billy replies.

"Strange that the world doesn't realize it needs a mother as well as a father," He rejoins.

Billy looks at She with "new respect," according to the stage directions.

"Nobody ever told me, ma'am," he says.

"Don't worry about it now, Billy," She reassures him. "It takes time for people to get used to it."

But there wasn't enough time to accustom the New England critics to such a radical notion, and they rejected it resoundingly. Elliot Norton of the *Post*, the dean of Boston critics and a reviewer who saw his job as much to point out how shows might be fixed, as to critique where they'd fallen short, pronounced the scene "just plain silly" and called it "a concept which is theologically and dramatically foreign to the New England of Billy Bigelow and alien to the whole tone of the play." Elinor Hughes of the *Boston Herald* was likewise skeptical. "It must be said, however unwillingly," she averred, "that *Carousel* represents a praiseworthy attempt to fit a fanciful and deeply touching play with a musical comedy frame and that so far the attempt has not really come off."

So more surgery was thus in order, with nightly pajama-clad conferences at which the actors would study their new lines. "We gotta get God out of the parlor," Hammerstein declared at one such meeting after the opening night. Mamoulian proposed adding a new character at the back entrance to heaven, a "Starkeeper" perched on a stepladder with a string of twinkling stars stretched out on a celestial clothesline. When the cast tried the new scene out the next day, it worked. Mamoulian would later claim that he came up with the lines that survive in the script, and that Hammerstein hadn't changed a word. His account is suspect, not only because he was a documented credit hog in the partners' eyes, but also because the dialogue sounds so much like Oscar: "The pearly gates are in front," the Starkeeper tells Billy. "Those are the back gates. They're just mother-of-pearly."

Agnes de Mille, for one, missed Hammerstein's original concept. "The first version had a dry toughness that the second lacked," she would recall, "and a quality that Oscar has frequently been forced to yield before audience hesitation or surprise." But by April 3, a week into the Boston run, Rodgers was optimistic enough to write to his wife, "Now I can write you because last night we had a SHOW! I am a very cautious kid, as you know, but there are certain bits of evidence that cannot be refuted. Best of all, I know how I feel, and I feel that there are many moments of extreme beauty here and that the public will want to see and hear them."

Still, *Carousel* wasn't out of the woods. Returning alone on the train to Connecticut after the Boston run, Dick had to lug his two heavy suitcases to the car himself, as no porters were present owing to wartime staff shortages. He went to bed without any ill effects, but when he woke the next morning, he coughed and was immediately seized by such excruciating pain that he collapsed on the floor. He had wrenched one of his lumbar vertebrae. He managed to drag himself to the final dress rehearsal at the Majestic Theatre in Manhattan, overseeing it as best he could from a stretcher placed in the center aisle.

The session went badly. "I left the theater thoroughly discouraged," Lawrence Langner would recall. "I went home and the next morning I remarked despondently to Armina, 'What an absurd occupation this is. Months have been spent on writing this musical, more months in producing it, $180,000 has been invested in it, yet, on the basis of one evening's performance, all this may go down in defeat. This is the very last play I will *ever* do.'"

Opening Night was Thursday, April 19. Rodgers was still laid up, sprawled on a stretcher hidden behind a curtain in an upper box, with only a partial view of the stage and so sedated with morphine that "I could not have appreciated what was happening even if I'd had the best seat in the house. In fact, so fortified was I against pain that I was also unaware of the laughter and applause, and was convinced that the show was a dismal failure. It was only afterward, when people came over to me—making me feel like an Egyptian mummy on display—that I realized *Carousel* had been enthusiastically received." After the show, Molnár approached Rodgers, who was speaking with his brother, Morty. "He may be your brother," the playwright said, patting the doctor's hand. "But he is my son."

The reviews were rapturous. Lewis Nichols in the *Times* declared that the pair "who can do no wrong continued doing no wrong," producing a score that was "on the whole delightful." Ward Morehouse of the *Baltimore Sun* said that *Carousel* was a play "of fragile beauty" with "an enchanting score," while John Chapman of the *Daily News* called it "one of the finest musical plays I have seen and I shall remember it always." The original production would run for 890 performances on Broadway and a national tour of two years. With the war in Europe now ending, and so many American households touched by years of death and loss, *Carousel* resonated in a darker, more visceral way than *Oklahoma!* had two years earlier. Now audiences were filled not with soldiers preparing to ship out to war but with veterans returning from the grim rigors of the battlefield. Jan Clayton would recall that at each performance when Billy rose from dead, "invariably you heard from the balcony, 'Oh, Jesus Christ! That's too much!'"

To the end of Rodgers's life, *Carousel* would remain his favorite score, his favorite show. "I think it's more emotional," he would say. "The whole subject matter cuts deeper. I feel it has more to say about human relationships. And I also think it's the best score we'd ever written. I have more respect for it. I just like it better."

CHAPTER 5

So Far

> It is a law of our civilization that as soon as a man proves he can contribute to the well-being of the world, there be created an immediate conspiracy to destroy his usefulness, a conspiracy in which he is usually a willing collaborator. Sometimes he awakens to his danger and does something about it. That is the story of *Allegro*.
>
> Oscar Hammerstein II

From almost the moment of *Oklahoma!*'s premiere, Rodgers and Hammerstein's creative energies would coexist with the exploding demands of their commercial enterprises. In the beginning, that was a high-class problem to have, and the partners embraced the extraordinary business opportunities that came their way with deliberation, discretion, and uncanny foresight. "Many of the old managers died broke," Dick would explain years later. "Oscar and I don't want to die broke." Starting in the summer of 1943, they contrived to make sure they never would.

The partners were ably abetted in that endeavor by Howard Reinheimer, the brilliant and meticulous lawyer who had been Oscar's lifelong friend. Reinheimer was, like his clients, a graduate of Columbia University—and of its law school—and he was an expert not only on intellectual property but on taxation as well. He was also thoroughly immersed in the world of New York theater, having represented Jerome Kern, Irving Berlin, Robert E. Sherwood, George S. Kaufman, Mary Martin, and Beatrice Lillie. He had even advised Margaret Mitchell on copyright matters pertaining to unauthorized dramatizations of *Gone with the Wind*.

A private and practical man who was so discreet, his son recalled, that he never breathed a word of his clients' business even to his family, Reinheimer also represented a few Hollywood stars. When he met the actress Carole Lombard at a party, neither her name nor her face made any impression. A week later she called asking him to represent her. "I want a lawyer who is not too immersed in moving pictures," she said. Reinheimer also represented Sigmund Romberg, who once remarked, "Business, business, all the time business, that's our Howard. I don't remember ever hearing him laugh . . . that is, to really laugh hard. It's a shame; otherwise, he's a very nice man."

Oscar Hammerstein's own legal training had made him more sensitive than most writers to the commercial realities of his creative work, while Dick Rodgers at once cultivated and disclaimed a reputation as the hardest of hardheaded businessmen. But Rodgers's daughter Mary would insist the myth was overblown. "He was an atrocious businessman," she would say of her father. "He just made a lot of money." It seems safe to say that neither Dick nor Oscar might have enjoyed the financial success they did without Reinheimer's sage advice, which boiled down to two core principles: first, whenever possible, the partners should own the rights to the works they created; and second, they should structure their business enterprises as an interlocking empire of nested partnerships and corporations, so as to take maximum favorable advantage of a federal tax code that then taxed personal income at marginal rates of 80 percent or more. Over the years, these entities would be established with such colorfully appropriate names as "Surrey Enterprises" and "The Siam Corporation," and Reinheimer and his law partner Irving Cohen would generate a mountain of memos, contracts, and financial reports memorializing the details.

But the partners' first decision was the crucial one from which all others would flow: in an era when sheet music sales were still a vitally important part of any songwriter's revenue stream, they established their own music publishing company, Williamson Music, named in honor of their fathers. Their partners in this enterprise were Max and

Louis Dreyfus, the brothers who owned and ran Chappell & Co., long the leading publisher of Broadway scores—including those of Rodgers and Hart and Kern and Hammerstein. Music copyrights typically lodged not with composers and lyricists but with their publishing houses, and so the new vehicle would be (as Oscar explained in a letter to his son Bill) "our device for owning title in our copyrighted songs," in addition to receiving royalties on music sales and public performance rights. The profits of the new enterprise would be split with the Dreyfus brothers, and Chappell & Co. would do the work of publishing and promoting the songs, including the creation of popular piano arrangements. The genius of this setup, for Rodgers and Hammerstein, was that they would make more money while being responsible for less administrative work, and the terms also called for the whole entity to be owned fifty-fifty by Rodgers and Hammerstein and their heirs after the deaths of the Dreyfus brothers.

"This is all pretty complicated," Oscar told Bill, "but you asked for it. The objective is on a long pull view for Dick and me and our heirs. I only wish I had similar rights in the songs I've been writing for the last twenty-three years—or so."

Sheet music was not the only way that mass audiences heard music in the 1940s, of course, and Rodgers and Hammerstein also signed an extraordinary recording contract with Jack Kapp, the head of Decca Records, to issue an album of 78 rpm recordings of the score of *Oklahoma!*, performed by the original Broadway cast and orchestra, complete with a souvenir booklet. Strictly speaking, this was not the first such undertaking; Marc Blitzstein's score for *The Cradle Will Rock* had been recorded with the original cast in 1938. But the huge popular success of *Oklahoma!* and the quality of the recording would engender a new standard industry practice that continues to the present day, one that would reap many millions of dollars in royalties. "No previous effort had captured quite so vividly on disc the sheer exhilaration of the Broadway musical experience from overture to finale, from the out-and-out hits to the less familiar character songs," wrote the musical theater historians Amy Henderson and Dwight Bowers. "More than anything, these recordings solidly confirmed that the music and lyrics for *Oklahoma!* are essential ingredients in the narrative structure of the show and not just a series of traditionally catchy, easily isolated popular songs."

The new business team of Rodgers and Hammerstein naturally required offices, which were promptly established in the RKO Building in Rockefeller Center, which housed Radio City Music Hall and the offices of Chappell & Co. Dick and Oscar hired Morris Jacobs, a savvy Broadway veteran, as their general manager, a job he would hold until his retirement nearly thirty years later. From Broadway to Hollywood, the new firm was swiftly known in alphabetical shorthand as "R&H."

As they reviewed the options for their own next show, the partners made yet another important business decision: to become producers of plays written by others. "We were anxious to keep active in the theatre and also to establish our names as a team," Rodgers would recall. It was a logical decision. After all, between them Rodgers and Hammerstein knew virtually all there was to know about the Broadway theater. Oscar had worked as a stage manager and director and had collaborated closely with his uncle Arthur, who produced so many of his early shows. Dick had been a silent producer of *Best Foot Forward* as his collaboration with Larry Hart wound down. Their own close partnership with the Theatre Guild and the phenomenal success of *Oklahoma!* had put them in the financial driver's seat in ways that few other creative artists enjoyed. They participated in all the Guild's casting sessions and would eventually establish their own regular weekly open auditions to find replacements for the Broadway and touring companies of their shows. They were awash in disposable income, and investing in a business they both knew well seemed as sensible as any alternative—and probably a good deal more fun.

Their first venture was a vehicle as homey and nostalgic as *Oklahoma!* In 1943, the writer Kathryn Forbes had published a collection of seventeen short stories—amounting to a modest novel—inspired by the quiet family joys and struggles of her Norwegian immigrant grandmother in turn-of-the-century San Francisco. Forbes's book, *Mama's Bank Account*, tapped into home-front America's wartime hunger for tales of a simpler time. The plots of the stories were delicate slivers of domestic life: how to handle the illness of a child; how to pay for a son's high school education; how to cope with the petty prejudices of polite society; how to help a grumpy alcoholic uncle to die with his dignity intact. The power of Forbes's book lay in its character study of Mama, whose resolute resourcefulness and calm in the face of every adversity resonated amid the sacrifices of World War II.

The teenage Mary Rodgers had read the book, then passed it on to her mother, who loved it and suggested to Dick that it would make a great play. He and Oscar agreed. To adapt the book for the stage, they signed John Van Druten, a British-born playwright and director who was even then enjoying just about the biggest success on Broadway outside of *Oklahoma!* with *The Voice of the Turtle*, his comedy of manners about the challenges of single life in wartime Manhattan. To play Mama, the producers hired Mady Christians, an Austrian-born actress who had emigrated to New York to escape Nazism and had made her mark in Lillian Hellman's *Watch on the Rhine* in 1941. Oscar Homolka played her crusty uncle Chris, while a twenty-year-old new-comer from Omaha named Marlon Brando made his Broadway debut as her son, Nels. Van Druten also directed the play, and in his quietly innovative staging, the narrator—the family's eldest, now-grown daughter Katrin—sits in a spotlight at the edge of the stage, breaking the theater's invisible fourth wall and reading aloud to the audience from a manuscript of her childhood memories. "For as long as I could remember, the house on Steiner Street had been home," she begins, before going on to catalogue her recollections, concluding, "But first and foremost, I remember Mama," just as the lights come up on the rest of the stage and the action begins.

I Remember Mama opened at the Music Box Theatre on October 19, 1944—while Dick and Oscar were in the middle of work on *Carousel*. The *New York Times* pronounced it "a delightful evening for the theater," and it would run for 713 performances before being turned into a successful 1948 film directed by George Stevens, starring Irene Dunne as Mama. It was an auspicious first outing for the new producing team.

Now, TEN MONTHS later, in August 1945, with *Carousel* up and running and the war ending at last, Dick and Oscar were again approached about a project to produce, and from the first the enterprise was a family affair. The inspiration came from Dorothy Fields, the most prominent female lyricist working on Broadway or in Hollywood, and the sister of Rodgers and Hart's onetime librettist, Herbert Fields. Already a two-decade veteran of collaboration with composers from Jimmy McHugh to Jerome Kern, with a gift for deft, conversational lyrics, Fields had written the words for such standards as "I Can't Give You Anything but Love" and "On the Sunny Side of the Street," and she had won an Academy Award for "The Way You Look Tonight." In addition to her family connections to Dick through her brother and her father, Lew Fields, she knew Oscar well from their shared involvement with the American Society of Composers, Authors and Publishers (ASCAP), the songwriters' collective that dispensed royalties for public performances of popular music.

Fields's current brainstorm was the result of a tip from an official at the New York branch of the Travelers Aid Society who told of a young sergeant who had come from Coney Island to Pennsylvania Station, "stoned, with kewpie dolls and lamps and cigars and candy, and across his tunic he had a row of sharpshooter's medals," Fields would recall. "And when I heard 'sharpshooter,' the idea struck: Wouldn't it be marvelous to have Ethel Merman as Annie Oakley?" Merman was already fifteen years into her long run as the Broadway musical's leading leading lady, and she was also a close friend of Dorothy's. Her brassy bravura and heard-in-the-last-row-of-the-balcony voice had made her a favorite of composers from George Gershwin to Cole Porter, and a darling of critics and audiences alike. She seemed a natural choice to play Oakley, the plucky sharpshooter who had made her name touring with "Buffalo Bill" Cody's Wild West show in the 1870s. Her colorful story was in keeping with the World War II–era wave of nostalgia that had swept popular entertainment from Broadway to Hollywood.

The real Annie Oakley had been dead for not quite twenty years, and young Oscar and Reggie Hammerstein had loved the Wild West Show when it played in New York. In yet another family connection, Dorothy Fields's other brother, Joseph, had written the screenplay for a fanciful 1935 film biography of Oakley starring Barbara Stanwyck.

Since Herbert and Dorothy Fields had a commitment to write a show for Mike Todd, Dorothy approached him first, but he was not interested. "A show about a dame who knows from nothing but guns?" was his skeptical reply.

"So Herbert said to me, 'Okay, we're going to go to somebody else,'" Dorothy would remember. "Now, there happened to be a meeting at ASCAP after our meeting with Todd, and the first person I saw when I came in was Oscar Hammerstein. I said, 'Ockie, what do you think about Ethel Merman as Annie Oakley?' He said, 'We'll do it.' That's all! And then he said, 'Talk to Dick after the meeting.' I talked to Dick and Dick said the same thing—'We'll do it.'"

There remained the small matter of getting the prospective star on board. Merman was in Doctors Hospital, having just given birth. Fields, herself the mother of young children, visited the star in the hospital. "I was having postoperative gas pains and felt like anything but a lady sharpshooter," Merman would recall. "I asked Dorothy to give me time to get out of the hospital." Fields did, and in short order, a salary offer of $4,500 a week plus 10 percent of the gross perked Merman right up and she said yes.

The project gathered steam. The Fields siblings would write the book, and Dorothy the lyrics. All that remained was to find a composer. Rodgers himself had no wish to work with anyone but Hammerstein, and all the parties agreed on their first choice: Oscar and Dorothy's old partner Jerome Kern, who was enjoying a satisfied semiretirement at sixty in Beverly Hills, working only when he wanted to. Dick and Oscar set out to woo him. IT WOULD BE ONE OF THE GREATEST HONORS OF MY LIFE IF YOU WOULD CONSENT TO WRITE THE MUSIC FOR THIS SHOW, Rodgers wired. For his part, Hammerstein held out the lure of a Broadway revival of *Show Boat*, his and Kern's greatest triumph. Finally Kern agreed, and he and his wife, Eva, came east at the beginning of November, spending the weekend with Oscar and Dorothy at Highland Farm, then heading to Manhattan. On Monday, November 5, Eva Kern had an appointment for lunch with Dorothy Fields, and Jerry decided to do some shopping. As he was heading around the corner of Park Avenue and 57th Street, he collapsed.

Kern was carrying no wallet and was at first taken to the city hospital on Welfare Island in the East River. But Kern did have an ASCAP membership card in his pocket, and the ASCAP offices eventually tracked down Oscar, who rushed to the scene, where his own doctor and old friend Harold Hyman told him that Kern had suffered a stroke and might never recover. Jerry was transferred to Doctors Hospital, where Oscar and Dorothy took a room. On Sunday the eleventh, Kern's breathing stopped. Oscar lifted the oxygen tent to whisper in his ear, "I've told ev'ry little star," a lyric from *Music in the Air*, but there was no answer. At the funeral, Hammerstein had not quite finished his eulogy when he broke down.

KERN'S DEATH LEFT the Annie Oakley project in limbo and its creative team at a loss. Dick Rodgers had already reached out to another old friend about directing the show: Josh Logan, whose collaboration with Rodgers and Hart had started with *I Married an Angel* in 1938. Just thirty-seven years old, Logan was already a consummate man of the theater. In the early 1930s, the Southern-born, Princeton-educated director had co-founded the University Players, a distinguished summer stock company on Cape Cod that drew such standout talents as Henry Fonda, Margaret Sullavan, and a college friend of Logan's, a skinny architecture major and accordion player named James Stewart. Logan had even studied briefly in Moscow with the father of modern method acting, Konstantin Stanislavski, observing the master's direction of grand opera—which aimed for a novel and "total integration of acting and music."

Logan also suffered from what was not yet known as manic-depressive bipolar disorder, in which bursts of incredible creativity alternated with periods of crippling doubt and depression, and he had had a serious breakdown in 1940. Still, he had uncanny instincts for showmanship, and during his tour of duty in the Army Air Corps he served as co-director of Irving Berlin's all-soldier revue, *This Is the Army*.

In a call with Rodgers from a pay phone at Camp Kilmer, New Jersey, where he was waiting to be mustered out of the service, Logan heard the awful news of Kern's death. Days later, he heard Rodgers's idea for a substitute composer: Irving Berlin. "Everyone agreed there was no point in asking him," Dick explained. "He's a boss. It's got to be his show all the way—his ideas, his money, his songs. He doesn't work for other people. So we started on down our list, when Oscar said, 'Wait! How can a man say no until he's at least asked to say yes?' So, we asked him and he said yes." So, Dick added, "Get out of that goddamned camp and let's get going."

If anyone could intimidate Dick Rodgers at this point in his career, it was Irving Berlin. He had had his first hit, "Alexander's Ragtime Band," in 1911, when Rodgers was just nine years old. And Rodgers remembered all too well Florenz Ziegfeld's surprise interpolation of Berlin's "Blue Skies" into Rodgers and Hart's score for *Betsy*—a stinging humiliation at the time. When Mary Rodgers, who was several years behind Berlin's daughter Mary Ellin at the Brearley School for girls, came home one day and asked, "Mommy, who is the most famous, Mary Ellin's father or my father?" Dorothy Rodgers was forced to reply, "I'm sorry to tell you but it's Mary Ellin's father."

But *Oklahoma!* had evened the score, and now it was Berlin whose confidence was shaky. He had been touring battle zones all over the world with *This Is the Army*, and he was exhausted. He was the past master of the old school: the hit Tin Pan Alley song, the elegant topical revue, the musical comedy in which songs could be inserted at will. The idea of an integrated score—what he called a "situation show"—was alien to him, and he was not sure he could do it. Plus, what did he know about hillbilly music? Then, too, there was the matter of credit; the project was too far along to allow it to become an "Irving Berlin Production." Berlin was an inveterate worrywart, fond of reciting a nervous couplet of self-awareness that he'd composed: "There goes Time with your last year's prize / Whittling it down to its proper size."

So Rodgers sought to reassure Berlin. Writing songs that grew out of plot situations and character would be *easier*, he explained, than plucking them out of the blue. (Indeed, the Fieldses had already sketched out such song ideas as "You Can't Get a Feller with a Gun.") Oscar's advice about how to write folksy music was just as direct: simply drop the g's on the ends of words. Berlin asked for a weekend to think it over, then asked to see the early draft of Herb and Dorothy's script. Finally, with his musical secretary, Helmy Kresa, he retreated to an

Atlantic City hotel to see what he could come up with. He felt confident enough to accept—and in a matter of days, he wrote a batch of songs. In one, Annie would explain her family's unlearned but wised-up ways in "Doin' What Comes Naturally." In another, she would bemoan the difficulty of getting a man with a gun. In a third, she would share a big romantic ballad, "They Say It's Wonderful," with her sharpshooting rival, Frank Butler.

The producers' reaction to Berlin's demonstration of the first songs was ecstatic, so he pressed on. But, still insecure, he thought one number had drawn insufficient appreciation and discarded it. Only when Josh Logan asked about the missing song at the next meeting did Berlin's secretary find the discarded manuscript under the office telephone. The title: "There's No Business Like Show Business." In the end, Berlin turned out a score of such power and shattering effectiveness that at least eleven of its fourteen numbers became hits completely outside the context of the show, which by now was titled *Annie Get Your Gun*. In no small part, he would have Rodgers and Hammerstein to thank. Years later, when asked why Berlin's score was such a standout, John Fearnley, Rodgers and Hammerstein's longtime stage manager and casting director, explained that Berlin would come into a meeting with a new song and excitedly announce, "This will sell tons because it has the same chord progression as 'White Christmas,' and once he played it for Dick and Oscar they would say, 'Irving, that's great. Now what we need here is a song between Frank and Annie when they . . .'"

Rodgers and Hammerstein might be the new kings of Broadway, but Berlin was an old street fighter. "I would say Irving Berlin wrote this tremendous score not just for himself but for Richard Rodgers," the conductor Jay Blackton would recall. "The extra reach, again and again and *again*, to show he still had it in him." And he showed he could be magnanimous, too: because his hiring had meant that Dorothy gave up the chance to write the show's lyrics, and because he was grateful for the Fieldses' inspiration in suggesting songs, he agreed to split the authors' royalties fifty-fifty instead of the usual one-third each to the writers of book, music, and lyrics.

Berlin also proved that Dick Rodgers had nothing on him when it came to speed of composition. At one story conference in Oscar's East

Side town house as the show was taking final shape, Josh Logan whispered to Oscar that he thought there should be a second-act duet for Frank and Annie, who had not sung together since their big first-act love song, "They Say It's Wonderful." In a flash, Berlin was at their side from across the room. "Listen, everybody," he insisted. "Josh wants another song. Josh, where do you see this song?" When Logan suggested the second act, Berlin demanded, "If they're not talking to each other in the second act, how can they sing together?" At this point Rodgers piped up. "Could they have a quarrel song or a challenge song?"

"Challenge!" Berlin exclaimed. "Of course! Meeting over. I've got to go home and write a challenge song."

The meeting broke up and Logan took a taxi back to his own nearby apartment. When he walked in the door, the phone was ringing. It was Berlin, who began singing "Anything you can do, I can do better . . ."

"That's perfect!" Logan shouted. "When in hell did you write that?"

"In the taxicab," Berlin replied. "I had to, didn't I? We go into rehearsal Monday."

Annie Get Your Gun would have none of the convention-breaking features of *Oklahoma!* or *Carousel*. There was no ballet, no soul-baring soliloquy, no pantomime prologue. Its depiction of Native Americans was cartoonish in its day and insensitive by modern lights. In the end, Annie would win her lover by purposely losing a shooting match—which could be seen as a gesture of traditional female acquiescence or a blow for female empowerment, depending on one's interpretation. But the play had other overriding assets: a star turn, flawless showmanship, and all those wonderful songs. It opened at the Imperial Theatre on May 16, 1946, and astoundingly the first-night critics found the score disappointing. "A great big, follow-the-formula, fetch-the-crowd musical," wrote *Time* magazine. "It bothers with nothing artistic or bizarre." Brooks Atkinson in the *Times* called Berlin's score "routine" and "undistinguished," though he allowed of Merman, "By the time she is finished with either a song or a part she possesses it completely and very nearly possesses all the other performers and has, at least, a lien on the scenery."

History would prove the skeptics wrong. The show ran for 1,147 performances, became an indestructible vehicle for many other actresses besides Merman, and its songs passed into the everyday rhythms of pop culture, especially "There's No Business Like Show Business," Berlin's hymn to the joys of performing, which became the entertainment world's unofficial anthem. Twenty years later, with Merman nearing sixty, Rodgers would produce a splashy revival for the Music Theater of Lincoln Center. The show was a hit all over again.

IN THE WAKE of *Annie Get Your Gun*'s resounding success, Dick and Oscar teamed up with Josh Logan for two slight, well-made comedies that were solid commercial successes, owing at least partly to Logan's canny direction. The first was *Happy Birthday*, a vehicle written for Helen Hayes by her friend Anita Loos. Hayes had tired of the hoopskirts and historical dramas that had made her famous and was looking for a lark. Loos, best known as the author of the Roaring Twenties novel *Gentlemen Prefer Blondes*, provided it with the story of Addie Bemis, a mousy librarian, who ventures into a dive bar in Newark, New Jersey, on a rainy night at twilight in search of the handsome bank teller on whom she has a secret crush.

Over the course of the evening, the teetotaling Addie falls under the spell of a few Pink Ladies and other pixilating alcoholic concoctions and blossoms into an alluring heroine who makes friends with all the raffish denizens of the bar. Through Jo Mielziner's scenic magic, the bar itself blossomed into an enchanted fairyland of twinkling lights and a telescoping bar stool on which Addie happily sways. She wins her guy, and even sings a jaunty tune, "I Haven't Got a Worry in the World," supplied, of course, by Rodgers and Hammerstein themselves.

But the Boston tryout was a disaster. Audiences were unsure how to respond to Addie's unsettling mix of sweetness and bitchiness. One night, everyone met in Oscar's suite at the Ritz-Carlton. Logan feared the team would close the play. Instead, displaying the steeliness that a quarter century in the theater had instilled in him, Oscar just said calmly, "Let's fix it."

"And," Dick added in the same level tone, "by Monday."

"I don't think I had ever seen dogged pride and fixed determination played in unison before," Logan would marvel. "I vowed secretly to be always as emotionally tough as they were that night."

Logan and Loos carefully excised every other line, removing Addie's nasty qualities while retaining her endearing ones. The show opened in New York on October 31, 1946, and ran for a year and a half—563 performances. It might have run longer if Hayes had not decided she'd had enough.

The second collaboration with Logan was a play recommended by the producer Leland Hayward, a comedy by Norman Krasna called *John Loves Mary*, which told the story of two army buddies dealing with complications in their return to stateside love. The show opened on February 4, 1947, and, while the critics were not especially impressed, it ran for 423 performances and became a film starring Ronald Reagan and a staple of summer stock and amateur productions for years afterward.

As IF THIS frantic pace of producing were not enough, Oscar was also growing busier by the day with his many commitments outside the world of the theater. He had never been one who could say no to what he saw as a good cause and was one of the entertainment world's most stalwart liberal voices. In his fallow years in Los Angeles, he had helped found the pro-Soviet Hollywood Anti-Nazi League and served as chairman of its cultural commission, helping to organize radio broadcasts and write articles to combat racial intolerance. After the Hitler-Stalin nonaggression pact of 1939 rendered the league obsolete, Oscar helped to found its successor, the Hollywood League for Democratic Action. In 1945, he helped start the Independent Citizens' Committee of the Arts, Sciences, and Professions—which promoted participation in the democratic process and would later be denounced as a Communist front organization. In 1946, he joined artists and writers like Paul Robeson and Woody Guthrie as a founding member of People's Songs, which organized entertainment for progressive causes.

Hammerstein had also been active in the Writers' War Board, a privately organized propaganda organization that worked in close coordination with a raft of government agencies to promote the Allied cause and combat racism and anti-Semitism on the home front. The group was instrumental in persuading the military to hire black medical workers and the Red Cross to stop classifying donated blood by race. Authors like Stephen Vincent Benét and Thornton Wilder wrote articles, essays, speeches, radio scripts, and books in support of the war effort. Oscar attended the group's weekly meetings every Wednesday, while also serving on committees to create a radio show and promote naval aviation. After the war, this group reconstituted itself as the Writers Board for World Government, a part of the growing World Federalist Movement. Under the leadership of Norman Cousins, the editor of the *Saturday Review of Literature*, and others, the movement advocated the formation of an international government stronger than the United Nations, and it would become the most passionate political cause of Oscar's later life.

At the same time, Hammerstein remained very involved in ASCAP, and he would also serve as president of the Authors Guild, an organization devoted to copyright protection and the preservation of writers' creative rights.

In Hollywood, Hammerstein's political and philanthropic activities had not impinged on his creative work, if only because there was not much challenging or satisfying work for him to do. Now, with *Oklahoma!* still playing to packed houses (and requiring regular auditions for cast replacements and touring companies) and *Carousel* having just closed, Oscar found he had less time for the painstaking process of writing.

Dick Rodgers was just as busy. "Even now, it is hard to write calmly about this extraordinary period in my life," he recalled in his memoirs. "There was just no letup. No sooner had we stopped one project than we began another. Most of the time, we worked on a number of shows simultaneously. Every day required an unending stream of decisions. Who would succeed Ethel Merman during her vacation? Which moving picture company offer should we consider for *John Loves Mary*? What record company should we choose for the original cast album of our next show? Could I afford the time to see the young interviewer from the *Los Angeles Times*?"

It was against this background that Oscar began to dig into what would become his most autobiographical, most deeply personal work, one that would bedevil him not only for the many months of its troubled creation but for the rest of his life.

HAMMERSTEIN HAD LONG had it in mind to write the story of one man's life from birth to death. In the end, he would settle for chronicling the span from birth to thirty-five years old. His protagonist was Joseph Taylor Jr., the son of a small-town midwestern doctor. Joe follows his father into medicine but falls under the spell of an ambitious and avaricious wife. She leads him to abandon his principles—and the art he was born to practice—for the empty life of a society doctor in Chicago, dispensing pills and rest cures, raising money, and making the scene. The title for the new show summed up the lead character's mad dash through an empty life: *Allegro*, the Italian musical term for a lively, brisk tempo. In Oscar's vision, Joe gets so caught up in the worldly swirl around him that he loses sight of what matters most.

It was perhaps no accident that Hammerstein chose to make his hero a doctor. His own doctor, Harold Hyman, had also been one of his closest friends since childhood, and he consulted him closely. Dick Rodgers was drawn to the subject because his father and brother were both distinguished physicians.

Allegro may be the only show in Broadway history whose creators set out to make it deliberately uncommercial. From the beginning, Hammerstein's notion was a minimalist musical, with a spare approach to storytelling that would take its inspiration from Thornton Wilder's *Our Town*. Naturalism would blend with a Greek chorus that would be "used frequently to interpret the mental and emotional reactions of the principal characters," as Hammerstein wrote in prefatory directions to the published script. There would be no walls, no windows, no conventional stage sets. Instead, "backgrounds for action" would be "achieved by small scenic pieces on a moving stage by light projections and by drops."

The new show would once again be produced under the auspices of the Theatre Guild, and Hammerstein had begun work on the script in the spring of 1946, when he and Dorothy were sailing to Australia to visit her relatives at the time of the Broadway opening of *Annie Get Your Gun*. When their ship docked in Brisbane, Oscar sent about a fifth of the draft script and several lyrics off to Dick. Typically, Rodgers immediately sat down and wrote three melodies. Years later, Oscar would describe his intentions in writing the play: "I was concerned when I wrote *Allegro* about men who are good at anything—writers, doctors, lawyers, business, and who are diverted from the field of their expertness by a kind of strange, informal conspiracy that goes on. People start pinning medals on them. People start asking them to join committees or chair committees. And the first thing you know, they are no longer writing, or practicing medicine or practicing law. They are committee chairmen. They are speechmakers. They are dinner-attenders. And this emaciates their achievements."

The script begins in 1905, with the lights rising on a mother in bed with a newborn child, and a chorus on the opposite side of the stage explaining:

> *The lady in bed is Marjorie Taylor,*
> *Doctor Joseph Taylor's wife.*
> *Except for the day when she married Joe,*
> *This is the happiest day of her life!*

Her husband enters and they "gaze down fondly at their first born," as the chorus intones:

> *His hair is fuzzy,*
> *His eyes are blue.*
> *His eyes may change—*
> *They often do.*
> *He weighs eight pounds*
> *And an ounce or two—*
> *Joseph Taylor Junior!*

Much of the show's first act leaned heavily on Oscar's memories of his own childhood—the death of his grandmother Nimmo and his mother's death. "I always felt his songs came out of his feelings about her," his son Bill would recall. He would spend more than a year on act one, drafting and revising in his usual painstaking practice. The dramaturgy was novel in several ways. After the grandmother dies early in the story, her spirit returns at crucial turns in the plot to sing or comment on the unfolding action. The chorus and other characters describe Joe Jr.'s childhood, but he himself is never seen. His character's voice is not heard until twelve pages into the script, and the actor portraying him does not appear in the flesh until he gets to college.

In all this, Oscar was plowing new ground. Though he wouldn't (and didn't) put it this way at the time, he was pioneering what would come to be called the "concept musical," a work in which avant-garde theatrical techniques and devices are used to comment on the action, and in which traditional linear narrative is often secondary to style, metaphor, or message. The problem for Hammerstein was delineating just what message he wanted to convey. He had proven himself a master adapter of existing dramatic or literary works with both *Oklahoma!* and *Carousel*, and *Show Boat* before that. He had also written original books for most of his other major collaborations with Kern, Romberg, and Friml. But here Oscar's narrative gifts seemed to elude him. In Joseph Taylor Jr., Hammerstein had a concept, all right. It is far less clear that he ever had a real character, a complex, flesh-and-blood human being like Curly or Billy Bigelow, who could explain and examine his motivations and feelings in song, as Oscar himself had now conditioned Broadway audiences to expect.

Throughout *Allegro*, Oscar would repeatedly commit the writer's cardinal sin of telling, not showing. In the beginning of the play, Joe Jr.'s parents and fellow townspeople sing about him. The chorus describes the process of his learning to walk in song—"One Foot, Other Foot"—but we never see the boy himself. His parents are given a beautiful ballad—"A Fellow Needs a Girl"—expressing the quiet contentments of married love, but Joe's first appearance is as a college freshman, singing this trivial (if admittedly catchy) song:

It's a darn nice campus,
With ivy on the walls,
Friendly maples

Outside the lecture halls,
A new gymnasium,
A chapel with a dome—
It's a darn nice campus . . .
And I wish I were home.

Joe's one and only sweetheart is his childhood friend Jennie Brinker, a grasping (and ultimately adulterous) woman, with more than a little of Myra Finn's mercurial character. His one big ballad of longing for her, "You Are Never Away," is first sung to *him* by the chorus. One of the show's best numbers, "So Far," an infectious Rodgers tune, set to lyrics about the early stages of a romantic relationship, is thrown away on a passing character named Beulah, a casual college date of Joe's who never appears again. Before the end of the first act, Jennie induces a heart attack in Joe's mother, who doubts the girl's love for her son and dies. The curtain falls at intermission with Joe and Jennie married before a congregation whose musings aloud reflect their own ambivalence, as a chorus sings ringing repetitions of the exhortation, "Wish them well."

HAMMERSTEIN SPENT EIGHTEEN months writing this first act, and as rehearsals loomed in the late summer of 1947, he churned out the second act in just two weeks. In it, Joe, now a doctor in his father's practice, bows to Jennie's urgings that he leave their small town for a job at a big hospital in Chicago, where his college roommate Charlie also works and has taken to drink out of boredom. Joe rises in the hospital hierarchy but derives less and less satisfaction from his work caring for hypochondriac socialites. He is oblivious to his wife's affair with a hospital board member, and takes his loyal and long-suffering nurse, Emily, for granted. Finally at the breaking point, he has an epiphany and is summoned home by the loving voice of his mother's ghost in a moving ballad, "Come Home," and takes Emily and Charlie with him as the chorus swells in a reprise of "One Foot, Other Foot." He is learning to walk all over again.

If that all sounds a bit baffling from a distance of seventy years, it was equally confusing to some on the creative team mounting the show. Four days before rehearsals began, Agnes de Mille, who had been engaged as both choreographer and director—the first woman to win such an assignment for a big Broadway musical—felt compelled to ask Oscar just what the hell the show was about. "It's about a man not being allowed to do his own work because of worldly pressures," Oscar replied. "That's not the play you've written," de Mille answered. "You haven't written your second act." Oscar's resigned reply was that the producers were already committed to the Majestic Theatre in New York in October.

Indeed, the whole project had gotten out of hand. Hammerstein's notion of a physical production so simple that college and amateur troupes might easily stage it had turned into something completely different. To make room for de Mille's dancers, the scenic and lighting designer Jo Mielziner had initially conceived a stylized set featuring a giant cyclorama with projected images. But he was dissatisfied with the projections and substituted painted drops, sliding platforms and realistic props like chairs and tables that could be moved on- and offstage. The elaborate scheme of treadmills, pendulum stages, curtains, loudspeakers, and projected images would require forty stagehands—twice the usual number.

Still, Mielziner was a genius, a superb artist who could draw freehand sketches of proposed sets to scale. He had built a working merry-go-round for *Carousel*, and for *Allegro* he had devised a serpentine, S-shaped curtain that ran along a continuous floor-to-ceiling track, allowing one scene to dissolve into the next, in cinematic fashion. This eliminated the usual need for some scenes to be played "in one," at the foot of the stage, while stagehands worked behind a fixed drop curtain. The concept was revolutionary but would prove very expensive.

Similarly, Oscar's vision of an *Our Town*–like ensemble cast had ballooned into a company worthy of the Metropolitan Opera: eighteen principals, twenty-one supporting players, twenty-two dancers, thirty-eight singers, and an orchestra of thirty-five players—requiring some three hundred costumes. All this spectacle sent the budget soaring above $300,000—more than three times the cost of *Oklahoma!*

That August, a reporter for *Cue* magazine was allowed to sit in on auditions, and the resulting story captured the feeling of the production team at work. Hammerstein declared that one actor "looks like a room clerk," while Rodgers was particularly taken with one young actress. "Let her read anything," he said. "I'm crazy about her. She's got more guts. The times she's been in here . . ." He addressed her directly, "Just sing it sweet, darling. Don't try to be comic," before telling his colleagues, "I'm in love with that silly little puss she has." Terry Helburn's deadpan reply: "But the body will have to be toned down."

Once more, the cast was made up mostly of unknowns. Annamary Dickey, who played Marjorie Taylor, had sung at the Metropolitan Opera, and John Battles, who played Joe Jr., had been in the original cast of *On the Town* in 1944. The newcomer Lisa Kirk, in the comparatively small role of the nurse, Emily, would become a star on the strength of the show's most enduring song, "The Gentleman Is a Dope," which her character sings in frustration at Joe's heedlessness.

A worm's-eye view observer of the proceedings was the seventeen-year-old Stephen Sondheim, whom Oscar had hired for the summer as a $25-a-week gofer after his first year at Williams College, fetching coffee, typing scripts, and soaking everything in. "It was a seminal influence on my life, because it showed me a lot of smart people doing something wrong," Sondheim would remember. The experience would also haunt his own creative work. "That's why I'm drawn to experiment," he would say. "I realize that I am trying to recreate *Allegro* all the time." In the short term, Sondheim was appalled by de Mille's handling of her first directorial assignment. She complained to Oscar that she couldn't devise new dances while also staging new songs and new scenes. So Hammerstein took on direction of the dialogue scenes (in addition to doing daily rewrites of the script starting at five a.m.), while Rodgers staged the songs. "It was not a satisfactory solution by any means," Rodgers would recall.

The opening night of the New Haven tryout, September 1, was one of the most famous train wrecks in Broadway history. First, a principal dancer, Ray Harrison, caught his foot in a scenery track on the floor of the stage, shredded the ligaments in his right leg, and was carried screaming from the stage. Then William Ching, playing Joe Taylor Sr., was right in the middle of "A Fellow Needs a Girl" when the scenery wall behind him started to collapse and he was forced to hold it up till the stagehands caught on. Lisa Kirk, singing "The Gentleman Is a Dope," also caught her foot in the curtain track and tumbled off the stage into the orchestra below. Luckily, the Shubert Theatre in New Haven had no traditional pit, so "the two cellists who caught her simply hoisted her back onto the stage and she didn't stop singing through the entire accident," Rodgers would recall.

"Need I tell you, the audience was giving her an ovation the Pope has never received," Sondheim would remember. "Everybody pushed her back onstage and she had to take two bows. Next day in *The New York Herald Tribune* . . . Billy Rose, of all people, said, 'A star is born.' Next night she comes back, gets to the same point in the song, and starts to fall again and the entire audience gasps because they'd all read the *Herald Tribune*. She recovers quickly, they all sigh and she gets another ovation. Oscar came backstage at the end and said, 'You do that a third time and you're fired.' "

Finally, at the climax of the evening, when the chorus began to sing to Joe, "Come home, come home, where the brown birds fly," smoke from an alley fire outside the theater began drifting in through doors propped open against the steamy September night, and perhaps fifty or sixty people made for the exits in fear before Josh Logan, in town to provide an impartial critique for Rodgers and Hammerstein, shouted an explanation and told them to stay put. Logan may have saved the day, but he could not save the show—though he tried, in two fevered letters to Oscar after seeing *Allegro* twice.

Even with the opening night mishaps, Logan wrote on September 4, "it's a wonderful job on everyone's part." But then he got down to brass tacks. "I hesitate to tell you again how much I dislike the grandmother," he wrote. "I felt a real and growing resistance to her in the audience and I believe this will increase." He urged Hammerstein to "get Joe on sooner." He complained that most all the songs were "unexcitingly staged and performed." He asked, "Do you or Dick feel that the chorus sings too much of 'You Are Never Away' before Joe sings it, thus robbing it of its full effect when he sings the whole thing?" "The mother dying on stage is hard to take and hard to set."

He concluded in all capital letters: "DON'T READ THIS IF YOU GET MAD EASY," before suggesting that Joe needed a "personal musical moment" in the second act. "It's just that I'm so fond of Joe, I hate to see other people take over moments that should be his—he's the story and he's the best actor in the show."

Two days later, Logan was even more emphatic: "The most important problem to solve is the whole development of Joe's final decision." Throughout the play, Logan judged, Joe had been weak and indecisive, influenced by his wife, mother, father, grandmother, and friends, but never taking a strong stand of his own. "His action as it now stands is a kind of cowardly retreat rather than a brave step." Mightn't it be better to have Joe consider returning home, but then resolve to stay in Chicago and run the big hospital the way he thinks it should be—with patient care at the heart of its mission? Logan offered to fly to Boston, where the show was set to open in two days, to work on the problems in person, and concluded, "I'm afraid that critically you will still be led to believe the show is packing more dynamite with the audience than it actually does. As it stands now it will get some rave notices and hysterical enthusiasm of numbers of people. What I am talking about is the mass effect which I feel the show can have if the points are really made so that everyone understands and feels them."

There is no evidence that Oscar took Logan up on his offer—or indeed, any record of his reply. On the contrary, it appears that Hammerstein made none of the changes Josh suggested, with the possible exception of softening Marjorie Taylor's death, which in the final script is implied but only wordlessly confirmed in a telegram Joe receives and reads silently at college. And the reaction of the Boston critics was just as Logan had predicted, veering wildly between praise and puzzlement. Elliot Norton in the *Post* pronounced it a "knockout." "It is romantic, realistic, fantastic, satirical, serious and gay all at once," he wrote. "It has hit tunes, bright jokes, fine singers, wonderful dancers, hilarity, hocus pocus, completely unconventional scenery, and a social conscience." He added, "It needs a little tinkering and tailoring. But even without tinker or tailor, it is the most remarkable musical show I have ever seen." But Elinor Hughes of the *Herald* predicted that there would be "no plain sailing ahead for this production."

————

ALLEGRO ARRIVED AT the Majestic Theatre in New York on October 10, with the biggest advance sale in Broadway history to date: $750,000, at a time when the top price of an orchestra ticket was no more than $6 and an advance sale of $100,000 was considered astronomical. The show had been featured in cover stories for both *Life* and *Time* magazines, but as de Mille's husband, Walter Prude, would recall, it went over with its opening night audience "like a wet firecracker."

The New York critics were just as divided as their Boston colleagues. "For at least half its length," Brooks Atkinson wrote in the *Times*, "it is a work of great beauty and purity, as if 'Our Town' could be written in music." Richard Watts Jr. in the *Post* found it "a distinguished musical play, beautiful, imaginative, original and honestly moving." But John Chapman of the *Daily News* complained, "They have set *Allegro* to an *andante* beat" (using the Italian term for a moderately slow tempo), while William Hawkins of the *World-Telegram & Sun* called the show "a vast disappointment," whose "realization crosses the stage like an impoverished sophomore class production."

In fact, as Stephen Sondheim himself would conclude years later, it was the muddiness and lack of sophistication of Oscar's writing—all the more glaring because of its contrast with the novelty and depth of his concept—that doomed the show. Indeed, Hammerstein had proved the point of the show by being too busy and distracted by other pressures to do his best work. "In *Allegro*, he was writing about the conflict between responsibility to your community and responsibility to yourself," Sondheim would recall. "He found that the more public appearances he made, the more speeches he gave, the more he traveled to support these causes, the less time he had for writing, the thing he was born to do. That is what he was trying to convey in *Allegro*. And nobody got it."

The *New Republic* archly observed that "the Messrs. Rodgers and Hammerstein bitterly regret being the richest and most successful people in the American theater and wish they could go back to Spirit, South Dakota, or Barstow, California, or some other suitable, small, simple community, and there devote their talents to playing the organ for the town glee club and composing songs for the high school football team." Rodgers's music came in for more than its share of scorn as well. While he was all but incapable of writing un-hummable melodies, Rodgers did write some of his least tuneful music for *Allegro*, especially in some of the ensemble numbers. "It seems the minute he leaves the métier of conventional musical comedy, in which he excels, and ventures into a more exacting area of theater music, he passes outside the limits of his technique and his ideas alike," wrote Cecil Smith in *Theatre Arts* magazine. "Even the best parts of the *Allegro* score misrepresent the composer who could command the wit of 'Bewitched, Bothered and Bewildered.'"

Allegro ran for 315 performances and was the top-grossing Broadway play of the 1947–48 season, but it was still a disappointment for Rodgers and Hammerstein. Near the end of the run, the company dropped eight chorus members and six musicians to cut costs. A scaled-down, sixteen-city tour ran for another seven months, but there would be no movie, no London company, no full-scale Broadway revival.

Cole Porter once remarked that Rodgers and Hammerstein's innovations had made musical theater harder for everyone else in the business. But they had made it harder for themselves, too. Josh Logan's take was that Dick and Oscar wanted to top not only themselves, but also Irving Berlin's smash success with *Annie Get Your Gun*. "They were overanxious," he said. "They wanted to do something sensational and they tried too hard."

In later years, in separate interviews, the partners sometimes seemed to indulge in fleeting mutual recriminations. Rodgers would agree with an interviewer that the show was "a bit pretentious," while adding in his own words, "I think it was too preachy, which was the one fault that Oscar had, if any. He tended to moralize a great deal, and this came across in *Allegro* more than in anything he ever did." For good measure, Rodgers added, "But I myself thought it moralized too much." For his part, Hammerstein said that the Greek chorus had not come out the way he envisioned it. "I intended Dick to write music for it but we wound up reciting the chorus instead," he said. "We also wound up with a great deal of scenery, with a stage that's not exactly a revolving stage but that shifts back and forth from the wings. Actually that was the reason the play didn't make money. I'm not blaming anyone, because we all accepted it, we all collaborated, we all liked the idea. But it was a mistake." To critics who claimed he had a naive affection for small towns, Oscar liked to point out that the most morally suspect character in the play—the ambitious and dishonest Jennie—is a small-town girl. But he could not quarrel with audiences' ultimate judgment. "Sometimes the audience writes your play for you, and rewrites it in the way you don't want it re-written," he would recall. "And if so, there is something wrong with you as a writer. It is as if a horse decides where he is going to take you, if he doesn't feel a strong enough grip on his reins."

It is difficult to know to what degree the failure of *Allegro* caused strains in the partners' relationship, if only because they maintained such a unified public front in all things. It may well be that Hammerstein was more inclined to experimentation than Rodgers, even if he was no more capable of ensuring that experimentation's success. In the end, Dick and Oscar were haunted by their failed effort. "Of all the musicals I ever worked on that didn't quite succeed," Rodgers wrote in his memoir, "*Allegro* is the one I think most worthy of a second chance. . . . I still keep hoping." Normally the most unsentimental of men about failure, Oscar could not let go of *Allegro*, either. "It is the only play that was not a big success that I have any loyalty toward, any desire to produce again and perhaps rewrite, give another chance to," he told an interviewer.

The plain truth is that Rodgers and Hammerstein would never again take such risks, never again push conventional boundaries so far. They would go on to resounding future successes and would continue to refine and sharpen and test the limits of the new genre of musical theater they had almost single-handedly created. But the era of innovation was over for them. The era of empire lay ahead.

CHAPTER 6

Enchanted Evening

The most commercial thing you can do is not to have your mind on commerce. One of our greatest qualities, I think, is the honesty we try to get into our work. Even those who didn't like *Allegro* couldn't say it was phony.

Richard Rodgers

By 1947, Joshua Logan was as much in demand as any director on Broadway, but even he lost a big fish from time to time. One of the most painful ones that got away was Tennessee Williams's *A Streetcar Named Desire*. Early in the year, its producer, Irene Mayer Selznick, had sent Logan the script to consider, but she sent it at the same time to Elia Kazan, whom Williams preferred. Logan was crushed, but not so permanently that he and his wife, Nedda, didn't eagerly attend the play's premiere on December 3, as guests of its scenic designer, their friend Jo Mielziner. Logan's mood was elevated by the knowledge that in just a few weeks a play of his own would be opening: *Mister Roberts*, a rollicking but poignant comedy about life aboard a navy cargo ship stuck in a backwater of the Pacific in World War II, based on the best-selling novel by Thomas Heggen. Logan had co-authored the script with Heggen and was set to direct, with Leland Hayward producing. Henry Fonda had signed on to play the title character, and Broadway was already abuzz with anticipation.

So it was not surprising, when the Logans repaired to Sardi's after the *Streetcar* opening, that Mielziner's brother Kenneth MacKenna, a former actor and veteran story editor at MGM, mentioned another new novel that might provide some scenic color for *Mister Roberts*. That book was *Tales of the South Pacific*, a loosely linked collection of nineteen short stories by James A. Michener, a navy veteran now working as a textbook editor at Macmillan. The MGM brass had passed on buying the movie rights, but MacKenna thought it had promise. Logan, who was headed with Hayward for a quick getaway to Miami Beach, picked up a copy to take with him and was immediately entranced by one of the stories, "Fo' Dolla," the tale of a passionate interracial romance between a marine lieutenant from the Philadelphia Main Line and a young Tonkinese native. He resolved at once to try to buy the dramatic rights to the book. But the next morning, Logan recalled, Hayward sensed that something was up, and that afternoon, while Logan was napping, Hayward swiped the book and read it himself, exclaiming when Logan woke up, "Josh, we're going to buy this son of a bitch!"

Whereupon Logan had an instant brainstorm: a musical adaptation by Rodgers and Hammerstein. "Of course," Hayward replied, "but don't you dare mention it to them. They'll want the whole goddamn thing. They'd gobble us up for breakfast." But Logan was nothing if not indiscreet, and a short time later, after returning to New York, he ran into Dick Rodgers at a cocktail party and could not resist blurting out a not-quite-true boast. "Don't tell anyone I've told you this, but I own a story you might want to make a musical of." Rodgers took out the little black notebook he always carried and jotted down "T. of the S. Pacific" and "Fo' Dolla." (Rodgers would later confess to having been puzzled by his own cryptic note. "Did I owe someone money, or did someone owe me? And why the devil had I suddenly started writing in dialect?")

A few weeks later, at the Philadelphia tryout of *Mister Roberts*, Logan ran into Oscar Hammerstein and mentioned *Tales of the South Pacific* to him. Two days later, Oscar called back, just as excited, having read the book himself, and having also talked to Rodgers, who assured him, "Oh, I was crazy about it, too, but some son of a bitch I met at a cocktail party owns it so we haven't got a chance."

Logan was the SOB in question, of course, but he had not locked up the rights, and now Leland Hayward hit the roof: the would-be producers would have to share their pet project with the two most powerful men on Broadway, who insisted on 51 to 49 percent control. Logan's indiscretion would cost him untold heartache in the months and years to come, but at the moment, the prospect of another collaboration with Rodgers and Hammerstein was too thrilling to turn down.

Hammerstein at first had trouble finding Michener to work out a deal with him, placing a frantic round of phone calls in Manhattan before finally realizing that the author lived on Harvey Avenue in Doylestown, a ten-minute walk from Highland Farm. Now Howard Reinheimer entered the negotiations and promptly poor-mouthed the property. "You know, Michener, your book has no story line," the lawyer said. "It has no dramatic impact." So Rodgers and Hammerstein couldn't possibly pay Michener the 1.5 percent of royalties that they and the Theatre Guild had given Lynn Riggs for *Green Grow the Lilacs*. After all, that had been a real play, with a cohesive plot and dramatic arc—not a ragtag collection of loosely linked tales. In the end, Michener accepted an offer of 1 percent of the gross box-office receipts in exchange for the rights to all of the stories and "never had regrets," he said. Michener had plenty of reason for optimism. He knew that Rodgers and Hammerstein were still smarting from the failure of *Allegro* and were determined to have a hit. "Those fellows are so mad," he would remember thinking, "they could make a great musical out of three pages of the Bronx telephone directory."

REINHEIMER WAS RIGHT about one thing: *Tales of the South Pacific* was a neither-fish-nor-fowl creation, not a standard novel with a beginning, middle, and end, but more an accumulation of atmospheric character sketches. The *New York Times* had pronounced it "truly one of the most remarkable books" to come out of the war, and its appeal lay in its granularity—in its depiction of American types interacting with South Sea island originals—more than in its inherent drama. Michener's wartime service in the Pacific had left him with a notebook full of vivid impressions and memorable characters. But Oscar Hammerstein would somehow have to hammer it all into a coherent libretto that could hold an audience for two and a half hours. The way forward was not immediately obvious, but there was no shortage of color.

"I wish I could tell you about the South Pacific," Michener's book begins, in an evocative passage that Oscar underlined in his own personal copy.

The way it actually was. The endless ocean. The infinite specks of coral we called islands. Coconut palms nodding gracefully toward the ocean. Reefs upon which waves broke into spray, and inner lagoons, lovely beyond description. I wish I could tell you about the sweating jungle, the full moon rising behind the volcanoes, and the waiting. The waiting. The timeless, repetitive waiting. But whenever I start to talk about the South Pacific, people intervene. I try to tell somebody what the steaming Hebrides were like and first thing you know I'm telling about the old Tonkinese woman who used to sell human heads. As souvenirs. For fifty dollars!

Indeed, it is just such a woman—a wily, betel-chewing entrepreneur and master of pidgin GI slang known as Bloody Mary—who features prominently in "Fo' Dolla," the longest story in the book. Making the acquaintance of handsome young lieutenant Joe Cable, she spirits him to the nearby island of Bali Ha'i, where the French planters have sequestered their daughters for the war, and where he promptly falls for Mary's own lovely daughter, Liat. With Mary playing an uncomfortable combination of matchmaker and procurer, Cable is drawn again and again to the mystic island. But despite his deep love for the girl, he knows he can never marry her or take her home to his family in Philadelphia. Bloody Mary's response as Cable heads off to duty in "Operation Alligator," a major assault on a Japanese-held island, is unsparing: "Lieutenant one bullshit goddam fool!"

Michener summons up a gallery of other compelling characters. There is Tony Fry, a swashbuckling American officer with a penchant for acting outside the regular chain of command. He figures in "The Cave," one of the most dramatic stories in the collection, about a group stationed on a small island, trying to keep the Japanese from retaking

Guadalcanal. They receive messages from the "Remittance Man," a British trader named Anderson, who has hidden out on a nearby island, secretly broadcasting Japanese troop movements to the Allies before being brutally killed. There is Lieutenant Bus Adams, an American bomber pilot who is shot down, and whose rescue mission costs the American taxpayers $600,000. "But it's worth every cent of the money," Michener's narrator notes, "if you happen to be that pilot." There is Luther Billis, a tanned, tattooed Seabee from the navy's construction battalion who is obsessed with a ritual native boar's tooth ceremonial on a neighboring island. There is Ensign Bill Harbison, a snappy, ambitious, married officer from Albuquerque who takes a shine to a navy nurse from Arkansas, Nellie Forbush, and, having briefly lost his head after a beach party, tries to rape her.

And finally there is Emile De Becque, a middle-aged French plantation owner, who falls in love with Forbush and asks her to marry him, in a story called "Our Heroine." Nellie agrees, until she learns that De Becque has eight mixed-race daughters by four different mothers, two Javanese, one Tonkinese, and one Polynesian. "A nigger!" the omniscient narrator exclaims in horror. "To Nellie's tutored mind any person living or dead who was not white or yellow was a nigger. And beyond that, no words could go!" But in the end, Nellie overcomes her fears and prejudices, returns to Emile, and joins him and his daughters in singing "Au Clair de la Lune."

It was a lot for a librettist to absorb, and with his usual meticulous attention to detail and his strong eye for plot and character, Hammerstein went through Michener's book story by story, underlining bits of dialogue, making red grease-pencil checkmarks in the margins, suggesting at one point that Cable, who never meets Nellie Forbush in the book, could have a scene telling her all about Bloody Mary's improbable proposal. On a sheet of yellow legal paper, with page numbers from Michener's book running down the left margin, he made notes of the characters' names: Nellie, Harbison, and so on. Oscar's work gained added impetus—and the whole project got a big shot in the arm—on April 27, with the surprise news that *Tales of the South Pacific* had won the Pulitzer Prize for Fiction.

THE FOLLOWING MONTH, Dick and Oscar went to Los Angeles to check up on one of their most important properties: the national touring company of *Annie Get Your Gun*, featuring Mary Martin, who was fast becoming a star to rival Ethel Merman herself. A onetime dance instructor from Weatherford, Texas, Martin had first met Hammerstein in Hollywood in the 1930s. At an audition at Oscar and Dorothy's elegant home in Beverly Hills, she sang for him "a song you probably don't know, 'Indian Love Call.'" When she finished, Hammerstein told her, "Young lady, I think you have something. I would like to work with you on lines and phrasing, if you could come to my house every week." Then he added, "Oh, and by the way, I know that song. I wrote it." Hammerstein promptly arranged for Martin to sing for Jerome Kern. She chose a flashy coloratura soprano selection, "Les Filles de Cadix" by the French composer Léo Delibes. Kern's advice was succinct. "Miss Martin," he asked, "why do you want to be a prima donna? They are a dime a dozen and most of them have better voices than yours. Why don't you find your own métier, your own style, and perfect it? Learn to be you."

Martin found her style, taking Broadway by storm singing Cole Porter's "My Heart Belongs to Daddy" in *Leave It to Me* in 1938. She performed the number's litany of risqué double entendres about a kept woman and her older patron with the straightest of faces, dancing the accompanying striptease with the most innocent of miens. The result was a sensation. When Rodgers and Hammerstein were in search of a star for the road company of *Annie Get Your Gun*, Martin and her manager-husband, Richard Halliday, made a proposal unusual for an actress of her rank: let her lead the national company, with her own softer, more gamine interpretation of the part, beginning in her home state of Texas. Dick and Oscar and Josh Logan leapt, and the tour had been a smash.

Now as the partners sat by the pool at the Hotel Bel-Air, they fell to talking about the Michener book. From the beginning, the interracial romance of "Fo' Dolla" had been envisioned as the central plotline of their show. But they were having second thoughts, concerned that the tale of Cable and Liat might come off as yet another twist on Puccini's *Madame Butterfly*. What about that other story, "Our Heroine," with its appealing Frenchman and the young navy nurse? That would be a novelty: two serious love stories in a single play, instead of comic foils like Ado Annie and Will Parker or Carrie Pipperidge and Enoch Snow.

What happened next seems too improbable even to have been scripted by a Hollywood screenwriter. That same day, out of the blue, Rodgers got a call from Edwin Lester, the West Coast's leading musical theater impresario and the founder of the Los Angeles Civic Light Opera. Lester had worked with Hammerstein for years, and was presenting the very touring company of *Annie Get Your Gun* that Dick and Oscar had come to see. Now, he told Rodgers, he had a big problem: He had signed Ezio Pinza, the beloved Metropolitan Opera basso, to a twelve-week, $25,000 contract in anticipation of producing a musical called *Mr. Ambassador*. The project had collapsed, but Lester was still on the hook for his guarantee with Pinza, who at fifty-six had decided to retire from grand opera.

"Do you and Oscar have anything cooking that might be suitable?" Lester wanted to know.

Years later, Rodgers would recall, "The whole picture suddenly began to take shape before my eyes. . . . I hung up and ran back to Oscar, who saw exactly what I saw." Ezio Pinza as Emile De Becque.

But what about Nellie Forbush? The perfect candidate was right in their own backyard: Mary Martin. But Martin was reluctant. For one thing, singing Irving Berlin's raucous songs for months on the road had lowered her vocal range. "What on earth do you want?" she asked. "Two basses?" The *Annie Get Your Gun* tour was ending in San Francisco that summer and Martin and Halliday would be driving home to Connecticut. The partners agreed to give her time to think.

Meantime, Dick and Oscar set to work in earnest. Rodgers had promised Martin that she would not have to sing in competition with Pinza, so instead of a standard duet, he and Hammerstein created a pair of "Twin Soliloquies" in which the lead characters would explore their growing attraction in parallel melodies. As usual, Oscar went straight to the original source. In his copy of *Tales of the South Pacific*, he had underlined a passage and penciled "Song//" in the margin next to it: "'I was looking at the cacaos,' Nellie said in a sing-song voice. To herself she was saying, 'I shall marry this man. This shall be my life from now on. This hillside shall be my home. And the afternoons he and I will sit here.' Aloud, she continued, 'They are beautiful, aren't they?'" From this, Hammerstein fashioned a lyric of tentative inquiry in which Nellie sings her private thoughts aloud:

> *Wonder how I'd feel,*
> *Living on a hillside,*
> *Looking on an ocean,*
> *Beautiful and still.*

Emile, unhearing, offers his own vision:

> *This is what I need,*
> *This is what I've longed for,*
> *Someone young and smiling*
> *Climbing up my hill!*

They go on, alternating verses, with Nellie acknowledging:

> *We are not alike;*
> *Probably I'd bore him.*
> *He's a cultured Frenchman—*
> *I'm a little hick.*

And Emile adding:

> *Younger men than I,*
> *Officers and doctors,*
> *Probably pursue her—*
> *She could have her pick.*

Nellie:

> *Wonder why I feel*
> *Jittery and jumpy!*
> *I am like a schoolgirl,*
> *Waiting for a dance.*

Emile:

> *Can I ask her now?*
> *I am like a schoolboy!*
> *What will be her answer?*
> *Do I have a chance?*

By the time the Hallidays got back to Connecticut, Dick and Oscar had finished two more songs, "A Cockeyed Optimist," in which Nellie sums up her sunny vision of the world, and "Some Enchanted Evening," in which Emile declares a love for Nellie that is as intense and instantaneous as it is improbable. Martin and Halliday were summoned to the Rodgerses' nearby country house to hear Josh Logan read the early dialogue, Dick play piano, and Oscar sing in his genial foghorn of a voice. It was a pleasant evening, and as the Hallidays headed home, Dick and Oscar asked for an answer within seventy-two hours. At three o'clock the next morning, Martin woke up Rodgers with a phone call: "Do we have to wait seventy-two hours to say, 'yes'?"

Now Rodgers and Hammerstein had only one problem: after reviewing the salary requirements of their two major stars, they concluded, "We had just cast ourselves out of a show." Given what they had already committed to pay Pinza, combined with Martin's established star salary from *Annie Get Your Gun*, "there was no way that South Pacific could be anything but an economic disaster, no matter how long it ran." After some initial reluctance on Pinza's part, both stars agreed to reduce their salaries and percentages, each settling for 7 percent of the gross box-office take, with a $2,000-a-week guarantee.

WITH HIS USUAL skills of synthesis, Oscar sketched a detailed outline of the show. Picking and choosing characters and incidents from Michener's stories, he wove together the lives of Nellie, Emile, Cable, and Liat into a single narrative. For comic relief, he seized on the character of Luther Billis from the story "Dry Rot" and asked Michener for some additional material on how a guy like that might operate. "I suggested that he would probably run a laundry of some kind," Michener would recall. Hammerstein softened Bill Harbison's character into the capable executive officer of a new character, Captain George Brackett, the local navy commander. He changed the number of Emile's children from eight to two (a boy and a girl); raided their names (Jerome and Ngana) from an unrelated story; and changed the spelling of the family's surname to use a lowercase *d*. He linked Cable and de Becque by making Cable's assignment the surveillance mission that Michener had described in "The Cave," and when Nellie rejects Emile's proposal of marriage, de Becque joins Cable on the mission, taking the role originally given to the plucky British trader Anderson ("the Remittance Man"). He flagged Operation Alligator, the pending assault on the Japanese-held islands, early in the action, allowing all the major characters to be caught up in its wake. In the end, Cable dies under enemy fire, but de Becque survives and returns to Nellie, who has overcome her biases and joins the Frenchman and his family as the curtain falls.

But as the summer of 1948 turned to fall, Hammerstein was stuck. Having been rejected for military service in World War I, he knew nothing of life in uniform. Meanwhile, Rodgers was getting antsy to compose the rest of the score, so he called Josh Logan and suggested he ask if Oscar needed some help. Hammerstein did. He had written just twenty-six pages: the opening scene between Nellie and Emile and one other.

"What do sailors do when young Lieutenant Cable comes onto the beach?" Oscar asked Josh. "I had them snapping to attention. But that seemed wrong."

"Good God, yes," Logan replied. "They'd pretend he wasn't there."

"I hate the military so much that I'm ignorant of it," Oscar explained.

Logan had no such problem. Not only had he been a cadet at Culver Military Academy in Indiana, where his stepfather was on the faculty, he had served in the Army Air Corps during the war and had just finished co-writing *Mister Roberts*. He offered to drive down to Doylestown to help. "Oh, please do, Josh," Hammerstein said. So Josh and Nedda and Jim Awe, Logan's secretary, arrived at Highland Farm, where Josh introduced Oscar to a new tool: a portable Dictaphone. They got to work fleshing out the story, with Awe and Oscar's secretary, Shirley Potash, transcribing the dialogue and Dorothy Hammerstein and Nedda collating the pages. A visit planned for only a couple of days stretched into ten as the collaborators worked every afternoon into the night, while Hammerstein spent the mornings focused on the lyrics. By Logan's later account, "I realized that Oscar was throwing me lines for Emile de Becque, Bloody Mary, and sometimes for Captain Brackett, and I was doing all the rest." It is difficult to gauge the precise extent of Logan's contributions, but some estimates suggest that he wrote as much as 30 to 40 percent of the finished script. It is beyond doubt that he did enough to count as a full collaborator—a point that his worried wife would make to him night after night as she urged him to ask Oscar for credit. Nedda Logan was especially sensitive to the point, as Josh had just finished a difficult collaboration on *Mister Roberts* with Tom Heggen, who had initially wanted to deny him a co-author credit. But Logan was so excited by the work with Oscar that he was reluctant to rock the boat, and he went back to Manhattan with the issue unresolved.

"If this isn't the damnedest show that's ever been written, I'll eat my hat," Josh said when they were done. And in fact, the show was shaping up with unusual excitement all around. One evening at the Logans' apartment, Rodgers first played Nellie's exuberant confession of love for Emile—"A Wonderful Guy"—for Mary Martin, sitting beside him at the piano, and she sang it with such growing enthusiasm that she fell off the bench at the end. "Never do it any other way," Dick said.

Rodgers had at first been worried about the music, because he hated the stereotypical sounds of what he took to be South Seas music: slack-key guitar, marimba, and so on. "This is a particularly mushy, decayed sound and one that is entirely abhorrent to me," he would recall. "The

prospect of having to deal with it for a full evening was far from entic-
ing." Rodgers met Michener for lunch to ask his advice, and "I could
hardly get my martini down because I was so anxious to find out just
what kind of steel guitar they used on Mr. Michener's particular island."
He was relieved to find that the only instrument Michener recalled was
some drums of hollow logs, but "no music in the accepted occidental
sense of tonality."

The emerging show was also a true collaboration among all the artists involved, as evidenced by "Bali Ha'i," Bloody Mary's song about
the alluring island to which Lieutenant Cable would be drawn. Oscar
had written a lyric and presented it to Dick at a production meeting
over lunch in Logan's apartment one day. "I spent a minute or so studying the words, turned the paper over and scribbled some notes, then
went into the next room where there was a piano, and played the song,"
Rodgers would recall. "The whole thing couldn't have taken more than
five minutes." But in recounting the tale in later years, Rodgers was also
typically defensive about the so-called speed of his composition. He had
spent weeks if not months thinking about the song, its place in the story,
the languorous Oriental feel it should have, the fact that it would be
sung by a contralto. All this suggested the use of notes from the five-tone
pentatonic scale common in Asian music. In fact, the first three notes of
the song, on the syllables "Bali Ha'i," repeated with insistent rapidity,
would become the first sound audiences heard at the beginning of Robert Russell Bennett's stirring overture, and a kind of leitmotif for the
whole show.

Meantime, Jo Mielziner was so excited by the new song that he
rushed to his studio to make a watercolor sketch of Bali Ha'i, with its
twin volcanoes rising in the distance. Not satisfied with his first effort,
he dipped his brush in water and blurred the tops of the peaks, as if
they were obscured by clouds. That in turn inspired Oscar to write
another verse:

> *Someday, you'll see me,*
> *Floatin' in de sunshine,*
> *My head stickin' out*
> *F'um a low-flyin' cloud . . .*

Mary Martin herself came up with another idea that turned into a song. As she was showering one day, it occurred to her that she had never seen any actress wash her hair, really wash her hair, onstage. She ran stark naked to ask her husband what he thought. "Don't you dare tell that to anyone," he said. "Not a soul. If you do, they'll go for it, and then you'll have to do it onstage eight times a week." But the next thing they knew, Josh Logan was on the phone and they promptly told him about the idea, swearing him not to pass it on to Dick and Oscar. "So, naturally," Martin recalled, "we all told them both. They said I was balmy but if I was willing to do it they loved the idea." "I'm Gonna Wash That Man Right Outa My Hair" became Nellie's brief declaration of independence from Emile. (And because Martin could never get all the soap out of her hair onstage, she washed it again in her dressing room after every performance, and then again at home before the next day's show, so she calculated that she wound up washing it not just eight times a week but more than twenty times—for three and a half years in New York and London.)

Martin was also the inspiration for another number, "Thanksgiving Follies," in which the nurses put on a morale-building show for the sailors. A friend had sent her an old picture, taken at a summer camp in Texas, of Martin in baggy men's striped shorts, a sailor hat, and necktie, and Hammerstein was so taken with the hapless image that he tucked a copy of it beside his shaving mirror with the caption, "This proves there is hope for everyone." Logan told Martin that she had come a long way in show business, but that for all her stardom and couture gowns, she was still a baggy-pants comedian at heart. He devised an oversize sailor costume with falling-down pants and tie to the knees, and planned a dance for Martin and Myron McCormick, who would play Luther Billis in a coconut bra and grass skirt, with a full-rigged ship tattooed on a bare belly that he had taught himself to undulate in a parlor trick to get free beer in college. Oscar had appropriate fun with the words for "Honey Bun":

My doll is as dainty as a sparrow,
Her figure is something to applaud.

Where she's narrow, she's narrow as an arrow,
And she's broad where a broad should be broad . . .

"I will never forget the half-embarrassed, very pleased look on Oscar's face when he first sang me the lyrics," Martin remembered. "Never in his life had he written such corny words but I shrieked with joy."

FOR OSCAR, PART of the strong appeal of Michener's book was its frank treatment of racial prejudice, which was anything but a theoretical issue for the Hammerstein family. Dorothy's sister Eleanor, nicknamed Doodie, was married to Jerry Watanabe, the son of a British mother whose father had once been his country's ambassador to Japan, and a Japanese father, who was a director of the industrial trading firm, Mitsui & Co. Jerry had been raised to be the very model of a proper Englishman, educated at Cambridge, and was a fine tennis player and golfer. When the United States entered World War II in 1941, he was working in the New York offices of Mitsui and, as a Japanese national, was interned at Ellis Island. Even after he was released, he could not find work, so Dorothy hired him to manage the accounts of her decorating business. During Jerry's internment, Doodie and their daughter, Jennifer, lived for a time with the Hammersteins in Doylestown, and when Dorothy and her sister took the girl to be enrolled at the local school, they asked the principal for assurances that she would not face discrimination. "She'll have to pay the price for her antecedents," the man answered, and Jennifer went instead to a local Quaker school and then to the George School in Newton, Pennsylvania (which Jimmy Hammerstein and Steve Sondheim also attended), where she was enrolled as Jennifer Blanchard.

In his work with the Writers' War Board, Oscar had also made a particular point of combating prejudice. And in 1949, Oscar and Dorothy joined James Michener and another Pennsylvania neighbor, the author Pearl Buck, in helping to create Welcome House, the country's first interracial, international adoption agency, begun with the particular mission of placing Amerasian children—many of them the offspring of broken wartime romances—in American homes.

Segregation was still a fact of life not only in the Jim Crow South but in much of the urban North as well. It had only been in 1947 that Jackie Robinson had broken big league baseball's color line. In the draft of the *South Pacific* script that Logan and Hammerstein completed in time for the first cast rehearsal, after Nellie has broken off her relationship with Emile in horror at his mixed-race children, and Cable finds himself unable to marry Liat, despite his love for her, the young Americans share their feelings.

"Damn it to hell!" Cable shouts to Nellie. "Why do you look so damned shocked? What's the difference if her hair is blonde and curly or black and straight? If I want her to be my wife, why can't I have her?"

"You can!" Nellie replies. "It's just that—people—I mean they say it never works. Don't they?"

"They do," Cable answers in disgust. "And then everybody does their damnedest to prove it. A hell of a chance Liat and I would have in one of those little gray stone and timber houses on the Main Line. 'Mr. and Mrs. Joseph Cable entertained, last Tuesday, with a house-warming. Nobody came!'"

This dialogue would be dropped before the first performance, perhaps considered too raw. But not the song that followed, which Cable sings in response to Nellie's assertion that her prejudice is "something that is born in me!" and Emile's insistence that it cannot have been. Indeed, Joe explains, "it happens *after* you're born":

You've got to be taught to hate and fear,
You've got to be taught from year to year,
It's got to be drummed in your dear little ear—
You've got to be carefully taught!

You've got to be taught to be afraid
Of people whose eyes are oddly made,
And people whose skin is a different shade—
You've got to be carefully taught.

You've got to be taught before it's too late,
Before you are six or seven or eight,

To hate all the people your relatives hate—
You've got to be carefully taught!
You've got to be carefully taught!

In Oscar's original draft, Emile continues the song, declaring, "Love is quite different. It grows by itself," and then singing:

It will grow like a weed
On a mountain of stones;
You don't have to feed
Or put fat on its bones;
It can live on a smile
Or a note of a song:
It may starve for a while,
But it stumbles along,
Stumbles along with its banner unfurled,
The joy and the beauty, the hope of the world.

Rodgers rejected the last verses as unnecessary (Hammerstein substituted words about Emile's feeling cheated "by a mean little world of mean little men") but stood lockstep behind the song.

ONE IMPORTANT MATTER remained to be resolved before the start of rehearsals: the question of Logan's credit for the script. After a run of sleepless nights, more hectoring from his wife, and a consultation with their doctor, Josh finally steeled himself for a confrontation with Hammerstein in which he stammered out a demand for half credit for the book. "Oscar's face was immobile but I thought he blushed slightly," Logan would recall many years later. "After the briefest of pauses, he said, 'I wish I'd said it first. I'm sorry you had to. Of course you must have credit. After all, you wrote it as much as I did. We'll work out the exact credits later.' "

But the next day, a stern-looking Oscar returned with bad news. After consulting with Dick Rodgers and presumably Howard Reinheimer, he agreed to co-credit for Logan, but with penalties. In their original contract, Logan's name as director was to have been in the same size type as Dick and Oscar's as authors. Now Logan's director credit would be reduced to 60 percent of that size, and his and Hammerstein's co-author credit would appear the same way. If that seemed petty, Oscar justified the punishment, telling Logan that the public had expected him to write the book alone and giving credit to a co-author had diminished him. Moreover, Oscar informed Logan that he would not share in the copyright or author's royalties of the play; only his director's royalties for the run of the original company. "Jesus, Oscar," a stunned Logan said, "that's a body blow." Hammerstein was pained but resolute. "Josh," he explained, "Rodgers and Hammerstein cannot and will not share a copyright. It's part of their financial structure. Including you would weaken our position." A memo from Irving Cohen in the Reinheimer office on February 1 spelled out Logan's new billing and noted matter-of-factly: "Your name shall appear in the foregoing form whenever and wherever the names 'Richard Rodgers' and 'Oscar Hammerstein II,' as authors, appear."

Logan was crushed but would remember that "I also saw by Oscar's expression how hard he must have fought to secure for me as much as he did, and how equally hard it was for him to look me in the eye as he said what he had to say." The decision would haunt Logan till his dying day.

But for the moment, there was work to be done. Besides Myron McCormick as Billis, the rest of the supporting cast had been rounded out. Betta St. John, who had been a replacement Louise in *Carousel*, would be Liat, and Juanita Hall, a mixed-race African American actress and singer who was a veteran of the original chorus in *Show Boat* and of the famed Hall Johnson Choir, was cast as Bloody Mary. William Tabbert, a young singer, took on the role of Joe Cable.

In addition to scenic designer Jo Mielziner, much of the established creative team was reassembled, including Russell Bennett to do the orchestrations and Trude Rittmann as vocal arranger and creator of the musical underscoring that would play beneath some of the dialogue, in the style of a movie.

The first rehearsal was on Monday, February 7, 1949, at the Majestic Theatre on West 44th Street. "The New York opening may be a musical's most exciting moment, but close to it is the first reading of the full score and book," Logan would recall. "Will it or won't it?" From the first moment, *South Pacific* did. Martin and Pinza sang their "Twin Soliloquies," and as the music swelled, Logan recalled, "This was the moment when for me the show became great." But he thought the number ended too soon. So he asked Trude Rittmann to improvise music based on what the actors were doing, and she added a thrilling orchestral climax that rose grandly up the scale as Nellie and Emile downed snifters of brandy.

LIKE RUSSELL BENNETT, Trude Rittmann was a vital part of the Rodgers and Hammerstein team, though her contributions to the sound of their music and the success of their shows have been even less acknowledged. She had first been recruited by Agnes de Mille to write the dance arrangements for *Carousel* and is believed to have contributed musical underscoring for some of that show's dramatic scenes as well. Now she would work hand in glove with Josh Logan to heighten the cinematic style of *South Pacific*. A native of Mannheim, Germany, classically trained in composition and piano, she had fled to England in 1933, eventually emigrating to the United States, where she was hired as a pianist for George Balanchine's American Ballet Caravan. She became de Mille's regular rehearsal accompanist in 1941 and would eventually work on more than sixty shows, sometimes writing dance music, sometimes vocal arrangements, sometimes incidental music, while often being credited for only one or two of those tasks, or even not at all. For *South Pacific*, Rittmann would write lush underscoring for the most intense dialogue scenes, going off at night to elaborate on themes from Rodgers's tunes and then rehearsing over and over with Logan until the music was set. De Mille herself would complain that Rittmann was sometimes treated like an electrician or seamstress, a technician needed only for a discrete task. "As her role in the shows increased," Rittmann's great-niece Susanna Drewry would recall, "she took great satisfaction in the creative collaboration with the choreographers she worked with. She grew to accept her lot but she also didn't want the limelight. She was very much an introvert, and she couldn't deal with the battles and intrigues of theater life."

Rittmann's own account of her contributions was matter-of-fact. "The composer usually has a certain wish as to what should happen to his songs," she would recall late in life. "Some of them—not everybody— but some of them—would have a certain vision of what he would like to do. Rodgers cared only that his song didn't disappear." Starting with *South Pacific*, she remembered, "He had made a carte blanche to me and said, 'Do.'" But like Russell Bennett, Rittmann was also under no illusions about the difference she made. She would continue to work with Rodgers off and on until the 1970s. Once, when she felt a new orchestrator was being mean to her, she asked Rodgers what he thought of the man. "Dick looked me right in the eye," she recalled, "and said, 'He's afraid of you.' And then he added, 'Sometimes, I'm afraid of you, too.'"

As THE FIRST reading continued, it was Pinza's turn to sing "Some Enchanted Evening." The song was always envisioned as the evening's big ballad, and it would become the undisputed hit of the show. It captured the power of Emile's instantaneous attraction to Nellie, and Hammerstein wrote it with the *coup de foudre* that had struck him and Dorothy on the boat to England all those years earlier clearly on his mind:

Some enchanted evening
You may see a stranger,
You may see a stranger
Across a crowded room.
And somehow you know,
You know even then,
That somewhere you'll see her again and again.

Even with just a piano accompaniment, the power of Pinza's voice was overwhelming. "We used to stand in the wings and marvel when he sang 'Some Enchanted Evening,'" remembered Don Fellows, the young actor who played Buzz (formerly "Bus") Adams, "because I swear we could feel it in our feet, you could feel the vibration."

The only problem was Pinza's appalling English pronunciation. "Enchanted" came out "enshonted" or, worse, "exchang-ed" in his thick Italian accent, while "sugar" was "sooker." Pinza himself would recall the rehearsal period as "the strangest and most trying month of my entire professional life." Everything was new to him: working with a living composer (instead of the long-dead author of a classic opera) and absorbing new music and dialogue almost daily, on the fly. "I had expected that I would have to make certain readjustments, but it had never occurred to me that they might be so difficult," he said. "No sooner would I adjust myself to the new changes than still newer ones would come, aglow with creative inventiveness, yet living hell and embarrassment for me." Rodgers would recall that at one point Logan and Hayward were so exasperated, they considered replacing Pinza, and Pinza himself acknowledged that as late as the eve of the first tryout in New Haven, he had considered dropping out of the show.

But for the rest of the cast, Logan's brisk direction could seem like magic. The creative team had long ago made the decision not to have any formal, choreographed dancing in a show that strove for realism. "You can't have a really moving and believable romance with a chorus line getting in the way," is how Rodgers put it. So Logan staged "There Is Nothin' Like a Dame," the sailors' lustful lament about their lack of female companionship, as an impromptu crosscurrent of prowling cats. "I started pacing as I imagined a caged animal would pace," Logan would recall. "The men followed me, restlessly pacing back and forth— killing time till the end of the war, till the chance of seeing women again. Then I asked Trude to repeat the song, and motioned one man to pace in one direction, another to go the other way, breaking the pattern constantly. Within fifteen or twenty minutes I had staged it. It didn't exactly fall into place, but it looked as if it had." The movements were so complicated that there was no way for a stage manager to note them; only the actors themselves knew the drill, and when an ensemble member was replaced, his predecessor was given a day's rehearsal pay to teach him the required steps.

Josh and Oscar had also made an important decision: Virtually every actor in the show would be playing a named character, with a specific rank or role. There would be no faceless singing-and-dancing ensemble. Logan sent the men in the cast who were veterans to the local army-navy surplus store with $25 each, and instructions to choose the sort of costume their character would wear. Don Fellows would remember that all the proceedings took place under Dick Rodgers's watchful eye. "Mr. Rodgers would sit in the rear of the theater and then we would hear, only occasionally, we'd hear, 'Josh, Josh, may I have a minute?'" Fellows remembered. "And Logan would trot up the aisle and they'd talk and talk and talk and talk, and then Josh would come down and say, 'Well, no, I think what we're gonna do . . .'"

Within a couple of days, much of the show was up on its feet. At this point Logan wanted to restore a second song for Bloody Mary, one that Oscar had called "Happy Talk," in which she would sketch out the agreeable life that might await Cable and Liat if they married. An early lyric fragment went like this:

> *Talk about breakfus' coffee and toast*
> *Opposite de one you love de most*
> *Dinner an' supper an' plen'y to eat,*
> *Gravy an' potatoes on your meat.*

Oscar told Logan he'd decided to scrap the song; he didn't see how it could be staged and didn't want to cause more headaches for the director. "You write it, I'll stage it," Logan rejoined cockily, and when he heard Oscar's words

> *Happy talk,*
> *Keep talkin' happy talk,*
> *Talk about things you'd like to do.*
> *You gotta have a dream;*
> *If you don't have a dream,*
> *How you gonna have a dream come true?*

sounding against the insistent rhythm of Dick's melody, he thought of two birds talking. Logan took Betta St. John, Juanita Hall, and Trude

Rittmann to the theater lobby and, putting his thumbs and forefingers together to mimic opening and closing beaks, promptly devised a charming pantomime for the song, with Liat resting her head on her open palms on the word "dream."

EVEN AS THE show took shape, work continued on the script and score. Hammerstein and Logan had debated how to handle the scene in which Cable and Liat first make love—an encounter that Michener had written offered "incarnadine proof" that the marine had taken the young girl's virginity. Oscar and Josh knew there would have to be a blackout at the moment of truth, but how to make sure the audience had not missed the point? Josh came up with the idea of having Cable remove his shirt during the blackout, so that when the lights came up again, it would be clear the couple had just had sex. "Well, you're nothing if not bold," the straitlaced Oscar exclaimed. "You're emphatic, aren't you?"

"Well, yes," Logan answered. "Would you rather not do it?"

"No, no," Oscar assured him. "It's a good idea. It's just that I had to catch my breath, that's all."

But there was still the matter of a song for Cable to sing to Liat when he realizes she has changed his life. At an early rehearsal one day, Dick and Oscar took Josh to the theater lobby and played and sang their proposal:

> Well, my friend,
> Our day is at an end
> Our next kiss will have to be our last.
> Soon, my friend,
> I'll be around the bend,
> Alone with a dream already past. . . .

"That's awful!" Logan blurted out. "That's the worst song I ever heard. Good God, that's terrible."

The partners responded in shock; Logan thought Dick's face looked "stricken." But the next day, they tried again, returning with a burbling schottische tune, a slow polka, whose lyrics began:

Suddenly lucky,
Suddenly our arms are lucky;
Suddenly lucky,
Suddenly our lips have kissed . . .

"When they finished," Logan would remember, "I was thinking so hard I didn't speak."

"Well, have we passed the test this time, Teacher?" Oscar demanded.

"You're close," Logan said. "I love the tune, but isn't that song a bit lightweight for a hot, lusty boy to sing right after making love to a girl who will change his life?" Remember, Logan added: *He's a marine.*

Rodgers rebelled, and "announced uncharmingly that he was not going to go on writing till 'this guy' agrees on a tune," Logan recalled. But Dick remembered an unused tune from *Allegro* that his wife and daughters had liked and still asked him to play from time to time. Its original title was "My Wife," and now Oscar wrote new lyrics:

Younger than springtime are you,
Softer than starlight are you;
Warmer than winds of June are the gentle lips you gave me.
Gayer than laughter are you,
Sweeter than music are you;
Angel and lover, heaven and earth
Are you to me.

At last Logan was satisfied. Generations of audiences would be, too.

JUST A FEW days later, another problem arose. Dick and Oscar had written a stirring march for Emile and Cable to sing as they at last agree to embark on the dangerous surveillance mission, "Now Is the Time."

Now is the time,
The time to act!
No other time will do.

Live and play your part
And give away your heart
And take what the world gives you.

But Logan was bothered. "If Cable and Emile were going on a mission to save Allied lives, why didn't they get a goddamn move on instead of standing and singing?" he asked. After seeing an early run-through of the show on February 20, Nedda Logan agreed. "As a matter of fact, my honest opinion is that Dick could get a better song here," she wrote in a memo to her husband. Something more on the order of Billy Bigelow's "Soliloquy" in *Carousel*. Josh had an idea: What if Cable and de Becque's mission came *out* of the song? Out of Emile's dejection at Nellie's rejection of him. Dick asked for a title line he could work on, and someone called out, "This nearly was mine."

"That's it," Dick said. "A big bass waltz." Oscar sketched an early fragment of just such a waltz:

I planned a lovely tomorrow
That someone lovely would share
But now tomorrow is fading
Like laughter on the air . . .

By February 25, the complete lyrics for "This Nearly Was Mine" had been typed out, and as usual, Oscar's refinements were an improvement:

I'll keep remembering kisses
From lips I'll never own
And all the lovely adventures
That we have never known . . .

JUST BEFORE THE company embarked for the out-of-town tryouts in New Haven, there was a near disaster. Mary Martin had been doing cartwheels since she was a kid, and in the dance break of "A Wonderful Guy" she had inserted a long, whirling cycle of them—clean across the stage. But on this day Logan had replaced the usual stage work lights with hot show lights, and Martin was temporarily blinded. She missed the edge of the stage and struck a glancing blow on the head of the conductor, Salvatore Dell'Isola, before thudding to a stop on top of Trude Rittmann at the piano. "Oh, God, my neck is broken!" Rittmann cried.

Fortunately it wasn't, and the next day Martin brought an apology, a football helmet covered with flowers—which Trude promptly plopped on her head. But from then on, Logan recalled, "We substituted a good, safe high note."

Only Rodgers, Hammerstein, and Logan knew the details of Logan's painful credit-sharing arrangement, but as the show took on the air of a sure-fire hit, there were rumblings along Broadway about whether Dick and Oscar had shortchanged James Michener with a mere 1 percent royalty. The columnist Walter Winchell called to say he was looking into the matter, but Michener begged him not to make a stink about the arrangement. That same night, after a full dress rehearsal, Oscar Hammerstein called Michener with an offer as generous as his treatment of Logan was stingy: while the producers could not change his royalty arrangement, they wanted to let him buy a share of the show, which would cost $4,500. "I don't have one thousand," Michener replied. Not to worry: the producers would advance him the funds, to be repaid when proceeds came in. "Tears came to my eyes," Michener would remember, "and I think Oscar knew it, for he waited for me to say, 'That's wonderfully generous.'" On March 5, Howard Reinheimer wrote a memo for the files, memorializing the "unusual courtesy" of granting Michener his stake, "by means of funds advanced by producers." In short order, the proceeds from that unusual courtesy would allow Michener to quit his day job at Macmillan and become a full-time writer, a career he would pursue with stunning success for the next forty-eight years.

THE NEW HAVEN opening was set for Monday, March 7. From Williams College, Stephen Sondheim sent a cheeky telegram of congratulations, asking, DO YOU NEED A GOOD BARITONE? But Josh Logan, whose emotions could veer wildly from exultation to despair, was on edge. On

Taft Hotel stationery, he scrawled a note to Oscar. "Thank you for the show & the fine time I had working with you—and the credit sharing and all the boosts and gooses," he said. "For God's sake don't let's make too quick decisions tomorrow night." Referring to the group of lawyers, investors, agents, and other kibitzers who were in town for the opening, he went on: "I will fix *anything* [underlined twice] in this show—toward the happiness of all three of us but I cannot give full satisfaction to Leland [Hayward], Nancy [Hawks, Hayward's wife], Gilbert Miller, Howard Cullman, Howard Reinheimer, Lew Wasserman, Morrie Schrier and people of that kidney."

As if validating his qualms, Logan watched that evening's performance with growing trepidation. First "I'm Gonna Wash That Man Right Outa My Hair," which he'd felt sure would be a smash, landed with a fizzle. Then "A Wonderful Guy," sung by Nellie and a bunch of nurses, also seemed to fall flat. His mood was not improved at intermission, when he learned from Nedda and his lawyer, Morris Schrier, that when the Reinheimer office had messengered his contract for signature the day before the first rehearsal, it came with a note stipulating that if it was not signed within two hours, Logan need not report for duty but would be replaced. Oblivious to the audience's applause, Josh retreated to his hotel room after the show, refusing all visitors and phone calls, until finally Dick Rodgers talked his way past Nedda to insist, "Josh, you don't seem to know we have a hit." Logan was somewhat reassured but still had the taste of ashes in his mouth. Rodgers himself was annoyed that Pinza had flubbed a line in "Some Enchanted Evening." "Oscar put it down as one of those minor errors," the playwright Marc Connelly recalled years later. "But Dick, oh Dick was relentless. What the hell was Dick so worried about? His notes weren't confused—it was the lyrics."

The next night, when "Wash That Man" and "Wonderful Guy" produced the same underwhelming reaction, Logan was again puzzled, until his friend Molly Williams, whose actor-playwright husband, Emlyn, had come to New Haven to help trim the show's running time, confessed that no one seated around her had heard "Wash That Man" at all because they were all abuzz, talking to each other and wondering whether Martin was really washing her own hair. Logan's solution was easy: Have Mary sing one full chorus of the song, to put over the lyrics, and *then* get out the shampoo. It took him about ten days, with the show in Boston, to solve the riddle of "Wonderful Guy." He thought the problem might be that Nellie was confessing her innermost thoughts to her fellow nurses, spoiling an intimate moment. "Too bad the song can't be a soliloquy," Josh mused to Oscar, who promptly agreed, and switched the pronouns in the song. "That night she tore the house apart," Logan would recall.

There were a few other small changes. On March 9, Oscar's old friend Essie Robeson (the wife of Paul Robeson) wrote to wonder why Archie Savage, the sole black dancer in the show, and a spectacular one at that, was always jitterbugging. "It is very possible that I am unduly sensitive, racially, but so are a lot of us, and it would help enormously that if just once he appeared with his comrades NOT cutting up." Oscar immediately replied, "Since you have seen the play, and before I received your letter, we have inserted an episode in which Archie Savage is *not* jitterbugging."

Hammerstein was less sympathetic to Lieutenant Commander Thomas McWhorter of the navy, who fired off an early broadside against the song "You've Got to Be Carefully Taught," asking that it be cut. "It is like drinking a scotch and soda and suddenly swallowing the ice cube!" McWhorter wrote. "You could not have interrupted the beautiful flow of entertainment any more effectively had you stopped the show for a VD lecture." Oscar wrote back, "I believe I get the point of your letter very clearly, and I realize very well the dangers of overstating the case. But I just feel that the case is not fully stated without this song. I wish it were true that all these things are accepted by the public. You say, 'the theme is wearing very thin,' but in spite of this, I see progress being made only very slowly."

The show opened in Boston on Tuesday, March 15, and Dick and Oscar could have written the reviews themselves. "More dramatic than their *Oklahoma!*, more solidly realistic than their *Carousel*, and bears no burden of social message as their happy *Allegro* did," was Elliot Norton's verdict in the *Post*. "It is like their other creations only in this: That it is wonderful." Don Fellows would recall knowing that the company had something special in hand when ticketless theatergoers outside the Shubert began offering cast members $100 for a pair.

THE NEW YORK opening was set for Thursday, April 7, 1949. Oscar happened to leave his overcoat in Ezio Pinza's dressing room, and by the evening's end considered it such a lucky omen that he left it there whenever he came to visit the show. The night was lucky in another way, too: Mary Rodgers introduced a young friend of hers named Harold Prince to Steve Sondheim, and within just a few years, they would make musical theater history of their own. Oscar and Dick were confident enough of the critics' verdict that they abandoned theatrical superstition and booked their own opening night party, an elegant supper dance at the St. Regis Roof, and ordered a couple hundred copies of the *New York Times* to pass out to their guests. They had not miscalculated: the critics offered raves all around. Brooks Atkinson in the *Times* called the play "a magnificent musical drama," Richard Watts Jr. of the *Post* found the show "an utterly captivating work of theatrical art," and Howard Barnes of the *Herald Tribune* pronounced it "a show of rare enchantment."

Predictably, "Carefully Taught" came in for its share of criticism, with John Mason Brown of the *Saturday Review* complaining that it smacked of "dragged-in didacticism," while the *New Yorker* found it "just a little embarrassing." But Rodgers and Hammerstein's theatrical peers and colleagues were ecstatic. Helen Hayes wrote Oscar and Dorothy Hammerstein, "Words won't do it—flowers failed to say it—there's just no way to express the gratitude I felt for last Thursday night. And for the many other wonderful times you've given me with your talent. I'm just humbly thankful to be living in the same period with you. 'South Pacific' tops everything you've ever done." For his part, James Michener paraphrased Lord Byron's famous response to his poem, "Childe Harold": "I went to bed an unknown and woke to find Ezio Pinza famous."

An advance sale of $500,000 quickly grew to $700,000 after the show opened. *South Pacific* had come in about $60,000 under its projected $225,000 budget, so the forty-eight original investors, who included the Hollywood director Billy Wilder, the philanthropist Albert

Lasker, and Kenneth MacKenna, the MGM story editor who had started the whole thing, not only got their first payout on opening night but stood to make back their entire investment by Labor Day, with the show's operating profit of around $12,000 a week. Howard Reinheimer had set up the production so it was owned by a corporation, which was in turn owned fifty-fifty by Rodgers and Hammerstein themselves. The advantage of this arrangement was that revenues from the show flowed into the corporate shell, where they were taxed at the rate of 38 percent, far lower than Dick and Oscar's personal income tax brackets. (And if, by some strange chance, the show had failed, the corporation would not have any limit on the losses it could deduct.)

Tickets immediately became all but unobtainable, and scalping was rife. At one point, New York City's commissioner of investigation threatened to close the Majestic Theatre's box office because its treasurer refused to answer questions about inflated prices, and for any given night's full house, Dick and Oscar estimated, theatergoers had paid $25,000 for tickets with a face value of $7,000. Each morning at seven o'clock, a line formed at the box office for the thirty standing-room seats available for that evening's performance. One day not long after the opening, Mr. and Mrs. George Fitzsimmons of Detroit arrived by train at Pennsylvania Station at 8:45 a.m., hopped into a taxi, got in line, and made the cut. It was their golden wedding anniversary, "and neither could think of a better way to observe the day," reported the *New York Post*. The demand was so intense that Michener himself stood in the wings to see the show, and as late as September 1951 he would tell the columnists Tex McCrary and Jinx Falkenburg that he had only seen it once from out front.

Even more than *Oklahoma!*, *South Pacific* became a huge cultural and social phenomenon. Virtually every American adult had some palpable connection to World War II, which meant that they also had a natural connection to the show. If *Oklahoma!* had satisfied wartime America's longing for a simpler time and *Carousel* had tapped into the returning servicemen's familiarity with death, *South Pacific* offered a dramatization of a conflict that was still visceral for millions. Souvenir shops sold fake ticket stubs, so that people who were unable to get in could display them on their coffee tables, as if to suggest they had seen the show.

The producers also licensed a wide range of consumer products with a *South Pacific* theme, from a "Knucklehead Nellie" doll, to a line of sheets, towels, pillowcases, and bathrobes; silk ties and clothing; toiletries; hairbrushes; compacts and cigarette cases; and a home hair permanent formula. Howard Reinheimer pointed out that never before had a Broadway play undertaken such merchandising for any purpose other than free publicity. Now *South Pacific*'s marketing licenses would soon bring in hundreds of thousands of dollars in revenues to the manufacturers—and tens of thousands in royalties to Rodgers and Hammerstein.

Everybody, it seemed, wanted a piece of the action. In September 1949, Norma Terris, the original Magnolia in *Show Boat*, who was then forty-five years old, wrote Oscar to inquire about playing Nellie in the national company. In the end, Janet Blair, a popular singer and film actress, got the part, and when the 118-city national tour opened in Cleveland in April 1950, there were 250,000 requests for 48,000 available seats. The problem was so severe that Oscar urged Claudia Cassidy, the powerful drama critic of the *Chicago Tribune*, to tell readers to write in for mail-order tickets to avoid disappointment. "I know it sounds arrogant to complain about there being too much demand for tickets to a play," Oscar wrote. But it was true.

In the spring of 1950, the show swept every major category at the fourth annual Tony Awards, and on May 1 came the crowning honor: *South Pacific* won the Pulitzer Prize for Drama, and not just a special citation, as *Oklahoma!* had received. *Of Thee I Sing* had won the prize in 1931 but, bizarrely, George Gershwin had not been cited for his music. Now Richard Rodgers was. But true to Josh Logan's worst fears, his name was missing from the citation. The error was corrected, but the oversight stung.

South Pacific ran for 1,925 performances on Broadway. Ezio Pinza left the cast for Hollywood when his contract was up in June 1950, but Martin stayed on another year, before leaving to head up the London company. She was replaced by Martha Wright, who was herself later briefly replaced by a lissome blond newcomer from Iowa named Cloris Leachman. Myron McCormick was the only principal from the original cast to stay with the show till the end. By the time of his one thousandth performance as Luther Billis, he had lived through three sets of actors playing the de Becque children; witnessed ten marriages in the cast (none to each other), and was on his third pair of shoes. He still had his original coconut bra, but the rope straps had been patched. On the closing night, January 16, 1954, he led the cast in singing "Auld Lang Syne" with tears in his eyes. By design, the curtain never fell, and the audience, hoping for one last promise of paradise, lingered on for half an hour, before finally drifting out into the night.

CHAPTER 7

Parallel Wives

> I think the point is that it isn't necessary to love one another. The
> necessity is to understand one another, because understanding, I
> think, is a block to hatred. We mustn't hate one another. But love
> is not the only alternative.
>
> Oscar Hammerstein II

It was not a press agent's fancy, just a much-remarked-upon coincidence, that Dick and Oscar had both married women named Dorothy,
who both happened to be skilled and successful interior decorators. And
in the summer of 1949, in the wake of *South Pacific*'s success, both
women had new homes to design: Dorothy Hammerstein an elegant
East Side town house at 10 East 63rd Street, just off Fifth Avenue, and
Dorothy Rodgers a new country estate on forty acres in Southport,
Connecticut—a rambling, gray-shingled Colonial house with white
chimneys called Rockmeadow, after a giant boulder in an adjoining
field.

Dorothy Rodgers had stumbled into her avocation by accident and
necessity. Returning from their three-year Hollywood sojourn in the
mid-1930s, she and Dick found their New York apartment, which they
had sublet, in shambles, with furniture gnawed by teething puppies,
carpets ruined by chewing gum, and a general state of wreckage. "'Oh,'
I moaned to Dick as I waved a tragic arm at the mess all around," she
would recall years later. "'I wish there were some magical place I could
call and say, "There it is—you fix it," and have everything back together
again.' 'Why don't you start one?' he countered quite reasonably." So

was born Repairs Inc., the first business of its kind in Manhattan, relying on an army of skilled craftsmen and -women that Dorothy had
assembled: experts in china, glass, and silver; cabinets, and carving;
needlework and reweaving; piano tuners and clock repairmen. With
offices on East 57th Street, the company quickly took off, attracting a
steady business from insurance companies forced to repair damages of
just the sort the Rodgerses had suffered, and performing such everyday miracles, she would recall, as "reactivating miniature waterfalls
and songbirds in a mad, marvelous Victorian clock that belonged to
Helen Hayes." Eventually clients wanted not simply to repair torn
draperies and stained carpets, but to redo rooms from scratch, so
Dorothy, who had studied sketching and sculpture as a teenager in
Paris, expanded into interior design. Her style was austere and formal,
though she did favor an eclectic blend of periods and provenances in
assembling the pieces of a room.

Her rooms—and her menus, and her wardrobe, and her hair, inevitably worn in a fashionable chignon—reflected a white-gloved meticu-
lousness that led the publisher Bennett Cerf, one of her beaux before
Dick, to christen her "La Perfecta." She would insist that this reputation
was overblown, but she did acknowledge that she Scotch-taped can-
celed checks back into her checkbook so she'd always have a record of
her expenditures, and she decreed that the medicine cabinet of any good
guest room should contain two drinking glasses, an emery board, an
orangewood stick, mouthwash, aspirin, disinfectant, Band-Aids, and
enough room for the guest's own toiletries. Her standard wedding present to the children of friends was the *Columbia Encyclopedia*.

Dorothy would wind down Repairs Inc. during the materials shortages of World War II, but she kept up her decorating business for such
clients as the writer Ben Hecht, for whom she produced a bathroom-
cum-writing room featuring flocked velvet walls and a marble wash-
stand. In the fifteen-room duplex cooperative apartment on East
71st Street that she and Dick had bought in 1945 when they outgrew
their cramped pied-à-terre at the Volney Hotel, nothing was ever out
of place, from the two grand pianos in the living room to the flowers
carefully arranged to mimic the palette of the paintings in front of which
they were placed. Indeed, she was such a germaphobe that she inven-

ted a disposable toilet brush—called the Jonny Mop—that could simply be flushed away when its work was done, without the user's having to touch it again. She won an arbitration case against Johnson & Johnson when it tried to tweak the design to avoid paying her for it. "I always felt that I hadn't washed carefully enough when I was with her," the lyricist Sheldon Harnick would recall. But under the perfect surface, Rodgers's daughters believed, she was uptight, anorexic, and a chronic abuser of laxatives and Demerol.

Dorothy Hammerstein had also begun her business by chance, when friends in Hollywood recognized her natural flair for design and asked her for help in decorating their houses. Her early clients included the RKO producer Pandro Berman, the silent movie star Norma Talmadge, and Oscar's old friend, Dorothy Fields. When Jules Stein built the MCA talent agency's lavish new Georgian headquarters in Beverly Hills, he asked Dorothy to do the interiors. But in sharp contrast to Dorothy R.'s restrained style, Dorothy H.'s approach was exuberant and informal, with a special fondness for features like wallpaper on the ceiling and vibrant tones of purple, her nephew John Steele Gordon would recall. She liked to mix English and American pieces with Chinese accents, and when searching for dining chairs would invariably ignore four perfectly matching Chippendales in favor of a mismatched assortment. She was a collector of valuable vintage porcelain and china but liked to say that she preferred a "slight dash of vulgarity" to keep a room from feeling sterile.

She was relaxed and earthy and bubbly, and she presided over a rollicking and ever-changing extended family with warmth and ease. She had a sly wit and a way of calming Oscar's occasional thundershowers of anger at the family table, though she was not above an occasional verbal misfire in the thick of an argument. One evening, she concluded a discussion of religious prejudice by declaring, "Well, I don't care whether a person is a Jew or a Mohammedan or a Buddhist or anything else, just as long as he is a good Christian!"

In later years, Dorothy Rodgers would publish a fat coffee table book of decorating and cooking advice called *My Favorite Things*, and would include back-to-back color photographs of her bedroom—in shades of soft pewter blue and plum brown—and the other

Dorothy's—done up in black-and-white cotton chinoiserie prints and a bold Bristol blue rug. "It is a handsome, exciting room—as perfect a background for Dorothy as it would be wrong for me," La Perfecta wrote with just the slightest whiff of condescension.

The two women had sharply different approaches to child rearing as well. Dorothy Rodgers made it plain that Dick was always her first priority. Both Rodgers girls had shown early musical talent—Linda was an especially gifted pianist—but neither parent particularly encouraged them, and in later years Linda would be reluctant even to play in front of her father. Mary, who had a gift for composition, was by now majoring in music at Wellesley but would soon leave college before graduation to marry—as, later, would Linda, who studied at Smith. The two older Hammerstein children—Billy and Alice—were now each remarried after divorces. Bill was working as a stage manager and fledgling director, the fourth generation to join the family business, while Alice had spent time as a script reader in Hollywood. Jimmy, Oscar's son with Dorothy, was now a student at the University of North Carolina at Chapel Hill.

It is an understatement to say that the two Dorothys—the onetime Jewish society girl from Manhattan and the former chorus girl from Tasmania—had little in common apart from their mutual brains, beauty, good taste, social standing, and famous husbands. "They were perfectly civil and pleasant, and would sometimes shop for antiques together when their husbands' shows were on the road out of town," Mary Rodgers would remember. "They just weren't close friends and I think there was a certain rivalry probably underneath the surface." Stephen Sondheim was blunter, observing that "the Hammersteins had virtually no social relationship to the Rodgerses."

But the two Dorothys did have at least one thing in common that would have important consequences for their husbands' careers: In 1944, both had admired a quirky and captivating historical novel by a Presbyterian missionary's wife named Margaret Landon. Its title was *Anna and the King of Siam*, and it told a highly fanciful version of the true story of a British schoolmistress who in the 1860s had been commissioned to teach the children of King Mongkut of Thailand. Both

Oscar Hammerstein II was born into the theater, the son and grandson of producers. As a young man, he learned every facet of the trade: office boy, play reader, stage manager, author, and producer.

Asked what he had done before he became a composer, Richard Rodgers once replied, "I was a baby." Raised in a passionately musical family, he was something of a prodigy and was composing by age nine.

Hammerstein's most important early collaborator was Jerome Kern (right), the quintessential American composer of popular music whose elegant, infectious melodies made European operettas sound antique.

Teaming up with the lyricist Lorenz Hart (left), Rodgers would recall, he "acquired in a single afternoon a career, a partner, a best friend and a source of permanent irritation."

COURTESY OF RODGERS & HAMMERSTEIN: A CONCORD MUSIC COMPANY, WWW.RNH.COM

Oklahoma! (1943) was the first musical to fully integrate song, story, and dance in the service of a realistic narrative and character development, revolutionizing the Broadway theater forever.

The sung dialogue of the "Bench Scene" in *Carousel* in 1945, with Jan Clayton and John Raitt, was the single most important moment in the development of the modern musical theater, in Stephen Sondheim's view.

PHOTOFEST

Agnes de Mille, the pioneering choreographer, brought the disciplined technique and narrative power of classical ballet to Broadway in the 1940s.

Robert Russell Bennett, the leading orchestrator of Broadway musical scores, was crucially responsible for creating what became known as the Rodgers and Hammerstein sound.

Before opening in New York, Broadway musicals had weeks of tryouts in New England. This photo of Rodgers and Hammerstein was taken in Boston's Public Garden during the tryouts for *Allegro* in 1947.

In *Allegro*, an experimental show without big-name stars or standout song hits, the newcomer Lisa Kirk made a sensational splash as a long-suffering nurse, singing "The Gentleman Is a Dope" about her distracted boss, an ambitious doctor.

Oscar Hammerstein's writing habits were as disciplined as Larry Hart's had been chaotic. He is seen here working in a favorite chair in his farmhouse study in Doylestown, Pennsylvania.

Rodgers and his wife, Dorothy, were both ambitious and competitive, but they did not encourage the musical interests and talents of their teenage daughters, Linda (far left) and Mary.

Irving Berlin (center), the past master of American popular song, was recruited to write the music and lyrics for *Annie Get Your Gun*, the hit musical that Rodgers and Hammerstein produced in 1946.

Howard Reinheimer was the principal architect of Rodgers and Hammerstein's wildly successful business and legal strategy.

ANN ROSENER/PIX INC./THE LIFE IMAGES COLLECTION/GETTY IMAGES

Jo Mielziner, peering through a scenic design on glass, was a genius who could draw freehand sketches of proposed sets to scale, and deployed cinematic techniques for scene changes in *Allegro* and *South Pacific*.

PHOTOFEST

COURTESY OF RODGERS & HAMMERSTEIN: A CONCORD MUSIC COMPANY, WWW.RNH.COM

RICHARD RODGERS and OSCAR HAMMERSTEIN, 2nd

LELAND HAYWARD & JOSHUA LOGAN

MARY
MARTIN

EZIO
PINZA

In the Pulitzer Prize Musical Play

South Pacific

Music by RICHARD RODGERS
Lyrics by OSCAR HAMMERSTEIN 2nd

Book by OSCAR HAMMERSTEIN 2nd and JOSHUA LOGAN

Adapted from JAMES A. MICHENER's Pulitzer Prize Winning "TALES OF THE SOUTH PACIFIC"

Directed by JOSHUA LOGAN

MYRON
McCORMICK

WILLIAM
TABBERT

JUANITA
HALL

MAJESTIC THEATRE

Ezio Pinza and Mary Martin (above) brought romance and a frank approach to racial tension to *South Pacific*; director Joshua Logan co-wrote the script with Hammerstein, but the original 1949 poster shows his reduced billing.

Joshua Logan, brilliant, mercurial, manic-depressive, was among the most successful Broadway directors of his day and a frequent (if sometimes frustrated) collaborator with Rodgers and Hammerstein.

The German-born arranger and composer Trude Rittmann devised dance music, scenic underscoring, and unforgettable vocal and choral arrangements for Richard Rodgers, often without receiving full credit for her contributions.

COURTESY OF THE HAMMERSTEIN FAMILY COLLECTION

Highland Farm in Doylestown, Pennsylvania, was Oscar Hammerstein's principal workplace and emotional refuge for the last two decades of his life. Here is where he wrote lyrics for almost all his collaborations with Richard Rodgers.

COURTESY OF RODGERS & HAMMERSTEIN: A CONCORD MUSIC COMPANY, WWW.RNH.COM

The partners and their parallel wives, "the two Dorothys"—Dorothy Hammerstein (center left) and Dorothy Rodgers (center right)—on a visit to Oklahoma in 1946.

COURTESY OF RODGERS & HAMMERSTEIN: A CONCORD MUSIC COMPANY, WWW.RNH.COM

Gertrude Lawrence and Yul Brynner in *The King and I* in 1951. They never so much as kissed but shared the sexiest polka ever danced.

RKO RADIO PICTURES INC/PHOTOFEST ©RKO RADIO PICTURES INC.

Gordon MacRae and Shirley Jones starred in the film version of *Oklahoma!* in 1955, together with Charlotte Greenwood (right), who had been the original choice to play Aunt Eller on Broadway but was unavailable in 1943.

Isabel Bigley (left) and Joan McCracken shared the spotlight in *Me and Juliet*, Rodgers and Hammerstein's 1953 backstage tale about life in a Broadway musical. It proved a big disappointment.

The original poster for *Pipe Dream*, Rodgers and Hammerstein's only out-and-out critical and commercial flop. The show about John Steinbeck's raffish denizens of Cannery Row opened in 1955, and the partners lost their entire investment.

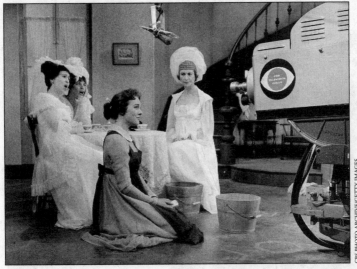

Rodgers and Hammerstein's *Cinderella*, an original musical for television in 1957, was the most-watched live broadcast in history to that point. Julie Andrews (center) played the title role even as she was starring on Broadway in *My Fair Lady*. Here she is seen with stepsisters Kaye Ballard and Alice Ghostley (left) and stepmother Ilka Chase.

Director Gene Kelly (front right, in cap) joins Rodgers and Hammerstein to watch a parade of costume tests for *Flower Drum Song* in 1958. The costume designer Irene Sharaff is at center, and the cast is visible in the mirror at rear.

Mary Martin (left) was nearing age forty-six when she starred in *The Sound of Music*, but onstage she could seem as bubbly and youthful as the seven von Trapp children she taught to sing eight times a week.

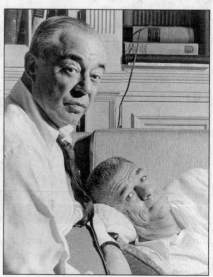

Rodgers and Hammerstein in a reflective pose, nearing the end of their collaboration.

Rodgers's collaboration with Stephen Sondheim (right) on *Do I Hear a Waltz?* in 1965 started pleasantly enough but soon turned sour over creative and personal differences.

A radiant Julie Andrews (center), charming children, and gorgeous Austrian scenery brought the screen version of *The Sound of Music* thrillingly to life and made it a box-office champion.

For nearly twenty years after Hammerstein's death, Rodgers, seen here with Dorothy at a gala in 1972, soldiered on. But he never again achieved the same degree of critical or commercial success.

Cinderella finally made it to Broadway in 2013, starring Laura Osnes and Santino Fontana, proving that fifty-six years after its debut, impossible things were still happening every day.

women thought it would make a fine subject for Dick and Oscar. "But Rodgers and Hammerstein rejected it individually and collectively," Rodgers's biographer David Ewen recounted. "They said that it was not their meat."

That was not the end of the story, however. As 1949 drew to a close, two powerful parallel forces would converge to bring the tale of Anna and the king back into the two Dorothys' field of vision—and into Dick and Oscar's, too. The first was Helen Strauss, a take-no-prisoners literary agent at the William Morris Agency who represented Margaret Landon and was looking for a new way to exploit her book, which had recently been made into a successful film for 20th Century Fox, starring Rex Harrison and Irene Dunne. The second was Fanny Holtzmann, a longtime lawyer and theatrical agent for the British stage star Gertrude Lawrence, who for a quarter century had been one of the leading lights of Broadway and the West End and was looking for a new vehicle as she headed into her fifties. Lawrence had just filmed a disappointing version of *The Glass Menagerie* for Warner Bros. and had turned down a feeler to star in Joseph L. Mankiewicz's production of *All About Eve*, at least partly on the grounds that its bitchy heroine, Margo Channing, would give an unflattering picture of life in Lawrence's beloved theater. At this juncture, a copy of *Anna and the King of Siam* landed on Holtzmann's desk, and an idea began to form.

At the same time, Helen Strauss happened to be discussing other publishing business matters with Bennett Cerf of Random House and mentioned that Landon's book might make a wonderful property for his friends Rodgers and Hammerstein. As it happened, Cerf was dining with Dick Rodgers that very night and agreed to mention the book. Strauss, citing Cerf's recommendation, sent Rodgers a copy of the book. (Leaving nothing to chance, William Morris himself sent a copy to Oscar as well.) Cerf then followed up, sending along yet a third copy, with a note inside saying, "This is the book I mentioned the other day. I think it would make a great musical." Flash-forward to late January 1950, when Fanny Holtzmann, having decided that the tale of Anna and the king would make a perfect project for Lawrence, was bustling along Madison Avenue. At 63rd Street, she caught sight of

Dorothy Hammerstein. "Can't talk now, Fanny," Dorothy called out. "On my way to Sammy's Deli to get a sour pickle for Ockie." *Of course*, Holtzmann thought to herself. *Dick and Oscar! Gertie! Anna!*

Here accounts diverge. Oscar's biographer Hugh Fordin reports that Holtzmann at first sent Dorothy a book about a Jewish actress married to a German general; others say the book was *Anna* itself. Dorothy wasn't impressed with the German Jewish romance and called Holtzmann to say so.

"Well, I'll think of something else," the redoubtable lawyer insisted. "But I definitely think the boys should do a show for Gertie."

"I don't know why they should," replied Mrs. Hammerstein. "She'll want it all."

Oscar, listening from the next room, couldn't stifle his admiration. "That's just what we would have said!" he later told Dick.

Holtzmann soon put yet another copy of *Anna and the King of Siam* in the Hammersteins' hands, and by now Oscar liked the idea a lot. Dick did, too, but he was wary. He and Oscar had had Mary Martin and Ezio Pinza in mind for *South Pacific* early on, but they had never before written a pure star vehicle, commissioned with only one actress in mind. And with Fanny Holtzmann and Helen Strauss in cahoots, it was clear that this project would be a package deal that included Lawrence or no one.

"We were concerned that such an arrangement might not give us the freedom to write what we wanted the way we wanted," Rodgers would recall. "What also bothered us was that while we both admired Gertrude tremendously, we felt that her vocal range was minimal and that she had never been able to overcome an unfortunate tendency to sing flat." So the partners arranged to see the Rex Harrison–Irene Dunne movie in Darryl Zanuck's Manhattan screening room. "That did it," Rodgers would recall, explaining that it was instantly obvious that the story "had the makings of a beautiful musical play." Lawrence herself had seen the film and admired the story and was now eager to play the part. So eager, by Helen Strauss's later account, that she let Howard Reinheimer sign her to a two-year contract to play Anna even before the dramatic rights were sewn up, which they soon enough were. On February 26, 1950, Holtzmann wrote Oscar, "Gertrude is pleased and is holding up all plans subject to ANNA AND THE KING OF SIAM."

FOR THEATERGOERS ON both sides of the Atlantic in 1950, Gertrude Lawrence was a name to make the heart beat faster. In light drawing room comedies and music hall romps with her good friend Noël Coward, she had lit up the stage in ways few performers ever do. Despite her vocal limitations, she had introduced such enduring standards as the Gershwin brothers' "Someone to Watch over Me." Not a conventional beauty, with an unhappily prominent nose, she nevertheless appeared ravishing behind the footlights. Her personal life was a swirl of caviar and champagne suppers, and she moved with the grace of a young deer. "Vitamins should take Gertrude Lawrence," was the verdict of Harold Cohen, the longtime drama critic of the *Pittsburgh Post-Gazette*.

"Oh, she was a fey creature—from and of another world," recalled the composer and conductor Johnny Green, who wrote the ballad "Body and Soul" for her. "Fascinating! Mercurial, volatile, enormously talented." Green added that Lawrence amounted to one of the unlikeliest instances of musicality he had ever known: "Awful voice, incapable of singing in tune, no breathing technique, sheer magic." Her longtime chum (and reportedly sometime lover), the novelist Daphne du Maurier, once wondered to their mutual friend Noël Coward, "Why, oh, why, should someone with the mind of somebody of ten, with whom one really had no thought in common, no topic of real conversation, no sort of outlook resembling one's own at all, who frequently lied, who never stopped doing the most infuriating things, yet have the power to so completely wrap herself around the heart that, because of her, one became bitched, buggered and bewildered?"

Lawrence would portray Anna Leonowens, a widowed schoolteacher of Anglo-Indian descent whose memoir, *The English Governess at the Siamese Court*, had sparked the imagination of post–Civil War abolitionists upon its publication in 1870. Leonowens offered what claimed to be an insider's account of life in the king's harem and of her own influence in moderating his semi-barbaric ways. But she also larded her purportedly factual firsthand account with a raft of self-serving fictions, hiding her mixed-race origins and romanticizing her late husband as a British army officer when he had actually been a civilian clerk.

Taking Leonowens's account at face value, Margaret Landon, a graduate of Wheaton College who had spent ten years in Thailand with her missionary husband, further embellished the tale with evangelical embroidery of her own, making Mrs. Anna not the instrument of the king's desire to modernize his country but the agent of his enlightenment under firm and benign Western influence. That was a message that resonated widely when her book was published in 1944, at the very moment when Allied troops were fighting fascism in Europe and envisioning a new era of influence in Asia. It's fair to say that it was also a message that would have resonated with that dedicated World Federalist, Oscar Hammerstein, for whom the power of Western liberal virtues to influence the rest of the world for the better was an article of faith.

In Landon's book, the relationship between Anna and the king is not even the central plotline, and he appears only episodically. Like James Michener's *Tales of the South Pacific*, *Anna and the King of Siam* is more a loosely linked collection of incidents than a cohesively plotted novel. But unlike the case of *South Pacific*, for which Hammerstein and Josh Logan had to fashion a dramatic narrative almost from scratch, there was already a strong and effective spine on which to base the new libretto: the screenplay of the 1946 film, by Sally Benson and Talbot Jennings, which wove Landon's vignettes into a coherent story and provided Rex Harrison's king with his distinctive, demotic, article-free version of English. Hammerstein would follow this lead, improving the result, as usual.

WITH THEIR STAR in hand, Rodgers and Hammerstein now began assembling the creative team for the show. They first offered the director's job, and full co-authorship of the book, to Josh Logan. But still smarting from his *South Pacific* humiliation, Logan turned them down, another decision he would regret for the rest of his life. So they settled for John Van Druten, whom they had known since the days of *I Remember Mama*, and whom Lawrence also knew and had worked with before. Much of the rest of the creative staff was familiar—Jo Mielziner to design the sets; Robert Russell Bennett to do the orchestrations; and the ever-reliable Trude Rittmann to arrange (and, as it would turn out, actually compose) the dance music. There were also two important newcomers: Irene Sharaff, one of Hollywood's top designers, to create the costumes using genuine Thai silks; and Jerome Robbins, a young choreographer who had made a name for himself both on Broadway and in ballet, to devise a planned second-act ballet in which one of the king's slaves would tell the story of *Uncle Tom's Cabin* in stylized dance.

But as the months wore on, Rodgers and Hammerstein still lacked a crucial element: a king. They had had several options in mind from the beginning, including an actor who'd already played the part. "I phoned Rex Harrison and he told me he had been in a couple of musicals and could do numbers, although he was no vocalist," Rodgers wrote his wife on February 19, 1950. "We're to have lunch with him next week to discuss it." But there was bad blood between Harrison and Darryl Zanuck in the aftermath of the film, and since Fox was set to be a major investor in the musical that would soon be retitled *The King and I*, nothing came of this idea. Dick and Oscar also thought of Lawrence's old co-star, Noël Coward, and sounded him out in June about the prospect of playing the king and directing the show, following up over a lunch in September, at which they presented him with a draft of act one, which he found charming. Rodgers fought Coward "like a steer" to try to persuade him to act and direct, but Coward had been at work on a comedy of his own with Gertie in mind and had no desire to appear in a play he had not written. Rodgers and Hammerstein then approached a singing actor whose work they knew intimately: Alfred Drake, their original Curly from *Oklahoma!* Over a lunch in the Oak Room of the Plaza Hotel they pitched the project to him. But by this point Drake, with a smash star turn in Cole Porter's *Kiss Me, Kate* under his belt, was fielding any number of attractive offers and did not want to commit to what already looked like an inevitable long run. Dick and Oscar left the Plaza and headed to the Majestic Theatre, where their casting director, John Fearnley, was holding auditions. Fearnley had invited a young actor to perform for the partners, an actor who had worked with Mary Martin in *Lute Song* and came highly recommended by her.

"He scowled in our direction, sat down on the stage and crossed his legs, tailor-fashion, then plunked one whacking chord on his guitar and began to howl in a strange language that no one could understand," Rodgers would recall. "He looked savage, he sounded savage, and there was no denying that he projected a feeling of controlled ferocity. When he read for us, we were again impressed by his authority and conviction. Oscar and I looked at each other and nodded. It was no more than half an hour after we had left Drake, and now, out of nowhere, we had our king."

His name was Yul Brynner, and he had decided he was "fed up with acting" and was directing television programs for CBS. Rodgers thought his "bony, Oriental face" would be perfect. Indeed, Brynner's appearance was exotic, and he had fashioned a biography every bit as embellished as Anna Leonowens's. He variously claimed to have been descended from Genghis Khan, to have run away from home at age thirteen to join the circus, to have a PhD from the Sorbonne. His birth year was reported as 1915, 1917, or 1920. The truth, while more prosaic, was yeasty enough. He was born in Vladivostok to a mother who was part Russian and a father who was part Swiss, and was raised there and in the Manchurian city of Harbin and eventually in Paris. He spoke Russian, French, Chinese, Romany Gypsy, and at least a smattering of other languages. He had trained as a circus clown, had worked as a substitute player on a jai alai team and as a lifeguard on the beach in Biarritz, and had studied acting in Paris before moving to Peking to spend time with his father. In 1940 he emigrated to America to study acting with Michael Chekhov, a nephew of the playwright, whose students over the years would include Anthony Quinn, Marilyn Monroe, Elia Kazan, and Clint Eastwood. He struggled to win small parts with Chekhov's touring troupe, and after the United States entered World War II he worked for the Office of War Information, producing French-language propaganda. He later kicked around

Broadway casting calls, and worked for CBS before getting his big break in *Lute Song*.

OSCAR WAS ALREADY well along on the script, as a surviving draft from July 1950 makes clear. Taking his cues from the Fox screenplay, which included a much-expanded role for the king and a ceremonial presentation of his wives and children to the new schoolmistress, Hammerstein refined and sharpened the characterizations and plot points. He would eliminate the death of Anna's son Louis in a horseback-riding accident, change the character of Tuptim from a haughty concubine to a sympathetic slave fascinated by Mrs. Anna's disquisitions on freedom and feminine dignity, and flesh out the role of the man who helps Tuptim escape, changing him from a priest to her lover. This created a dynamic that echoed *South Pacific*, in which the secondary characters would be played not for laughs but as tragedy. And just as Cable and Liat's ill-starred romance is the intellectual heart of *South Pacific*, Tuptim's quest for freedom is the crux of *The King and I*.

By midsummer, Hammerstein was sketching out detailed ideas for songs without yet committing lyrics to paper. In his July draft, he explained the purpose of a proposed soliloquy for Anna, who, alone in her bedchamber, pours out her frustrations that the king considers her his servant and forces everyone in his presence never to have their heads above his but to prostrate themselves in obeisance. This song, Oscar wrote, would "reveal Anna's character, the well-bred and genteel Victorian surface, and the inner strength and haughtiness of this woman, her pride, her deep love for the royal children, and the Siamese people, to whom she has become attached, and her admiration and affection for the king, however reluctantly she admits it right now. This number then is designed, not only to give added dimension to the character but to afford the actress the opportunity to loosen up and go beyond the bounds of propriety within which a lady had to keep herself in 1862. Here is a chance for more lusty comedy than she can reveal in other scenes of the play." The finished number, "Shall I Tell You What I Think of You?," written in six distinct sections, which Rodgers set to different melodies, is as compact a piece of dramatic exposition as Hammerstein ever wrote and an important window into Anna's thinking and motivations, as she alternately gives the king a piece of her mind in an imaginary confrontation, then indulges in her own reflections and self-doubt.

> *Shall I tell you what I think of you?*
> *You're spoiled!*
> *You're a conscientious worker*
> *But you're spoiled.*
> *Giving credit where it's due*
> *There is much I like in you*
> *But it's also very true*
> *That you're spoiled!*
> *Everybody's always bowing*
> *To the King,*
> *Everybody has to grovel*
> *To the King.*
> *By your Buddha you are blessed,*
> *By your ladies you're caressed*
> *But the one who loves you best*
> *Is the king!*

By the fall, Oscar would be exchanging detailed letters with Jo Mielziner and John Van Druten about the technical aspects of the script. He had sounded out Mielziner about the possibility of using a live elephant onstage, but the report from Fairfield Osborn, the head of the New York Zoological Society, was not encouraging: even the best-trained elephants prefer to work in groups; they tend to shift their weight from leg to leg unpredictably (with potentially dangerous consequences for anything but the most strongly reinforced stage) and are exceedingly sensitive to cold temperatures. "I hope my memo to you on the emotional idiosyncrasies of the elephant did not get to you just at the point when you had decided to use a live animal in the show," Mielziner wrote a few days later.

On December 5, Oscar wrote to Van Druten to say that Irene Sharaff needn't worry about how to get Lawrence out of her cumbersome
Victorian hoop skirts to sing her soliloquy about the king; she could
just undress to her bodice. But Oscar also confided his own frustrations. "I have had a very tough time with the lyrics so far," he wrote.
"They have not come very well. I *can* tell you that I think I have sketched
in Anna's background rather well in lyrics leading up to the song 'Tom
and I.' I am about to embark on the King's song, 'Sometimes I Nearly
Think I am Not Sure etc.' 'Tom and I' held me back a long time. I am
spending all my days on the lyrics now, and at night when I am not too
tired, I go back to the script."

The "King's song" to which Oscar referred would be the bookend to
Anna's own monologue, a soliloquy in which the monarch could confess feelings of doubt he is unable to share with Anna or his son, Crown
Prince Chulalongkorn, who is outraged that the new schoolteacher has
explained that the world is a "round ball which spins on a stick through
the middle," when "everyone knows that the world rides on the back
of a great turtle, who keeps it from running into the stars."

"How can it be that everyone knows one thing, if many people
believe another thing?" the king tentatively asks his son.

"Then which is true?" the puzzled prince demands.

"The world is a ball with stick through it . . . I believe," the king
answers.

"You believe?" the prince counters. "Does that mean you do not
know? But you must know, because you are king."

"Good," the king says, settling the question. "Some day you, too,
will be king, and you too will know everything."

But the moment he is alone, the king's tune changes abruptly, and
he sings his soliloquy, now titled "A Puzzlement."

When I was a boy
World was better spot.
What was so was so,
What was not was not.
Now I am a man—

World have change a lot;
*Some things **nearly** so,*
*Others **nearly** not.*

There are times I almost think
I am not sure of what I absolutely know.
Very often find confusion
In conclusion I concluded long ago.
In my head are many facts
That, as a student, I have studied to procure.
In my head are many facts
Of which I wish I was more certain I was sure!

As deft as that song was, the one that Hammerstein called "Tom and I" would become a minor masterpiece. Oscar struggled mightily with the number, in which Anna attempts to explain her background to the king's head wife, Lady Thiang, and describes her great love for her late husband, whose picture she wears in a locket. Lady Thiang has just told Anna that the slave Tuptim, a gift to her husband from the king of Burma, is secretly in love with another man and is foolish for being so. "But you can't help wishing for a man, if he's the man you want," Anna replies, before launching into a gentle reminiscence that makes her sympathies with Tuptim clear. By Oscar's own account he had spent a month on this single song, writing at least five separate versions, not all of them for the same melody. Finally, in a forty-eight-hour burst of effort, he produced this final version, its refrain a mix of two tempos, a six-bar barcarolle (a staple of operetta) followed by eight bars of a classic Rodgers waltz:

When I think of Tom,
I think about a night
When the earth smelled of summer
And the sky was streaked with white,
And the soft mist of England
Was sleeping on a hill—
I remember this,

And I always will . . .
There are new lovers now on the same silent hill,
Looking on the same blue sea,
And I know Tom and I are a part of them all,
And they're all a part of Tom and me.

Hello, young lovers, whoever you are,
I hope your troubles are few.
All my good wishes go with you tonight—
I've been in love like you.
Be brave, young lovers, and follow your star,
Be brave and faithful and true;
Cling very close to each other tonight—
I've been in love like you . . .

Hammerstein was uncharacteristically proud enough to send the typed lyric to Rodgers by special messenger, with instructions to wait for a reply. None came. For three days. Finally, on the morning of the fourth day, Dick called to discuss some other business. Only at the end of the conversation did Rodgers allow, as an afterthought, "Oh, I got that lyric. It works fine."

Oscar was crushed. Shaking with emotion, he summoned Josh Logan and demanded, "It's my best lyric, isn't it, Josh?"

"Well, certainly I've never read anything better," Logan replied. "But why do you seem so upset? You should be happy."

Oscar explained, pouring out years of frustration, insisting that Logan was the only one who could understand. Finally, he stopped abruptly and stuck out his hand.

"Okay," he said. "That's it. You've helped me. Thanks."

MEANTIME, RODGERS WAS having troubles of his own. In a November 28 letter to John Van Druten, he confessed, "Work on the score is coming along very, very slowly indeed. I spent a good part of today trying to get some incidental music and found myself turning out stuff that sounded as though it had been composed for a stage show at the

Music Hall. This doesn't exactly satisfy me, and I'm praying for better luck." An initial challenge was how to produce an Oriental-sounding score that would not be off-putting to American ears. He approached the problem in his typically sure-footed way, "writing the best music I could for the characters and situations without slavishly trying to imitate the music of the locale in which the story is set." Since tinkling bells, nasal strings, and percussive gongs could not create the desired effect, Rodgers decided to handle the problem "the way an American painter like Grant Wood might put his impressions of Bangkok on canvas. It would look like Siam, but Siam as seen through the eyes of an American artist." The technical trick was a liberal use of intervals of open fifths (without the intervening third tone of the scale) and their inverse, open fourths, for songs sung by the Asian characters, while reserving more traditional diatonic melodies for Anna and her son. The effect of an open fifth on Western ears is an incomplete, unresolved, exotic sound. Rodgers also harmonized the Asian characters' songs using chords well outside the usual vocabulary of the keys in which they were written. This, too, has the effect of making those melodies sound otherworldly. Finally, Rodgers, ever stretching his craft and always striving to surprise audiences by now accustomed to the standard thirty-two-bar format of a typical popular song, set some numbers in unexpected tempos. For example, the words of "We Kiss in a Shadow," a duet for Tuptim and her lover, suggest by their natural stresses a waltz in three-quarter time:

> We *kiss* in a shadow,
> We *hide* from the moon,
> Our *meetings* are few
> And *over* too soon . . .

But Rodgers set the lyric in four-four time, with even emphasis on each word.

One song that blended East and West musical sounds—indeed, in the same way its singer and subject did—was set to a soaring Rodgers melody, in which Lady Thiang begs Anna (in the aftermath of her angry soliloquy) to help defend the king against foreign accusations that he

is a barbarian. She explains her loyalty to her husband, even when he
disappoints her:

> *This is a man who thinks with his heart,*
> *His heart is not always wise.*
> *This is a man who stumbles and falls,*
> *But this is a man who tries.*
> *This is a man you'll forgive and forgive,*
> *And help and protect, as long as you live . . .*
>
> *He will not always say,*
> *What you would have him say,*
> *But now and then he'll say*
> *Something wonderful.*
> *The thoughtless things he'll do*
> *Will hurt and worry you—*
> *Then all at once he'll do*
> *Something wonderful . . .*

As always, Rodgers contributed to the overall shape of the show in
ways that went far beyond the music alone, notably with the second-
act ballet. In November, writing from Paris, Jerome Robbins told Hammerstein that he had been to see some Indonesian dancers and had
been transfixed by the pulsating minimalism of their movement, and
by one piece in particular in which a man and woman stood on opposite sides of the stage, never making contact, but still creating an effect
he found "terrifically sexy," almost "as if he had been touching her all
over." This performance also got Robbins thinking about a broader
role in the production. "I am completely pleased to do just the ballet,
but in reading the script over and over I felt very much that all the
movement should be of a particular style, and maybe by this time you
have arrived at the same idea yourself," he proposed. "I think that
the entrances of the servants and the entrances of the children and the
manner of deportment around the court should all be of one style
which should really be connected with the ballet ultimately."

Robbins would hire Yuriko Kikuchi, a Japanese American veteran of Martha Graham's dance company, as principal dancer for the ballet, and he devised movements of flexed feet and hyperextended fingers that, while not authentically Thai, created an impression of Eastern exoticism. Nevertheless, Robbins struggled to find the right tone for the ballet, and Rodgers arrived for an early rehearsal one day to find him sitting alone on the stage, seemingly stumped. The scene was one in which the king, like Claudius in *Hamlet*, would be forced to watch a play that depicted his own misdeeds—in this case, Harriet Beecher Stowe's *Uncle Tom's Cabin*, which would be a pointed commentary on the king's status as an enslaving autocrat. But Rodgers suggested that the ballet need not be ponderous; what if Robbins approached the ballet from a comic viewpoint—and yet delivered its serious message? The result was a stylized cartoon, now titled "The Small House of Uncle Thomas," in which masked dancers play Simon Legree's pursuing bloodhounds and the runaway slave Eliza crosses a frozen river of shimmering silk scarves suddenly pulled taut.

Rodgers sometimes chafed at Trude Rittmann's elaborations on his melodies in her dance and vocal arrangements, insisting at one point, "It's *Rodgers* and Hammerstein, not Rittmann and Hammerstein." But in *The King and I*, he allowed Robbins and her far greater leeway than he had ever given Agnes de Mille, whose ballets invariably used strung-together versions of Rodgers melodies, adapted to the dramatic or rhythmic needs of the dance. In this case, Rittmann would create a wholly new composition for the ballet, while being credited only with "arranging" the dance and incidental music. True, Rittmann would quote both "Hello, Young Lovers" and "A Puzzlement," the latter rendered dissonantly as Prokofiev might have composed it, but the great bulk of the music in the fifteen-minute ballet was hers alone, even if the name on the published score was Richard Rodgers.

THE KING AND I was budgeted at a lavish $360,000, much of it going to pay for Irene Sharaff's resplendent costumes. She had worked with Jim Thompson, a former American OSS officer in World War II who had settled in Bangkok after the war and almost single-handedly revived the moribund Thai silk industry. Jo Mielziner's sets were fairly spare and simple, using drops and small movable pieces to create the king's study, Mrs. Anna's schoolroom, and other locations. And as with every show since *Oklahoma!*, the partners once again had no trouble raising money. They could rely on their now-regular stable of angels, plus the single largest chunk—$40,000—from 20th Century Fox. In fact, Rodgers and Hammerstein had to turn down would-be investors, including Helen Strauss and their friend the playwright Russel Crouse, who had attempted to buy shares for his children, Timothy and Lindsay, whom he described in a letter to Rodgers as "your two most satisfied angels." "Having had plenty of experience trying to get money for shows when none was forthcoming," Rodgers wrote back, "it's kind of heartbreaking to have to turn down people like you, especially in view of the fact that inevitably we will need help sometime in the future."

Abetted as always by Howard Reinheimer's eagle eye on the bottom line, Dick and Oscar were in a stronger position than ever to dictate terms to their investors. In January 1951, Reinheimer wrote to the show's backers, explaining that unlike the typical arrangement, the producers of *The King and I* would share only in "first class rights" in the United States and Canada—meaning the major New York production and subsequent national tour—and would have no piece of the sales of subsidiary rights—for motion picture or foreign productions—which would be "reserved to the authors for their own account."

Despite the high anticipation about the new show—or perhaps because of it—its creators were insistent that the public should understand what the play was intended to be, and what it was not. On January 11, 1951, Helen Strauss passed along to Oscar a letter from Margaret Landon, who had not liked the libretto Hammerstein had allowed her to see. In essence, her complaint was that *The King and I* lacked the charm of *South Pacific*. This was a line of critique sure to irritate Hammerstein, who unwaveringly rejected the comparison out of hand. "I'm sorry that Miss Landon did not like my play," he replied, "but I cannot help feeling that there is much more to my script than meets her eye. I hope when she comes up to New York to see it on the stage that she will be pleasantly surprised." In fact, Hammerstein insisted to anyone who would listen, "By its very nature, the story will not permit the pace and lustiness of a play like *South Pacific*, and I am now sharpening a very long knife for the first one who tells me that it hasn't the qualities of *South Pacific*. It is a very strange play and must be accepted on its own terms."

Rehearsals got under way that same month, and from the start Dick Rodgers stepped off on the wrong foot with Gertrude Lawrence. The day before the first all-company rehearsal, the composer showed off the score for his star. In an effort to make sure his music was heard to the best effect, he asked Doretta Morrow, a ravishing lyric soprano who had been hired to play Tuptim, to sing it. That was a big mistake. Lawrence listened politely but was already insecure about her vocal capacities, and Rodgers's choice left her feeling worse. At the next day's rehearsal, she greeted Oscar and other cast members warmly, but "cut me dead," Rodgers would recall. A chill set in that would last for weeks—indeed, in some ways, for the rest of her run in the play.

By January 18, the production team was confident enough to play the score for Josh Logan. He was so thrilled that he stayed up until three a.m. composing his thoughts. He pronounced "Hello, Young Lovers" "the single greatest dramatic song I have ever heard in my life, and probably ever will," topping even "If I Loved You" and the "Soliloquy" from *Carousel*. But he had one major qualm. "I am also a little bit worried to hear that there is going to be no mass singing in the first act, and no dancing except for a tiny bit at the opening," he wrote Dick and Oscar. "May I make a suggestion? Is it possible in the school room scene when the children are learning that they could be a given a dancing lesson by Gertie and a gay, happy dancing song with a lot of kids singing with her? If this could be inserted and give some chance for a little more fun in this act. It would be nice to have something quite Western, as for instance a polka or gallop or whatever could be done in that period." That would turn out to be prescient advice.

One of the joys of the production was the large cast of children, many of them Puerto Rican, made up to look Asian. But in close quarters in the winter weather, they were a breeding ground for colds, and by February, as the company prepared to decamp to New Haven for the first tryout, much of the company, including Lawrence, was sick. In the week of February 14 alone, Oscar's friend and doctor Harold

Hyman and his colleagues paid a total of fourteen house calls to the star, plus two fourteen-hour visits to New Haven after the company arrived there.

Lawrence's longtime understudy, Constance Carpenter, played the dress rehearsal, and by the New Haven opening on February 26, Lawrence was running a fever of 103 degrees but went on anyway. Lawrence had asked the partners to delay the opening, but they refused. The curtain rang down after nearly four hours, a stretch for any audience and a certain financial disaster since the show had to be over by 11:30 p.m. or it would incur crippling overtime costs for musicians and stagehands. The reaction of the New Haven critics: The show was no *South Pacific*. It was not for the tired businessman. It was forty-five minutes too long. Its score was not written with an eye toward the Hit Parade.

Leland Hayward's verdict was the most dire: he told Dick and Oscar that they should close the show rather than risk bringing it into New York. Robert Emmett Dolan was more sanguine, writing to Oscar on the day after the opening with only minor complaints. He wondered if Lawrence was playing Anna as too young. He couldn't always hear all of "A Puzzlement" and wished that Brynner were a better singer. He praised Rodgers's score. "This show represents a real striking out for new forms on Dick's part and I think he has been very successful." Still, the company had its work cut out for its three-week run in Boston, which would begin on March 5. There, *The King and I* would undergo more pre-Broadway changes than any other Rodgers and Hammerstein show. Five songs would be cut entirely, along with several stanzas of others.

One early number, "Waiting," was to have been sung by Anna, the king, and the king's prime minister, the Kralahome, about her long wait for an audience with the king after her arrival in Bangkok; instead the wait would merely be described in a couple of lines of dialogue. Another song, "Why, Why, Why," a broadside by the king that dismissively catalogued the absurdity—to Eastern eyes—of prevailing Victorian customs, was jettisoned in favor of a new second-act opening number, "Western People Funny," in which Lady Thiang and the harem, struggling with hoopskirts in preparation for an elegant banquet to entertain visiting British dignitaries, bemoan the same phenomenon.

To prove we're not barbarians
They dress us up like savages!
To prove we're not barbarians
We wear a funny skirt! . . .

Western people funny,
Of that there is no doubt.
They feel so sentimental
About the Oriental,
They always try to turn us
Inside down and upside out!

The critical doubts, the changes, her illness, and Rodgers's seeming dissatisfaction with her singing had by now left Gertrude Lawrence shaken. She poured out her feelings to Rodgers in a long, handwritten note on Ritz-Carlton stationery. "There seems to be an idiotic impression around that there is a 'feud' between us—you & I, and it strikes me as an extremely unhappy and most unfortunate situation," she told him. "For my part the explanation lies in the deep-rooted feeling which has been settled in my heart since our early rehearsal days that you were not happy with my portrayal of 'Anna' or even of my presence in the whole play. As you know, I have never had a 'big' voice—but ever since 'Lady in the Dark' I have been studying to correct my faults in placement & to at least improve my breathing and thus to sing on pitch." She acknowledged that there had been gaps in her lessons, but added, "To my horror you seemed to bite your nails to the quick every time I sang before you & so my throat would close up & my heart has been sore with disappointment." In closing, Lawrence insisted,

My only desire is to please you, but I am a very shy person & would rather crawl into a hole somewhere than face disapproval. I have not changed in any way—but you have in some manner—to the extent that you no longer seem the warm-hearted friend that you used to be but rather a big businessman with much at stake—which seems to be all my fault!! I have no wish to "vocalize" but I have endeavored to improve & repair a fault simply because I wanted to be worthy of your music

& it has been saddening to watch you walk away during rehearsals, even as late as Tuesday afternoon when the new arrangement came for Lovers. You didn't even seem interested. I will work until I drop in my tracks, but a kind word is worth more than all the glowing and gushing of others. *Please* be my chum again and let's dispel this idea of a feud between us.

She reported that the conductor, Frederick Dvonch, "seems very happy over the music now, & I am getting more relaxed in the singing of it, but my heart just aches inside me when I think that you are unhappy. I would rather *leave altogether* than go on this way. 'Mrs. Anna.' "

Lawrence was not the only one with doubts. Her entourage shared Josh Logan's feeling that the first act lacked warmth and that there ought to be a musical number for her and the children. Mary Martin, who claimed to have seen the first performance in New Haven—a somewhat doubtful possibility since she was still playing nightly in *South Pacific* in New York—had the perfect tune in mind, the discarded "Suddenly Lucky" from her own show. Oscar got to work, and in short order found the perfect matching syllables with which Anna could greet her new charges:

Getting to know you,
Getting to know all about you,
Getting to like you,
Getting to hope you like me.

As Rodgers would note, the song not only immediately became a high point but served as a vivid and charming articulation of the show's East-meets-West theme. And the composer's relations with Lawrence seemed to improve as well. There is no record of his reply to her anguished letter, but sometime after she wrote it, he evidently reassured her, because she wrote again, to thank him for his "sweet letter," and borrowing a line of dialogue between Mrs. Anna and the king, to assure him, "I am so much happier now that 'everything seems to be going well for us.' "

———

FROM THE BEGINNING, Oscar Hammerstein had realized that an unspoken sexual tension and mutual attraction between Anna and the king would be the emotional center of the show. As early as his July 1950 draft of the script, he was outlining "a new song which will be Anna's attempt to describe a romantic love totally foreign to the king's idea of relations between man and woman." The moment comes at the climax of the play. The dinner for the visiting British, which Anna has helped plan, has been a smashing success, scotching any European notion of making Siam a protectorate, and the king in his gratitude gives Anna a ring.

In Yul Brynner's words, the king was "the most refined barbarian you've ever seen . . . if his jacket was off, he did not look naked, like, like a panther cannot look naked." But all during the dinner, the king has been fascinated by the sight of Anna's bare shoulders in her ball gown, because it does not conform to his own impressions of Western propriety. Now they tangle over the very idea of monogamy as he sings:

> *A woman is a female who is human,*
> *Designed for pleasing man, the human male.*
> *A human male is pleased by many women,*
> *And all the rest you hear is fairy tale.*

To which Anna counters:

> *Then tell me how this fairy tale began, sir.*
> *You cannot call it just a poet's trick.*
> *Explain to me why many men are faithful*
> *And true to one wife only—*

"They are sick!" the king concludes.

Anna then endeavors to explain to the monarch that, just as he is king, so every man and woman falling in love the world over feel themselves the same. She summons memories of the dances of her youth, when shy couples meet:

> *We've just been introduced,*
> *I do not know you well,*

But when the music started
Something drew me to your side.
So many men and girls are in each other's arms—
It made me think we might be
Similarly occupied.

And then she launches into a joyous, vibrant polka:

Shall we dance?
On a bright cloud of music shall we fly?
Shall we dance?
Shall we then say good night and mean goodbye?
Or, perchance,
When the last little star has left the sky,
Shall we still be together
With our arms around each other
And shall you be my new romance?
On the clear understanding
That this kind of thing can happen,
Shall we dance?

The teacher undertakes to instruct her employer, and they count to the "one, two, three and" beat of the polka, holding hands in the innocent manner of a square dance. But suddenly the king stops, insisting that this is not the way the visiting Englishmen had danced with their ladies. Anna acknowledges that it is not, and after a pregnant moment, the king grasps her waist, draws her close, and they fly gloriously from side to side across the open stage. Until. Until they are interrupted with the news that the fleeing Tuptim has been caught—and that her lover presumably soon will be, too. Tuptim rushes into the room, begs Anna for mercy, and faces the king's wrath. To Anna's disbelief, the king proposes to whip Tuptim into submission. He says perhaps she will believe he can do it when she hears the slave's screams as she runs down the hall. Anna refuses to oblige him, vowing to stay and declaring "You *are* a barbarian!"

The king tears off his jacket, raises the whip, but freezes as he sees Anna's eyes, then flees in humiliation.

"You have destroyed king," the Kralahome tells Anna before shout-ing with what Oscar's stage directions describe as "heartbroken rage," "I wish you have never come to Siam!"

"So do I," Anna sobs. "Oh, so do I!"

Anna has indeed destroyed the king, and in the scene that swiftly follows, Lady Thiang delivers a letter in which the king tells Anna that he is dying. "You have spoken truth to me always," Anna reads aloud, "and for this I have often lost my temper on you. But now I do not wish to die without saying this gratitude, etcetera, etcetera. I think it very strange that a woman shall have been most earnest help of all. But, Mrs. Anna, you must remember that you have been a very difficult woman, and much more difficult than generality." Anna rushes to the king's study, where he orders Prince Chulalongkorn to describe his first planned acts as the new king. The crown prince announces that he will end the custom of crouching "like lowly toad," and the king points an accusing finger at Anna, saying this edict is her fault. "Oh, I hope so, Your Majesty," she replies. "I do hope so." As the strains of "Something Wonderful" swell, the king quietly slips from life. Anna takes his hand and kisses it as the curtain falls.

The dramatic demands of this quick change for Lawrence were intense, and now it was Oscar's turn to receive a wrenching supplica-tion from the star. He had cut a transitional scene in which Anna's son and the crown prince play chess and discuss their parents, and Law-rence not only had to change heavy costumes while still dripping wet from the vigorous dance, but to compose herself for the high emotion of the final scenes. "Dearest Occie," Lawrence wrote. "Please I beg of you put back the chess scene for the reading of that most important letter—until you can get some further cuts elsewhere." But the cut remained.

THE NEW YORK opening was Thursday, March 29, 1951, and for all the tensions and doubts on the road, anticipation was high. John Van Druten would later say that it was in such situations that Gertrude Lawrence knew just what she was capable of, once the curtain went up at last. The effect was electric. "On the opening night she came on the stage with a new and dazzling quality, as though an extra power had been added to the brilliance of her own stage light," Van Druten would remember. "She was radiant and wonderful." Fanny Holtzmann, sitting next to Billy Rose in the orchestra, watched "Getting to Know You" for the first time and surprised the impresario with a sharp, delighted dig in the ribs. "We're in, Billy, we're in!"

Howard Dietz, the lyricist and MGM publicist, was so excited that he ducked into a bar after the show and scribbled a note to Oscar on a scrap of paper, calling *The King and I* the "most tasteful show I've seen and I think it will be a big hit and will make other writers careful not to be too vulgar." Oscar's old partner Sigmund Romberg called it "a monumental piece of work," and Dorothy Fields described the show as "beautiful, touching, charming and funny."

But as Oscar had feared, the critics were more restrained.

"No match for *South Pacific*," was the verdict of Brooks Atkinson in the *Times*, though he allowed that "strictly on its own terms, it is an original and beautiful excursion into the rich splendors of the Far East, done with impeccable taste by two artists and brought to life with a warm, romantic score, idiomatic lyrics and some exquisite dancing." And with a myopia that seems incredible in hindsight, many critics found the score wanting. In the *New Republic*, Harold Clurman was especially dismissive, calling it "probably the weakest of the Rodgers scores."

The show would win five Tony Awards—for best musical, best actress, best featured actor, best costumes, and best scenic designer—and would prove an unquestioned commercial and popular success, racking up 1,246 performances on Broadway and 926 in London. But now it was Dick Rodgers's turn to have hurt feelings, and he did. A chill settled over the partnership. No rupture was publicly announced or even acknowledged. But for the rest of 1951, Dick and Oscar went their separate ways, their collaboration at least temporarily on ice. They would resume it gingerly, and with the scars to show for it.

CHAPTER 8

Catastrophic Success

There's a vast difference between being what's known as a "Businessman" with capital letters and being a fool. And I don't think I'm a businessman, nor, I must admit, do I think I'm a fool. I put my business in the hands of people who know how to handle it.

Richard Rodgers

The commercial success of *The King and I* meant that Rodgers and Hammerstein once again had back-to-back hits running on Broadway, with *South Pacific* still packing them in at the Majestic, and Brynner and Lawrence doing capacity business at the St. James. It meant, too, that Dick and Oscar had reached the stage in their partnership at which they were just as apt to be celebrated for the remarkable feats they had already accomplished, as for any achievement they might yet turn out to top themselves. One such occasion was a two-part tribute to Oscar on Ed Sullivan's *Toast of the Town* television program on CBS. Rodgers and Hammerstein had been guests on Sullivan's very first show in 1948 and made frequent appearances thereafter. It had provided superb, free, nationwide publicity that cemented Dick and Oscar in the public mind as an inseparable team. Now, in the second installment of the Hammerstein tribute show, on Sunday, September 16, 1951, Oscar insisted that there was no magic formula for success in the theater. "The next five plays we write could well be flops," he said.

He offered a heartfelt tribute to his partner. "This fella Dick to whom I keep referring—he's my collaborator," Hammerstein said. "In the eight years of our association, we've never disagreed about anything at all. It sounds too good to be true, but it is true, and I'm reporting it here for the record. I think good things should be reported just as well as bad things. A cynic might say that, of course we have a happy partnership because we've had so much success. But I suggest that part of our success has been due to the fact that we have a happy partnership. I've never sat in a room with Dick and told him how grateful I am to be working with him. I think I'd be too self-conscious to do that." Here Oscar permitted himself a sly smile and went on, "But somehow or other, standing up here, being looked at and listened to by a good proportion of this country's population, I'm not self-conscious at all. And I find it a great and easy pleasure to publicly announce that I'm proud and happy and lucky to have him."

At this, Sullivan welcomed Dick himself to the stage. Rodgers stuck out his hand in the self-conscious manner of a man averse to any public display of affection or emotion. He then stammered awkwardly for a moment, shifting his weight, searching for words, and looking at his feet, before finally blurting out, "I think he's the greatest."

It was a revealing moment, reflecting in its way the complexities that lay beneath the surface of the partners' public facade. In 1951, Rodgers and Hammerstein would each earn something on the order of $1 million—when the average wage was about $3,500 and a new car cost $1,500—from their shows then running and from ASCAP royalties on past works. Not for a moment did either of them have the slightest desire to rock the boat, and certainly not in public. "I don't believe the firm of Rodgers and Hammerstein was full of problems between them," Robert Russell Bennett would recall. "They were both products of a practical, commercial age and they probably agreed that temperamental clashes would be bad for business. I once saw them together with tears in their eyes, but they were tears of joy after the first performance of *South Pacific*." It is worth noting, in an era of greater social reserve, that each man invariably signed his correspondence to the other with a single word, "Love."

Still, there *were* tensions. Josh Logan once reported that Dorothy Hammerstein would sometimes wonder aloud to her husband why the Hammersteins were forever relegated to the second-best suite, or the second-largest stateroom, or the second-plushest Pullman compartment when traveling with the Rodgerses. Oscar, ever mindful of his eleven lean years before teaming up with Dick, would reply that this subordination was simply the cost of doing business—and the price of enjoying a much higher income and much greater degree of success than he otherwise might have. Dick, for his part, seemed never to forget that he'd had an unbroken run of success when he took Oscar on as his collaborator—he once said that he'd feared Broadway would assume his mere teaming with Hammerstein meant he was washed up, too—and assumed top billing above his older, more experienced partner as his due, just as he had with Larry Hart. It was by no means a Broadway or Hollywood convention that the composer's name should come first, and indeed it did not with such songwriting teams as Lerner and Loewe, Dubin and Warren, or Cahn and Styne (and later Cahn and Van Heusen). In all those cases, the lyricists' credits came first (and in alphabetical order, to boot). Rodgers once told the arranger Don Walker that his billing—in each partnership—had been determined by a coin toss, a claim Walker found hard to believe. Even in *The Rodgers and Hammerstein Fact Book*, a massive compendium assembled by the partners' longtime public relations team, Rodgers's credits are listed first, though Oscar had been at work in the professional theater while Dick was still in high school. Indeed, Oscar would sometimes chafe at promotional copy that dated their success to the premiere of *The Garrick Gaieties*, Dick's first hit in 1925, when Oscar's first professional play had debuted six years earlier. In the film *Main Street to Broadway*, a slender 1953 backstage drama that amounted to an excuse for cameos by the theater's biggest stars, Rodgers and Hammerstein appear as themselves. When Josh Logan introduces Dick to a stage full of chorus girls, he luxuriates in their applause. But when Oscar arrives moments later and is given a similar greeting, Dick sardonically cuts the clapping short with a wave of his hand, saying, "That's enough."

The partners invariably treated each other with respect, but little annoyances had a way of creeping in. During the preparation of the text for *The Rodgers and Hammerstein Songbook* in the late 1950s, Oscar wrote to Henry Simon, their editor at Simon & Schuster, unhappy with his treatment at the hands of Newman Levy, who had contributed brief interstitial essays about the creation of their major shows. "You will note that throughout these articles, Dick seems to play a more prominent part than I in making decisions," Hammerstein wrote. "Newman Levy also quotes him several times, and I am given the feeling that I am sort of a junior partner. On this particular page, for instance, it is Rodgers who whispers, 'There's our King,' when we see Yul Brynner. Well, as a matter of fact, we both recognized immediately that that was our King and it really wasn't Dick who turned to me and said it. I think I spoke first. Although this doesn't make any difference, it seems to me that in this one place, perhaps, we do not have to ascribe the discovery to Dick. He has enough credit in the course of the articles, and I have little enough. Maybe I should say, "There's our King." As a matter of fact what I did say was, 'Papa, I want him.' " It was typical of Oscar's loyalty, though, that in the next breath he objected to Levy's description of "The March of Siamese Children" as a "Prokofieff [sic] type march," adding, "It seems to me that it is a wonderful Rodgers march, with really no debt to any other composer." The book's finished text is a testament to the kinds of compromises that kept the partners together: in it, it is Oscar who says, "There's our King," while Levy describes the Siamese march as "one of Rodgers' happiest achievements."

On rare occasions, the partners would confess their anxieties and frustrations—to others. Dorothy Hammerstein told Stephen Sondheim that Oscar "would come home from a working session with Dick so tense that he wouldn't be able to talk to her until he'd had a drink and a chance to cool down." On the other hand, Dorothy Rodgers once told Mary Martin that Dick could be so tense after playing a song for the first time that he would go in a bathroom to throw up. When Rodgers learned from a stage manager that the Hammersteins would not be attending the opening of *Annie Get Your Gun*—it had been postponed due to structural damage at the Imperial Theatre—because they'd be on their way to Australia, he was deeply hurt that Oscar hadn't told him himself. If Oscar was capable of wearing his emotions on his sleeve from time to time, Dick was much more guarded. Their office secretary, Lillian Leff, once told Russell Bennett of Rodgers, "I've seen him cry, I've seen him happy, worried, angry, thrilled, even. But never once did I know what was going on inside. With the other man I always felt I could help him think, if he needed me, but not with Rodgers."

It's a poignant truth that the two men seemed able to confess their shared vulnerabilities only to third parties. After Hammerstein acknowledged to John Van Druten that his lyrics for *The King and I* were coming very slowly, and Rodgers made the same admission about the music, a sympathetic but bemused Van Druten wrote Oscar in reply, "I am sorry that the lyrics have been giving you trouble. I had a letter from Dick, telling me that the score was giving *him* trouble, too. You two, whom I always took to be such highly inventive boys!"

IN THE WAKE of the chill that descended after *The King and I*, the partners went their separate ways, each to pursue projects of his own, much as they had done after *Oklahoma!*, when they were first finding their way. They had already stopped producing plays written by others, after two big disappointments—*The Heart of the Matter*, based on a Graham Greene novel, which closed out of town; and *Burning Bright*, by the novelist John Steinbeck, which ran for just thirteen performances in New York.

Oscar's new project was a revival of *Music in the Air*, his 1932 hit with Jerome Kern, with his brother, Reggie, as producer, Billy Rose as sole backer, and his son Jimmy as second assistant stage manager. For the new production, given post–World War II sensibilities about Germany, Hammerstein transferred the story's setting from Bavaria to Switzerland, cut some of the book, and interpolated "All the Things You Are" from *Very Warm for May* into the score. For James Hammerstein, the experience was a revealing window not only into the practical mechanics of production but into the world in which his father was most relaxed and most at home: the theater. He remembered watching a disastrous technical run-through during the end of summer tryout at a regional theater in Olney, Maryland, and was impressed to see that Oscar, who was directing, remained calm and stoic for four hours, speaking up only when necessary. The show opened on Broadway on October 5, 1951, and ran for a disappointing fifty-six performances.

"Mr. Hammerstein was writing tender, effortless lyrics in those days, with a little star-dust shaken over them," Brooks Atkinson wrote in the *Times*. "But the plot has a lot of hackneyed playwriting in it. He writes with much greater simplicity now."

Dick took up two solo efforts, both of which proved much more substantial. The first was a smashing revival of *Pal Joey* that starred Vivienne Segal repeating her original role as Vera; Harold Lang, a brilliant dancer and fine vocalist who had made a big success in *Kiss Me, Kate*, as Joey; and Elaine Stritch in a tour de force performance as Melba, the reporter who interviewed the stripper Gypsy Rose Lee. The passage of time had more than vindicated Rodgers and Hart's and John O'Hara's original faith in the material, and Brooks Atkinson recanted his original critique. "No one is likely now to be impervious to the tight organization of the production, the terseness of the writing, the liveliness and versatility of the score and the easy perfection of the lyrics," he wrote. The revival opened in New York on January 3, 1952, and ran for 540 performances—the longest Broadway run of any Rodgers and Hart show.

Rodgers's second outing was farther afield. In the fall of 1951, Sylvester "Pat" Weaver, the head of NBC's entertainment division, approached Dick about writing a musical score to accompany a twenty-six-part documentary film series that the network had commissioned about the Allied naval campaign in World War II, to be called *Victory at Sea*. At first, Rodgers was wary. The project would require something approaching thirteen hours of music, by most measures the longest single symphonic suite ever composed, comprising nine major movements—longer, as the critic Deems Taylor pointed out—than Richard Wagner's scores for *Tristan und Isolde*, *Die Meistersinger*, and *Parsifal* combined.

Of course, Rodgers composed nothing like that much music himself. The best estimate is that he wrote about an hour's worth. "I had neither the time, patience nor aptitude to sit in a cutting room hour after hour going over thousands of feet of film with a stopwatch in my hand in order to compose themes that fit an inflexible time limit," he would recall. Instead, the series' producer-writer, Henry Salomon, created written logs of the on-screen action, for which Rodgers composed "musical themes" appropriate to the situation—a landing on an aircraft carrier, a fleet of ships under way. These tunes were given evocative names like "Song of the High Seas," "Guadalcanal March," "Theme of the Fast Carriers," and "Under the Southern Cross," a seductive tango that would soon make an encore appearance on Broadway. "For the difficult task of timing, cutting and orchestrating," Rodgers acknowledged, "I turned to my old friend Russell Bennett, who has no equal in this kind of work. He fully deserves the credit, which I give him without undue modesty, for making my music sound better than it was."

Rodgers's self-deprecation is charming, and there was nothing clandestine or unacknowledged about Bennett's contributions. Indeed, his efforts were crucial to the project's success. But in his memoir, Bennett would acknowledge the extent of his work, noting that it would be difficult to describe where Rodgers's efforts left off and his own began.

Victory at Sea aired Sunday afternoons from the fall of 1952 to the spring of 1953. For his efforts, Rodgers won Emmy and Peabody awards, and the navy's Distinguished Public Service Award. He also won the undying loyalty of one very prominent fan: Richard M. Nixon, who two decades later would retreat to the Lincoln Sitting Room of the White House during some of the darkest moments of his presidency, crank up the air-conditioning, light a fire, and play the score of *Victory at Sea* into the wee hours of the morning.

EVEN AS THEY pursued their own projects, Rodgers and Hammerstein could not ignore their obligations to the partnership's ongoing ventures. The London company of *South Pacific*, starring Mary Martin, opened in the fall of 1951, after yet another unhappy tangle with Josh Logan, who had thrown Martin into a tizzy by trying to restage scenes and songs that Dick and Oscar thought had worked just fine. British critical reaction was muted, with many reviewers expressing puzzlement that such a fuss was made over interracial romance, which was hardly unheard of in British colonial outposts, and others just finding the story slow-going ("South Soporific," in one estimation). But audiences embraced Mary Martin, and the show ran for 802 performances. The British production was also notable for marking the professional debut of two young actors who would go on to bigger things. The first was Martin's own son, Larry Hagman. The second was a Scotsman who would never be known for his singing but who had the perfect kind of beefcake physique for Logan's burly chorus of Seabees. His name was Sean Connery.

Of course, Dick and Oscar also had to tend to the day-to-day realities of *The King and I*'s sold-out Broadway run. There was a nightly parade of celebrities backstage—General Douglas MacArthur, Farley Granger, Joan Crawford—and requests for tickets from the likes of Ogden Nash and Gloria Swanson. And from almost the opening night, there came new demands from the show's breakout star, Yul Brynner, who by May 1951 was seeking a $500-a-week raise, doubling his salary, retroactive to the Boston opening. And soon there were further demands: additional weekly raises on a set schedule to bring his salary to $2,000 a week by the end of 1952; co-star billing under the title (Gertrude Lawrence's name remained above the title); the same $75 a week for his dresser that Lawrence got for her maid; and two separate ten-week leaves of absence to make movies. This last request was not an idle notion: Cecil B. DeMille appeared backstage at intermission one night to offer Brynner the part of Ramses in his forthcoming film of *The Ten Commandments*, and he was willing to wait till the star was free. In the end, Brynner got the raises, but only one eleven-week vacation in the spring of 1952, when he was spelled by Alfred Drake.

Soon enough, Brynner was given to other displays of star temperament, chief among them a propensity, when tired or not feeling well, to skip his character's main musical number, "A Puzzlement." This became such a problem that the stage manager, John Cornell, would complain that "there are periods when it is out as much as it is in." Cornell wondered whether the management should consider sending Brynner's understudy on a few times to shame him. In the fall of 1953, a father whose daughter had seen the show wrote to Rodgers, complaining that the number had been dropped and adding that orchestra members had told his daughter that Brynner, a demon baseball fan, had skipped it to watch the World Series on television in his dressing room. The accusation was forwarded to Cornell, who thought it was unlikely to have occurred. "Well as I know and mistrust this man and his motives," Cornell wrote,

"it is simply inconceivable to me that he would cut a 5-minute number to watch a ball game." Still, by the end of the Broadway run, Brynner had skipped the number 116 times, according to one count.

As for Gertrude Lawrence, she was doing her best. Days after the
opening in April 1951, Oscar wrote to thank her for the gift of a lucky
gold piece. "This is my official and documentary expression of thank-
ing you for generous behavior," he wrote in the voice of the king. "This
does not, however, give you right to ask me for new cue to 'Young Lovers' of which I have already given exorbitant sum." Days later, Lawrence wrote him to thank him for "everything," and adding, "'Getting
to know you' has been a most warm and remarkable milestone in my
career—and your great patience and understanding has caused me
constant solace."

The summer of 1951 was beastly hot in New York, a special burden for Lawrence in her heavy hoopskirts, as the temperature in her
dressing room often reached the mid-nineties. "The Messrs (and I mean
the word) Shubert only put ice in the front of the theater once a day
around 11 AM," she wrote John Van Druten. "This is fanned into nothing by 3 o'clock on matinee days, so from then on the odor of frying
ham is terrific but hardly succulent." But she soldiered on, borrowing
an air-conditioned town house from a socialite friend. That fall, she
took on an outside assignment teaching drama at Columbia University,
which seemed to restore her. Only at Christmastime did an attack of
pleurisy force her to miss performances. After the death of King George
VI in February 1952, she hung on even harder, determined to take
The King and I to London for Queen Elizabeth II's coronation season
the following year.

But it was not to be. An attack of bronchitis followed the pleurisy,
and by the spring of 1952 Lawrence's singing had deteriorated to such
a marked degree that audiences were beginning to murmur during her
performances, and discontented theatergoers were writing to Rodgers
and Hammerstein to express their displeasure and concern. In April,
Dick and Oscar asked Noël Coward to intercede. "Lunched with
Gertie," he recorded in his diary on April 29. "Advised her to leave *The
King and I* for good. I did not say they were anxious to get rid of her

because of her singing, but I think I convinced her that she ought to do a straight play." Her friend Daphne du Maurier would later write to Coward of Gertie's "dreadful straining after the high notes," so much that "one's belly ached in agony for her."

By May 20, Rodgers and Hammerstein had come to the end of their rope. They had got no satisfaction from Lawrence's agents Fanny and David Holtzmann, and had tried in vain to arrange a meeting with the star herself. Writing from Oscar's return address in a stern voice that sounded very much like Dick at his most exasperated—and that, for better or worse, amounted to a unified front—they told Lawrence, "We are sorry that you were unable to see us either Monday or Tuesday, because we were anxious to record with you our deep concern over what seems to us a crisis in your theatrical career." They said that while her dramatic performance as Mrs. Anna was better than ever, her singing was not, and then they lowered the boom:

> Eight times a week you are losing the respect of fifteen hundred people. This is a serious thing to be happening to one of the great women of our theatre, and it would be dishonest and unfriendly of us to stand by any longer without making you aware of the tarnish you are putting on your past triumphs, and your future prospects. Whether you want to face up to this problem, or allow the situation to drift on as it is doing, is a decision you will have to make. It may be that you will resent our telling you this. If you do it will be childish on your part. We have neither motive nor desire to worry you. We are trying to protect you from a danger that faces you, and at this moment, as we do this, we are the best friends you have. Our love, always.

The surviving copy of this agonizing letter is marked "Not Sent." Lawrence hung on until her scheduled summer vacation, when Celeste Holm replaced her. Lawrence wrote Dorothy Hammerstein from Cape Cod that she had "found it very hard to get un-wound when I got here," but she felt well enough to resume her role on August 11. Three days after her return, however, she doubled over in pain while arranging flowers at home, and two days after that, after the Saturday matinee on

August 16, she collapsed while crossing the stage and told her dresser she could not go on that night. After a few days in New York Hospital, doctors diagnosed hepatitis, a debilitating but seldom grave disease of the liver. But Lawrence herself had a premonition, telling Fanny Holtzmann, "I don't think I'm going to get out of this place, Fan," and adding, "About the play—see that Connie Carpenter steps in. She has waited so long for her chance. See that she gets the role. And see that Yul gets star billing. He has earned it." On Friday, September 5, Howard Reinheimer wrote Holtzmann a stern letter, saying that Lawrence was obviously now much sicker than previously known, and that she must return to the play within three weeks or withdraw permanently. If she withdrew, Reinheimer said, Rodgers and Hammerstein were willing to keep paying her 5 percent of the box-office net for the balance of her contract, "as a gesture of goodwill." Otherwise, he warned, they would have no choice but to ask Actors' Equity to break her contract and relieve them of any further obligations.

Lawrence died the next day.

Only after an autopsy did her doctors realize that a virulent cancer of unknown origin had taken over her liver. She was fifty-four years old. She would be buried in Irene Sharaff's billowing mauve ball gown from "Shall We Dance," and her star-studded funeral was held at the Fifth Avenue Presbyterian Church. Oscar delivered the eulogy.

BY THE SUMMER of 1952, Dick and Oscar had patched up, or at least papered over, whatever temporary freeze had divided them and were ready to work together again. Dorothy Hammerstein chartered a Circle Line boat in honor of Dick's fiftieth birthday on June 28, and a glittering black-tie crowd of friends and celebrities cruised up the Hudson after nightfall, stopping along the way to be serenaded by the chorus of "Siamese children" from *The King and I*. Oscar wrote a gently teasing tribute to his partner for *Town & Country* magazine, noting that becoming fifty was only a "mild achievement." "A better reason for doffing one's hat to you is the fact that at the age of fifty you are Dick Rodgers," Hammerstein wrote. "I think this is a very good thing to be. . . . I congratulate you for your capacity to enjoy all the lovely things you have written, and I thank you—on behalf of the world—for the enjoyment that all the rest of us have had from them."

The team's next project was Dick's idea, and at first Oscar was not at all enthused. The notion was one that had long appealed to Rodgers—a backstage musical that might explore the realities of daily life in the theater. "One of our aims was to avoid all the clichés usually found in backstage stories," Rodgers would recall. "The backer didn't pull out, the star didn't quit and the chorus girl didn't take over." The show could depict action on two planes at once: a musical play onstage, and the trials and tribulations of the cast and crew backstage. Oscar couldn't see it, but he had talked Dick into *Allegro* and now felt an obligation to meet his partner halfway. He, too, told an interviewer that the goal was "to do our utmost to avoid the usual clichés of show business musicals." As it happened, those were the clichés of Hollywood musicals *about* Broadway; with the exception of *Kiss Me, Kate*, there hadn't really ever been any backstage musicals on Broadway. Unfortunately, the original libretto that Oscar produced amounted to an overheated melodrama more suited to a Hollywood B-movie than a first-class Broadway show. The story centers on Jeanie, a chorus girl who aspires to stardom, and Larry, the assistant stage manager who loves her. When Bob, a stage electrician who is Jeanie's former lover, learns of her new relationship, he is so consumed with jealous rage that he drops a sandbag from the flies in an effort to kill Larry. It was hardly the stuff of Cable and Liat, or Tuptim and Lun Tha.

Perversely, the partners once again fell prey to some of the same mistakes that had dogged them on *Allegro*, locking in the Majestic Theatre for an opening in May 1953, forcing Oscar to rush the book, and conspiring with the ever-resourceful Jo Mielziner to devise an elaborate series of two-sided set pieces that could show multiple locations at once, but that sent the budget ballooning to $350,000. In all, there would be twelve separate sets, together with some three hundred costumes designed by Irene Sharaff.

Still, Rodgers was excited, seeing a chance to write the kind of snappy tunes that had been the hallmark of his work with Larry Hart—and there would be a live jazz trio onstage. Don Walker—not the stately Russell Bennett—was signed to do the orchestrations, which would employ the sexy wail of saxophones for the first time in a Rodgers score since *By Jupiter*. To direct, the partners enlisted that past master of the rollicking, lighter-than-air musical comedy, George Abbott. But when Oscar sent Abbott a draft of the script in the early fall of 1952, the director had his doubts—particularly about *Me and Juliet*, which was the title of the play within the play and ultimately became the name of the whole show. The show inside the show was a gauzy, semi-surrealist story featuring characters named Carmen, Don Juan, and Juliet, much of it told in dance. It was meant to look so distinctive as to be instantly recognizable as something other than the actual action of the plot. But sixty-five years later, even repeated close readings of the published script leave the point of the effort profoundly unclear.

"Where is this?" unseen voices demand at the beginning of the internal show.

"It doesn't matter," Juliet replies in a kind of spoken verse.

The scene of the play
Is neither here nor there.
All the things
About to happen
Are things that are always happening everywhere.

"From the start we ought to have known that was no good," Abbott would recall. "It was based upon the fact that there was a show within a show—a show onstage and there was a show offstage. The symbolism of the ballets made no sense whatsoever. So the damn thing was a pipe dream. I thought that Oscar had some notion that he was going to develop here, but he never did—it didn't mean anything." Abbott hoped that when the action, which was barely described in the script, was fully staged by the veteran choreographer Robert Alton, the show would come alive. He swallowed his doubts and forged ahead.

Jeanie was to be played by Isabel Bigley, a soprano fresh from her success as Sarah Brown in *Guys and Dolls*. Bill Hayes, a young actor making his name on Broadway and in television, took the role of Larry, while Mark Dawson would play the murderous Bob. To play the characters in the show's comic subplot—Mac, the stage manager who makes it a policy never to date any woman in one of his shows, and Betty, the saucy dancer who woos him—Rodgers and Hammerstein cast Ray Walston, who had made a most effective Luther Billis in the national and London companies of *South Pacific*, and Joan McCracken, a brilliant dancer who had first won their hearts as the girl who took a pratfall in "Many a New Day" in *Oklahoma!* Oscar was still working on the book when chorus auditions began on March 10, 1953. There were forty-two parts for singers and dancers, who would be paid $90 a week in Manhattan and $100 a week on the road. More than a thousand hopefuls showed up.

The first rehearsal was March 19, and by mid-April, Hammerstein was engaged in furious rewrites, with the way forward not entirely clear. "In some quarters we may be criticized because it is not as highfalutin' as our more recent efforts," he wrote John Van Druten. "It is, in fact, an out and out musical comedy. If this be treason, make the most of it." For his part, Rodgers would recall, "Anybody can fix things with money. It's when things need brains that you have a little trouble." A week before the out-of-town tryouts began, two production numbers were dropped, including the original opening number, "Wake Up, Little Theater," which began with the less than poetic phrase, "Julius Baum is sweeping up the stage." Oscar was also discreetly functioning as an informal director outside Abbott's purview. Bill Hayes would recall that while Abbott always demonstrated precisely how he wanted Hayes to deliver line readings, "Hammerstein would wait for a quiet moment to whisper, 'Think of it this way' . . . and then he would explain succinctly and precisely how the character was feeling." Rodgers was also his usual punctilious self. He had set "Under the Southern Cross" from *Victory at Sea* to a lyric by Oscar; "No Other Love" would become the only hit to emerge from *Me and Juliet*.

No other love have I,
Only my love for you,
Only the dream we knew—
No other love . . .

Into your arms I'll fly.
Locked in your arms I'll stay,
Waiting to hear you say:
No other love have I,
No other love!

"To this day, if I sing it," Hayes would remember, "or even just hear it playing in the background of some restaurant I hear Dick Rodgers saying 'No, Bill. It's written eighth-quarter-eighth-quarter-eighth, with the whole note preceded by an exact eighth-note syncopation. . . . Don't linger on the word "love" and then come in on the downbeat. Do it the way I wrote it, thank you.'"

Throughout the rehearsal process, Oscar dictated notes on yellow legal pads: "Larry's waistcoat should be a sweater." "Bigley's bodice should be fitted." "Take the tag off stepladder." Hammerstein also wrote a lyric that offered a revealing window into his view of the theater, and of the one critic that he had always believed could never be wrong, the audience:

A big black giant
Who looks and listens
With thousands of eyes and ears,
A big black mass
Of love and pity
And troubles and hopes and fears;
And every night
The mixture's different,
Although it may look the same.
To feel his way
With every mixture
Is part of the actor's game. . . .

That big black mass
Of love and pity
And troubles and hopes and fears,
Will sit out there

And rule your life
For all your living years.

Because Mielziner's sets were so cumbersome—eighty-five tons of scenery on five giant tracks with synchronized motors—the first out-of-town tryout was booked not into the Shubert in New Haven but into the more commodious Hanna Theatre in Cleveland. Opening night was April 20, and Dick and Oscar took up their usual positions: Rodgers in the last row of the orchestra, Hammerstein down front to listen for signs of trouble in the crowd. In rehearsals, Oscar tended to be impassive, waiting to deliver notes at the end of the performance, while Dick flitted everywhere. Now, their demeanors were reversed, with Dick calm the moment the curtain went up and Oscar agitated. But Cleveland seemed to love the show. "Nobody could ask for more!" Rodgers shouted backstage to anyone in earshot.

The show then moved to Boston, where the rewriting continued, and it wasn't going well. Jimmy Hammerstein, who joined the company there as an assistant stage manager, would recall telling his father in their suite at the Ritz-Carlton one night that the show wasn't working, only to have Oscar explode in a "slam-bang" fight that sent Jimmy from the room in tears.

The Boston critics were divided: three strongly positive and one mildly unfavorable. *Me and Juliet* headed to its May 28 opening in New York with trepidation all around. The second-act opening number, "Intermission Talk," had been intended as Rodgers and Hammerstein's winking take on the vagaries of audience reaction. They had always believed that if theatergoers talked about anything *other* than the show at intermission, it was a bad sign. So their song had a woman arguing with her husband about a bill from Saks; another patron complaining about garlic breath wafting from the couple behind him; a bored businessman hoping for a tax cut . . .

I think the production is fine,
The music is simply divine!

The story is lovely and gay—
But it just isn't my kind of play.

The number proved prophetic. Brooks Atkinson judged that *Me and Juliet* "has just about everything except an intelligible story." John Chapman of the *Daily News* allowed that there were "many lovely and miraculous things. . . . Yet it does not strike me as a major work because its story is either too involved or incapable of competing with the remarkable scenic plot." Walter Kerr in the *Herald Tribune* called it "perilously close to . . . a show-without-a-show," one that "seems more deeply in earnest and a lot less lighthearted than their more significant works."

If Rodgers had wanted to recapture some of the carefree sparkle of his days with Hart, the result was disappointing. On the strength of its $500,000 advance sale, *Me and Juliet* managed a ten-month run of 358 performances, and turned an eventual profit of $100,000, followed by a seven-week engagement in Chicago. Its greatest legacy may well have been its employment of a nineteen-year-old redheaded dancer from Richmond, Virginia, named Shirley MacLaine. In his memoir, *Musical Stages*, Rodgers devoted just two terse pages to the show. Oscar's verdict was even more succinct. Returning to his town house after checking out a matinee one day, he stopped in the ground-floor office of his secretary, Mary Steele, who asked him how it had gone. He paused for a moment or two, then said, "I hate that show."

IN THE SUMMER of 1953, Oscar's worries went beyond the artistic. When his passport expired that July, in order to receive a new one, he was required to sign and file an affidavit attesting that he was not then, and never had been, a member of the Communist Party. Even then, he was issued a limited passport—good for only six months, and not the two years that was then standard. He was told that the State Department had information that reflected on his loyalty as an American, and that in order to be eligible for a regular passport again, he would have to file a statement of his beliefs. His first reaction, according to family and friends: "The hell with them."

That response was hardly surprising. Hammerstein had been a political liberal—and a staunch civil libertarian—for years. In the 1930s and during World War II, he had supported any number of left-ist causes that, in the harsh light of the Cold War, would come to be seen as reflecting "pre-mature anti-Fascist" views, in the Orwellian ter-minology of the day. When Oscar's old friend the screenwriter and pro-ducer Hy Kraft returned to New York after being blacklisted in 1950 for taking the Fifth Amendment before the House Un-American Activ-ities Committee, Oscar and Dorothy made a point of inviting him to dinner and a movie, and then insisting that the three of them drop by Sardi's afterward for a drink. "The gesture of hosting a Fifth Amend-ment friend was a defiant commitment that raised plenty of eyebrows," Kraft would remember.

Over the years, Oscar and Dick had employed such Communists or former party members as Howard Da Silva, the original Jud Fry in *Oklahoma!*, and Jerome Robbins, the choreographer of *The King and I*. But while Dick had taken a hands-off approach to most political issues, Oscar had been much more outspoken. In 1950, as president of the Authors League—a consortium made up of the Dramatists Guild, the Radio Writers Guild, and the Screenwriters Guild—Oscar had spo-ken out strongly against the Hollywood blacklist, saying that to "black-list writers on the basis of their personal political views, however repellent those views are, is more in accord with the practices of the Soviets than with our democratic traditions." In February 1953, when a touring company of *South Pacific* began a one-week engagement in Atlanta, some members of the Georgia state legislature denounced the song "Carefully Taught" and proposed a bill to outlaw entertainment works having "an underlying philosophy inspired by Moscow." Oscar told reporters he was surprised by the notion that "anything kind and humane must necessarily originate in Moscow."

Now, Hammerstein's outspoken advocacy was catching up with him. He could not have known the full details, but confidential gov-ernment records show that senior officials of the Federal Bureau of Investigation had been interested in Oscar's political views for at least two years. On June 29, 1951, Alan H. Belmont, the head of the bureau's domestic intelligence division, notified D. M. Ladd, the agency's No. 3

official under J. Edgar Hoover, that Hoover's deputy Clyde Tolson had been advised that an unnamed member of the Senate Subcommittee on Internal Security had raised questions about Oscar. Scrutiny at this level was no idle matter. Ladd, himself the son of a Republican senator from North Dakota, had been an expert on German espionage in World War II and had served as the FBI's head of counterintelligence, supervising its investigations into Alger Hiss and Julius and Ethel Rosenberg.

Belmont's memo went on to note that Oscar had been "affiliated with or participated in the activities of seventeen organizations" that had been cited as Communist by the attorney general of the United States, the House Un-American Activities Committee, or the California Senate Subcommittee on Un-American Activities. These suspect organizations included the American Committee for Protection of Foreign Born, the Civil Rights Congress, the National Negro Congress, National Committee to Win the Peace, and the United American Spanish Aid Committee. The memo quoted a snarky 1950 newspaper column in the *Daily Mirror* by the scurrilous Hearst correspondent Lee Mortimer, who reported in an article headlined, "Reds, Pinkos and Fronters in Entertainment Field," that "the name Oscar Hammerstein II appears frequently, but I find no record of his advocacy of sharing the profits from his big hits."

Belmont recommended that the bureau's Internal Security Section should initiate an investigation of Hammerstein, to determine if he should be recommended for listing in the FBI's security index of known risks. Tolson initialed the memo with his approval. But in December 1951, still another memorandum, this one from the special agent in charge of the New York office, informed Hoover that, "inasmuch as all leads in instant investigation have been covered this case is being placed in a closed status by the New York Office." The following month, some unnamed army official asked the FBI again for information on Hammerstein, prompting yet another memo from Belmont, with a regurgitation of the earlier notes.

What had changed by 1953 was that Dwight Eisenhower had been elected president and he was eager to appease the Republican Party's right wing, large segments of which believed the federal government was riddled with Communists and fellow travelers. Secretary of State John Foster Dulles had installed a former FBI agent and Republican Senate aide named R. W. Scott McLeod as assistant secretary for security and consular affairs, with a mission to root out miscreants and potential security risks from the foreign service. On McLeod's watch, Ruth Shipley, the longtime head of the passport division, denied or restricted the passports of anyone who might be a security risk. Oscar was caught in the net.

Because Hammerstein had important business interests in England that might require spur-of-the-moment travel—four Rodgers and Hammerstein productions were then running simultaneously in London—he reconsidered his initial reluctance to defend his patriotism to the authorities in Washington. In a draft letter dated October 1953, he began by making just that practical point about his business interests. But in a thirty-page typewritten affidavit written the following month, he abandoned this line of reasoning and couched his arguments on a higher plane. He staunchly defended his patriotism, explaining his membership in the Hollywood Anti-Nazi League in the 1930s by noting that it was one of the few American organizations willing to take on Hitler at the time. He wrote that he never saw Communist influence in the league's affairs, but he acknowledged:

> It would be dishonest of me not to confess that on several occasions I was warned that there were Communists in the anti-Nazi league. I remember what my answer was. I said in effect: "My interest now is to do all I can to stamp out Nazism, which I think is the greatest threat to our culture and our safety. If there are Communists in this organization and they are willing to help me do this, I can work with them without being a Communist myself. If there were a forest fire outside of Los Angeles and we all ran out with buckets to pour water on it, I would not ask the man at my shoulder what his political philosophy was."

Oscar also allowed that in 1949 and 1950, he had made $2 annual contributions to the Veterans of the Abraham Lincoln Brigade, who had fought for the Loyalist cause in the Spanish Civil War. But when Howard Reinheimer, whose office had made the payments, noticed that the organization had appeared on the attorney general's list of suspect organizations, the donations were stopped. Oscar reaffirmed his opposition to all forms of discrimination. He quoted from such all-American songs as "Ol' Man River" and "Getting to Know You," cited "The Last Time I Saw Paris" as an expression of solidarity with democratic allies everywhere, and noted that *State Fair* was reportedly the favorite movie of both Generals Douglas MacArthur and George C. Marshall. He said that his principal post–World War II charitable causes had included the National Association for the Advancement of Colored People, the United Negro College Fund, and Catholic Charities, and explained that his principal civic engagement had been with the World Federalist Movement—which was itself anti-Communist and had been denounced as such by the party.

"I should emphasize that if I have been careless in the past in lending my name to organizations with high-sounding titles, I no longer make this mistake," Hammerstein wrote. For good measure, he added that he had supported both the Marshall Plan to aid struggling democracies in Europe and the American-led international "police action" in Korea, and noted that despite supporting the New Deal, he had become disenchanted with President Harry S. Truman and voted for Thomas E. Dewey, the Republican presidential candidate, in 1948. He denounced Communism as "the worst gold brick that has ever been sold to the underprivileged."

"My plays and songs are either in praise of human dignity, or just plain romantic and happy," Oscar wrote. "I have helped write many of the songs of this nation, and I do not think I have let the nation down or endangered its security." In conclusion, he said he hoped that the State Department would not look upon him "as a second or third class citizen, and that it will acknowledge my right to the same two year passport to which every loyal American is entitled."

Oscar's affidavit was typically eloquent. But the preposterousness of his having had to offer it up was underscored by the fact that on the very day he drafted it—November 23, 1953—he and Dick were appearing in Washington as avatars of Americanism at the fortieth anniversary dinner of the Anti-Defamation League of B'nai B'rith. They had organized the evening's entertainment, and their fellow celebrants in the ballroom of the Mayflower Hotel included President Eisenhower, five justices of the Supreme Court, the chairman of the Joint Chiefs of Staff, Attorney General Herbert Brownell, and J. Edgar Hoover himself. The show featured Lucille Ball and Desi Arnaz, Eddie Fisher, Helen Hayes, and Rex Harrison. Jane Froman sang "You'll Never Walk Alone," and when it was the partners' turn to speak, Ethel Merman introduced them, counting off their hit shows on her fingers.

"I think the theater has a better right than almost any other influence in America, to speak for democracy," Rodgers began.

Oscar chimed in. "We have no intolerance on the American stage, so we can plead for tolerance everywhere else."

"In other words," Dick added, "our house is in order. We're at no loss in the theater for blistering names to call each other—but they're never based on color or religion."

"Another thing," Oscar said, "nobody tells us what to write."

"The public tells us what it likes—and that's democracy for us," Dick concluded.

In his own remarks, Eisenhower could not have been more supportive of Dick and Oscar's comments. "I would not want to sit down this evening," the president said, "without urging one thing: if we are going to continue to be proud that we are Americans, there must be no weakening of the code by which we have lived; by the right to meet your accuser face to face, if you have one; by your right to go to the church or the synagogue or even the mosque of your own choosing; by your right to speak your mind and be protected in it. Ladies and gentlemen, the things that make us proud to be Americans are the soul and the spirit."

Oscar's regular passport was eventually restored. But the FBI continued to keep him in its sights until December 1959, when the bureau noted that someone—it is unclear who—was once again requesting the file generated by the original 1951 investigation.

THE MUTED REACTION to *Me and Juliet* did not deter Rodgers and Hammerstein from seeking out their next project. In the early 1950s, virtually every idea for a Broadway musical came to their door, and they turned down many of them, including the shows that later became *My Fair Lady* and *Fiddler on the Roof*. Instead, they fell for an unlikely project that had been bubbling along for months. In 1952, the producers Cy Feuer and Ernest Martin, who had scored back-to-back Broadway successes with Frank Loesser's *Where's Charley?* and *Guys and Dolls*, approached the novelist John Steinbeck with a proposition. How about a musical play based on some of the raffish characters in the novelist's *Cannery Row*, set in the fishing port of Monterey, California? Feuer and Martin were especially attracted to the story of Doc, a marine biologist, and of the Bear Flag Cafe, a friendly local whorehouse. In fact, their proposed title for the play was *The Bear Flag Cafe*, and they asked Steinbeck to write a libretto. He was game at first but soon realized he was uncomfortable with the mechanics of dramaturgy and made a counterproposal: he would write a novel based on those characters—he would call it *Sweet Thursday*—and that could be the basis of Feuer and Martin's show. From the first, the producers had only one actor in mind to play Doc: Henry Fonda, who was dividing his time between Broadway and Hollywood but had never appeared in a musical. Feuer and Martin sent Fonda to singing lessons and approached their old partner Frank Loesser about writing the score. But Loesser was already consumed by other projects.

It was at this point that Rodgers and Hammerstein entered the picture. Dick and Oscar knew Steinbeck well, both professionally and personally. The failure of Steinbeck's play *Burning Bright* had not impaired their friendship, and Steinbeck's wife, Elaine, had been assistant stage manager on the original production of *Oklahoma!* The partners were intrigued by Feuer and Martin's idea, with the usual caveat: they would have to be sole producers, but they would cut in Feuer and Martin for a share of the profits. Almost from the start, however, there were complications. Despite some six months of singing lessons, Fonda would recall, "at the end of it, I still couldn't sing for shit." Rodgers, never one to compromise in the vocal department, agreed. "It would be a mistake," he told Fonda after a painful audition. What's more, Hammerstein was not thrilled with the idea of working with Fonda, who was by now his son-in-law, having recently married Dorothy's daughter, Susan.

So the team went back to the drawing board. Steinbeck began send-ing Oscar installments of his novel on color-coded pages, and Rodgers and Hammerstein started sketching out their own vision for the libretto and the score. In the spring of 1954, *Sweet Thursday* was published—to tepid reviews—and by this time Oscar had written five scenes of the first act, with accompanying lyrics, lifting liberally from Steinbeck's text. Steinbeck's story was basic. Doc, who had always been a carefree type, has returned from World War II restless and discontented, and his friends decide that what ails him is loneliness. They contrive to fix him up with Suzy, a defensive but sweet-at-heart hooker whom Fauna, the local madam, has taken under her wing. The plan blows up when Suzy realizes that Doc is reluctant to fall in love with a whore, and she breaks off their budding romance before love wins out in the end.

Once again, there were early warning signs of trouble. Oscar wrote Dick that he found Steinbeck's characters very interesting, and Rodgers answered expressing concern about one point. "Whether we can get away with a factual house of prostitution and make one of the leading characters a working prostitute is something else again," he worried. It would turn out that they could not. Hammerstein's early drafts of the libretto closely follow Steinbeck's unvarnished dialogue. When Suzy first arrives in town, Fauna sizes her up, guessing at the tough life she's lived: "Lousy home—fighting all the time. Not more than fifteen or six-teen when you married the guy—or maybe he wouldn't. You left home just to get away from the guy." (Even in this version, Oscar omits Suzy's pregnancy, which ends in a miscarriage.) In Oscar's finished script all such explicit dialogue is gone, and Suzy and Fauna's occupations are only hinted at in a genteel way.

The problem is neatly distilled in an exchange of letters between Steinbeck and Hammerstein in the summer of 1955. On July 20, Stein-beck wrote Oscar to pass on a story he had shared with his wife about a hooker who'd worked at the real Bear Flag Cafe. "She was good and popular and on a good night she might turn twenty to thirty tricks," he wrote. "But as soon as the joint closed every night or rather morning, she piled into an ancient car and drove eighteen miles to Salinas. Once we asked her why. 'I got a guy over there,' she said. 'I have to get it once for love or I don't sleep good.' End of story. I find it pretty romantic but don't imagine the Watch and Ward [the Boston censorship authority] would." Six days later, Oscar wrote back about this "romantic girl." "I like her," he said. "I don't see how I can wedge her in at the moment, but you never know what will turn up as you go along."

As if to signal that this project would be the polar opposite of *Me and Juliet*, Rodgers and Hammerstein signed up Harold Clurman, a veteran of the pioneering Group Theatre in the 1930s and the director of such serious plays as Carson McCullers's *Member of the Wedding*, to direct the new show, which would ultimately be called *Pipe Dream*, after the abandoned boiler pipe into which Suzy moves when she breaks up with Doc. And they had settled on a new star to headline the show: the Wagnerian opera diva Helen Traubel, who had recently been fired from the Metropolitan Opera for moonlighting as a nightclub singer. Oscar and Dick had seen her perform and agreed that she would make a busty, lusty madam. This was another miscalculation. Traubel's voice was fading; she would eventually be miked from the stage. By the summer of 1955, with the show headed into production, the two other lead roles were cast. Bill Johnson, who'd played the male baritone leads in the London companies of *Annie Get Your Gun* and *Kiss Me, Kate*, was signed as Doc. And for Suzy, Dick Rodgers had been mightily impressed with Julie Andrews, a nineteen-year-old English ingénue who'd made a splash in Feuer and Martin's production of *The Boy Friend*, but she was snapped up by Lerner and Loewe for their Pygmalion adaptation. So Judy Tyler, whom Dick had noticed as Princess Summerfall Winterspring on television's *Howdy Doody Show*, would play the role. Tyler's belting singing style annoyed Clurman, who thought it made her character seem hard and unsympathetic. "Doesn't that belting disturb you?" he asked Rodgers. But Dick replied, "She's so pretty I can't even think about that."

DURING THAT SAME summer of 1955, a far graver complication arose. Dick Rodgers had been experiencing pain in his left jaw and made periodic visits to his dentist, who was not concerned. Then one day in September, the dentist suspected more serious trouble and Rodgers was packed off first to his own doctor, and from there to a specialist in head and neck surgery. As Dick and Dorothy waited anxiously outside the office, Morty Rodgers (a physician himself) was closeted in lengthy consultations with the surgeon. "The wait was interminable and I knew something serious was going on," Dick recalled. The verdict was bad: cancer of the jaw, no doubt the result of the years of Dick's heavy smoking and drinking. The surgeon was measured. "It isn't too early but it still isn't too late," he told Rodgers.

Dick's family's impressions of the effect of his illness would vary significantly. "When he finally got cancer of the jaw, I think he was relieved," Mary Rodgers thought. "Because he'd been waiting for something terrible to happen for so long, when it finally happened he was like, 'Oh, well, Now I've got that over with,' and he was always rather curiously happy when he was in the hospital, being taken care of." But Daniel Melnick, who was then married to Linda Rodgers, drew the opposite conclusion. "Before that happened, he was still very outgoing, and in years to come he started to retreat," Melnick would remember. "For someone of that period, cancer was the plague, a death sentence. So when it hit him, it had a disproportionately devastating effect."

The diagnosis came on a Friday. Rehearsals for *Pipe Dream* were to start the following Tuesday, and surgery was scheduled for Wednesday. Over the weekend, Dick wrote one new song and finished three piano manuscripts. He got permission to stop by the Tuesday morning rehearsal before entering the hospital for surgical prep. When he awoke Wednesday, "The next thing I knew I was conscious again in the recovery room, minus one malignant growth, a part of one jaw, and numerous lymph nodes." The surgery was gruesome; all the teeth on the left side of his jaw were removed, he drooled uncontrollably at first, and the metal piece that replaced his jawbone would leave his face (and his radiant smile) permanently a bit lopsided, with the result that he would henceforth prefer to be photographed in profile from the right side. In public, he was typically resilient. "I can't say the surgical and medical procedures of my hospital experience were enjoyable, but there was nothing horrible about them, either," he would write years later. On the tenth day after the operation, while still spending his nights in the hospital, he showed up at rehearsal.

———

FOR DOC'S OPENING number, Oscar had written a lyric that reflected
the biologist's wonder at the natural order of the marine world—and
Hammerstein's own philosophy about humanity.

> *It takes all kinds of people to make up a world,*
> *All kinds of people and things.*
> *They crawl on the earth,*
> *They swim in the sea,*
> *And they fly through the sky on wings.*
> *All kinds of people and things,*
> *And brother, I'll tell you my hunch:*
> *Whether you like them*
> *Or whether you don't,*
> *You're stuck with the whole damn bunch!*

As the company packed up for the first out-of-town tryout in New
Haven on October 22, 1955, Steinbeck was feeling satisfied. "I am
delighted with *Pipe Dream*—with book and score and direction and
cast," he had written Oscar a month earlier. "It is a thing of joy and
will be for a long time to come." But as the tryouts continued and moved
to Boston on November 1, Steinbeck grew increasingly uneasy at
Rodgers and Hammerstein's softening of the show's tone. "*Pipe Dream*
became full of doilies, and both of them were responsible, not just
Oscar," Cy Feuer would recall.

Oscar had changed the source of Doc's discontent from his war service to his first discomfiting meeting with Suzy. In the scene when Suzy
arrives in Monterey, supposedly a dusty road kid, she sings a plaintive
song, set to a haunting Rodgers melody, "Everybody's Got a Home
but Me":

> *I rode by a house*
> *With the windows lighted up,*
> *Lookin' brighter than a Christmas tree,*

And I said to myself
As I rode by myself,
Everybody's got a home but me.

Steinbeck imagined Suzy as the kind of woman who has been ridden hard and put away wet, but she was dressed in a neat blue frock and looked, Steinbeck complained, "like an off-duty visiting nurse." In a long string of memos to Hammerstein, the novelist elaborated:

> One of the most serious criticisms is the uncertainty of Suzy's position in the Bear Flag. It's either a whore house or it isn't. Suzy either took the job there or she didn't. The play doesn't give satisfaction here and it leaves an audience wondering. My position is that she took the job all right but wasn't any good at it. In the book, Fauna explains that Suzy's no good as a hustler because she's got a streak of lady in her. I wish we could keep this thought because it explains a lot in a short time.

In fact, Oscar's second-act opening number for Fauna, "The Happiest House on the Block," made the Bear Flag Cafe sound a bit like a USO outpost:

> *The happiest house on the block*
> *Is quietly sleeping all day,*
> *But after eleven*
> *Our little blue heaven*
> *Is friendly and foolish and gay.*

Oscar's reputation for prudishness was well known among his peers. He had, after all, been born in the Victorian era, and in important ways he remained shaped by those times. The sole dirty joke he was known to approve of was a subtle one, told by Dorothy's son, Henry Jacobson: A man walks into a store and asks the clerk, "Excuse me, Miss, do you keep stationery?" She replies, "Yes, until the very last minute, and then I go crazy!" So it is perhaps a paradox that even as he shrank from describing Suzy's true trade, he himself around this point in his life had apparently embarked on an extramarital affair with Temple Texas, a striking showgirl who played Agnes, one of the Bear Flag girls in the show. Her photograph appears in the endpapers of the published script of the play, the most prominently featured member of the ensemble. A onetime model, born in Arkansas as Dora Jane Temple, Texas was a veteran of a couple of Broadway musicals and was the sort of girl who used one of her diamond bracelets as a collar for her miniature poodle, Floosy. Her comings and goings were regular fodder for the Broadway columnists Walter Winchell and Dorothy Kilgallen in the 1940s and 1950s. In later years, she would find work as an entertainment press agent and settle down to married life as the wife of Joe Shribman, a prominent music industry manager in Los Angeles, with whom she adopted two children. She would count Ethel Merman among her close pals.

It isn't clear precisely when her relationship with Oscar began or ended, but Dick Rodgers was apparently aware of it, and was "very protective" of it, according to his niece Judy Crichton. Texas's son, Owen Shribman, would recall that his mother never explicitly confirmed an affair with Oscar, but always spoke in the warmest terms about the importance of their relationship, and before her death at age sixty-two in 1987, she gave her son a man's signet ring that Oscar had given her. "When she did speak of her time in *Pipe Dream*, she always had a smile on her face," Shribman would recall. "Make of that what you will."

Dorothy Hammerstein's daughter, Susan Blanchard, once said that her mother was the sort of woman who "contemplated calling a lawyer" if Oscar danced with the same woman twice, but it is not clear whether she was aware of Oscar's dalliance. By all accounts, the Hammersteins' marriage was close and compatible; after more than two decades together, they still held hands when they rode in a car together, and Oscar would often sneak up behind Dorothy and kiss her. But at their twenty-fifth wedding anniversary party at the Pierre Hotel in 1954, at least one guest, Moss Hart, had detected a surprising lack of feeling in the room, noting that while Oscar had made a speech that briefly warmed up the mood, the proceedings had felt more dutiful than celebratory. What is beyond dispute is that a marriage that had begun with a thunderclap of love at first sight—and a tempestuous affair—would endure until Oscar's death.

NOW, WITH DICK unwell and Oscar perhaps more distracted than usual, it may be no wonder that *Pipe Dream* was having more than its share of problems. Many of Rodgers's tunes were lovely, but he was not always present to hear them. Oscar did his best to supplement Harold Clurman's wavering direction. But the killer team that had once coolly known how to fix a show, "and by Monday," suddenly seemed at a loss. Because the conflict between Doc and Suzy—his rejection of her as a prostitute—was never spelled out, Steinbeck complained that the would-be lovers had been reduced to "two immature people who are piqued at each other." In Boston, Steinbeck wrote a pained letter to Oscar that laid it all on the line, and summed up the crux of the problem the show now faced. Noting that the respected Boston critic Elliot Norton had pronounced the show "conventional," Steinbeck seized on that critique:

> I have heard others describe the same thing as sweetness, loss of toughness, lack of definition, whatever people say when they feel they are being let down. And believe me, Oscar, this is the way audiences feel. What emerges now is an old fashioned love story. And that is not good enough for people who have looked forward to this show based on you and me and Dick. When Oklahoma came out it violated every conventional rule of Musical Comedy. You were out on a limb. They loved it and were for you. South Pacific made a great jump. And even more you were ordered to go ahead. But Oscar, time has moved. The form has moved. You can't stand still. That's the price you have to pay for being Rodgers and Hammerstein.

And when the show opened at the Shubert Theatre on November 30, 1955, the New York critics largely shared Steinbeck's assessment. "Except for nice music, it is pretty much of a bust," wrote *Time* magazine. "It is so warm-hearted about a cold world, so high-minded about its lowlifes as to emerge more hootch-coated butterscotch . . .

what is meant to be low-down seems more like a hoe-down." Walter Kerr in the *Herald Tribune* had a discerning and perceptive take. He noted that in the song "The Man I Used to Be," Doc complains that he's not having as much fun as he used to because he's "got a mission now" in his scientific research. "I wonder if something strangely similar isn't beginning to happen to Rodgers and Hammerstein," Kerr mused. "The authors seem unable to keep their minds on cheerfulness. Philosophy keeps breaking in. . . . Someone seems to have forgotten to bring along that gallon jug of good, red wine."

Despite its $1.2 million advance sale, the largest of any Rodgers and Hammerstein show to date, *Pipe Dream* would have the shortest run of any of the pair's collaborations, just 246 performances. There would be no national company—and, as with *Allegro*, no London production, no movie version, and precious few amateur or stock revivals in years to come. Because Dick and Oscar had broken their long-standing rule against investing in their own shows by backing this one, they lost their whole investment—and the hopeful Feuer and Martin never saw a cent. Even in the weeks after the show opened, Oscar would still be rewriting—a fact noted by Ed Sullivan in a tribute to *Pipe Dream* on February 5, 1956, when he charitably described the show as Rodgers and Hammerstein's latest "smash." Oscar told Sullivan that there was no reason not to try to make any show better, even one that the public was already paying to see. But they never managed to get this one quite right.

In a letter to the casting director John Fearnley years after the show's failure, Steinbeck said the die had been cast when Dick Rodgers told him they'd decided to call it *Pipe Dream*. "That name indicated that R+H didn't believe in it," he wrote. "They were telling the audience it wasn't true before they started. . . . If you will read *Sweet Thursday* again you will see that I believed every word of it and played it as though it were the most important thing in the world. *Pipe Dream* didn't convince anyone."

Billy Rose's verdict was more succinct. "You know why Oscar shouldn't have written that?" the veteran showman said. "The guy has never been in a whorehouse in his life."

CHAPTER 9

Beyond Broadway

You ask too much of people who have been successful and they're human, too. I'm tremendously worried right now about the next show. This isn't because Pipe Dream only ran one year instead of five, it's a natural wariness at the nature of the business. It's very easy to fail and I've always known that.

Richard Rodgers

In the spring of 1954, the dean of Boston drama critics, Elliot Norton, addressed the University of Massachusetts's spring convocation. He noted that while the American theater had produced a first-rate crop of modern playwrights—Eugene O'Neill, Thornton Wilder, Arthur Miller, Maxwell Anderson, and Tennessee Williams among them—"only one person in fifty" among the general population "would be able to identify them."

"But," Norton added, "the names of Rodgers and Hammerstein," the convocation's honorees that year, "are almost literally household words. However, people don't merely *know* these names, they know the works these men have done. When you mention Rodgers and Hammerstein to almost any normal American with a sound heart and good hearing he thinks at once of songs and scenes and shows which they have written and which have given him great and abiding pleasure. In their work these two men have touched and enriched the lives of more people than any other American dramatic writers."

This was no exaggeration. But even as Norton spoke, Dick and

Oscar were hard at work assuring that their words and music would soon reach millions more people, at home and all over the world. They would move beyond the familiar stretches of West 44th Street in Manhattan and Drury Lane in London that had been their home for a decade, and that had made their names so famous. In doing so, they would further enrich their bank accounts and extend their brand. They would also sow seeds that helped to stifle their creativity and diminish their critical and artistic reputations in years to come. How? They went Hollywood.

At first, the rewards were apparent, but not the risks. Having for years steadfastly resisted all entreaties to sell their shows to the movies, as the tenth anniversary of *Oklahoma!*'s Broadway premiere passed, Rodgers, Hammerstein, and their ever-reliable legal and business adviser Howard Reinheimer made plans to conquer the next logical frontier. And they made certain to do so in the only way they liked to work: with the maximum degree of creative and financial control. The first step was to buy back all of the rights to *Oklahoma!* from the Theatre Guild and the show's original investors for the impressive sum of $851,000—more than $7.5 million in 2017 dollars—to be paid out in six installments beginning in the summer of 1953.

Hollywood's interest in *Oklahoma!* as a film property had been so intense, Rodgers would recall, that at one point Paramount Pictures had offered the partners 100 percent of any movie's profits, so convinced was the studio that it could make a fortune on the distribution rights alone. But true to form, and still wary of the ways of the Hollywood they had loathed two decades earlier, Dick and Oscar decided to do it themselves, forming a corporation, Rodgers and Hammerstein Pictures, Inc., to produce and package the film. With the old Hollywood studio system collapsing in the face of competition from television, and with moviemakers striving for ever-greater special effects with wide-screen formats like Cinerama, not to mention novelties like 3-D, the partners made the strategic decision to embrace a brand-new format themselves: Todd-AO.

Todd-AO was a partnership between the producer Michael Todd and the American Optical Company of Southbridge, Massachusetts. Todd had been captivated by Cinerama, an early wide-screen process

that used three interlocked cameras and three separate strips of
35-millimeter film stock to produce a panoramic image on the screen.
But the technique had flaws, including a tendency for the picture to
blur at the seams, and Todd was convinced that there had to be a better
way—a system that would, as Todd put it with typical bluntness,
amount to "Cinerama out of one hole." The resulting image would be
projected on a wide, deeply curved screen that would extend partway
around an auditorium's walls, giving the viewer the sensation of being
in the picture.

Rodgers and Hammerstein's partner in producing the film using the
new format would be the Magna Theatre Corporation, whose directors included Todd, the longtime Fox executive Joseph Schenck, the
producer Arthur Hornblow Jr., and the veteran movie exhibitor George
Skouras. Hornblow was one of the few Hollywood producers Rodgers
trusted completely, and he played a crucial role in the production team's
next choice—of Fred Zinnemann as director. Hornblow had worked
with Zinnemann since the 1930s, and though he had never made a
musical, Zinnemann had gained respect for his work on films like *High
Noon* and *From Here to Eternity*, which would win the Academy
Award for Best Picture of 1953, with Zinnemann taking home a statu-
ette as best director. Shuttling back and forth between New York and
Hollywood, Zinnemann threw himself into the work of screen tests
and casting, with constant oversight from Dick and Oscar, who by now
had *Me and Juliet* up and running on Broadway and were also preparing the London production of *The King and I*. There was hardly a
promising young actor on either coast who was not considered at one
time or another for a part in *Oklahoma!* Some of the ideas now seem
far-fetched. Richard Burton as Jud Fry? Elsa Lanchester as Aunt Eller?
Frank Sinatra as Ali Hakim? But other options amount to a tantalizing list of might-have-beens.

Josh Logan was especially enthusiastic about a young actor who
was then appearing on Broadway under his direction in William Inge's
Picnic. Fred Zinnemann was less impressed. "Paul Newman is a handsome boy but quite stiff, to my disappointment," he wrote to Oscar. "He
lacks experience and would need a great deal of work. Still, in the long
run he may be the right boy for us. He certainly has a most winning

personality although I wish he had a little more cockiness and bra-vado." Zinnemann was more impressed with Newman's future wife, Joanne Woodward. "Joanne has a lovely quality," he told Hammer-stein. "It may be that she is a bit too wistful for the part, and perhaps she doesn't have quite the kind of radiance and vitality required for Laury [sic]. However, I was amazed at her ability to play the part believably—as though she were a very young and naïve teenager."

Zinnemann also tested another young actor just then making his name in live television, James Dean. "Dean seems to me to be an extraordinarily brilliant talent," he told Hammerstein. "I'm not sure he has the necessary romantic quality. Just the same, I shot his scenes with great detail because I felt that with an actor of his calibre a standard of performance would be set up which would later on become very help-ful as a reference and comparison." Not every contender earned a screen test, but Zinnemann considered a raft of other names for Curly, among them Robert Stack, Vic Damone, Jeffrey Hunter, Van Johnson, Montgomery Clift, Robert Ryan, and Robert Alda. He was especially taken with Eli Wallach's audition for the role of the peddler but also considered Hoagy Carmichael, Buddy Ebsen, Danny Thomas, and Ray Bolger. Lee Marvin and Jason Robards Jr. were both considered for Jud, and among the potential Ado Annies were Debbie Reynolds and Rosemary Clooney. For the all-important lead role of Laurey, the list included Piper Laurie, June Allyson, Doris Day, June Haver, and Janet Leigh.

But Hammerstein wrote to Joe Schenck on October 22, 1953, reviewing Zinnemann's screen tests and auditions. "We didn't find our-selves sufficiently enthusiastic about any of the candidates to make us want to proceed further with them." He acknowledged this was some-what worrisome, but there was no alternative but to keep plugging away. What Oscar didn't say was that since that July, he and Dick had had an ace in their back pocket, a sparkling nineteen-year-old soprano from Smithton, Pennsylvania, named Shirley Jones. She had shown up at one of the weekly open auditions at the St. James Theatre. These casting calls, presided over by John Fearnley, had become a Broadway institution and a necessity for Rodgers and Hammerstein, who had to find replacement casts for their long-running New York shows and touring companies. Among the other young talents who were spotted through this farm system were Florence Henderson, Edie Adams, and Julie Andrews.

Dick and Oscar had been so impressed with Jones's crystalline soprano voice—and her creamy, blond good looks—that she became the only performer ever to be placed under a long-term personal contract by the team. She was promptly put in the chorus of *South Pacific* and would later join the road company of *Me and Juliet*. But from the moment they saw her, Dick and Oscar had considered her a potential screen Laurey.

MEANTIME, THERE WAS plenty of spadework to be done, including raising the financing for the film, and Rodgers and Hammerstein remained skeptical about their new Hollywood partners. After a lunch with George Skouras that fall, Dick wrote to Oscar, "You and I seem to be standing firmly in the middle of that pail of snakes that we talk about so often. It seems to be endless backbiting among all of them, and I think we'll have to be very careful not to lose our heads." And Oscar, belying his reputation as the easygoing half of the team, told Joe Schenck that he and Rodgers were determined to strike the best possible bargain for the rental of soundstages to shoot the picture. They would prefer the capacious facilities at MGM in Culver City, he said, but not at any cost. "We cannot pretend to have very much knowledge of our own as far as the details of a question like this are concerned," Hammerstein wrote, "but one thing we can do is count, and if one studio is going to cost us two or three hundred thousand more than another we are not going to want to go there."

By early 1954, final casting choices were coming together, some of them unconventional. For Ado Annie, Zinnemann picked Gloria Grahame, who'd played a blowsy string of bad girls in noir films but who also had a gift for comedy. Rod Steiger, a New York method actor who had won widespread acclaim as a mobbed-up union official in *On the Waterfront*, would be Jud. Eddie Albert, a veteran song and dance man, was cast as Ali Hakim, and Gene Nelson would play Will Parker. Charlotte Greenwood, the veteran Broadway star who had been unavailable to play Aunt Eller on Broadway in 1943, finally got her intended part. And by spring, Rodgers, Hammerstein, and Zinnemann had settled on their Curly: Gordon MacRae, a handsome Broadway and radio baritone who had co-starred with Doris Day in musicals at Warner Bros. MacRae had a winning personality and a gorgeous voice, but at age thirty-three was already showing the puffy and paunchy effects of a lifelong problem with alcohol. In late March, during the broadcast of a televised tribute to Rodgers and Hammerstein, MacRae performed songs from *Oklahoma!* with Florence Henderson as Laurey, and backstage, Jan Clayton asked Oscar if they were "going to give Gordy the part" in the film. "And he said, 'Yes,' and I said, 'Why don't you tell the poor lad?' " Clayton would recall. "He said, 'We're trying to worry a few more pounds off him.' " At virtually the same time, Shirley Jones, in Chicago with *Me and Juliet*, got a phone call from her agent. "Hello, Laurey!" he said.

For Jones, it was a Cinderella story that seemed too wonderful to be true. Soon enough, though, she experienced the darker side of her good fortune: Rodgers invited her into his office, closed the door, and made "a cold-blooded pass," as she later recalled. Over the years, Jones would recount slightly varying versions of her response, but the gist of it was that she told Rodgers, who was thirty-one years her senior, that she would always think of him as her father or, worse for his ego, her grandfather. "It is a tribute to Richard Rodgers's professionalism," she would say, "that he didn't take steps to fire me or ensure that *Oklahoma!* was the last movie I would ever make."

Location shooting began on July 14, 1954. Oklahoma itself had been ruled out as too full of telephone lines and other signs of civilization to pass for Indian Territory, circa 1907. So had Iowa. But Arthur Hornblow had seen some spectacular pictures of the San Rafael Valley near Nogales, Arizona, just north of the Mexican border. At a cost of $100,000, the scenic designer Oliver Smith built a replica of a working farm for Aunt Eller, complete with a cheery yellow farmhouse, a red-sided barn, and a rough-hewn smokehouse made with recycled lumber from an abandoned miner's shack. Crews had planted seven acres of waving wheat, a peach orchard, and ten acres of specially irrigated corn, overseen by the University of Arizona's agriculture department and guaranteed to be high as an elephant's eye by the time of shooting. At its peak, the traveling company of actors and technicians numbered more than three hundred, with seventy trucks and trailers and a portable workshop to keep the expensive Todd-AO cameras in fighting trim. The encampment taxed Nogales's resources so severely that the local chamber of commerce warned would-be visitors to stay away.

Because the Todd-AO process was still untested, Zinnemann and the producers felt they needed a backup plan, and so decided to shoot every scene two ways: in Todd-AO and in the more tested Cinema-Scope format. Needless to say, this prolonged the shooting schedule and complicated everyone's lives. Dick and Oscar kept a close watch on every aspect of the production, from Shirley Jones's weight to Gene Nelson's singing. "Richard—boy, you sang it the way it's supposed to be sung, or not at all," Nelson would recall years later. Walking around the Arizona landscape during breaks in the shooting, Hammerstein tried to work on the lyrics for *Pipe Dream*, which was then in the planning stages, but confessed he did not make much progress.

Zinnemann was acutely conscious of the obligation he had taken on in directing such a beloved property. The annotations on his shooting script reflect his ideas about the story and spirit of the show. "Naïve. Not sophisticated. Primitive," Zinnemann wrote in notes to himself. "Actors do not condescend to material. Feeling that songs are *improvised* sung for the first time right now." And he added this note, "Get weather into picture!" That last desire proved both easier and harder than the director might have anticipated, because near-daily thunderstorms often interrupted shooting, as puffy white clouds built to enormous afternoon thunderheads before calm returned late in the day "with brilliantly clear and soft afternoon sunlight," in which some of the cinematographer Robert Surtees's best shots were made, Zinnemann would recall.

Back in Culver City, the Skidmore ranch—the scene of the box social—was built on one of MGM's largest soundstages. Agnes de Mille had been hired to re-create her dances and the signature dream ballet, and Rodgers would recall that she proved to be the most temperamental member of the production staff, tangling with both him and Arthur Hornblow. "On one occasion," he would remember, "she had the door locked on a sound stage during a dance rehearsal and made Arthur and me—both her employers—wait outside until she deigned to let us in."

Rodgers himself tangled with Malcolm Kingsberg, the Magna Theatre Corporation's treasurer, over what Kingsberg viewed as the extravagance of a $50 lariat, with Rodgers explaining that it was a trick prop, made easy to twirl—and that the $50 had purchased more than one, to boot. Kingsberg also complained about spending $200 for custom-made posters of the burlesque girls in Jud's smokehouse, only to have Rodgers explain that they had to be specially drawn to match the faces of the girls who come to life in Laurey's dream. Kingsberg's reply: "Why must they come to life?" As might be expected, Rodgers also kept an eagle eye on the music, setting out detailed notes for what he wanted from the seventy-five-piece orchestra that would play Russell Bennett's orchestrations under the direction of the original Broadway conductor, Jay Blackton. The movie's opening sequence had been carefully planned, with the camera moving silently through that field of priceless corn before emerging into an open meadow to reveal Curly on horseback, singing "Oh, What a Beautiful Mornin'."

"Before anything appears on the screen," Rodgers wrote to Hornblow, Zinnemann, and Bennett on October 29, "I suggest that we hear a faint rustle coming from an outsize string section. After this rustle has had a chance to establish itself, we ought to get the first glimpse of the tall corn. As the camera starts to move through the corn, the rustle should grow to a murmur, and the murmur should gradually increase in volume until the camera breaks through the corn, and as we look out over the valley there should be a tremendous outpouring of sound from the entire orchestra while Curly starts riding up the hill toward us."

That same week, George Skouras saw a rough cut of the film and was worried. "I see a beautiful picture with beautiful paintings which will call forth from the audiences exclamations of appreciation," he reported to Dick and Oscar, "but, it seems to lack the suspense, excitement and virility which are the very elements of making a motion picture a *great box office attraction*." Skouras proposed a prologue for the movie that would begin with Dick and Oscar rehearsing the

Oklahoma! company in New York, then announcing that the cast would all be flying on location to the state of Oklahoma itself. He suggested borrowing a DC-7 from whichever airline would supply it for free, filming scenes of the craft flying past the George Washington Bridge (and almost hitting it), before heading west. "I feel that by this time the audience will not only have been greatly thrilled by the process, but it will have experienced an intense enough sense of participation to be ready to relax and enjoy the picture."

Dick and Oscar's reaction to this outlandish idea is not recorded, but in the end, the film would be preceded in its theatrical showings with a special short subject, *The Magic of Todd-AO*, in which filmgoers were treated to a camera's-eye view of a roller-coaster ride and other thrills, lest they underestimate the possibilities of the new wide-screen process.

Zinnemann finished shooting on December 6, 1954, and while the film's release had originally been anticipated for early 1955, repeated delays caused by the new equipment forced the postponement of its premiere to October 11. But the delay did not dim the critics' enthusiasm. The movie "magnifies and strengthens all the charm that it had upon the stage," wrote Bosley Crowther of the *New York Times*, and the public lapped it up. The film opened in limited road show release in select, specially equipped theaters and played for fifty-one consecutive weeks at the Rivoli on Broadway, grossing $1.5 million there alone. Total box-office receipts were $9.5 million, making it the fourth-highest-grossing film of the year.

Late in life, though, Rodgers would remain ambivalent about the final result, finding the wide-screen process not so effective in the intimate scenes and complaining that the casting was not "totally satisfactory." In the future (except for *South Pacific*), he noted, "Oscar and I left moving pictures to moving-picture people and stayed clear of any involvement."

THERE WERE CLEAR practical and legal reasons for Rodgers and Hammerstein's comparative noninvolvement in the next two film adaptations of their work. But they would pay a lasting artistic price for

staying on the sidelines. By virtue of having filmed the 1946 Rex
Harrison version of *Anna and the King of Siam*, 20th Century Fox
had right of first refusal on any film version of *The King and I*, and
the studio chose to exercise it. And because Fox's European arm had
made the 1934 French-language version of *Liliom* starring Charles
Boyer, it also had a claim on *Carousel*, whose film rights Rodgers and
Hammerstein had bought back from the Theatre Guild for $165,000 in
May 1955. Both movies went into production that year, even as the
finishing touches were being put on *Oklahoma!*

At first, Fox's ideas for *Carousel* seemed promising, even daring.
For the long-suffering Julie Jordan, one name turned heads right away:
the long-suffering Judy Garland, Hollywood's greatest, though deeply
troubled, musical star, fresh from her triumph in Warner Bros.' remake
of *A Star Is Born*. But Garland had a newborn baby son, and nothing
ever came of the notion. Fox's production chief Darryl Zanuck had
another idea just as riveting: America's favorite singing bad boy, Frank
Sinatra, as Billy Bigelow. And Sinatra wanted the part. Zanuck told
Oscar that he hoped the studio could begin location shooting by late
summer and that Sinatra "was born to play this role." Zanuck added,
"He has all of the necessary larceny and yet he has the tenderness and
he has developed into a remarkable actor, which has already won him
one Academy Award. He is hounding me because he has so many other
offers and he wants to leave free time in case we decide to take him. I
think perhaps if we played him opposite the girl you have in OKLA-
HOMA this might be an ideal combination." Oscar replied that he and
Dick agreed that Sinatra could make "a very interesting and offbeat
approach to the casting" but urged Zanuck to consider Gordon MacRae
as well. He liked the idea of Shirley Jones as Julie but warned Zanuck
that she was about to leave for Paris in a special goodwill touring production of *Oklahoma!* to be directed by Rouben Mamoulian, and she
would thus be occupied through midsummer. Five days later, Zanuck
was back to Oscar with another idea. "I think it would be a terrible
mistake for us to use the same cast you have in OKLAHOMA," he wrote,
instead suggesting that Julie be played by the British actress Jean Simmons, who had just wrapped up the role of Sarah Brown in *Guys and
Dolls* for Sam Goldwyn. "In the case of CAROUSEL I assume we would

have to dub her," Zanuck noted, but added that she and Sinatra would make a perfect "motion picture cast," adding, "You have no idea how valuable this will be to us in Europe."

In the end, Zanuck settled on Sinatra and Jones, which would have been a sexy, summer-and-smoke pairing. But when Sinatra showed up on location via limousine in Boothbay Harbor, Maine, he professed shock that the director, Henry King, would be shooting the picture two ways, à la Fred Zinnemann, this time in standard 35-millimeter CinemaScope and in Fox's new CinemaScope 55, a 55-millimeter, six-track stereo format. "I signed to do one movie, not two," the Voice declared, and got back in his limo and headed for the airport. (In her memoir, Jones also floated an alternate reason for Sinatra's disappearance: his battling wife, Ava Gardner, was threatening to have an affair.) Carousel's producer Henry Ephron, who with his wife, Phoebe, was also co-author of the screenplay, had "tears rolling down his cheeks," Jones recalled, and asked her if she knew how to reach Gordon MacRae. From a pay phone, Jones called MacRae in Lake Tahoe (where he was performing a nightclub act) and asked him if he'd like to play Billy. "Give me three days," he replied. "I gotta lose ten pounds."

So the studio settled for a rematch of Jones and MacRae, but the sunny chemistry that had worked in Oklahoma! proved off-key for Carousel. The Ephrons concocted a tricked-up screenplay that began the story not with the stunning pantomime of "The Carousel Waltz" but with a hokey prologue before the opening credits, with Billy in Heaven preparing to tell the Starkeeper his story in flashback. Rodgers's magnificent score was truncated and the sung exchanges between Julie and Billy in the bench scene eliminated in favor of spoken dialogue. Hammerstein was also forced to come up with bowdlerized lyrics to replace some of his saltier phrases to satisfy the movie censors—only to see most of the alternatives eliminated altogether in the final cut. There were distracting technical glitches: the sight of motorboats in the background of the location scenes in Boothbay Harbor, and MacRae singing Billy's "Soliloquy" amid the crashing rocks and waves of Paradise Cove in Malibu, with the sun setting *behind* him—an impossibility on the Atlantic coast.

But the biggest problem was the overall sanding down, even the dumbing down, of a story that had always been both delicate and dark. What the Ephrons didn't do by way of messing up the screenplay, the enforcers of the Motion Picture Production Code did themselves, asking Fox for the elimination of even such mild oaths as "damn," "by God," and "what the hell," and insisting that Billy could not be allowed to kill himself to avoid arrest but must fall on his knife accidentally, because the code's prudish strictures required that suicide "should never be justified or glorified or used to defeat the due processes of law." The result, seen by millions of people, and eventually replayed on television, was a *Carousel* that lacked the subtlety, sophistication, and grace of the Broadway original—and that would in the long run help to cement R&H's reputation as purveyors of safe, sickly sweet, middle-of-the-road fare. When the film opened on February 16, 1956, *Time* magazine's assessment was tough but not off the mark: "The melodies have all their clovered freshness still, but if film fans lick their lips over anything else . . . it will be because they can't tell sweet from saccharine. . . . In a word: goo." *Carousel* would prove to be the only one of Rodgers and Hammerstein's major films not to be nominated for a single Academy Award.

Dick and Oscar had no greater involvement in the production of *The King and I*, but the result was much better, in part because of the strong hand of Jerome Robbins, who re-created his Broadway dances; the gorgeous costumes of Irene Sharaff; and perhaps most of all, Yul Brynner's brilliant and commanding performance as the king. The director was Walter Lang, who had directed *State Fair* a decade earlier, and the Fox music department under the direction of Alfred Newman did justice to the score, though in the end several songs did not appear in the final print. Deborah Kerr made a fine Mrs. Anna, credibly and effectively dubbed by Marni Nixon, who worked closely with Kerr to mimic her speech patterns. Trude Rittmann's chorus featured the future opera star Marilyn Horne, while Rita Moreno, chosen after Fox's first choice—Dorothy Dandridge—fell through, was an appropriately exotic Tuptim, albeit Puerto Rican, not Thai. (In a reflection of the questionable prevailing practices of the day, Moreno's own perfectly strong singing voice was also dubbed.) Rittmann had a screen credit as arranger of the ballet music—"not the correct one thanks to Mr. Rodgers," she ruefully wrote to her sister, "but still my name's there in connection with the picture."

Brynner himself, never one to suffer fools gladly, played a key role in keeping things on track, though the veteran television director chafed at the hidebound ways of a studio that he would later dismiss as "16th Century-Fox." Together, he and Hammerstein conspired to fend off the studio's idiotic suggestion that the king's death be explained as the result of his having been gored by an elephant. "The king dies because he has no will to live any longer," Brynner explained to the producer Charles Brackett. "He dies of a broken heart, if you wish to put it in a common language. But he truly dies because he cannot fulfill his desire to become a modern king that can modernize and bring something to his country that is better for his son. . . . The studio, they laughed at me when I said, 'He dies of a broken heart.' They said, 'Oh, come on, you're really just a kid.' "

The film opened on Dick Rodgers's fifty-fourth birthday, June 28, 1956—just four months after *Carousel*—and the reviews were uniformly strong. "It has the full content of that charmingly droll and poignant book that Mr. Hammerstein crystallized so smartly," wrote Bosley Crowther in the *New York Times*. "It has, too, the ardor and abundance of Mr. Rodgers's magnificent musical score." But in an unhappy postscript, the movie cost Dick and Oscar their long professional association with Jo Mielziner, who sued them and Fox for appropriating his stage designs, including the colorful schoolroom map in which Siam looms larger than all its neighbors. More than two years later, he would settle his case for $21,000, with $10,000 contributed by the studio and $5,500 each by Dick and Oscar. Mielziner, who had designed every Rodgers and Hammerstein show since *Carousel*, would never do another.

ONE OF THE most appealing realities about Dick and Oscar, and doubtless one of the secrets of their enduring success, was that while they took their work very seriously, they were never snobs about it— or about the mass popular culture that had embraced it. Moreover, despite their spectacular good fortune, they remained alert to fresh ideas. A case in point was television, the brash new medium of the day. "I look at television a great deal," Oscar told an audience gathered at Swarthmore College for a lecture, "Art and Mass Media," in February 1957. "And I resent the kind of snobbish attitude that people have toward it. I get into a great many dinner party fights with people who say they won't have television in their house. What will it do to their children and things like that! Well, I don't think it harms the children any more than funnies or comics." Moreover, Hammerstein contended, unlike the movies, which since the dawn of sound had stolen talent from the Broadway stage, the production of live television drama, then centered in New York, had "used theatrical talent and created more," with both films and legitimate plays increasingly starting out as television productions.

The topic was far from theoretical for Hammerstein, because he and Dick Rodgers were immersed in creating *Cinderella*, their original ninety-minute live musical for CBS. And he made it clear that he did not consider the assignment in any way a come-down or an invitation to produce second-tier work. He noted that it typically took him and Dick about a year to write a two-and-a-half-hour play, and explained that they would be spending the proportionally equivalent amount of time— about seven months—on *Cinderella*. Indeed, he said, "if there is any difference it's that we are using more care because we are entering a new medium. We do not want to fall on our faces, we want to do the very best we can; and we're very conscious of those sixty or seventy million people who are going to be looking at the television sets that night."

Some of the early collaboration took place by mail, because Oscar and Dorothy Hammerstein were in Australia. In a letter to Dick on November 10, 1956, Oscar asked him to send a copy of *Variety*'s review of the recent out-of-town opening of a new Max Gordon production, *Everybody Loves Me*, in Princeton, New Jersey. Oscar didn't explain the reason for his request, but he didn't have to: the play—which would never make it to Broadway—starred Jack Carson and featured Temple Texas.

From the beginning, the prospect of working on a *Cinderella* built around Julie Andrews had been all but irresistible. In fact, Rodgers and Hammerstein would produce one of their most scintillating scores for

the show. Rodgers's stirring main march and his swirling, foamy "Waltz
for a Ball" are as memorable, and as effective in their place, as any
music he ever wrote. Cinderella's opening ballad, "In My Own Little
Corner," is a plaintive, poignant expression of wistful wish fulfillment,
as the character dreams of what her life might be. In writing the lyrics,
Oscar went through his usual painstaking process of refinement. An
early draft,

> I'm a sailor in the battle of Trafalgar
> I'm a countess who is kidnapped in Peru
> I am taken by the Incas to the mountains
> And I have to eat and drink as Incas do . . .

gave way to lines more appropriate for a brave but lonely girl, and
more ruefully funny, too:

> I'm a huntress on an African safari
> (It's a dang'rous type of sport and yet it's fun).
> In the night I sally forth to seek my quarry
> And I find I forgot to bring my gun!

While both partners made a point in interviews of saying they had
no wish to mar the classic story with anachronistic modern touches,
the genius of Hammerstein's book is that he made Cinderella's stepmother and stepsisters more comic than evil, and he sprinkled other
deft touches throughout. In the lyrics for "The Prince Is Giving a Ball," a
spoof of medieval pageantry that would ultimately open the show,
Oscar gave his royals an impossible mouthful of Ruritanian names,
each capped by a borscht belt topper. Hence:

> TOWN CRIER: *His Royal Highness*
> *Christopher Rupert*
> *Windermere Vladimir*
> *Karl Alexander François*
> *Reginald Launcelot*
> *Herman—*

SMALL BOY: *Herman?*

TOWN CRIER: *—Herman Gregory James*
                  Is giving a ball!

Hammerstein initially named his king "Maximillian Godfrey Ladislaus Leopold *Elvis*" before thinking better of it and substituting "Sidney" instead.

Oscar's fairy godmother was not an elderly granny but the young and sexy Edie Adams, who was even then appearing on Broadway as Daisy Mae in *Li'l Abner*. She, too, had gotten her big break through one of Rodgers and Hammerstein's open auditions a few years earlier. They had nothing for her at the time, but George Abbott did, and she originated the role of Eileen in *Wonderful Town*. For "Impossible," the song in which the godmother explains to Cinderella that her dreams really can come true, Hammerstein sketched out a rough idea:

> *Impossible*
> *For six little mice*
> *To be turned into six large horses*
> *Such balderdash/poppycock, of course, is impossible*

followed by a list of synonyms: "Fol de rol, fiddle faddle, twaddle, poppycock, drivel, moon-shine, balderdash . . ."

That sketch became this finished lyric:

> *Impossible*
> *For a plain yellow pumpkin*
> *To become a golden carriage!*
> *Impossible*
> *For a plain country bumpkin*
> *And a prince to join in marriage!*
> *And four white mice will never be four white horses—*
> *Such fol-de-rol and fiddledy dee of course is*
> *Impossible!*

The song's conclusion summed up as well as anything Hammerstein's essential philosophy:

> But the world is full of zanies and fools
> Who don't believe in sensible rules
> And won't believe what sensible people say,
> And because these daft and dewy-eyed dopes
> Keep building up impossible hopes,
> Impossible things are happ'ning every day.

"When You're Driving Through the Moonlight" is an extended
musical scene in which Cinderella, who has just returned from the
ball, though her stepsisters do not know it, surprises them by correctly
imagining just what it must have been like. Its sung dialogue is a lighthearted echo of the bench scene in *Carousel*, and it gives way to "A
Lovely Night," a joyous celebration of the evening, accompanied by a
raucous ragtime piano obbligato.

In later years, Julie Andrews would reflect that she barely appreciated at the time what legends she was working with or what an
extraordinary opportunity she'd been given. In February and March
1957, she was sandwiching rehearsals for *Cinderella* between her
eight performances a week in *My Fair Lady*, and trying to sing and
dance on a television set so crowded that every move was "a bit of
a scuffle." It was all she could do to keep up. Instead, she would
remember the small moments, like watching Howard Lindsay and
Dorothy Stickney, theatrical royalty who played the king and queen,
eat their brown bag lunches at rehearsal, or standing backstage one
day idly whistling "The Last Time I Saw Paris," only to hear Oscar's
gentle voice behind her saying, "I really meant that when I wrote it,
you know," and having to confess that she'd had no idea it was his
song.

Just one number was cut in rehearsal, a song for Howard Lindsay,
called "If I Weren't King." It's hard not to see in its wistful lines a
reflection of Hammerstein's growing desire to take things easier in his
own life:

If I weren't King,
What a drifter I would be!
Like a kite without a string,
Irresponsible and free.
While the King was busy opening some bazaar,
I'd be nonchalantly leaning on a bar.
When the monarch made a speech,
I'd be lying on a beach,
Holding seashells to my ear to hear them sing.
And when cornerstones were laid,
They'd be laid without my aid—
If only I weren't a King!

Critical reaction to the show was overwhelmingly positive—"It had a gossamer beauty, a tender grace, plus the incomparable sheen of a child's dream world," wrote Harriet Van Horne in the *World-Telegram & Sun*—and the ratings were spectacular. Two days after the Sunday night broadcast, CBS took a full-page ad in the *New York Times* to brag. "At the stroke of 8, on Sunday night, nearly every home in the nation witnessed an act of electronic magic that only television can perform," the copy read. "By capturing and enthralling virtually an entire population at the same instant, it demonstrated again the medium's unique power to satisfy the public's increasing interest in television and the advertiser's need for vast audiences."

Because videotape had not yet been perfected, the show could not be rebroadcast, but Oscar told journalists he hoped to see it in the legitimate theater one day soon. The following year, it was in fact produced as a traditional Christmas "pantomime" in London, with the stepsisters in drag and some interpolations from other Rodgers and Hammerstein shows, plus an original number by its antic star, Tommy Steele. In 1965, under Rodgers's supervision, CBS would produce a much inferior videotaped version starring Leslie Ann Warren, which would be rebroadcast annually over the next decade. In 1997, ABC would reimagine the property again, with Whitney Houston as the fairy godmother heading an interracial cast. Not until 2013 would *Cinderella* finally fulfill Hammerstein's wish of getting to Broadway, in a splashy, elegant, and successful production with a new book by Douglas Carter Beane and costumes by William Ivey Long that amounted to a miracle of stage magic. After fifty-six years, it seemed proof that impossible things *were* still happening every day.

BUT FOR RICHARD Rodgers, the success of *Cinderella* rang hollow. With no fresh project in sight—and perhaps with the still-unprocessed trauma of his cancer surgery weighing on him—he fell apart. As early as November 1956, while still at work on *Cinderella*, he had written to Oscar about a puzzling illness. "Apparently I picked up a bug or got some bad food and in some mysterious manner my central nervous system was affected," Rodgers told his partner. "I couldn't retain my balance, I walked unsteadily and kept bumping into things. I couldn't even sign my name properly." Rodgers resisted his doctor's advice to consult a neurologist or another specialist, hoping that the symptoms would resolve themselves spontaneously, which they eventually did.

What did not resolve itself was a serious depression—one that to all evidence had been years aborning. It is impossible to know just how Rodgers's outlook may have been affected by the disappointment of *Me and Juliet* and the failure of *Pipe Dream*—or, for that matter, by the stupendous success of the rival Lerner and Loewe's *My Fair Lady*, which was now the hottest ticket on Broadway. He thought it was best to forget about criticism "and just go on with your work—but again, being human, you read what's said about you and you listen to what's said about you and you're pleased by it or you resent it." But his daughter Mary would come to believe that her father's personality underwent a sea change as he aged. "I get a very peculiar feeling that gradually over the years he changed from somebody who had a wonderful time to somebody who had a terrible time," she remembered. Rodgers's dark mood was clearly compounded by the deadening effects of alcohol. As his letters to Dorothy from Hollywood in the mid-1930s showed, he had been wrestling with alcohol for the better part of two decades, alternately going on the wagon and going overboard. Given the intense frustration, bordering on disgust, with which he had viewed Larry Hart's benders, and the way alcohol had impaired their collaboration, it is remarkable that Rodgers's own heavy drinking had so seldom affected his productivity.

Indeed, precisely because Rodgers did not disappear, because he did not fail to do his work, and because he was in no sense a stereotypical falling-down drunk, his problem remained a closely guarded secret during his lifetime. Yet there were clues. In early 1957, Moss Hart and his wife, Kitty Carlisle, dined in the Rodgerses' apartment and, after Dorothy went to bed early, stayed up late with Dick listening to an all-Rodgers program of music on the radio. Hart began counting the number of after-dinner scotch and sodas Dick consumed, and eventually tallied up sixteen. Rodgers may have sugarcoated the question of his drinking, but he did not minimize the crippling effects of what he called his "mystifying" depression. "I began sleeping late, ducking appointments and withdrawing into long periods of silence," he would write. "I lost all interest in my work and barely spoke either to Dorothy or to my children. I simply didn't give a damn about doing anything or seeing anyone."

Rodgers's younger daughter, Linda, recalled that his typical pattern in this period was to simply retreat and fall asleep at family gatherings, doubtless aided by the tranquilizers his doctors had prescribed. Finally, by the Fourth of July weekend at Rockmeadow, Linda remembered, "He had ground to an absolute halt. Essentially he was not there anymore." When his family suggested he check into the Payne Whitney psychiatric hospital on Manhattan's Upper East Side, Rodgers did not object, and he committed himself. Linda scrambled to buy pajamas with no strings, because her father had been put on a suicide watch. "I voluntarily separated myself from my family, from my work, from life itself," Rodgers would recall of this "extremely baffling and frightening period of my life."

In the mid-1950s, Payne Whitney was not only what Margo Channing, Bette Davis's character in *All About Eve*, would have called a "well-padded booby hatch," but a gilt-edged retreat for elite patients suffering from mental illness. Breakfast was made to order, and tables were set with sterling silver flatware and damask napkins. Over the years, celebrity patients from Robert Lowell to Marilyn Monroe would seek treatment there. Talk therapy appointments alternated with the application of soothing hot wet packs; actors practiced their lines in front of unbreakable mirrors; famous opera stars sang arias in the showers. Rodgers himself played cards, read, chatted with fellow patients, and received regular visits from Dorothy and occasional ones from Oscar. His stay lasted three months by his own account—and perhaps a month longer. "After a self-imposed exile of twelve weeks," he would recall, "I returned to my family and my work as if nothing had happened."

The letters that Rodgers saved from sympathetic friends paint perhaps a fuller portrait of the depth of his despair. "You've piled mountaintop on mountaintop of success," his former neighbor Edna Ferber wrote him. "There's never been anything like it in the history of the theatre, in this country or any other country. Your successful operation of two years ago, so marvelously overcome, was treated by you really with less respect than it should have been rated. . . . The advantage of this enforced leisure time is that the process of thinking and readjustment almost imperceptibly takes place. You will know yourself better. You will even write better or more wonderful music, if that is possible." Moss Hart, himself a survivor of a crippling depression just three years before, wrote, "I think you know, Dick, that I, too, have had a taste of the frightening and unpleasant experience you have been going through, and I know how deeply painful it can be. It passes. And even the pain is sometimes hard to recall, afterwards. I hate to say this, but it is not always an unmixed blessing—when it goes, one tastes and relishes every sunny day more keenly."

The most astute analysis may well have come from the erudite writer, editor, and radio and television host Clifton Fadiman, who sent a long, handwritten letter assuring Rodgers that summer, "I've had a couple of bouts of what I *think* a near-cousin to your trouble." Fadiman noted that some of his friends, including the editor Van Wyck Brooks, had experienced similar depressions, and he reflected on the knife's edge on which creativity is sometimes balanced. "You must have noticed that longshoremen don't suffer from depression," he wrote. "They suffer from discouragement or frustration or bafflement; but not from the vague constellation of downbeat feelings sometimes oddly known as 'a nervous breakdown.'" Fadiman added, "The fact is that the trouble often *follows* a triumph, or a succession of great successes; which seems paradoxical, doesn't it? . . . For a first-rater like yourself, it is a very serious and crucial moment when one has done what one sets out to do. The second-rater who satisfies his ambitions is often contented, or at least fatuously complacent." For the genius, Fadiman suggested, the challenge is different. "It is at this point—*precisely when he has everything* that he begins to question what he has, that is, if he is a person of complex mental organization."

Rodgers back wrote to thank Fadiman for his encouraging words but offered little by way of detailed introspection or insight into what he had experienced in treatment. "The hospital has done amazing things for me," Dick wrote, "and I am now ready for work and to pick up the threads of a very happy life. Things are clear to me now that I never quite understood with the result that I'll fare better and avoid the possibility of future trouble." Alas, he would not—not really, anyway—and in the coming years, his drinking, depression, and a range of other physical ailments that almost certainly grew out of them would take an increasing toll on his creativity.

RODGERS'S HOSPITALIZATION MEANT that he was mostly sidelined for production on the film version of *South Pacific*, which began in the summer of 1957. This property was especially dear to Oscar and Dick, and to film it they reasserted the kind of creative authority they had been compelled to surrender to 20th Century Fox on *Carousel* and *The King and I*. The production should have been creatively foolproof, filmed under the now-familiar auspices of Fox with the veteran Buddy Adler as producer. Josh Logan—by now a successful film director of such hits as *Picnic* and *Bus Stop*—held out for a percentage of the box-office receipts (more than making up for what he'd lost out on the stage version) and agreed to direct once more. Outside of Dick and Oscar themselves, no one knew *South Pacific* better or had a deeper emotional connection to the material.

But almost from the beginning, there were problems with a project that would turn out to be ill conceived and overblown.

First there was the matter of casting. Ezio Pinza was now too old for the part (and would die in May 1957), so Logan and company looked to the forty-year-old Italian film star Rossano Brazzi, who had played opposite Katharine Hepburn in the 1955 romantic drama *Summertime*. Brazzi had sung for Rodgers and Hammerstein a few years earlier, and they had thought he sounded all right. But in February 1957, Oscar wrote to Logan that he and Dick had heard a recent Italian recording by Brazzi and decided his singing voice "did not sound good at all." They resolved to dub his songs with Giorgio Tozzi, the Metropolitan Opera basso who had been cast to star with Mary Martin in a road company of *South Pacific* at the Los Angeles Civic Light Opera.

Picking a Nellie Forbush was more fraught. Logan's first choice, Elizabeth Taylor, was reduced to a nervous croak when she tried to sing for Rodgers, who closed his eyes, winced, and pronounced the idea of dubbing Nellie's voice "absolutely impossible." The fallback candidate, Doris Day, whose wholesome blond good looks and natural on-screen exuberance would have seemed to make her a natural, alienated Logan by refusing to sing for him when they met one night at a party at Rosalind Russell's house. Eventually, Logan turned to Mitzi Gaynor, a bright and brassy Hungarian American from Chicago who had held down singing and dancing roles in musicals at Fox and was filming *The Joker Is Wild* with Frank Sinatra. Everyone seemed happy with the choice—everyone, that is, but Mary Martin. Martin had recently made yet another Broadway (and television) triumph as an ageless Peter Pan; she and her husband and manager, Richard Halliday, not so quietly seethed at being passed over.

"Mary and Dick are cool to us," Oscar wrote Dick Rodgers that summer after seeing Martin in *South Pacific* on tour in Los Angeles. "We have all noticed it. Smart as they are in most things, they are blinded about this one thing. They don't realize that she is not young enough to play Nellie in the movie. This is regrettable. Age is not, in my opinion, the only deterrent. I did not like her performance, although God knows the audience did. She was 'cute'—very much as Peter Pan is! The little dry crack in voice was over-used. The comedy was well served. The emotional quality—much of it—was lost." Halliday was even colder to Mitzi Gaynor, who had recently gone to see the Civic

Light Opera's production of *South Pacific* with her husband, Jack Bean, along with Josh and Nedda Logan and Rossano Brazzi and his wife, Lydia. "He hugged Nedda, kissed Josh, introduced Lydia, shook hands with Rossano and said, 'Come on in, Mary's dying to see you,'" Gaynor would recall of Halliday. "Closed the door on Jack and me. That was it."

More familiar figures rounded out the cast. Ray Walston, who had made such a good Luther Billis in the national and London companies, reprised his role, and Juanita Hall returned as Bloody Mary, though Rodgers decreed that her vibrato was now frayed, so her songs would be dubbed by Muriel Smith, Broadway's original Carmen Jones. John Kerr, who had shot to fame in the stage and movie versions of *Tea and Sympathy*, played Cable (with *his* voice dubbed by Bill Lee). A newcomer, France Nuyen, would be Liat.

After four weeks shooting background material in Fiji, the production team headed to Kauai, Hawaii's "Garden Isle," where the lush vegetation, soaring mountains, and dramatic beaches made a natural and authentic location. The company of nearly two hundred people took four cargo ships full of material and built thousands of square feet of concrete roads and loading aprons, spending nine weeks and exposing some two hundred thousand feet of Todd-AO film, including extensive coverage of a real navy and marine training exercise that would stand in for "Operation Alligator," before returning to California to finish interiors on four soundstages at Fox.

But from the beginning, Logan made a fatal mistake. The director's manic streak sometimes led him to conclude that more was more. Just as he and Jo Mielziner had borrowed the technique of the cinematic lap-dissolve for the scene changes in the stage version of *South Pacific*, so he now sought a way to echo the mood-altering power of stage lighting for the songs in the film. His solution, in consultation with the skeptical cinematographer, Leon Shamroy, was to use color filters in front of the camera to tint the negative itself, with the result that when Nellie sings about a sky of "bright canary yellow," the scene itself turns a bilious hue. What is more, solo shots of the singers would be framed in a gauzy-edged border. At first, Logan and Shamroy shot each scene protectively, with and without filters—in much the way that Fred

Zinnemann had photographed *Oklahoma!* in both Todd-AO and CinemaScope. But soon enough, by Logan's later account, Buddy Adler decreed that any undesired color could be removed in the photographic lab in postproduction, and that the picture could be shot much more quickly and cheaply without double takes. "As he left," Logan would recall years later, "I watched him with a funny feeling that I had just had my head cut off with a sharp razor—so sharp it seemed painless."

Logan was nervous enough about the process that he asked Hammerstein for his "definite" opinion. But Hammerstein hedged. "This could be wonderful and truly blazing," he wrote Logan, but added, "On the other hand there is some merit in asking the question, why should we stick our necks out too far, when by simply not sticking them out we are going to have a smashing success."

One contemporary witness who remained highly skeptical of the color was Ken Darby, the film's associate music director. He was playing chess on location with Oscar one day when Hammerstein made a move that trapped him on the board. Darby acknowledged Hammerstein's skill but said his chess move had produced "not nearly the trap that Josh and Shamroy are building with their damned color filters." Why? Oscar wanted to know. "Because," Darby explained, "with the filters in front of the lens, the *negative* is being tinted irrevocably, and that's a mistake. If they shot the film normally, without filters . . . the laboratory back in Hollywood could add any degree of rainbow tint Shamroy or Josh or Buddy Adler thought was effective . . . and they wouldn't be trapped with a pre-printed negative. It's like . . . in recording . . . you can put reverberation *into* a track when you record it, but you can never take it out once it's in." During the next break in shooting, Hammerstein walked over to consult with Logan and Shamroy, and Darby could see vigorous hand gestures and an apparently heated discussion. Soon enough, Hammerstein returned, confessed that he had fingered Darby as the source of concern about the filters, and passed on the word that Logan had shouted, "Go back and tell Darby to keep his nose where it belongs—in the music! *I'll* shoot the picture!"

When the film opened on March 19, 1958, the critics had a field day with the filters. William Zinsser in the *New York Herald Tribune* wrote that Fox had "wrapped a fancy package—and lost the story inside," while John McCarten of the *New Yorker* allowed that the film was "full of technical razzle-dazzle, but it never comes anywhere near expressing the simple charm of the work from which it stems." *Time* was perhaps the toughest, noting that it was "almost impossible to make a bad movie out of it—but the moviemakers appear to have tried," especially with Logan's decision to "smear 'mood' all over the big scenes by shooting them through filters."

For his part, after the premiere, Logan sent Darby a terse telegram: YOU WERE RIGHT. In later years, Rodgers would say he found the movie "awful" and the use of color "atrocious." But the story was indestructible, Gaynor and Brazzi gave authentic performances, and the public made the film a worldwide blockbuster. The soundtrack album stayed in the No. 1 slot for a year. The film would make more money than all of Logan's other movies and plays put together and, because of his percentage deal, would help him survive a long career dry spell during the last two decades of his life. "Unfortunately," he would confess, "that doesn't make me feel any better about it."

IN THE SUMMER of 1957, during *South Pacific*'s production, Oscar wrote Dick, then still at Payne Whitney, discussing the possibilities for their next project. "I went over my personal income figures with my accountant," Hammerstein reported. "They must be similar to yours. The income, without a major theatrical company running for us, was staggering. God knows, we don't need money!" The movie of *South Pacific* would soon bring in even more. So, Oscar continued, "I am reminding myself and you that we have no time pressure—only our permanent desire to write something when we find something we want to write and to produce it when we damn please!"

As it happened, the next project grew out of a chance encounter in the Fox commissary between Hammerstein and his old friend Joe Fields, the eldest of the theatrical Fields siblings. Like his brother, Herbert, and sister, Dorothy, Fields was a veteran playwright—the co-author of such Broadway hits as *Gentlemen Prefer Blondes* and *Wonderful Town*—and he was now negotiating to buy the stage rights to *The Flower Drum Song*, a recently published novel by C. Y. Lee. The book

told the story of a Chinese American family in San Francisco grap-
pling with the challenges of assimilation and generational conflict.
Oscar read the novel and liked it, describing it as "sort of a Chinese
Life with Father." Dick liked it, too, and they decided to make it their
next musical. Oscar was willing to collaborate with Fields on the book,
with Fields acting as an associate producer.

Turning the novel into a dramatic musical play would require a
good deal of the trademark Hammerstein skills of compression. Lee's
book had highlighted the family patriarch, Wang Chi-yang, a traditional Chinese paterfamilias who is resistant to Americanization and is
exasperated by his elder son, Wang Ta. Ta is himself torn between three
women: May Li, an old-fashioned Chinese girl; Linda Tung, a thoroughly Americanized playgirl; and Helen Chao, a serious-minded friend
who has long been pining for him—and who eventually commits suicide when he rejects her. Hammerstein and Fields put the spotlight on
Ta and invented a new character, Sammy Fong, a slang-slinging nightclub owner who is Ta's rival for Linda's affections. (They also renamed
this character Linda Low.) The newly spelled Mei-Li became a Chinese "picture bride" whom Sammy's tradition-minded wealthy parents have arranged for him to marry—and whom Sammy attempts to
fob off on Ta instead. The elder Wang's meddling sister-in-law, Madam
Tang, was renamed Madame Liang, and the two of them became slightly
befuddled comic foils for the younger generation of Chinese Americans.
And Helen Chao, an elegant dressmaker and seamstress, would no longer kill herself when Ta jilts her; she simply disappears from the story. In
the end, Ta realizes that it is really the sweet and tender Mei-Li he loves,
and Sammy and Linda wind up together, too. It was a slender enough
reed of a plot—an old-fashioned musical comedy story about two
couples and love conquering all. No one dies, no one bares his soul,
and the prevailing weather—even in foggy San Francisco—is sunny and
fair.

By April 1958, Dick Rodgers could give Arthur Hornblow a progress report on the new show. "We have some score finished, and a
large chunk of the book is completed, too," Rodgers wrote, "but it's a
pretty difficult job, especially where casting is concerned. We want to
cast the piece as much as possible with Orientals as we both feel that

a lot of the fun would go out of it with a conventional cast made up to look Chinese. The score is less of a problem in this direction and the difficulties in writing it are actually easier to cope with." Indeed, opportunities for Asian actors had been so limited that of the principal cast, only two characters would be played by Chinese Americans: Key Luke, who had long portrayed the detective Charlie Chan's "No. 1 Son" in the movies would be the patriarch Wang Chi-yang, and Arabella Hong, an opera singer, was cast as Helen Chao. Pat Suzuki, a Japanese American nightclub performer who had been interned in World War II, would play Linda Low, making a splash with her sexy (if sexist, by modern lights) solo, "I Enjoy Being a Girl." (Years later, Rosemary Clooney would insist that the song's lines about a "brand-new hairdo" and "a pound and a half of cream upon my face" had been inspired by Temple Texas's beauty routine.) A Hawaiian-born actor, Ed Kenney, won the role of Wang Ta. Mei-Li would be played by a winsome young Japanese-born actress, Miyoshi Umeki, who had been discovered on *Arthur Godfrey's Talent Scouts* and cast by Joshua Logan in *Sayonara*, his film adaptation of James Michener's novel about interracial romance during the Korean War. She and Red Buttons had won Supporting Actor Oscars for their portrayals of doomed young lovers, and Rodgers approved of her "slight but adequate voice." For the role of Madame Liang, Dick and Oscar chose an old reliable: Juanita Hall, the original Bloody Mary. Sammy Fong would be played by a Caucasian actor, the rubber-faced comic Larry Storch.

To round out the creative team, Rodgers and Hammerstein hired a younger generation of talent: Oliver Smith, a veteran scenic designer for ballet whose work on the film of *Oklahoma!* they had admired; Carol Haney, a hot young Broadway dancer from *The Pajama Game* as choreographer; and Gene Kelly, who had not worked on the Broadway stage in years, as director. Their first choice had been Yul Brynner, but they hired Kelly in late April, a choice that Rodgers would acknowledge was "unexpected." Years later, Kelly himself would recall the assignment as "one of those things that I, I did without any other idea but, 'Hey, this is a good idea—to work with Dick Rodgers and Oscar Hammerstein and do this lovely story about the Chinese girl.' It seemed to me so lovely, and such a good change of pace."

The show's score was a mash-up of pentatonic, Oriental-sounding numbers, hot American show tunes, and nightclub pastiche songs, and not all of it was top-drawer by Rodgers and Hammerstein's standards. Oscar's lyrics for "Chop Suey," in which Madame Liang explains to Mei-Li the rich melting pot of modern American life, are a case in point:

> *Chop Suey,*
> *Chop Suey,*
> *Living here is very much like Chop Suey:*
> *Hula Hoops and nuclear war,*
> *Doctor Salk and Zsa Zsa Gabor*
> *Harry Truman, Truman Capote and Dewey—*
> *Chop Suey!*

But other efforts were striking. For Mei-Li's first-act solo, "I Am Going to Like It Here," Hammerstein used a Malay verse form called pantoum, in which the second and fourth lines of each stanza become the first and third lines of the next, creating a kind of elegant, lazy-eight effect and requiring considerable skill and economy to propel the song forward:

> *I am going to like it here.*
> *There is something about the place,*
> *An encouraging atmosphere,*
> *Like a smile on a friendly face.*
>
> *There is something about the place,*
> *So caressing and warm it is—*
> *Like a smile on a friendly face,*
> *Like a port in a storm it is!*

The preproduction period had its challenges. In July 1958, Oscar underwent a gall bladder operation and then the removal of his prostate, which resulted in some painful urological complications and left him hospitalized and out of commission for a month with the score unfinished. Rehearsals began in September, with Oscar still recuperating at home and Dick sometimes so apt to drowse off that the crew would have to turn off the houselights in the theater to avoid the indignity of having the composer be seen snoozing. The truth is, the partners were slowing down and showing their age. In mid-September, Dick wrote to Dorothy, who had gone to Europe, "Oscar has slowed up again, Joe is doing nothing, Gene is paying too much attention to details in directing, and I'm the only one who's faultless. Aren't you proud?" In fact, Kelly, long accustomed to the atomized working realities of Hollywood, was having trouble directing for the stage, and it showed. Jimmy Hammerstein would remember that Kelly sometimes seemed confused and uncertain, and as Oscar recuperated, he played his usual quiet role of backstop director behind the scenes. Kelly tried to keep up a good front and to buck up the cast. "Think of the fun we're having," he exhorted after one late-night rehearsal. Rodgers's progress reports to Dorothy continued to sound grim, with complaints that the score was coming very slowly, with not enough music for him to teach the assembled cast. "The show is horribly rough," he wrote in late September. "But the cast, badly unrehearsed, is full of charm and potential talent. Even the intrinsic book doesn't appear to be too bad for this stage."

But the pressure was definitely on. The advance sale had now topped $1 million, and the work continued as the Boston tryouts began on October 27 in anticipation of a December opening in New York. While the show was in Boston, Joe Fields suffered a heart attack. Larry Storch's characterization as Sammy Fong was not working out, and he was fired, to be replaced by Larry Blyden, Carol Haney's husband and an old college friend of Jimmy Hammerstein's. Blyden asked for a new comic number to be sung with Umeki. Dick and Oscar delivered the song, "Don't Marry Me," in under two hours, with Dick working out the tune on a piano in the ladies' lounge of the Shubert Theatre. "Dick was always fast," Gene Kelly would remember, "but so was Oscar that day." There were other problems, though. Perhaps the most beautiful song in the show, a soaring Rodgers ballad called "Love Look Away," is sung in the second act by Helen Chao, who realizes she can never have Ta and later vanishes from the plot. Haney had created a de Mille–

like second-act ballet, in which Ta is torn between his potential lovers, and winds up dancing off with Helen—a muddled affair that the theater historian Dan Dietz would acidly describe as "Ta Doesn't Quite Make Up His Mind Because Despite His Choice in the Ballet He Later Chooses Someone Else."

The company more or less held its breath and the show opened on December 1 at the St. James Theatre in New York. Critical reception was decidedly mixed. Walter Kerr in the *Herald Tribune* called it "a modest and engaging leaf from a very full album." Brooks Atkinson of the *Times* pronounced it "not one of their master works" but allowed that it was "a pleasant interlude among some most agreeable people." But Kenneth Tynan, the *New Yorker's* newly appointed critic, delivered what may have been the first-ever all-out mockery of a Rodgers and Hammerstein show. In a review titled "Tiny Chinese Minds," he noted that *Flower Drum Song* contained "more than a smidgen of pidgin," and he didn't stop there. He viewed the show as "a stale Broadway confection wrapped up in spurious Chinese trimmings." Insidiously comparing it to *The World of Suzie Wong*, Paul Osborn's recently opened Broadway adaptation of the popular novel about a British artist and Chinese prostitute in Hong Kong, Tynan concluded that "Rodgers and Hammerstein have given us what, if I had any self-restraint at all, I would refrain from describing as a world of woozy song."

And yet audiences flocked to the show, the advance sale held up, and it would run for 600 performances, with a London company opening in 1960 and clocking 508 performances of its own. The play was made into a commercially successful film in 1961—notable for being the first Hollywood movie made starring a virtually all-Asian cast. Today, *Flower Drum Song* is often considered old-fashioned, even condescending, but to a younger generation of Asian American artists the show became a kind of cultural touchstone, an affirmation that Asians could have a place in popular culture beyond slant-eyed villains and exotic half-castes. For a 2002 Broadway revival, the playwright David Henry Hwang, who had discovered the movie on television, radically overhauled the play's book and proved that the property was worthy of a respectful rehearing.

Oscar Hammerstein understood just what a bullet *Flower Drum*

Song had dodged. It was skillful but retrograde entertainment in a changing Broadway environment—an environment that only the year before had seen the gritty, pathbreaking realism of *West Side Story*, with lyrics by his protégé Stephen Sondheim. "I've had some unlucky flops in my life," Oscar told his son Jimmy a month or so after the opening. "I've had some plays that deserved to run better than they did. And then I've had some well-deserved hits. But this is the first lucky hit I've ever had." For Dick Rodgers, the show represented something else: confirmation that he had conquered his depression. "My only thought was to keep on doing what I was doing," he would recall, "and I saw nothing in the future that could stop me."

CHAPTER 10

Auf Wiedersehen

I'm not very interested in urban irony. I'm not that kind of man, I'm not very ironic, I'm not very urban. I love trees. I hope I'll never stop loving them. Trees, green meadows ... who cannot love them?

Oscar Hammerstein II

Rodgers and Hammerstein had their next project lined up well before *Flower Drum Song* was even finished. It came to them as a package deal from their most reliable star—Mary Martin—who, in the years since *South Pacific*, had not only scored a major Broadway triumph in a musical version of *Peter Pan* in 1954 but had become a celebrated television performer in a series of one-off "spectaculars." These included two live broadcasts of *Peter Pan* for NBC, a TV version of *Annie Get Your Gun* co-starring John Raitt for the same network in 1957, and *Together with Music*, a ninety-minute music and comedy special with Nöel Coward for CBS in 1955—in addition to the 1954 all-network tribute to Rodgers and Hammerstein sponsored by General Foods, for which she played hostess. Still another small-screen outing was her 1955 appearance in Thornton Wilder's *The Skin of Our Teeth*, with Helen Hayes and George Abbott. The director of that project was a former actor named Vincent J. Donehue, who by 1958 had gone to work as a story scout at Paramount Pictures and had come across a property that the studio had optioned, which he thought would be a perfect stage vehicle for Martin.

Donehue's find was *Die Trapp Familie*, a 1956 German film that told the only-slightly-too-good-to-be-true story of the famous Austrian singing group that fled Hitler on the eve of World War II and became a touring sensation in the United States and beyond with its choral performances of madrigals, motets, and folk songs. The family had eventually settled in Stowe, Vermont, where it ran a summer music camp and built a ski lodge. Donehue saw the von Trapps' story as a dramatic play, with Martin portraying the young postulant who marries a widowed naval officer with seven children. Martin and her husband, Richard Halliday, agreed, and they sought out their old colleague Leland Hayward as producing partner, and Howard Lindsay and Russel Crouse, who were to straight Broadway plays what Rodgers and Hammerstein were to musicals, to write the script. The original idea was to include authentic Baroque music from the real von Trapp family repertoire in the play. Then someone—most accounts say it was Hayward—had a bright idea: Why not commission a new song or two from Dick and Oscar to round out the tale?

That instantly struck Rodgers, who was confident of his own abilities but had no wish to compete with musicians named Bach and Mozart, as a bad idea. He and Hammerstein agreed that hybrid scores never worked. They watched the German film and liked the story, and they offered a counterproposal: they would write their own original score. The only problem was that they were committed to *Flower Drum Song* and told the Hallidays and Hayward that they could not turn to a new project for at least a year. "They came back," Rodgers would recall, "with the two most flattering words possible: 'We'll wait.' "

Meantime, there was plenty of work to do in securing the rights to the von Trapps' story—and what a story it was. Indeed, the most dramatic aspects of the family's tale were true, even if many of the particulars differed from the German film.

The real Maria Augusta Kutschera was born not in the mountains outside Salzburg but on a train between Vienna and the Tyrol in 1905. She was orphaned by age nine, and a college-age religious conversion sent her as a postulant to Nonnberg Abbey in Salzburg, where her high-spirited personality (she really did whistle on the stairs) proved a poor fit. In 1926, she was sent as a teacher to one of the von Trapp children, not all seven—as it happened, a girl named Maria who was recuperat-

ing from scarlet fever. Captain Georg von Trapp, a widower, whose
first wife was the English granddaughter of the inventor of the modern
torpedo, did use a bosun's whistle to summon his children, but he was
not a joyless martinet. Indeed, he was a dedicated music lover. He really
did break off his engagement to a princess, and though at first Maria
wasn't sure she loved him, she did realize she was not cut out to be a
nun. She and Captain von Trapp married in 1927 and would eventually have three more children. The captain was, in fact, embarrassed
by the family's professional singing career, which began under the tute-
lage not of Maria alone but also of a friendly local priest, Father Franz
Wasner. His chagrin owed at least partly to the reality that his children
were forced to become performers after he lost his fortune by prop-
ping up an Austrian friend's bank during the Depression.

Captain von Trapp opposed the Nazi annexation of Austria, and
the family was forced to flee the country in 1938, eventually settling in
America. They first struggled as a formal choir, but after taking a more
informal approach to performing, rechristening themselves the Trapp
Family Singers, they were soon crisscrossing the country in a big blue
bus, hopscotching from college campus to concert hall throughout
World War II.

Georg von Trapp died in Vermont in 1947, and his widow published her first memoir, *The Story of the Trapp Family Singers*, two
years later. Halliday and Hayward assumed that they would need her
permission to adapt the family's saga for the stage, and they set about
tracking her down. Accounts of their quest vary. In one telling, the baroness was doing missionary work in Australia, Tahiti, Samoa, and
New Guinea, and at each port of call kept ignoring letters from someone named Mary Martin, whom she'd never heard of. When her ship
at last docked in San Francisco, this story goes, Halliday was waiting,
and invited her to see Mary perform in a touring production of *Annie
Get Your Gun*. Maria was said to have loved the show but to have had
trouble envisioning Martin playing her onstage. In another account,
Martin's biographer Ronald Davis reported that Maria was finally
tracked down in her sickbed in a hospital in Innsbruck, Austria, where
she was recuperating from malaria she'd contracted in the Pacific. In
any event, the dramatic rights to her life story were no longer Maria

von Trapp's to convey: she had sold them outright to the German film company.

So Hayward and H. William Fitelson, the Hallidays' theatrical lawyer, commenced negotiations with the German company, as Paramount's option on the German film had lapsed. The film had broken box-office records in Europe, and its commercial success had made its star, Ruth Leuwerik, into the most popular female actress in German cinema. *Die Trapp Familie* (and a sequel, *Die Trapp Familie in Amerika*) belonged to the *Heimat,* or homeland, school of German filmmaking popular after World War II, a genre that focused on the pastoral pleasures of prewar German life. And while the film did not sugarcoat the rise of Nazism, it was directed by Wolfgang Liebeneiner, who as a functionary in the Nazi propaganda machine had made a film promoting the euthanasia of patients with multiple sclerosis.

One fanciful account of the sale to Halliday and Hayward has the German producers, who spoke no English, and Hayward, who spoke no German, conducting the final negotiations in Yiddish. But since Hayward was a WASP who'd been born in Nebraska, that seems unlikely. In the end, a price of $200,000 was agreed to; to raise the needed sum, the Hallidays asked NBC for an advance on Martin's multiyear contract with the network. And as a gesture of goodwill, they gave the Baroness von Trapp a three-eighths share of their own royalties from the planned show—a move that would reap unimagined benefits for the real Maria in years to come.

BY 1958, THERE were no more experienced commercial playwrights on Broadway than Howard Lindsay and Russel "Buck" Crouse, who had been working together for more than a quarter century and had produced not only the all-time longest-running nonmusical play on Broadway, *Life with Father,* but also the Pulitzer Prize–winning political satire *State of the Union*—together with the books for such musical hits as Cole Porter's *Anything Goes* and Irving Berlin's *Call Me Madam.* Lindsay's maxim—that "an audience must go away from your play feeling rewarded, or purged"—had proved highly reliable.

Now Lindsay and Crouse sketched a sixty-page outline of the proposed libretto for a show whose first working title was *The Singing Heart*. From the beginning, their script would lean heavily on the German film screenplay. Their von Trapp villa, like the one in the film, would feature a spacious living room with a curved staircase and balcony running above it. Their philosophical nuns, like the ones in the movie, would be fond of saying, "When God closes a door, he opens a window." And as in the German film, the von Trapps would make their escape wearing hiking clothes and carrying rucksacks. (Never mind that the real von Trapp family escaped Austria via a train to Italy, not by hiking over the mountains to Switzerland, which is hundreds of miles from Salzburg.) But the playwrights also made important changes. They eliminated the role of Father Wasner and invented a new character, an impresario named Max Detweiler, to launch the von Trapp children's musical career. Baroness Elsa Schraeder would take the place of "Princess Yvonne" as Captain von Trapp's fiancée, and together she and Max would serve as politically accommodating foils for the captain's proud Austrian patriotism. Lindsay and Crouse would also give all the children new names and would replace the family's eldest son, a medical school graduate named Rupert, with a teenage daughter named Liesl.

Martin herself would play a crucial role in the creation of the character of Maria, through her own improbable but enduring friendship with a Dominican nun who headed the drama department at Rosary College in River Forest, Illinois. Sister Gregory, born Katherine Eleanor Duffy and educated at the University of Iowa and Catholic University, took her vows in 1939 and was assigned to teach at Rosary (now called Dominican University) three years later. A dedicated theater buff, she traveled to New York each summer to see the latest Broadway offerings and wrote to Martin after seeing the original production of *South Pacific*, expressing particular admiration for the play's theme of racial tolerance. The sister and the star struck up a friendly correspondence, and when Sister Gregory returned to Manhattan the next year, Martin invited her backstage. "She didn't act like a nun, or the way we poor ignorant souls thought nuns acted," Martin would recall years later. "She was bouncy, enthusiastic, with an ambling walk like a good baseball player. She also had beautiful, clear skin and sparkling, snapping brown eyes. We all fell in love with her." Sister Gregory's advice when she heard about the von Trapp play was succinct: "Don't make nuns sanctimonious."

As work on the show progressed, Sister Gregory would become a trusted adviser, not just to the Hallidays but to Rodgers and Hammerstein as well. In February 1958, she wrote a five-page, single-spaced typed letter to Halliday and Martin, outlining her views of the story. "The whole purpose of life, it seems to me," she wrote, "is pin-pointed in Maria's struggle to choose between two vocations. Like every adult human being, she must find the answer to the question: 'What does God want me to do with my life? How does He wish me to spend my love?'" She took some pains to explain that, in her view, nuns (and priests) are neither afraid of love, nor incapable of sharing it, but were drawn to their vocation "because they keenly appreciate the gift of life, and have a tremendous capacity to love.

"A religious is neither afraid of sex nor disgusted with it," she added, "but rather recognizes it as one of God's greatest gifts, and therefore, in consecrating it to His service, one reflects the measure of one's love." Sister Gregory allowed that a priest might actually have a better perspective as a technical adviser, since he would have been apt to have observed nuns in varied settings, and explained that she herself would have been "terribly reticent" to try to explain her views to Lindsay and Crouse but trusted the Hallidays implicitly. It was a trust that would be repaid in kind, as many of Gregory's observations—and even a few of her verbatim lines of dialogue—made it into the final script.

That same spring of 1958, even as Hammerstein was at work on *Flower Drum Song*, his friend the conductor and arranger Robert Emmett Dolan warned him about what he saw as some of the pitfalls of the new project. "You and Dick have already done a show about a woman who becomes a governess to a man's children," Dolan pointed out. "What made that story come alive was the fact that the man was quite a man equally, if not more, interesting than the woman." Moreover, Dolan noted, he had qualms about "the very American Mary Martin playing the very Austrian Baroness."

But even more than Gertrude Lawrence had driven the train on *The King and I*, Mary Martin was the motive force behind this new show.

She was also a big part of the muscle, investing $200,000 for a 25 percent ownership share, which gave her and Halliday just the kind of say-so that Rodgers and Hammerstein preferred not to grant to their actors. The collaboration would prove tense. Richard Halliday was a semi-closeted, sexually ambiguous alcoholic, and he was a querulous and unpredictable partner, ever on the lookout for any perceived slight to his wife. (Martin herself was apparently sexually ambidextrous and reportedly maintained a long and discreet relationship with the actress Janet Gaynor.) Halliday was given to late-night drunken tirades, which endeared him to no one. "As time goes on, Halliday is going to be the one who drives everybody nuts," Russel Crouse's son, Timothy, would recall. "Halliday would have a snoot-full and he'd call my father and scream at him and my father just hated it."

Nevertheless, by January 1959, a month after the opening of *Flower Drum Song*, the four writers had begun meeting to work on the show that was now tentatively titled *Love Song*. (Howard Reinheimer warned them that this title was so common for both stage and screen works that it would be impossible to defend under copyright law. "PLEASE, PLEASE, PLEASE get a new title!" he begged.) As that winter turned to spring, the collaborators quickened the pace, meeting once in January, five times in February, six times in March. Lindsay and Crouse usually worked on the book at Lindsay's town house on East 94th Street, then would join Oscar and Dick for broader conferences at Hammerstein's house on East 63rd Street. Oscar told his son Jimmy that he was happy to be relieved of the burden of writing the book, and would have given that task up years earlier if he had found collaborators of the caliber of Lindsay and Crouse. By all accounts, it was the happiest of partnerships. "The four guys loved the material, loved working together," Timothy Crouse would recall. "I don't think it's an exaggeration to say that they loved each other."

Free to concentrate only on the lyrics, by early March Oscar had laid out the placement of songs using mostly dummy titles—except for the first one, which he reported to Crouse on March 2: "The Sound of Music." The other numbers would take shape in pretty much the order he listed them to begin with:

Sad Song
Happy Song
First Singing Lesson
Duet (Young Lovers)
Yodeling Song (to drown out thunder)
Sophisticated Love Song (Captain and Elsa)
Children's Farewell Song
Face Life: (Abbess to and With Maria)

OSCAR AND DOROTHY Hammerstein spent a month in Jamaica that winter, at a house they had recently bought there. There, in the Caribbean sun, Oscar wrote the words for "The Sound of Music" and began work on the inspirational song that would end the first act. In it, the abbess would tell Maria, who fears she is falling in love with the captain, that she must return to the von Trapp villa to find out where her heart truly lies. "Don't think that these walls shut out problems," the abbess says in an early draft. "You have to face this decision. You have to face life, wherever you are." Then the playwrights appended a cheeky parenthetical note: "(At this point she also has to face Rodgers and Hammerstein.)" What Maria had to face in the end, of course, was "Climb Ev'ry Mountain," a solemn, stirring, uplifting anthem in the mold of "You'll Never Walk Alone," in which the abbess urges Maria to discern how she wishes to spend her love, in Sister Gregory's memorable phrase.

Climb ev'ry mountain,
Ford ev'ry stream,
Follow ev'ry rainbow
Till you find your dream

More than for almost any other show, Oscar kept detailed worksheets of his draft lyrics, so it is possible to track the evolution of his thinking. For the play's opening number, in which Maria is discovered reclining in a tree, this was his early effort:

To laugh like a brook
When it trips on a stone,
To hum like the leaves on the vines
To pray in the dark
Like a nightingale
To sing through a storm like the pines
The hills give me strength
When my heart is lonely
And lost in the fog
Of a thousand fears
The hills fill my heart
With the sound of music
And my heart wants to sing,
My heart wants to sing,
My heart wants to sing
Every song that it hears.

Only after Dick wrote the accompanying tune, which required some metrical changes in the words, did Oscar settle on the final version:

To laugh like a brook
When it trips and falls
Over stones in its way,
To sing through the night
Like a lark who is learning to pray—
I go to the hills
When my heart is lonely,
I know I will hear
What I've heard before.
My heart will be blessed
With the sound of music
And I'll sing once more.

On April 4, Oscar would report that he'd finished the song—and that he'd also decided that "The Sound of Music" must be the title of the show itself—to the relief, surely, of Howard Reinheimer. By early

May, Hammerstein was working on "First Singing Lesson," and his worksheets show that he quickly came up with the idea of using the Italian syllables that marked the notes of the scale:

A word for every note
A note for every word
Da fa mi re sol fa re
What a very lovely day

Then he explored English equivalents for those musical tones, listing initial thoughts, often scratching through them with better ideas. "Doe is a very young deer" became "Doe is a female deer." "Ray" is alternatively "a light that comes from the sun," or "a very bright light from the sun," while "Me" is either "a thing I call myself" or "what I call myself." Likewise:

Sow is what you do with wheat
La will always follow so
Tea you drink when cake you eat
Now we go right back to Do

Rodgers contributed a melody that skittered appropriately up and down the scale. But it was Trude Rittmann who created the clever choral arrangement—"Do-Mi-Mi / Mi-So-So / Re-Fa-Fa / La-Ti-Ti"— that mimicked the sound of Swiss bell ringers, and that would lodge happily and permanently in the heads of listeners the world over. "You ask after the relationship between Rodgers and me," Rittmann wrote to her sister. "Pretty good as a whole (no fights whatsoever on the whole show)—rather distant. He was overjoyed about my choral arrangements—they do sound pretty gloriously."

For the nuns' song lamenting what to do about Maria's coltish, irrepressible behavior, Oscar asked Lindsay and Crouse if he could pilfer some lines of dialogue they'd written—about Maria's having curlers in her hair under her wimple. Seventeen days later, he'd finished "How Do You Solve a Problem Like Maria?"

Meantime, Sister Gregory was weighing in right along. In a letter to the Hallidays, she objected to the line about the curlers on the grounds that it "dramatically changes the image I've formed of Maria— that of an untrammeled youngster, something of a tomboy, and completely unconscious of her physical beauty and of the power that beauty could exert." She lost that battle but in the same letter won another. She suggested that Maria should not ask the abbess for permission to say she's beautiful as she prepares for her wedding to the captain, but instead should simply burst out with a spontaneous declaration, only to have the abbess cut her off: "Do not be vain, my daughter. Let me say it for you. You are indeed beautiful, my dear." Those lines would appear in the final script verbatim. Finally, Sister Gregory begged of the portrayal of the nuns: "Please don't have them giggle. Chuckle, laugh— and even explode with laughter, but *not* giggle. When laughter wells up we are inclined to either smile or go all the way and laugh wholeheartedly."

PERHAPS NO COMPOSITION in Hammerstein's whole career has a more carefully documented record of its creation than the catalogue of happiness-inducing objects and experiences that he initially called "Good Things." It was to be sung by Maria and the abbess as the postulant works up her courage to leave the abbey to care for the von Trapp children, and the two women recall a song that both had known in childhood. Critics have mocked the song for celebrating the prosaic and quotidian, but Oscar's notes show that he labored over it with the care of a master craftsman. He began the lyric in late June, making lists of pleasing phenomena: kittens, mittens, small baby's fingers, ice cream and cake, little boys who smell like boys. Then he sketched a quatrain:

Sun on a Mountain
Lights in a fountain
A crisp apple strudel
A soft yellow noodle

On other pages he listed still other pleasures, each steadily more concrete and specific: cream-colored ponies, white muslin dresses with pink satin sashes, "snowflakes that fall on my nose and my eyebrows (eyelashes)." Then a breakthrough came, with these words neatly typed on lined paper:

> *Raindrops on roses and whiskers on kittens*
> *Curling my fingers in warm woolen mittens,*
> *Riding down hill on my big brother's bike*
> *These are a few of the things that I like*

But he thought better of the last word, "like," a hard word to sing on a sustained note, a bad word with which to end a line. Instead, he scribbled beside it: "My favorite things." (Similarly, he changed "pink" satin sashes—another pinched short vowel sound—to "blue" satin sashes, a long vowel that could resonate.) Then he made a list of words that rhymed with "things," including clings, kings, rings, sings, springs, strings, slings, and wings—and wrote the phrase "Brown paper packages tied up with strings."

Then he put his lists together, each refrain ending with the signature line, "These are a few of my favorite things." But the litany still lacked meaning; it was only a list. So he gave it a final twist, scrawling in a barely legible hand:

> *When the dog bites,*
> *When the bee stings,*
> *When I'm feeling sad,*
> *I simply remember my favorite things*
> *And then I don't feel so bad!*

"This makes it a song with a reason," says Mark Horowitz, a senior music specialist in the music division of the Library of Congress, who has studied Hammerstein's work closely for years. "One thinks of favorite things—singing—when something bad happens, or one is sad. In a way, singing becomes a blessing, a relief, like a prayer."

But Hammerstein's worksheets also show that he was far from infallible, that the deftness of his final product was usually purchased at a painstaking price. Hawaii became the fiftieth state in the union on

August 21, 1959, and within days Oscar wrote these lines for "So Long, Farewell," the von Trapp children's good night song to their father's party guests:

> So long, farewell
> Auf wiedersehen, aloha

And then he proposed that Marta, the second-youngest daughter, chime in: "I hate to say the time has come to go-ha," before "she does a little hula step and exits." An object lesson for hasty writers everywhere on the merits of a second draft.

FROM THE BEGINNING, Sister Gregory had worried about how Richard Rodgers would handle the music for the convent scenes. She told the Hallidays that too much use of Gregorian chant would be tiresome, while too much Broadway razzle-dazzle would be inappropriate. It turns out that Rodgers was worried, too. "Given my lack of familiarity with liturgical music," he would recall, "as well as the fact that I was of a different faith, I had to make sure that what I wrote would sound as authentic as possible." So he did something unusual for him: He undertook some musicological research. Through a friend, he arranged to hear a special concert of liturgical music—traditional chant, together with modern religious works—at Manhattanville College in Purchase, New York.

Then, in lieu of a standard overture, he decided to open the show with an a cappella nuns' chorus at prayer with "Dixit Dominus," the Latin words for the text of Psalm 110: "The Lord said unto my Lord: Sit thou on my right hand, until I make thine enemies thy footstool." This would be followed by a ringing "Alleluia," which fades into Maria's rendition of "The Sound of Music." Sister Gregory enthusiastically approved of the final result, writing the Hallidays that she and some fellow sisters had taken the sheet music and dug into Rodgers's "Praeludium," as he called the piece, until it "really orbited and soared all over the place."

But it's at least possible that Rodgers did his research too well—and failed to credit his sources properly. In an unpublished monograph written late in her life, Agnes de Mille would insist—with the tacit backing of Trude Rittmann, who read the paper and altered other passages but not this one—that Rodgers lifted his prelude from a work by Orlando di Lasso, a sixteenth-century Franco-Flemish composer, "which he claimed without hesitation to the astonishment of musicologists."

For the rest of the score, Rodgers would write, "It was essential that we maintain not only the genuineness of the characters, but also of their background." The melodies apparently came as easily to him as always—and, indeed, they do not sound like songs written by a fifty-seven-year-old man. They evoke the spirit of childhood and play, whether in "Do-Re-Mi" or "The Lonely Goatherd," which is sung by Maria to buck up the von Trapp children during a frightening thunderstorm—the spot in the plot where "My Favorite Things" is sung in the film. And in what was by now the prevailing Rodgers and Hammerstein pattern, virtually all the songs were packed into the first act, with only two new numbers after intermission—"No Way to Stop It," a political dialectic between Max and Elsa and the Captain, and "An Ordinary Couple," a duet for Maria and the Captain when they realize they're in love. The rest of the second-act score consisted of various reprises, including the stirring final rendition of "Climb Ev'ry Mountain."

By MIDSUMMER, IT was Maria von Trapp's turn to weigh in on the draft script. On July 21, she told Dick Halliday on the telephone that the portrait of her husband was "so marshaling," and insisted, "He wasn't like this." It was a criticism she might equally have made of the German film, but this was her last chance to do anything about her story. "Please rectify my husband's picture," she begged Halliday, according to his notes of the conversation. "Now he looks like a Prussian officer." Sister Gregory, too, thought the character of Captain von Trapp was too cold and unsympathetic for the bulk of the play, making his sudden transition to a warm father at the story's end surprising and implausible. "Anything that's attractive about the Captain is told us," Sister Gregory wrote. "We never see it. Elsa tells us. The housekeeper tells us, 'He never used to be that way.' Maria tells us, when she tells the Abbess. But we never see it ourselves. I think you have to prepare the audience for the change." In the end, the change *would* be visible, and it was one that Howard Lindsay dated to the earliest story conferences; it was, he recalled, "to be music—the sound of music—that first broke the Captain's self-imposed shell." Just after Maria confronts him about his failings as a father, the Captain hears his children singing, allows himself to be moved, and joins in. If the authors never quite succeeded in making this character as multidimensional as they might have, no one could argue that they had not provided musical and emotional subtext.

Simply casting the part was proving challenging enough. From the beginning, the decision had been made not to have Martin essay an Austrian accent, but the producers did wonder if it might not make sense to cast a Mittel-European actor as her husband. A number of actors were considered, including—by his later account—Christopher Plummer, who was not yet quite thirty years old. (Martin would turn forty-six just after the play opened.) The producers auditioned the Hollywood actor Leif Erickson (who despite his Scandinavian-sounding name had been born William Anderson, in Alameda, California), but he didn't seem quite right. Eventually they saw Theodore Bikel, a thirty-five-year-old Vienna-born actor and singer whose Jewish family had fled Austria for Palestine in 1938. Bikel was shooting a movie in the Netherlands, but Halliday and Hayward flew him to New York for an audition. He sang Frank Loesser's "My Time of Day" from *Guys and Dolls*, but then the producers asked him to sing a folk song, and he played his own guitar. "And apparently," Bikel would remember, "while all this was happening, Mary Martin leaned forward, tapped Dick Rodgers on the shoulder and said, 'We don't have to look any further, do we?' " He won the part.

As it happened, Bikel had been a friend of Martin's son, Larry Hagman, when Hagman was stationed in London with the US Air Force. Bikel viewed Martin as a complete professional and would find it tough to work with her in only one way. "She was kept in a glass bowl, wrapped in cotton, as it were," he would remember. "She was so guarded and taken care of, surrounded by blow-softening material." To make up for the difference in their ages, Bikel was sent to the society hairdresser Kenneth Battelle, known professionally as "Mr. Kenneth," to have a single gray streak dyed in his hair. The treatment would be repeated every couple of weeks during his entire run in the part.

Casting the seven children posed yet another challenge. In the end, Vincent Donehue would recall, more than three hundred youngsters auditioned, before a group of unknowns were chosen. "They had to emanate health and joy and, of course, they had to sing," Donehue said. In the end, Donehue chose well enough. The children would be jointly nominated for a Tony Award for their performances (in the best featured *actress* category, as it happened).

For her part, Martin trained like a fighter in that summer of 1959—literally slugging a punching bag while singing aloud in order to strengthen her abdominal muscles under the lash of her vocal coach, William Herman. She also did Pilates exercises—then little known to the general public, but already favored by dancers—to strengthen her core and improve stamina and balance. And she spent two weeks with Maria von Trapp in Stowe, where the baroness gave her the one room in the family lodge with an en suite bathroom. Martin not only learned how to cross herself and kneel properly, but posed for a series of striking black-and-white pictures for the noted *Life* magazine photographer Toni Frissell, running through the Vermont hills in a dirndl dress in what amounted to priceless advance publicity for the show.

REHEARSALS BEGAN ON the morning of September 1 at the Lunt-Fontanne Theatre, and Oscar approached the task with the sangfroid of an old hand. "I think this will be the 46th time I have sat down with a cast to a first reading of a play I have written—not counting plays we have produced or foreign companies of plays," he wrote his old friend and onetime collaborator Harry Ruby. "I guess this makes me a veteran. I feel like one too; otherwise I would not be calm enough to be dictating letters this morning." But barely two weeks later, Hammerstein's natural optimism would be tested as never before. On September 16, he went for a checkup with his regular doctor, Benjamin H. Kean, who had taken over Oscar's care when Harold Hyman retired. After the exam, Kean pronounced Hammerstein in fine health but asked if he had anything he wanted to discuss. At first, Oscar said no, but as he was leaving, he ducked his head back in the door to say, "You know, I've been awakening in the middle of the night hungry. I take a glass of milk and then it's fine." Kean thought for a moment, then chased Oscar out onto Park Avenue to say that he'd like to run tests for an ulcer, just to be on the safe side.

Oscar walked the few blocks home and as he came through the door of the town house on East 63rd Street, he gave rare voice to his frustrations with Dick. "God damn it!" he said. "I have an ulcer. That son-of-a-bitch has done it to me." But it wasn't an ulcer. The tests found stomach cancer, and surgery was promptly scheduled for September 19 at New York Hospital. Lindsay and Crouse sent Hammerstein a cheery note, urging him not to worry and borrowing a line from his love duet for young Liesl and her suitor, Rolf: "Dear Oscar: We are sixty, going on seventy, and you can depend on us. Get well soon. Love, Howard and Buck."

On the day before the surgery, with the extent of his condition still a secret, Oscar met Mary Martin at the Lunt-Fontanne's stage door with a folded piece of paper, explaining that it contained some lines for the show, though he wasn't yet sure where they would go. "Don't look at it now," he told her. She went to her dressing room, where Rodgers gave her the bad news and said they'd all just have to do their best. When she unfolded Oscar's piece of paper, Martin saw the words he had originally written as a verse for "Climb Ev'ry Mountain" and that would now introduce Maria's second-act reprise of "Sixteen Going on Seventeen," in which the new stepmother reassures Liesl about the joys of true love.

> A bell is no bell till you ring it,
> A song is no song till you sing it,
> And love in your heart wasn't put there to stay—
> Love isn't love
> Till you give it away . . .

To the end of her life, Martin would treasure the words.

The postoperative prognosis was grim; the cancer was Stage IV, meaning that it had spread. The surgeon, Dr. Frank Glenn, had removed three-quarters of Oscar's stomach and advised Dorothy that her husband would be dead in six months to a year. He had taken her aside to tell her the news, and when the children, waiting nearby, saw her slump, they knew the word was bad. But when Oscar asked Dorothy what the doctors had said, she finessed the question, answering, "They just cut it all out," and he did not press her. Hammerstein would remain in the hospital until October 4, and then spend another ten days recuperating at home.

Meantime, *The Sound of Music* was coming together, but there was work to be done. Years later, Mary Martin would recall the demands of her part. "The treatment had to be very skillful, totally controlled. It was one of the most disciplined shows I ever did. You could never do a kidding thing, never play it broadly. I had to remember the character always, keep a tight rein on my emotions and my performance." It was also a workout: she appeared in eighteen of the show's nineteen scenes; had fourteen costume changes, sang ten times, and climbed flights of stairs on six occasions. Halliday put a pedometer on his wife at one point and calculated that she walked—all but ran, really—three miles per performance.

Martin was also receiving steady reassurance from an important source. She and Halliday had sent Sister Gregory the music for "Climb Ev'ry Mountain" and on September 17, she wrote to tell them, "It's a beautiful song and drove me to the Chapel," adding, "(Relax chums, I'm sure it will not effect [*sic*] your audiences in the same way)." Rather, she explained, the song had moved her to prayers of gratitude for all those who find their true vocation, and she marveled that she had found her own. "How from all the gay, glittering and gilded avenues that beckoned I found the secluded by-way that has brought such unbelievable happiness for over twenty years, only God knows."

On September 25, while Oscar was still in the hospital, the scenery was hauled to New Haven, for the opening and weeklong run beginning October 3. It was in New Haven that the creative team—minus Hammerstein, of course—decided that the second-act appearance of Nazis in brown shirts and swastika armbands was too heavy-handed. Henceforth, they would mostly be heard offstage, and would wear blue uniforms or light brown shirts when they did appear, and would say only "Heil!" not "Heil, Hitler!"—a softening choice that Theodore Bikel did not approve of but had no power to influence. It's worth noting that the mere appearance of any Nazi character was enough of a rarity in *any* Broadway play in 1959 that the producers' qualms were perhaps understandable.

It was also in New Haven that Dick Rodgers and his collaborators decided that the character of the Captain needed a stronger moment in the second act to underline his growing warmth—and to take advantage of the skill with the folk guitar that had won Bikel the part in the first place. Rodgers worked out a simple tune to await words from Oscar when he was well enough to work.

The Boston opening was Tuesday, October 13, and the critics were decidedly mixed. Elliot Norton, as always the most influential of the Boston reviewers, complained about the "silliness, stiffness and corny operetta falseness of the script," but Elinor Hughes of the *Herald* called it "a wonderful addition to this or any season," and audiences loved the show from the start. So did Oscar Hammerstein, when he first saw it a few days into the Boston run. He sat in a box with Dorothy, who found Russel Crouse at intermission. "'I have only seen Oscar'—Poppy, she called him—'cry once in my whole married life . . . and he's been crying,'" Crouse's wife, Anna, would recall years later. Backstage, after the show, as she watched Oscar give the cast meticulous and supportive notes on their performance, it was Dorothy Hammerstein's turn to cry.

With the dispatch that the situation required, Oscar set to work on the lyrics for the Captain's new song, which was to feature a hardy Alpine flower that was a symbol of Austrian pride. It is a member of the daisy family—its Latin name, as Oscar noted, is *Leontopodium alpinum*—and its common name is edelweiss. In his notes sketched out on a small pad, Oscar wrote:

"No hothouse flower"
"A toughie"
"Not easily licked by weather, storm, wind or snow"
"A tiny white flower that can mean so much"
"All that is good in a great country."

One early draft contained these lines:

> *Edelweiss, edelweiss*
> *I'll come back and I'll find you.*
> *Small and white*
> *Clean and bright*
> *On the mountain behind you . . .*

And, doubtless mindful of his own precarious situation, Oscar's early idea for the bridge went like this:

> *Look to your lover and hold him tight*
> *While your health you're keeping.*

In a room furnished with a piano at the Ritz-Carlton, Dick and Oscar worked out the final version, with its simple last line—"Bless my homeland forever"—and the song went into the show. It clicked immediately, and Bikel would recall that a fan once stopped him at the stage door to say, "I love that Edelweiss," adding, "Of course I have known it for a long time, but only in German." It was the last lyric Oscar ever wrote, his 1,589th.

Meantime, Rodgers had had his fill of the querulous Richard Halliday. One of Halliday's early suggestions had been to have Maria catch her bloomers on the tree in her opening number. Dick and Oscar rejected the notion, infuriating him. "You know what's wrong with you guys?" Halliday demanded. "All *you* care about is the *show*!" In Boston, Rodgers finally let Halliday have it. Just what prompted the blowup is unclear, but the result was that the composer didn't speak to either his co-producer or his star for a few days, and at the Boston opening night cast party at the Ritz, the Hallidays and the Rodgerses sat on opposite sides of the room, incommunicado.

THE NEW YORK opening was Monday, November 16, and the advance sales had climbed to $2.3 million. The first-night audience was the usual glittering gang: Helen Hayes, Claudette Colbert, Ethel Merman, Marlene Dietrich, Katharine Cornell, Gypsy Rose Lee, and, in a green satin gown—a gift from Mary Martin—Maria von Trapp herself. Once again, as they had been with *South Pacific*, Dick and Oscar were confident enough to book the St. Regis Roof for the after-show party. This time, however, when the reviews came in, the evening was less than enchanted. The good news: Brooks Atkinson in the *Times* judged that "Mr. Rodgers has not written with such freshness of style since *The King and I*. Mr. Hammerstein has contributed lyrics that also have the sentiment and dexterity of his best work." The *New York Post* wrote that "the score and the lyrics are particularly rich in freshness and imagination," and *Variety* agreed: ". . . Rodgers has composed the sort of richly melodious score for which he's famous, and . . . Hammerstein has provided some of his most graceful lyrics."

But the bad news was worse, and it preponderated. Atkinson found it "disappointing to see the American musical stage succumbing to the clichés of operetta" and complained that "the revolution of the Forties and Fifties has lost its fire." Walter Kerr of the *Herald Tribune* called the show "not only too sweet for words but almost too sweet for music." And Kenneth Tynan's verdict was the most acid of all: "To sum up un-controversially, it is a show for children of all ages, from six to about eleven and a half."

The Hammersteins attended the opening with Herbert Mayes, the editor of *McCall's* magazine, and his wife, who were their upstairs tenants in the top-floor apartment at 10 East 63rd Street. Their homecoming that night was a glum one. "Herb told me later that, as they were going up in the elevator, they heard Oscar give a heartfelt sigh of despair," Anna Crouse would recall. "It just broke my heart."

Rodgers and Hammerstein—and Lindsay and Crouse—were paying the price of their long success. Broadway was no longer their oyster, and if *The Sound of Music* seemed out of step and old-fashioned, it was because it suffered by comparison with its contemporary competition: *Fiorello!*, a sharp satire of New York politics that would win the Pulitzer Prize for Drama; *Gypsy*, the gritty story of the stripper Gypsy Rose Lee's indomitable stage mother (with lyrics by Stephen Sondheim and

Ethel Merman in the lead); and *Once Upon a Mattress*, a cheeky twist on "The Princess and the Pea" with fetching music by Rodgers's own daughter, Mary.

But the next night, the producers and authors were back at the Lunt-Fontanne, and Oscar watched the audience closely as always. By intermission, he assured his collaborators that the Big Black Giant had delivered an altogether different verdict. "Make no mistake about it!" he insisted, Anna Crouse remembered. "This is a hit. . . . Just look and listen to that audience! They couldn't care less about the reviews. I promise you, this is a smash hit!" Oscar—and the people—were right. The show would run for three and a half years on Broadway—1,443 performances—and nearly twice as long in London, where it set a new record as the West End's longest-running musical.

Rodgers and Hammerstein were sensitive to the criticism, which differed so sharply from the genuine popular embrace. They were doubt-less aware that *The Sound of Music* would be their last show and would weigh heavily on their reputations. "Anyone who can't, on occasion, be sentimental about children, home or nature is sadly maladjusted," Rodgers complained. But Dick and Oscar needn't have worried. Just twelve days after the opening, the publisher Max Schuster wrote them a note that has stood the test of time. "As in all your other shared creations," Schuster said, "the whole is greater than the sum of the parts. It adds up. It sings. It parses in the grammar of the heart."

COLUMBIA RECORDS RECORDED the cast album on the Sunday after the opening, as was the usual practice, and the album would occupy the No. 1 spot on the Billboard charts for four months—and remain a bestseller for 276 weeks, almost long enough to share space with the soundtrack of the film version, which would itself stay on the charts for another four and a half years. Taken together, those record sales made *The Sound of Music* the best-selling Broadway score of all time.

The Hallidays' profits from the show were so staggering that their accountant eventually persuaded them (in that era of high marginal tax rates) to sell their 25 percent stake for a onetime capital gain—a decision that deprived them of participation in what would prove to be the vast profits from the film version. Those rights were eventually purchased by 20th Century Fox, whose president, Spyros Skouras, was in the audience opening night, seated next to the Hollywood agent Irving "Swifty" Lazar. Lazar wound up selling Fox the film rights for a cool $1.25 million, but also added a provision that no one thought mattered much at the time: the stage producers would receive 10 percent of the gross box-office receipts after the movie made a profit of $12 million. After all, what movie had ever made such a profit? Rodgers and Hammerstein and Lindsay and Crouse—and their heirs—would have reason to thank Lazar beyond their wildest imaginings in years to come.

As *The Sound of Music* settled in for its long run, there were some amusing moments. When some nuns came backstage to see Martin after one performance, the dance director, Joe Layton, mistook them for actresses in the chorus. "God damnit!" he shouted. "You girls know you're not supposed to stand out here in the hall in your goddamned costumes. Now get back to your dressing room right this minute and get them off." He was suitably horrified when his mistake was pointed out. For her part, Mary Martin was terribly nearsighted but had always resisted wearing contact lenses. When she finally broke down and got a pair, Bikel noticed that her performance suddenly came alive. When he asked her why, she sheepishly confessed that she could really see him for the first time. When a young Jon Voight joined the company as a replacement Rolf (and fell in love with and married his Liesl, Lauri Peters), he was astounded at how fresh Martin kept her part, after playing it over and over. And having been warned in no uncertain terms that he should never upstage the star, Voight was astounded, too, at how effortlessly Martin could still upstage others. Martin would win the Tony Award for Best Actress for her performance, beating out Ethel Merman's Mama Rose in *Gypsy*. But Merman was philosophical, famously telling the producer Cheryl Crawford, "How are you going to buck a nun?"

Barely a month after the show's opening, on December 18, 1959, Dick Rodgers could write to Oscar, who had flown to Jamaica with Dorothy for a rest, that business was getting steadily better as the songs became more popular from radio and record play and sheet music sales. "Do-Re-Mi" alone had sold eighty-five hundred sheet music copies that week. "It is increasingly apparent that we have something very big here and that's all fine," Rodgers wrote.

The Hammersteins' children joined them in Jamaica for Christmas, and Oscar felt well enough to begin work on a proposed film remake of *State Fair* for Fox, and on a project that sparked greater personal passion: a television adaptation of *Allegro* in which he would at last try to work out the problems that had dogged the second act. Hammerstein sketched an outline that would borrow from some of Josh Logan's long-ago suggestions for improving the book. He would revise the character of Jennie to make her more sympathetic and reduce the antagonism between her and Joe Taylor Jr.'s mother. He would eliminate Marjorie Taylor's death but would have Joe and Jennie, their marriage on the rocks, get word that Joe's father is dying. In the end, Joe and Jennie would reconcile, and he would decide to stay in Chicago but practice medicine the way his father had. The teleplay would open with the title song before shifting to Joe Jr.'s birth. Oscar had big ambitions for the casting, listing Rock Hudson and Pat Boone as options for Joe Jr.

The Hammersteins even felt up to joining Dick and Dorothy Rodgers in London in March 1960 for the West End opening of *Flower Drum Song*. On his return to the states in April, Oscar wrote Dick, who was still in England, with some firm casting ideas about any future film of *The Sound of Music*. He reported that both Jack Warner and Universal were interested in the movie rights but said that if the Universal offer should come with Doris Day attached to play Maria, he would be "very leery" about that idea.

"I realize that right now she is one of the hottest stars on the screen," Oscar wrote. "But we are not producing the picture right now. I think she is a little too old to play the part now, and how old she will be before we are able to release it is more than anyone can say." Having countenanced the forty-six-year-old Mary Martin as the original Maria, he added, "I think we should be adamant about having nothing but young girls play the part from now on, in pictures, in London, on the road."

By early summer, as he felt worse and grew weaker, Oscar told Dorothy he knew that the cancer surgery had not cured him and he

realized that he was going to die. He took steps to put his affairs in
order and to make his farewells. On July 12, his sixty-fifth birthday, he
wrote a journal entry that he hoped might serve as the start of the
memoir he had long promised his son Billy he would one day write.

"This is the accepted age of retirement," he wrote.

> I do not want to retire, am in no mood to retire. This is considered a
> good time to come to a stop. Perhaps it is, but not for me. . . . I make
> no room to die with my boots on. Some day I may leave the theatre. But
> I couldn't walk out suddenly; I would have to linger a while and take a
> few last looks. I would have to blow a few fond kisses as I edged towards
> the stage door. I would have to look around and sigh, and remember a
> few things, a few people—No, many things, many people.

He played a game of tennis with Jimmy, who was determined not to
concede any weakness in his father by holding back his own volleys,
but when they were through, Oscar announced that he couldn't remember when he'd been so tired. From then on, everyone at Highland Farm
played croquet instead. Hammerstein was unsentimental with his own
children to the last.

"Goddamnit!" he burst out one day when Jimmy started crying.
"I'm the one who's dying, not you." The younger Hammerstein sensed
that it was hard for his father to acknowledge the end. "I've had a very
happy childhood," Hammerstein told his son. "I've had a good time as
a young man. And I've had a terrific middle age. The only thing that I'm
disappointed in is that I was looking forward to having a really good
old age, too." Oscar summoned the family for a lunch at the 63rd Street
town house and passed out studio portraits of himself. Stephen Sondheim asked Hammerstein to autograph his copy. Oscar thought for a
moment, before allowing himself a slight smile and inscribing a tender
message that nodded to the verse of "Getting to Know You." ("It's a
very ancient saying, but a true and honest thought, that if you become
a teacher, by your pupils you'll be taught.") "For Stevie," Hammerstein
wrote. "My friend and teacher." Sondheim had trouble making it
through the meal.

One day that summer, Oscar asked Dick to lunch in the Oak Room of the Plaza Hotel, one of their regular meeting spots. He urged Rodgers to find a new and younger collaborator to work with when he was gone. He made it clear that he intended to go home to Doylestown to die. "We discussed many things that day," Rodgers would recall, "two somber, middle-aged men sitting in a crowded restaurant talking unemotionally of the imminent death of one and the need for the other to keep going." At one point, a man who'd been sitting nearby came and asked the partners to autograph his menu. He told them he couldn't imagine why they looked so sad; they were so successful, they shouldn't have a worry in the world.

As late as July, Oscar was still getting suggestions for new shows. Robert Kitchen, a reader of the *New Yorker* from Philadelphia, wrote to commend a short story that the magazine had recently published, "The Light in the Piazza" by Elizabeth Spencer. "It would be difficult, I believe, for us to adapt it as a musical play," Oscar replied. "But it is a tempter."

On August 15, Dick wrote to Jerry Whyte, who had worked for Rodgers and Hammerstein since *Oklahoma!* as a stage manager, touring company director, and all-around major domo, to say that Oscar was "now in no condition to see anybody or at any rate he doesn't wish to." "I understand this perfectly well," Rodgers went on. "He's lost weight terrifically and doesn't want anyone to see him in this condition or be sympathized with. Frankly, I have no desire to see him myself. There is nothing I can do and I am not constituted so that I wish to deliver myself a beating if it can be avoided." There was no way of knowing how long it might be until the end, Dick added. "We do know that he has no pain whatsoever and is quite heavily drugged nearly all the time so that he is neither too worried about himself nor too unhappy. How rugged it is for the rest of us I leave to your imagination."

On Oscar's last office visit to Benjamin Kean, his doctor urged him to reconsider and take some radiation therapy to stave off the cancer even a bit longer. The next day, Hammerstein told him, "Ben, I have considered very carefully your recommendation. In this showdown I must really decide whether to die, possibly a little later, in the hospital, or on Dorothy's pillow. I'm really lucky and never knew how much until now."

As the days wore on, Oscar lay in his second-floor bedroom at the farm, eating hardly anything and sipping essence of sarsaparilla. Dorothy stayed by his side for hours. On the evening of Monday, August 22, Harold Hyman, who continued to check in on his old friend and former patient, told Dorothy to take a break and entered the bedroom only to find Oscar murmuring the names of some of his beloved Yankees, "Ruth . . . Gehrig . . . Rizzuto," just as he had muttered the names of baseball heroes more than thirty years earlier during the breakdown before he decided to marry Dorothy. A short time later, his breathing eased by an extra dose of morphine, Oscar died. Hyman broke the news to the family.

Less than forty-eight hours later, there was a small funeral service in a chapel at Ferncliff Cemetery in Hartsdale, New York, where Oscar's remains were to be cremated. Harold Hyman read from *Leaves of Grass*. The Reverend Donald Szantho Harrington, a Unitarian minister who had been active with Oscar in the United World Federalists, paraphrased Saint Paul: "In this life we have three great lasting qualities—faith, hope and love. But the greatest of them is love." Howard Lindsay delivered the eulogy.

"No man can work as long as Oscar did in a public medium without making a complete disclosure of himself," Lindsay said. "So he is there, undisguised, in the lyrics he wrote. There you find his basic qualities: simplicity, integrity and compassion. He was so simple and so honest that it never would have occurred to him to have what Winston Churchill once called 'the craven fear of being great.' As certain as one can be about a contemporary, I am certain that Oscar Hammerstein had greatness."

Condolence letters flooded in to Dorothy from every corner of show business and every sphere of Oscar's life—from Johnny Green, and Jose Ferrer and Rosemary Clooney in Hollywood; from Nelson Rockefeller and Vincent Sardi Jr. in New York; from Richard Nixon, Pearl Buck, Harpo Marx, Harold Prince, Joan Crawford, John Steinbeck, Noël Coward, and Maria Augusta von Trapp. Moss Hart assured Oscar's widow, "I would sometimes see him looking across the room at you at a party—sometimes begging to be rescued, sometimes just resting his eyes on you with love and pride." Edna Ferber's note was typically brisk. "I shan't pretend to you that I think it's all for the best, and that sort of nonsense," she wrote. "His going is wasteful and utterly stupid, and a deprivation to the entire world." But it may have been Agnes de Mille, who called Oscar "a gentleman in a profession where there were few enough," who saw Hammerstein's loss—and his legacy—most clearly. "What a heritage he left us! How bonny and wise, how darling and deft, how inescapable so many of his lyrics!" she wrote. "Girls and boys are going to talk with his words, with his point of view, long hence, and may perhaps not be aware whom they quote. He will be in the air they breathe."

On September 1, at 8:57 p.m., by order of Mayor Robert F. Wagner, the lights of the Broadway theater district were extinguished in Oscar's honor, and a bugler sounded taps.

EXPECTED THOUGH IT was, Oscar's death hit Dick Rodgers like a hammer blow. The *World-Telegram & Sun* described him as "near collapse from grief," quoting an unnamed spokesman as saying, "The guy is falling apart." Mutual friends confided to Dick that Oscar had worried about what would happen to his partner—and had wondered, too, right up to the end, just what Rodgers really thought of him. "He had come to the conclusion that he did not again want to go through the strain of doing another show and he was so deeply concerned as to how you would take this decision," the producer Eddie Knopf wrote Rodgers in early September. "Although Oscar was full of sentiment he so rarely became sentimental in his discussion of human relationships. But on that day, Dick, he was deeply sentimental about you. He told me that of all the composers he had ever worked with, you had given him so much more than anyone. And he was not speaking only of music. He told me that somehow you had the ability to bring out the best that was in him. And he wondered whether he'd done the same for you, and would his unwillingness to continue writing affect you adversely."

With uncanny acuity, Sister Gregory wrote to Dick surmising that his surface reaction to Oscar's death surely only began to reflect his deepest feelings. "I would guess that it was a little easier for him to release his inner warmth than for you," the nun wrote. "But yours is reflected with equal strength in your work and in your face." Indeed, Dick's letters to even close friends in those weeks reflect a grim, unyielding stoicism. "There isn't very much to say beyond the things that have been written because they are all true," he told the playwright Sam Behrman. "It's been a difficult time, but I suppose nearly everything is capable of being survived." To Jan Clayton, he allowed, "I suppose patience is a lesson we must all learn but it's damn tough, isn't it?"

For the next year, Rodgers would tell people, "I am permanently grieved." But, at the age of only fifty-eight, he would also recall, "I could not imagine spending the rest of my days reliving past glories and withdrawing from the vital, exciting world that I loved." So he walked through the storm, with his chin up high—and for most of the next two decades, he would struggle to prove, to the world and to himself, that his best days were not behind him.

CHAPTER 11

Walking Alone

I'm on a new road, whether it's with Joe Doaks as a collaborator, or alone. This has got to be a third career, or I've got to die.

Richard Rodgers

Oscar Hammerstein's death left Richard Rodgers bereft, perhaps all the more so because it forced him to confront the dynamics of their professional collaboration and their personal relationship in ways that both had largely avoided for eighteen years. In the last year of his life, Oscar had asked Stephen Sondheim, "What do you think of Dick?" When Sondheim wondered why he'd inquired, Hammerstein replied, "Because I don't know him at all. We've worked together all these years and I don't really know him." Hammerstein found Rodgers emotionally opaque. "Dick's life is the office or the box office or the theater. I just don't understand." For his part, Rodgers would confess to Hammerstein's biographer Hugh Fordin years later, "I was very fond of him— very fond of him—and I never did find out whether he liked me or not. To this day I don't know." Late in their partnership, Rodgers learned that the Hammersteins were planning a trip to Jamaica only by over-hearing word of it in the office one day. Later, Oscar and Dorothy invited the Rodgerses to join them, but the damage had been done. "I let it brush over but it bothered me," Rodgers acknowledged. "It was all very placid. For the most part, the shows were successful so we didn't fight about them."

But whatever private frustrations the partners had papered over to preserve their well-oiled machine, Dick now found himself alone, and that was far worse. As it happened, he at least had a short-term project to divert him: *The Valiant Years*, a documentary for ABC Television based on the memoirs of Winston Churchill. In September 1960, Rodgers wrote to Edna Ferber that he had taken up the work with almost a hunger, adding, "I don't think we need a psychologist to tell us where this hunger comes from." Rodgers wrote incidental music for the twenty-seven episodes that aired that fall and through the spring of 1961, with Richard Burton reading Churchill's words. Dick won an Emmy for his work.

Finding a new collaborator, and a show he could sink his teeth into, was a bigger challenge. "With Oscar gone it was simply too much to expect that I could adjust to anyone else without a lengthy interval between," Rodgers would recall, adding: "Under the circumstances, there was only one logical path: I had to try to write my own lyrics." In fact, Rodgers had sometimes been forced to come up with lyrics on his own when Larry Hart was AWOL, and in the years since Hart's death had sometimes been asked to provide updated lines for revivals of their shows. His first efforts—not memorable—were for an undistinguished remake of *State Fair* that Fox had cooked up for Ann-Margret and Pat Boone, shifting the story's locale from Iowa to Texas and losing most of its charm in the process. The five new songs Rodgers wrote for the film included "More Than Just a Friend," for Abel Frake to sing to his champion boar. But soon enough, Rodgers had a better idea, one all his own.

It came one evening in April 1961, while he was watching *The Jack Paar Show* on NBC. Parr's guests that night included Diahann Carroll, a stunning young black actress and singer whom Rodgers had first noticed in Harold Arlen and Truman Capote's Broadway musical, *House of Flowers*, in 1954. He had considered Carroll for the lead in *Flower Drum Song* but could not contrive how to make her look Asian enough. Now it struck Rodgers that Carroll was chic enough to have stepped off the cover of any fashion magazine. With the civil rights movement gathering steam across the country, why not cast her as a sophisticated woman of the world? "She would not represent a cause or be a symbol of her race," Rodgers would remember, "but a believable human being, very much a part of a stratum of society that the theatre thus far had never considered for a black actress."

Thus inspired, Rodgers invited Carroll for a drink the next day, to discuss the idea. He quickly enlisted Samuel Taylor, whose play *The Happy Time* had been produced by Rodgers and Hammerstein in 1950, to devise a book. Taylor's story, titled *No Strings*, would center on the characters of Barbara Woodruff, an American fashion model working in Paris, and David Jordan (to be played by Richard Kiley), a Pulitzer Prize–winning American novelist who has gone to live a dissolute expatriate's life in France. The couple meet, fall in love, but part in the end because Jordan realizes he must return to his roots in Maine if he is ever to write again, and a successful interracial marriage seems as impossible to him as it had to Lieutenant Joe Cable twelve years earlier. That was a debatable proposition by 1961, and Carroll and Kiley debated it vigorously with Taylor and Rodgers: Why couldn't the lovers end up together? The compromise—which Carroll would later call "absolutely brilliant"—was to end the play just as it had begun, with the two lead characters singing onstage, each unaware of the other's presence, "making everything that came in between a fantasy, a love story that may or may not actually have happened."

The sinuous song that Rodgers wrote for the opening and closing numbers, "The Sweetest Sounds," is a remarkable statement of optimism and confidence for a man at his stage in life. It begins in a minor key and ends exultantly in major:

> *The sweetest sounds I'll ever hear*
> *Are still inside my head.*
> *The kindest words I'll ever know.*
> *Are waiting to be said.*
> *The most entrancing sight of all*
> *Is yet for me to see.*
> *And the dearest love in all the world*
> *Is waiting somewhere for me,*
> *Is waiting somewhere, somewhere for me . . .*

Rodgers's own take on his new lyricist was sly: "I was always there when I wanted me." More seriously, he viewed the work as "occupational therapy," and he would confess that "as any songwriter will tell you, writing lyrics is more demanding than writing music," because music is "created with broad strokes on a large canvas, whereas lyrics are tiny mosaics that must be painstakingly cut and fitted into a frame." He worked several ways, sometimes writing snippets of words first and then music, and sometimes the reverse. The one method he never used was the one he'd most relied on with Hammerstein: he never wrote a complete lyric and then set it to music. And in keeping with the show's title and theme—*No Strings*—Rodgers also settled on another novelty: there would be no orchestra in the pit; the musicians would appear onstage and in the wings, and except for a harp there would be no stringed instruments at all—only brass, woodwinds, and percussion, lending the show the cool feel of a jazz ensemble.

If the tunes still came as easily as ever, Rodgers was defensive about the show's book. In a letter in October 1961 to his son-in-law Daniel Melnick, who had apparently suggested a deeper development of the main characters' motivations, Rodgers cited one of the nation's leading authorities on civil rights law in his own defense. "Thurgood Marshall is wildly enthusiastic about the substance and development of the play," Dick wrote. "He said to me, 'Anyone who tries to solve this problem is crazy. Only time and contact will provide the solution.' I myself feel strongly that we must not try to resolve the situation. We must leave the girl more or less as we found her, relieved to be away from discrimination and poverty, unwilling to return to the discomfort she knew as a child. The man, through sleeping with the girl, has developed the real set of male organs and these finally extend to his work and his resolve. I think this is more than enough for any play to say, regardless of words or music."

In two months of out-of-town tryouts—in Detroit, Toronto, Cleveland, and New Haven—Diahann Carroll would be more impressed with Rodgers's talent than she was with his character. She would never forget the seeming delight with which he informed her that there would be no opening night party for the cast in Detroit because the would-be hostess, a friend of his, had declined to invite black guests to her home. Rodgers did not seem bothered by his friend's racism, Carroll would recall. "It only confirmed that he accomplished what he set out to accomplish, which was to present this glamorous, very desirable black woman in a vehicle that would startle the white community," she remembered. Rodgers went to the friend's house himself, while Carroll held a party for the cast in a restaurant across the street from the theater. "As time passed, I came to the conclusion that he was really incapable of hearing someone's point of view without regarding that person as a potential adversary and his frequent insensitivity was appalling."

No Strings opened in New York on March 15, 1962, and most critics found the book underwhelming. "The musical is a show in which the actors never have to go anywhere," wrote Walter Kerr. "Everything comes to them. Everything except an idea." But Howard Taubman of the *Times* declared that "Rodgers has lost neither his zest nor his art." The show was a solid hit, clocking 580 performances and producing a national tour and a London production. Rodgers also won the Tony Award for Best Original Score, and Carroll won for Best Actress in a Musical. "But most important to me," Rodgers would recall, "was the assurance it gave me that I could pick up the pieces of my career and start all over again with new people and new techniques."

IT IS A paradox that while Rodgers had almost nothing to do with the next project that came his way, it would have more to do—for better or worse—with cementing his and Hammerstein's worldwide reputations than anything else he ever did: the film version of *The Sound of Music*.

Twentieth Century Fox had owned the movie rights since shortly after the Broadway opening, but the sale contract had stipulated that no film of the play could be released before December 31, 1964, or until all Broadway and touring productions had closed, whichever came first. But in 1962, this became a moot point. Fox was awash in red ink from the cost overruns on its production of *Cleopatra* starring Elizabeth Taylor and Richard Burton; it had sold off its back lot in the middle of west Los Angeles to create the shopping and housing complex that would become Century City; and Richard Zanuck, the son of the studio's longtime chief, Darryl Zanuck, had been installed as head of production, presiding over a skeletal staff. As Dick Zanuck rummaged through his script library for a vehicle that might bail the studio out, he turned to *The Sound of Music*. "It was just an obvious thing to do," he would recall years later. But it did not seem so obvious to everyone else at the time.

In December 1962, Zanuck secured a first-rate screenwriter, Ernest Lehman, who had not only written *North by Northwest* for Alfred Hitchcock but had successfully adapted *West Side Story* for the screen, but Lehman was having a terrible time finding a director. Billy Wilder pooh-poohed the whole idea, declaring, "No musical with swastikas in it will ever be a success." Stanley Donen and Gene Kelly, two of Hollywood's leading directors of musicals, turned Lehman down cold. William Wyler was interested, but after a visit to New York to see the play and a flight to Salzburg to scout potential locations, it turned out that he was more interested in making an anti-Nazi drama about World War II than the story of the Trapp Family Singers. Finally, Lehman turned to Robert Wise, who had directed *West Side Story* and had already passed on *The Sound of Music*. Wise still had his doubts, but he turned for advice to his friend Saul Chaplin, a veteran composer and music director who had worked with him on *West Side Story*.

Chaplin had seen the show on Broadway and hated it. He was prepared to feel the same way now, but as he read Lehman's draft script, he found himself enchanted. "The characters were more clearly defined, it was more charming, and he had invented a truly exciting and suspenseful finish," he would recall of Lehman's treatment. Chaplin's comment is emblematic of a long-running debate between the partisans of the Broadway and film versions of *The Sound of Music*, one that persists to this day. The Broadway advocates contend that the filmmakers stripped the show's subtleties and sanded down its politics, removing "No Way to Stop It," Elsa and Max's exhortation to Captain von Trapp to go along to get along with the Third Reich. Wise and Lehman and their allies argue that the movie version leached away saccharine and schmaltz in the service of greater realism. The debate need not be resolved here, but its import for Richard Rodgers was that the moviemakers wanted two new songs: a love duet for the Captain and Maria to replace "An Ordinary Couple," and a new solo for Maria to sing as she leaves the abbey to take up her duties at the von Trapp villa. Rodgers happily supplied "Something Good" as the new duet, and Chaplin and Wise loved it. But Maria's new song gave him trouble.

Rodgers's first effort was short—just sixteen bars—and in a lugubrious minor key. It was not at all what Chaplin had in mind. Returning to Hollywood, he wrote Rodgers a diplomatic letter explaining his ideas. In response, Rodgers produced the bubbly refrain the world knows: "I have confidence in sunshine! I have confidence in rain!" which would serve as the third part of "I Have Confidence," but ignored Chaplin's request about the first two sections, in which Maria would first express doubt, followed by tentative resolve. After half an hour of polite telephone jousting in which, Chaplin would recall, "either he didn't want to write the new material, or he wanted me to offer to do it," Chaplin agreed to try. He sent Rodgers a demonstration recording, using motifs from the original verse of "The Sound of Music," which would not be sung in the film. Rodgers wired back something like "Prefer my version. Okay to use yours if that is the decision," Chaplin would recall. Only long after the movie's opening did Chaplin work up the courage to tell Julie Andrews, who played Maria, that she'd been singing an amalgam. "Suddenly everything made sense," Andrews would recall decades later, "as I'd had a hard time with that song in general, finding that the lyrics didn't quite resonate for me!"

Andrews's performance in the film has become so iconic that it seems impossible to imagine anyone else in the part, but a wide range of other actresses—from Audrey Hepburn and Anne Bancroft to the inevitable Doris Day—either sought the role or were considered for it. Wise, Lehman, and Chaplin made up their minds for good after seeing some early footage of Andrews in *Mary Poppins* on the Walt Disney lot. "We went right back to the studio and said, 'That's our girl,'" Wise would recall. "Sign her." At twenty-nine, Andrews may not have been quite young enough to be an actual postulant, but she was more than youthful enough to satisfy Oscar Hammerstein's late-in-life wish that only young actresses play Maria. Christopher Plummer, six years her senior, was cast as the Captain. (The studio's first choice had been the sixty-year-old Bing Crosby, but the producers never took that idea seriously.)

The Austrian locations, wide-screen photography, and Chaplin's carefully planned musical numbers—most notably a "Do-Re-Mi" that ranged wonderfully through the streets and gardens of Salzburg—brought the stage play indelibly to life for an eager new generation of movie audiences, and for their children and grandchildren. The story proved as indestructible as ever.

Rodgers never visited the Austrian locations or the Fox soundstages, but he was by Julie Andrews's side at the New York premiere on March 2, 1965. The New York critics mostly savaged the film, taking the criticisms of the play a step or two further. The headline on Judith Crist's review in the *Herald Tribune* warned, "If You Have Diabetes, Stay Away from This Movie," and her verdict was that "the movie is for the five to seven set, and their mommies, who think their kids aren't up to the stinging sophistication and biting wit of *Mary Poppins*."

The catcalls couldn't have mattered less. *The Sound of Music* quickly became the all-time American box-office champion to date, beating the dollar record of *Gone with the Wind*, which had held the honor for twenty-five years. It won the Oscar for Best Picture, the soundtrack album stayed in the Billboard Top 10 for 109 weeks, and the trade journal later named it its No. 2 all-time album. The film was first released on home video in 1979 and holds the comparable record for longevity of sales in that medium. On the movie's fiftieth anniversary in 2015, Lady Gaga performed the title song live at the Academy Awards, and was greeted by a surprise onstage visit from Andrews herself as an encore.

"Everyone on the film was unified in their passion to make it the best it could be," Andrews says today, attempting to explain its endless, enduring appeal. "We shared an unspoken commitment to making a beautiful story while recognizing the dangers of being overly saccharine. I think that is one of the main things that contributes to the film's longevity—that, plus a heady combination of life-affirming elements, like glorious music and lyrics, the Austrian Alps, triumph over adversity in a critical period in history. Plus, children, nuns, family, and above all, a great love story. What more do you need?"

———

WHILE THE HOLLYWOOD filmmakers were immersed in the gemütlich world of "My Favorite Things," Rodgers was enduring the Sturm und Drang of a new Broadway musical in formation. The path to the project had been anything but straight or smooth. In the wake of *No Strings*, Rodgers had explored a new vehicle for Diahann Carroll set in ancient Egypt and based on the life of Nefertiti, but nothing came of it. Then he agreed to collaborate with Alan Jay Lerner, whose partnership with Frederick Loewe had ended in recriminations after *Camelot* in 1960. Dick and Alan discussed several ideas, but the one they settled on was to be called *I Picked a Daisy*, and it was an exploration of Lerner's long interest in extrasensory perception. But Lerner's attraction to the story could not overcome a hopeless case of writer's block, and an impatient Rodgers moved on. (Lerner would later write the show, renamed *On a Clear Day You Can See Forever*, with the composer Burton Lane.)

Rodgers's next choice of collaborator was not altogether un-expected: Stephen Sondheim. Dick had known Stephen since he was a twelve-year-old boy, and the possibility of their collaboration had been germinating for years, encouraged by Oscar Hammerstein before his death. In 1962, Sondheim had at last fulfilled his wish of writing both lyrics and music for Broadway—with *A Funny Thing Happened on the Way to the Forum*. While that show was a hit, his next outing, *Anyone Can Whistle*, with a book by his *West Side Story* and *Gypsy* collaborator Arthur Laurents, had closed after nine performances. Laurents now had another idea: a musical version of his 1952 play, *The Time of the Cuckoo*. It told the story of an unattached American woman of a certain age who finds unexpected—and unresolved—love on a vacation in Venice. Hammerstein himself had been interested in the property as a prospect for him and Dick, but he believed the 1955 film version, called *Summertime* and starring Katharine Hepburn and Rossano Brazzi, was too fresh in audiences' minds. Now the project—retitled once more as *Do I Hear a Waltz?*—looked too good to pass up: a proven vehicle, with established collaborators and a lush Rodgers score. Though Sondheim would once again be writing lyrics only, he could content himself with the thought that he was paying a posthumous debt to his mentor, and everyone stood to make a lot of money.

At first, Sondheim would remember, the collaboration was easy and friendly. But soon there were problems, the central one, in Sondheim's eyes, that the lead character was so emotionally repressed that she shouldn't be able to sing—at least until the very end of the show. Rodgers was unable to get his head around such an idea, and instead cast Elizabeth Allen, a brassy brunette with a clarion voice, in the pivotal role. Since he was the producer, he had the final say, and behind his back Sondheim, Laurents, and the show's British director, John Dexter, took to calling him Godzilla. That those three men happened to be gay added to the complicated dynamics. Long used to the routines of late nights, chorus girls, and being one of the guys, Rodgers felt ganged up on and left out. "The more we worked on the show, the more estranged I became from both writers," he would recall. "Any suggestions I made were promptly rejected, as if by prearrangement." Rodgers was also drinking secretly—and heavily—and Sondheim and Laurents came to feel that he responded to their own suggestions with a churlishness that bordered on contempt. In a joint interview with Sondheim, Rodgers joked—but only sort of—that the charming little boy he'd known had grown into a "monster."

Somehow the show limped into New York. "Unfortunately, when we put our touching, intimate story on the stage, we found that instead of a musical, we had a sad little comedy with songs," Rodgers would recall. "It simply didn't work." In fact, the score has some ravishing songs, including the title number and "Moon in My Window," a haunting trio for the three lead female characters.

The show opened on March 18, 1965, barely two weeks after the film premiere of *The Sound of Music*, and while the reviews were mixed, the show would run for a respectable 220 performances and Rodgers was philosophical about the backstage conflicts. "Someday, when we see each other again, I will be able to tell you more about Mr. Sondheim's lyrics and his personal problems," he wrote Sister Gregory a few weeks after the opening. "The latter didn't exactly make for an ideal relationship but now that the show is opened, and apparently will succeed, I am in a wonderfully charitable mood to forget everything I didn't like and remember the things I enjoyed."

RODGERS KEPT BUSY in other ways as well. He had agreed to take on the leadership of the Music Theater of Lincoln Center, housed in New York's new performing arts center. The goal was to produce first-class revivals of classic works in a two-show summer season. The first two productions, in 1964, were *The King and I* and Dick's old childhood favorite, *The Merry Widow*. The show's mountings were lavish, and sometimes new cast albums were produced. The most successful venture was a smash 1966 reimagining of *Annie Get Your Gun* with Ethel Merman once again in the title role and featuring "An Old Fashioned Wedding," a brand-new contrapuntal showstopping duet by Irving Berlin, the last hit he would ever write.

And even as he aged and grew more artistically conservative, Rodgers showed he could keep up with the times. Belying his reputation as a fierce foe of jazz interpretations of his works—he had reportedly reacted to Peggy Lee's driving, up-tempo Latin version of his and Larry Hart's "Lover" in 1952 by lamenting, "I don't know why Peggy picked on me when she could have fucked up 'Silent Night'"—he had warm words for Dave Brubeck's 1965 album of his songs, *My Favorite Things*. "'Oh, What a Beautiful Mornin'' would, I think," he wrote Brubeck, "have lasted a whole three months if only orthodox versions had been permitted." In a similar letter to the pop songwriter Burt Bacharach, Rodgers was also full of praise. "What you are doing," he wrote, "is to open a window and let fresh air into a room that has become too noisy in one way and too stuffy in another."

Rodgers's next project was a 1967 television version of *Androcles and the Lion* for NBC, starring Noël Coward, and to write it, he would recall, "I simply went back to my *No Strings* collaborator—me—and we got along just fine." The show was a mild success but produced no memorable songs. That same year, Rodgers's sixty-fifth birthday was celebrated with glowing tributes from friends and colleagues, but he could no longer deny the toll that advancing age, and decades of smoking and drinking, had taken on his health. On July 22, 1969, he suffered a serious heart attack. But a mere myocardial infarction could not dull Rodgers's perpetual quest for the next show; in fact, he was already at work on a new project, an adaptation of Clifford Odets's 1952 comedy, *The Flowering Peach*, a *Yiddishe* version of the story of Noah and the flood. Cast as Noah was Danny Kaye, the zany Hollywood song and dance man who had cut his teeth as a borscht belt tummler in the Catskills more than thirty years earlier. But Rodgers proved reluctant to emphasize the quintessentially Jewish quality of the material. His collaborators, lyricist Martin Charnin and librettist Peter Stone, had brought him the project in the first place, but, without telling them, Rodgers had acquired the rights himself, "which meant we were not only working with him, but working for him," Charnin would recall. Stone and Charnin were forced to defer to the boss, but they remained puzzled and found Rodgers hard to pin down. "If you wanted to talk to the composer he had on his producer's hat," Stone would recall. "And when you wanted to talk to the producer, you got the composer."

The director Joe Layton, who had first worked with Rodgers as dance director on *The Sound of Music*, devised an elaborate scenic concept in which the cast would disassemble the timbers of Noah's house at the end of the first act, only to reassemble them into the ark as the second-act curtain rose. Charnin found the whole idea cumbersome, and it required endless rehearsals. But Rodgers managed to turn out a number of good songs, including a beautiful ballad for one of Noah's sons, "I Do Not Know a Day I Did Not Love You." And despite his heart attack, Dick was also still openly—evenly shamelessly—chasing the girls in the company, including a young Madeline Kahn, who made fun of him to her fellow cast members.

The show, *Two by Two*, opened on November 10, 1970, and the critics were not kind. "Its badness is total," wrote Jack Kroll in *Newsweek*. Kaye's name on the marquee assured brisk enough business at the box office, but three months into the run, he injured his leg coming down a ramp during a performance. He returned to the show in a cast and wheelchair, and began a nightly series of ad-libbed dialogue and bits of comic business that turned the play into *The Danny Kaye Show*. Charnin and Stone were appalled and Rodgers was none too happy, but audiences flocked to the novelty and Dick kept the show running to return his investment. Kaye took to making curtain speeches in which he said, "I'm glad you're here, but I'm glad the authors aren't." The show ran for eleven months, clocking 351 performances, before Kaye gave up the ghost.

It is to Rodgers's credit that even such a disappointing experience did not diminish his appreciation for the most exciting show on Broadway that year: Stephen Sondheim and George Furth's *Company*, an acid examination of a commitment-phobic bachelor and his circle of married friends. Writing to Sondheim and the show's producer-director, Harold Prince, Rodgers called the show "triumphant" and said that in all his years of theatergoing, he had rarely been as impressed. "This is a unique talent that you walk around with," he told Sondheim, setting aside their past quarrels, "and I think you are absolutely right in your insistence that you must write both words and music." He concluded, "I think COMPANY is to cynicism what THE SOUND OF MUSIC is to sentimentality. This is not only artistically proper but publicly acceptable, as we all know perfectly well by now. There's room for both in the theatre and I am delighted with your success."

But the entente was to be short-lived. In a 1973 interview with *Newsweek*, Sondheim described Hammerstein as a man of limited talent but infinite soul, and Rodgers as a man of infinite talent but limited soul. Asked for comment, Dick replied, "The less said, the better."

IN 1972, DOROTHY Rodgers had a serious heart attack, which kept her hospitalized for weeks, but Dick kept plugging away. The latest potential project was a musical version of *Arsenic and Old Lace*, the popular 1940s black comedy about two elderly sisters who poison lonely old men and then bury them in their cellar. There was some suggestion that Ethel Merman and Mary Martin might be coaxed out of retirement to play the leads. The lyricist Sheldon Harnick, who had just ended his partnership with the composer Jerry Bock, which had produced such shows as *Fiddler on the Roof*, thought the play was so tightly plotted that there was no room for songs. A number of writers took a crack at the book, including the British playwright Tom Stoppard, before Rodgers decided it could never work and gave up.

But soon enough, Rodgers was at work on another project with Harnick, suggested by the producer Richard Adler, based on the life of Henry
VIII. In the spring of 1974, while at work on the show, Rodgers complained to Liza Minnelli that he had a case of "galloping laryngitis." It
would turn out to be something much worse: cancer of the larynx. That
July, Rodgers underwent surgery to remove his vocal cords. Grim as the
cancer of the jaw had been nearly twenty years earlier, this was worse,
literally robbing the composer of his voice. He could have used an electronic voice box but opted for the much more challenging course of
learning "esophageal speech," which requires gulping in air and then
belching it back through the oral passages. This not only took time and
enormous effort but also deprived Rodgers of one of his greatest pleasures, the witty riposte, the outrageous pun, the bon mot. By the time he
could gulp in and belch out, the moment had been lost. It was a major
achievement when Rodgers marched into the office of his doctor and the
nurse announced he had something important to show the doctor. Rodgers paused a bit and then began singing, "Doe—a deer, a female deer."

At first, Harnick assumed the Henry VIII project was doomed, but
Rodgers craved the work. "When he was able to function again, he
just, he had such drive to go forward," Harnick would recall. They
worked in the Rodgers and Hammerstein offices on Madison Avenue,
with Harnick usually writing the lyrics first. He was nervous about
showing Rodgers his first effort—a lullaby for the newborn Princess Elizabeth. Rodgers scowled fiercely—his usual expression when
concentrating—and said, "Well, let me see what I can do." "And I
thought, 'He hates it,'" Harnick remembered, "but I'll go on to the
next one." Rodgers could no longer dash off a tune in half an hour, but
a few days later, he invited Harnick to the office and dragged himself
to the piano. (By this point, he was also suffering the aftereffects of an
apparent stroke.) "And he got halfway there and he turned to me and he
said, 'I'll probably fuck it up.' And I thought, he is as nervous as I am.
And he played it and I thought it was just gorgeous." Until that moment,
Harnick had always called his new collaborator "Mr. Rodgers," but
"When he finished, I said, 'Oh, Dick, that's beautiful!' And literally his
shoulders sank. And he said, you know, when I left the house this morning, Dorothy said, 'Oh, I hope he likes it.'"

But the show, now called *Rex*, was heavy sledding. The librettist Sherman Yellen had larded the book with long expositions of Tudor history. The British actor Nicol Williamson, who had been cast as Henry, was having trouble in his marriage and drinking heavily, arriving late for rehearsals and leaving early. Rodgers managed to produce at least one lovely ballad, "Away from You," but the show simply wasn't working. When *Rex* opened on April 25, 1976, the verdict was grim. Clive Barnes in the *Times* said the show "has almost everything not going for it." It closed after just forty-eight performances.

The last thing anyone expected was for Rodgers to attempt another show. In 1975, he had published an autobiography, *Musical Stages*, ghostwritten by the theater historian Stanley Green. The book had flashes of Rodgers's wit, especially in its telling of his earliest days in the business, but it also had a tepid, denatured feel, and sales proved disappointing. As ever, though, Dick kept abreast of the competition, writing to Michael Bennett, the director of Broadway's latest singular sensation, "I didn't just have a good time at *A Chorus Line*, I laughed and cried and had that wonderful feeling way deep inside that can only be there in the presence of something great and new." There were still some high moments, notably a splendid revival of *The King and I* starring Yul Brynner that arrived in New York from a national tour in time for Dick's seventy-fifth birthday in 1977. The following year, Rodgers was among the first group of five artists to be awarded the Kennedy Center Honors, which would become one of the nation's highest rewards for creative achievement. Florence Henderson, an occasional lunch companion in these later years, would recall that even as he grew frailer, relying on a cane to walk, he lost neither his dignity nor his pride. "When he'd go to get in his car, his limo, he said, 'Don't help me,' he said to the guy, and he said, 'I just hate it because people try to help you and then the cane goes out from under you and you fall again.' "

Still, the shadows were lengthening. So it is perhaps not so surprising that when the producer Alexander Cohen approached Dick about writing a musical version of *I Remember Mama*, the play Rodgers and Hammerstein had first produced in 1944, Rodgers said yes. The show was the brainchild of Martin Charnin, who since the days of *Two by*

Two had scored a smash hit with *Annie*. Charnin had written both music and lyrics, with a book by his *Annie* collaborator Thomas Meehan, but Cohen thought the show needed a Rodgers score, which Dick agreed to provide. Cohen and Charnin saw the show as a perfect vehicle for the Swedish film star Liv Ullmann, who, as it turned out, could not really sing. Cohen eventually fired Charnin as the director and brought in Cy Feuer, who wanted to recruit the Hollywood songwriter Sammy Cahn to write some new lyrics. Dorothy Rodgers vetoed that idea, pronouncing him not "theater." Once upon a time, Dick would never have countenanced such involvement by his wife, but now he depended on her, and he deferred.

I Remember Mama opened on May 31, 1979, and hung on through the summer for 108 performances, closing on the Sunday before Labor Day. It was Rodgers's fortieth original Broadway show—and his last. For by now the curtain was falling on Dick himself. He was deeply depressed, beset by crippling headaches for which his doctors could find no cause. That October, he suffered a major seizure with convulsions. At times, he hallucinated. Much of the time, he was sedated with a powerful cocktail of morphine, Demerol, and codeine. He would sit, his daughter Linda would recall, "like a baby" in front of the television set, alone in his room while the rest of the family ate lunch.

In early December, there was one last drop of golden sun: a new touring revival of *Oklahoma!*, directed by Bill Hammerstein, was opening on Broadway. Agnes de Mille, by then herself coping with the effects of a severe stroke, wrote Dick an emotional letter. "Thirty-eight years ago you and I stood hand in hand at the back of the St. James waiting to see what would happen," she remembered. "Your arms were around me at the end of 'Farmer' and the world broke open." She expressed deep gratitude for the career that Dick and Oscar had helped to launch, and concluded, "Thursday night my hand will again be in yours. We are both broken now and badly dented if not daunted but we know we were right and we know what we are doing today and we can take joy in that knowledge."

But it appears that Rodgers was too ill to attend the opening on December 13. The new production, starring a mix of comparative newcomers and the great character actress Mary Wickes as Aunt Eller, won widespread critical praise and an appreciative intergenerational audience that rediscovered the show's irrepressible charms. "As I went up the aisle at intermission," Walter Kerr reported in the *Times*, "I noticed one and all were beaming. Some were smiling because they remember. The others were smiling because they will." Seventeen days later, on the next to last day of the last year of the 1970s—his sixth decade in the professional theater—Rodgers died quietly at home. As had been done for Oscar Hammerstein nineteen years earlier, the lights of the Broadway that Richard Rodgers had changed forever were darkened in his honor.

THE EXPECTED CONDOLENCES poured in from all over. "It must be gratifying to know that his music will give pleasure for whatever forever there is," Lauren Bacall wrote Dorothy. Perhaps unaware of her opinion of his pedigree, Sammy Cahn wrote to her as well. "No one, I repeat, no one," he declared, "will ever nearly match his great contributions." There were notes from New York's mayor, Ed Koch, and Jerusalem's, Teddy Kollek. Ginger Rogers, Beverly Sills, and Frank Sinatra all wrote, the last giving Dorothy his private telephone number should she need anything at all. "His medium was his music, and that lasts," Agnes de Mille told Rodgers's widow. "That is with us. His music will be with us for hundreds of years, fresh, ebullient, persuasive, adorably rhythmic, incomparable." One note stands out years later. "Dear Dorothy," it reads. "In spite of our differences, please accept my condolences and let me add that it was a privilege not only to work with Dick but also merely to be around when such a composer was alive. Sincerely. Steve (Sondheim)."

The funeral at Temple Emanu-El on Fifth Avenue was private but the congregation was filled with famous faces. Helen Hayes wrote Dorothy to apologize for bungling by mistake (with Lillian Gish) into the family's private gathering place before the service. Shirley Verrett, the Metropolitan Opera mezzo-soprano, whose musical education Rodgers had quietly helped to finance, sang. The presiding rabbi, Ronald Sobel, eulogized Rodgers as "a very gentle man" and "a very private person."

"I don't think anybody ever knew who he really was, with the possible exception of one of the five psychiatrists he went to," Mary Rodgers would recall many years later. "And I'm sure they didn't know either. And he certainly . . . I don't think he knew. He was just all locked up in there grinding out gorgeous stuff."

In fact, he wasn't all locked up, at least not always. A decade before his death, he received a remarkable letter, handwritten on stationery from the Waldorf-Astoria, from a woman named Terrell Dougan, who had seen him in a Manhattan restaurant that day.

Dear Mr. Rodgers,

There you were, having lunch at Le Valois today, when you see a lady across the room recognize you. You smile and nod to her.

Did you notice the stupid lady start to cry?

That particular moment happened because all my life I have felt your music so much a part of me.

I would like nothing more, when I come to be older, than to think it has mattered very greatly that I have lived at all; to see that it has mattered so much to a girl from Salt Lake City that she burst into tears at the sight of me would help.

It is important to me that you know this, even though I must be one of millions who would agree.

Days later, Rodgers sent an equally remarkable reply.

I remember the short scene at Le Valois very well indeed. I should tell you that I thought you had either recognized me or that you were someone I had known slightly in the past. But in any event, I felt that it was important that I should smile. I had no idea that this would, or did, make you cry, but I am delighted that you did. This ability to let an emotion have its way is all too rare in this restricted life that we lead and I must congratulate myself for being the cause of it in this case. You must lead a satisfactory life to be able to react in this way and I hope you'll keep on doing so.

Epilogue

BLOOM AND GROW FOREVER

Richard Rodgers lived long enough to see his own best work recognized as immortal, but also long enough to see the musical theater that he had revolutionized and dominated pass him by. Fairly or not, the critical eclipse had begun with Rodgers and Hammerstein's last shows. The sophisticated critics and creative forces that came to dominate Broadway in the late 1950s, '60s, and '70s increasingly looked askance at Dick and Oscar's achievements. A combination of factors was in play: the too often second-rate, middlebrow film versions that minimized their shows' sophistication and maximized their schmaltz; the rise of "concept" musicals that emphasized style over plot; and, of course, *The Sound of Music*.

Even as a twelve-year-old boy in 1959, Timothy Crouse could sense the attitude inherent in the smart set's dismissal of the show his father helped create. "I'm talking about people in the business who acted as if Rodgers and Hammerstein and Lindsay and Crouse were one of those big food conglomerates who do testing in the lab to create a snack with just the right combination of salt and fat and especially sugar to make it a tour de force of empty calories that consumers can't stop eating," Crouse says. "It was as if the four authors had sat around saying, 'Oh, we'll toss in so many grams of nuns, and so many grams of Nazis, and so many of adorable kiddies, and we'll have the hit of all time.' People really thought that. What these people were incapable of seeing was that the key ingredient of the secret sauce was sincerity. Whether or not you agree with the vision offered by *The Sound of Music*, it was a sincere vision, sincere on the part of all four guys. They believed in what they'd written."

Rodgers himself contributed to the calcification of the canon, often insisting that revivals and touring companies display an amber-like fidelity to the original staging. Barbara Cook would recall how when she played Carrie Pipperidge in a revival of *Carousel* in the 1950s, Rodgers wanted her to waddle her bustle just the way Jean Darling had done in the original production. "And I said, 'Well, I don't want to do that because that's the only time she ever walks like that, it's not true, right?' And he said, 'No, you're right,' and he went along with me."

By 1967, the critic Martin Gottfried would judge that Hammerstein's plays were "embarrassing and childish, but considering the ludicrous boy-meets-girl books of the period, his were at least attempting to do more than kill time between songs and dances," before giving way to "increasingly cynical money makers" in the late 1950s. "If Hammerstein's books were soggy, cliché-ridden, unadventurous melodramas," Gottfried wrote, "his lyrics were their equal. Reflecting his foursquare morality and greeting-card sentimentality, they marched evenly along to the even-tempoed thoughts that matched Rodgers's increasingly even-tempoed scores.

"But while their seriousness was middlebrow," Gottfried allowed, "it was not sham. The team believed it. They were convincing the public that a musical could be serious, and perhaps it was just as well that it was they who did the convincing. A little elevation mixed with a lot of pap was needed and the only way it would work was if the creators could swallow it themselves without throwing up." Those were harsh words, but they set a trajectory that critics would increasingly follow as Vietnam and Watergate divided the country, and Stephen Sondheim, Harold Prince, and Michael Bennett revolutionized the Broadway musical in thrilling but dark works like *Follies* and *Sweeney Todd*. Some scholars went so far as to suggest that the romantic views of

Southeast Asia—and of Western exceptionalism—promoted in *South Pacific* and *The King and I* had a hand in forming the mind-set that led to America's misadventure in Vietnam.

On the occasion of the fiftieth anniversary of *Oklahoma!* in 1993, Stephen Holden of the *New York Times* would write that Rodgers and Hammerstein had celebrated "a kind of secular catechism that sweetly but firmly instructed people on the rules of behavior in a world where America knew best and good triumphed over evil." In that "wholesome, cheery land," Holden wrote, employing a mash-up mouthful of Hammerstein's lyrics, "nothing could be more desirable than to be as corny as Kansas in August and as normal as blueberry pie. If you kept on whistling a happy tune, you would never walk alone. And on some enchanted evening, you might even find your true love. Those who climbed every mountain, beginning with foothills that were alive with the sound of music, would surely find their dreams." Holden concluded that the Rodgers and Hammerstein shows reflected a perspective "that was considered liberal in the 1940's and 50's but that in the light of today's sexual and racial politics seems slightly right-of-center, especially in treating relations between men and women."

YET EVEN AS Holden wrote those stinging words, the Rodgers and Hammerstein catalogue was poised for a striking critical comeback. The previous year, in 1992, the Royal National Theatre in London had staged a stunning revival of *Carousel*, the play that Holden had implied was most outdated in its outlook. Directed by Nicholas Hytner, the production had explored the doomed relationship of Billy Bigelow and Julie Jordan with a sexual frisson that seemed fresh in the age of *Fatal Attraction*. The show featured Clive Rowe, a black actor, as Enoch Snow, an unconventional casting choice that the eighty-three-year-old Dorothy Rodgers had at first adamantly opposed. Bill Hammerstein was skeptical, too, but James Hammerstein and Mary Rodgers were all for the experiment, as was Ted Chapin, the young theater executive who had been recruited to head the Rodgers and Hammerstein office in the early 1980s, after Dick Rodgers's death. After Hytner said that he would cancel the production (and would explain why, if asked), Dorothy Rodgers relented. Two years later, Lincoln Center Theater imported the Hytner production to Broadway, where it featured an African American new-comer named Audra McDonald as an indelible Carrie, and won raves. "Forget every other *Carousel* you may have seen," Vincent Canby wrote in the *New York Times*.

"I think it's all about the productions," says André Bishop, who oversaw the Lincoln Center *Carousel* and later produced equally pioneering revivals and re-imaginations of *South Pacific* and *The King and I*. "I think what happened was that the Rodgers and Hammerstein shows in the sixties and seventies and early eighties were mostly in summer stock and in tours with stars—Robert Goulet in *South Pacific*, Brynner in *The King and I*—and the fact of the matter is, a lot of them weren't very good. And these shows seemed earnest and rather long for an audience that had changed since the 1940s and 1950s. Somehow the shows were not being done in a way that reflected that change.

"There had been huge changes in theatrical craft—how you move scenery, how you move lights—and a whole new visual way, and a faster way of presenting these shows," Bishop adds. "Directors like Bartlett Sher have dug into those books and realized that they're superbly well-crafted, and extremely political. They've uncovered things that maybe people never knew were there when the shows were first produced. They have managed to bring new things to these shows, while still honoring what they are, treating them with reverence but not sanctimoniousness."

Some critics had never wavered, of course. Nearly twenty-five years after the premiere of *South Pacific*, Brooks Atkinson wrote that, compared to the froth of most musical comedy, "The fundamental humanity of *South Pacific* cannot be ignored. It is interested in the character of its chief men and women. It discusses race prejudice in ethical terms. It belongs to the literature of the human race in music as well as in words." Whatever instinct guides creators to know just which stories will make satisfying and successful musicals, Dick and Oscar possessed it in spades. Like even the greatest sluggers, they produced their share of doubles. But their home runs have more than withstood the sternest test of all: the test of time.

By 2006, the revolution in Rodgers and Hammerstein's reputation was so complete that when Andrew Lloyd Webber produced a revival of *The Sound of Music* at the London Palladium, the critical reaction was one of overwhelming approval. Reading the London papers the morning after the opening, Ted Chapin and Mary Rodgers were astounded.

WELL INTO THE twenty-first century, Rodgers and Hammerstein remained very much a family operation. Dorothy Hammerstein died in 1987, and by then her stepson Bill had long since become his family's representative on company business (and had stepped in to run the office during Rodgers's final illnesses). After Dick's death, Bill worked with Dorothy Rodgers, who died in 1992 and was succeeded by her elder daughter, Mary, who was not only a composer but also a successful novelist, the author of *Freaky Friday*, a charming tale of mother-daughter role reversal that surely owed something to her own complex relationship with her mother. James Hammerstein took over from the aging Bill in the late 1990s but died unexpectedly of a heart attack in 1999, and Bill died two years later, leaving his sister, Alice, to represent the Hammerstein interests.

When Ted Chapin took the reins in 1981, it seemed as if the Rodgers and Hammerstein repertoire might be relegated to summer stock, star tours, and high school and community theater productions. There was a reluctance among a new generation of top-notch theater artists to reexamine the venerable shows in first-class productions. That all changed with the Royal National Theatre's *Carousel*. In the meantime, Chapin extended the brand by taking on the management of the catalogues of other artists—most notably the works of Irving Berlin—and paving the way for the first-ever Broadway production of *Cinderella* in 2013. Among the latest experiments: an Oregon Shakespeare Festival production of *Oklahoma!* featuring gay, lesbian, and transgender characters in the principal roles.

In 2009, with Dick's and Oscar's surviving children aging and their grandchildren's generation scattered and pursuing careers of their own, the families sold the business for a reported $225 million to the Imagem Music Group, the investment arm of a giant Netherlands-based pension fund. Mary Rodgers died in 2014; Linda Rodgers and Alice Hammerstein died the following year. In 2017, Imagem was in turn acquired by Concord Bicycle Music, a recording and music company whose holdings include the catalogues of Paul Simon, James Taylor, and Creedence Clearwater Revival.

Still, the DNA of Richard Rodgers has a prominent place in the contemporary Broadway theater. In 2005, Mary Rodgers's son Adam Guettel won the Tony Award for the Best Original Score for his original production of *The Light in the Piazza*, the tender story of a mentally disabled girl who falls in love in Florence—the same property that the dying Oscar Hammerstein had found such a "tempter" forty-five years before.

TODAY, THE SOUND of Dick and Oscar's music is as ubiquitous as ever, generating tens of millions of dollars in annual revenues. On a single spring evening in 2014, in the United States alone, there were 11 productions of *Carousel*, 17 of *The King and I*, 26 of *South Pacific*, 64 of *Oklahoma!*, and 106 of *The Sound of Music*.

"If a composer is to reach his audience emotionally," Rodgers wrote in his memoir, "and surely that's what theater music is all about, he must reach the people through sounds they can relate to." In some nine hundred songs, that is just what he did. In the estimation of the critic Jonathan Schwartz, Rodgers ranks as the most-played composer of any kind of music, ever.

As for Hammerstein, the naked simplicity that his detractors are so quick to mock may be the very quality that has given his work such staying power. "Hammerstein rarely has the colloquial ease of Berlin, the sophistication of Porter, the humor of Hart and Gershwin, the inventiveness of Harburg or the grace of Fields," Stephen Sondheim once wrote. "But his lyrics are *sui generis*, and when they are at their best, they are more than heartfelt and passionate, they are monumental. . . . The flaws in Oscar's lyrics are more apparent than in those of the others because he is speaking deeply from himself through his characters and therefore has no persona to hide behind. He is exposed, sentimental warts and all, every minute and in every word, especially in the songs he wrote with Kern and Rodgers. In the end, it's not the sentimentality but the monumentality that matters."

"They thought big, and wrote about important, and quite often uncomfortable themes," Julie Andrews says simply. "Bigotry in *South Pacific*, for instance, or cultural and societal differences in *The King and I* and *Flower Drum Song*—which was brave and gave each musical a spine. Rodgers's music was always melodically glorious, simple yet soaring. It hooked you and lodged in your gut with huge satisfaction. His waltzes were as beautiful as any of Strauss's. Hammerstein's lyrics were equally rich, brilliantly constructed and so very specific to the worlds they created together. Their shows managed to be both timely and timeless—the epitome of classic."

Will people ever tire of the compelling dramatic stories Rodgers and Hammerstein created together? Will they ever tire of their somber, soaring, sentimental, sly, sad, sunny, uplifting songs? The evidence of three-quarters of a century suggests that "many a new day will dawn, many a red sun will set, many a blue moon will shine" before they do.

NOTES

Unless otherwise specified, all quotations of lyrics and libretti from Rodgers and Hammerstein's plays are taken from authoritative published versions of those works, or from *The Complete Lyrics of Oscar Hammerstein II*, and are used with permissions listed in the back of this book.

The Library of Congress holds the vast bulk of Oscar Hammerstein's writings and Richard Rodgers's musical manuscripts, while the New York Public Library for the Performing Arts at Lincoln Center holds an important collection of Rodgers's correspondence. The Hammerstein collection arrived piecemeal at the Music Division of the Library of Congress in the decades after Oscar's death, and at the time of this research, it was open to scholars but had never been fully catalogued or processed—with material on any given subject scattered widely among dozens of cardboard shipping containers and archival boxes. As this book was being finished, the library was undertaking a comprehensive reorganization of the collection, which means that many, if not most, of the citations to boxes and folders listed here will be out of date. Whenever possible, I have included the date on which documents were created, and the library's new classification scheme should ultimately make everything much easier to find.

The following abbreviations are used in the notes:

AMPAS   Academy of Motion Picture Arts & Sciences Margaret Herrick Library

CU   Columbia University Oral History, widely available in reference libraries, including AMPAS Library.

DBH	Dorothy Blanchard Hammerstein
DFR	Dorothy Feiner Rodgers
JLL	Joshua Lockwood Logan
LOC	Library of Congress
NYPL	New York Public Library for the Performing Arts
OH	Oral History
OHII	Oscar Hammerstein II
R&H	Richard Rodgers and Oscar Hammerstein II
RR	Richard Rodgers
SMU	Southern Methodist University, Ronald L. Davis Oral History Collection

PROLOGUE: ALL THEY CARED ABOUT WAS THE SHOW

1   This evening's production: Harold Messing, "The CBS Television Production of Cinderella" (unpublished master's thesis, Stanford University, 1957), on file in R&H office.

3   Rodgers and Hammerstein had first met Andrews: Bonus interview track, Rodgers and Hammerstein's *Cinderella*, Image Entertainment, 2004.

4   "I just thought it was going to be the greatest train wreck": Ibid.

4   "That boy in the second row": Ibid.

4   The special effects were crude: Messing, *The CBS Television Production of Cinderella*, pp. 25–28.

5   The final run-through ended: Ibid., p. 56.

5   "I walked outside the theater": Bonus interview track, *Cinderella*.

7   By the time the two men finally teamed up: OHII OH, CU, p. 28.

7   At the height of the partners' success: David Ewen, *Richard Rodgers* (New York: Henry Holt, 1957), p. 18.

7   As for Hammerstein: Philip Hamburger, "The Perfect Glow," pt. 1, *New Yorker*, May 12, 1951, p. 35.

9   "Dick loved money more": Ballard interview, SMU.

9   For eighteen years: Oscar Hammerstein II, *Lyrics* (Milwaukee, WI: Hal Leonard Books, 1985), p. 7.

9   Hammerstein once complained: Laurence Maslon, script for his American Masters PBS documentary, *Richard Rodgers, The Sweetest Sounds*, 2002; RR to Johnny Carson on *The Tonight Show*, March 8, 1963.

10   A glimpse of the careful, starchy formality: R&H Archives, New York. See also RR NYPL.

11   "I guess like Gilbert and Sullivan": Irving telephone interview with author.

1: THE SENTIMENTALIST

16   "There is no limit to the number of people": Frederick Nolan, *Lorenz Hart: A Poet on Broadway* (New York: Oxford University Press, 1994), p. 54.

16   By one later account, he went home: Hamburger, "The Perfect Glow," pt. 1, p. 35.

17   Oscar would later attribute his love: Hamburger, "The Perfect Glow," pt. 2, *New Yorker*, May 19, 1951, p. 46.

17   He didn't like the theater: Letters to William Hammerstein, Box 28, OHII LOC.

17   "He seldom scolded me": Ibid.

17   "She was my friend, my confidante": Ibid.

17   Allie's death from a botched abortion: Hugh Fordin, *Getting to Know Him: A Biography of Oscar Hammerstein II* (New York: Random House, 1977), p. 23.

18   "I never feel shaken by death": Arnold Michaelis interview with OHII, circa 1959, transcript in OHII LOC, pp. 13–14.

18   "whatever order or form I have got": OHII to William Hammerstein, January 18, 1953, Box 28, OHII LOC.

18   Indeed, Stephen Sondheim: Hammerstein, *Lyrics*, p. xv.

19   "Oscar is a comedian": Fordin, *Getting to Know Him*, p. 28.

20   "It's in my blood," Oscar insisted: Hamburger, "The Perfect Glow," pt. 2, p. 50.

20   *"Make yourselves at home"*: Fordin, *Getting to Know Him*, p. 35.

21   "In those days, it was more of a free-for-all": OHII OH, CU, p. 2.

21   "I don't think I had any high-minded notions": Ibid.

21   when white dinner jackets were in vogue: Mitzi Gaynor interview with author.

21   "not that he was a dandy": Fordin, *Getting to Know Him*, p. xii.

22   "While I was sitting there, an idea came": Ibid., p. 38.

23   The music was "catchy": Stanley Green, ed., *Rodgers and Hammerstein Fact Book: A Record of Their Works Together and with Other Collaborators* (New York: Lynn Farnol Group, 1980), p. 255.

23   This discovery gave birth to a lifelong conviction: Fordin, *Getting to Know Him*, p. 44.

24   He likened the construction: Ibid., p. 47.

24   Harbach would not only impress: Stephen Sondheim, *Finishing the Hat: Collected Lyrics (1954–1981) with Attendant Comments, Principles, Heresies, Grudges, Whines and Anecdotes* (New York: Alfred A. Knopf, 2010), p. 36.

24   The show opened in New York: Green, *Fact Book*, pp. 258ff.; Fordin, *Getting to Know Him*, p. 48.

24   The next four years: Green, *Fact Book*, pp. 262–89.

25   Many years later, Oscar himself: Fordin, *Getting to Know Him*, p. 50.

25   "A Long Island commuter, I prided myself": Hammerstein, *Lyrics*, p. 35.

26   Though she pines only for the trapper: Green, *Fact Book*, pp. 291ff.

27   "The fertile brain of Oscar Hammerstein": Ibid.

27   "'when do I do my tap specialty?'": Fordin, *Getting to Know Him*, p. 62.

29   "It isn't just the controversial subject matter": *Oscar Hammerstein II: Out of My Dreams*, PBS documentary, 2012.

29   Catching them all singing one day: Edna Ferber, *Show Boat* (Garden City, NY: Doubleday, Page, 1926), p. 123.

30   "If a listener is made rhyme-conscious": Hammerstein, *Lyrics*, p. 21.

30   "This was great music": Edna Ferber, *A Peculiar Treasure* (New York: Doubleday, Doran, 1939), p. 306.

30   Richard Rodgers, attempting to contrast: Arnold Michaelis interview with RR, circa 1959–60, R&H office files.

31   That purity went hand in hand: Sondheim, *Finishing the Hat*, p. 36.

31   Hammerstein himself once explained: Hamburger, "The Perfect Glow," pt. 1, p. 46.

31   *Show Boat* opened: Green, *Fact Book*, pp. 52–53.

32   But the next morning: Fordin, *Getting to Know Him*, p. 75.

32   "He looked at me": *Out of My Dreams* documentary.

33   "Oscar snapped": Fordin, *Getting to Know Him*, pp. 92–93.

33   Two months later, Dorothy told Oscar: Letters to Dorothy Box, OHII LOC.

34   At the end of his life: Statement of May 28, 1959, Box 29, OHII LOC.

34   James, the son he had: Ethan Mordden, *On Sondheim: An Opinionated Guide* (New York: Oxford University Press, 2016), p. 3; *Out of My Dreams* documentary.

35   "They are not companionable to each other": OHII to Myra Finn, November 13, 1934, Box A, OHII LOC.

35   "Pretty soon we were all shipped back on the Chief": OHII OH, CU, p. 12.

36   After its failure, Oscar asked Jerry: Fordin, *Getting to Know Him*, p. 128.

36   So the Hammersteins returned: Ibid.

36   "Their chief interest is developing me": Letter to Myra Finn, Box A, OHII LOC.

36   "The saddest word I know is 'but'": OHII to Norman Zierold, August 7, 1954, Box 2 of 3, OHIII LOC.

36   "I was selling words instead of gambling with them": OHII OH, CU, p. 20.

37   "In Hollywood above all other places": OHII to Myra Finn, June 11, 1934, Box A, OHII LOC.

37   Later that year, in a letter to his lawyer: OHII to Reinheimer, November 13, 1934, Box 8 of 9, OHII LOC.

37   But he would never forget this fallow period: John Mosher to OHII, July 1, 1936, Box A, OHII LOC.

37   "Forgive me for not writing sooner": OHII to Hy Kraft, November 28, 1938, Box 29, OHII LOC.

38   Wolcott Gibbs in the *New Yorker* pronounced it: Green, *Fact Book*, pp. 493–94.

38   "I was pretty blue": Hamburger, "The Perfect Glow," pt. 2, p. 59.

38   On January 2, 1942: Max Gordon to OHII, January 2, 1942, Box 6 of 9, OHII LOC.

2: A QUALITY OF YEARNING

39   Richard Rodgers was once asked: Charlotte Greenspan, "Richard Rodgers: Collaborator," *Musical Quarterly* 98, nos. 1–2 (March 1, 2015): 81–99.

39   Like Oscar Hammerstein, he spent his early childhood: RR OH, CU, p. 41.

40   "there was music every day": James Day interview of RR, May 13, 1974, http://www.cuny.tv/show/dayatnight/PR1012249.

40   By age six, he was fiddling around: Meryle Secrest, *Somewhere for Me: A Biography of Richard Rodgers* (New York: Alfred A. Knopf, 2001), p. 22.

41   Decades later, he would wonder: Richard Rodgers, *Musical Stages: An Auto-biography* (New York: Random House, 1975), p. 14.

41   "The Kern scores had the freshness": RR OH, CU, p. 52.

41   "The sound of a Jerome Kern tune": Rodgers, *Musical Stages*, p. 20.

42   In his autobiography: Ibid., p. 24.

42   Dick's vivid first impressions: Ibid., p. 27.

43   But what really dazzled: Samuel Marx and Jan Clayton, *Rodgers & Hart: Bewitched, Bothered, and Bedeviled* (New York: G. P. Putnam's Sons, 1976), p. 38.

43   As Dick would famously recall: Rodgers, *Musical Stages*, p. 28.

43   Lorenz Hart was born: Robert Gottlieb, "Rodgers and Hart's Dysfunctional Partnership," *Atlantic*, April 2013; Secrest, *Somewhere for Me*, p. 32.

44   "In all the time I knew him": Max Wilk, *They're Playing Our Song: Conversations with America's Classic Songwriters* (Westport, CT: Easton Studio Press, 2008), p. 49.

44   at a time when homosexual acts were still a crime: Marx and Clayton, *Rodgers & Hart*, p. 190.

44   "It wasn't much of a splash": Rodgers, *Musical Stages*, p. 30.

45   "The world was going to have to get along": Ibid., p. 61.

46   "This show's gonna run a year!": Ibid., p. 66.

46   The reviews were raves: Green, *Fact Book*, p. 25.

47   She did, and the *Gaieties* ran: Rodgers, *Musical Stages*, pp. 65ff.; Green, *Fact Book*, pp. 20–27.

47   "No, Larry," Dick replied: Rodgers, *Musical Stages*, p. 67.

47   While Rodgers did not need a piano: Marx and Clayton, *Rodgers & Hart*, p. 86.

48   "Our fights over words were furious": Richard Rodgers, preface to *The Rodgers and Hart Songbook* (New York: Simon & Schuster, 1951), p. 3.

48   What made a Rodgers song?: Alec Wilder, *American Popular Song: The Great Innovators, 1900–1950* (New York: Oxford University Press, 1972), p. 163.

49   The result is that thousands of songs: William Knowlton Zinsser, *Easy to Remember: The Great American Songwriters and Their Songs* (Jaffrey, NH: David R. Godine, 2001), p. 44.

50   "There's a sigh in the music that's emotional": Pomahac interview with author, Racine, Wisconsin, July 24, 2017.

50   The music critic Winthrop Sargeant: Secrest, *Somewhere for Me*, p. 383.

50   Rodgers once told an interviewer: Michaelis interview with RR, New York, circa 1960, widely available in reference libraries and Rodgers and Hammerstein archives, see for example: https://www.jstor.org/stable/25602279. 4–8.

50   "I knew exactly what was happening to me": Ibid., p. 2–2 (same page numeration system as in above note).

50   Decades later, he would insist: Tony Thomas interview with RR, January 28, 1960, https://www.youtube.com/watch?v=e8UpXPU_myw.

51   "Larry and I used to thrash around": RR OH, Columbia, p. 109.

52   It would make an equal impression back in New York: Margaret Case Harriman, "Words and Music," pt. 1, *New Yorker*, May 28, 1938, p. 19.

52   Only one song: Green, *Fact Book*, p. 93.
52   Asked why he wanted to grapple: Gary Marmorstein, *A Ship Without a Sail: The Life of Lorenz Hart* (New York: Simon & Schuster, 2012), p. 148.
52   The veteran Broadway music director Buster Davis: Ibid., p. 150.
53   "My prepubescent fantasies": Rodgers, *Musical Stages*, p. 17.
53   From his teenage years on: Ibid., p. 44.
53   "Although I had seen her at the theatre": Ibid., p. 74.
54   Dorothy and Dick had many mutual friends: Dorothy Rodgers, *A Personal Book* (New York: Harper & Row, 1977), p. 50.
54   Not realizing he'd intended to start a conversation: Secrest, *Somewhere for Me*, p. 111.
54   When the notion of marriage first came up: Ibid., p. 135.
55   His letters to Dorothy when they were apart: RR to Dorothy Feiner Rodgers, August 9, 1934, Boxes 6,7, RR NYPL.
55   "There is in Rodgers's music": Crouse e-mail to author, July 5, 2017.
55   "it was a lot to take on a ménage à trois": Dorothy Rodgers, *A Personal Book*, p. 69.
56   Dorothy would flee upstairs: Ibid., p. 73.
57   "What we had in mind": Richard Rodgers, *Musical Stages*, p. 150.
58   Dick summed up their entire output: Ibid., p. 164.
58   "As a matter of clinical fact": RR to DRF, July 4, 1933, RR NYPL.
59   Around the same time, he confided: RR to DFR, August 1, 1934, Box 6, 7, RR letters, NYPL.
59   It was in these dark days: RR OH, Columbia, p. 155.
60   "I didn't know a thing about choreography": Richard Rodgers, *Musical Stages*, p. 175.
61   The other notable Rodgers and Hart show: Ibid., p. 199.
62   The most famous first-night review: Green, *Fact Book*, p. 219.
62   Gene Kelly would recall waiting: Gene Kelly OH, SMU.
62   Still, the show ran for eleven months: Green, *Fact Book*, p. 221.
63   The Broadway publicist Gary Stevens: Secrest, *Somewhere for Me*, pp. 101–2.
63   "Had dinner with the shrimp last night": RR to DFR, May 7, 1937, Box 6, 7, RR letters, NYPL.
64   But by 1941, Hart was barely functioning: Richard Rodgers, *Musical Stages*, p. 204.
64   Suddenly that summer: Fordin, *Getting to Know Him*, p. 174.
64   Over lunch, Dick poured out his worries: Ibid., p. 185.

3: AWAY WE GO

65   "Indeed, the subtitle might almost be": Phyllis Cole Braunlich, *Haunted by Home: The Life and Letters of Lynn Riggs* (Norman: University of Oklahoma Press, 1988), p. 73.
66   He would call his drama: Lynn Riggs, *Green Grow the Lilacs* (New York: Samuel French, 1958), p. 7.
66   Brooks Atkinson of the *New York Times*: Braunlich, *Haunted by Home*, p. 97.

66 "After the show, Terry came backstage": Max Wilk, *OK!: The Story of Oklahoma!* (New York: Applause Theater & Cinema Books, 2002), p. 25.

67 There were "prospects of utter disaster": Lawrence Langner, *The Magic Curtain* (New York: E. P. Dutton, 1951), p. 368.

67 Years later she would confess: Theresa Helburn, *A Wayward Quest* (Boston: Little, Brown, 1960), p. 283.

68 Rodgers called his bluff: Richard Rodgers, *Musical Stages*, p. 216.

68 Hart went off to Mexico: Ibid., p. 217.

68 Meantime, backstage at the Shubert: Author conversation with Rose Inghram, circa 1990.

68 At this point, two developments occurred: Fordin, *Getting to Know Him*, p. 184; "Road to Oklahoma."

69 Strawberry festivals, sewing parties, quilting bees: Hammerstein, *Lyrics*, p. 8.

70 "It is a radiant summer morning": Riggs, *Green Grow the Lilacs*, p. 3.

71 "Well," Rodgers would recall: RR OH, Columbia, p. 228; Fordin, *Getting to Know Him*, p. 189.

71 He would not sing in the standard: Jack Viertel, *The Secret Life of the American Musical: How Broadway Shows Are Built* (New York: Sarah Crichton Books, 2016), p. 30.

72 Now those old lines: Hammerstein, *Lyrics*, pp. 10–11.

72 Rodgers was similarly open: Mark Eden Horowitz, "The Craft of Making Art: The Creative Processes of Eight Musical Theatre Songwriters," *Studies in Musical Theatre* 7, no. 2 (June 2013): 274.

72 Oscar was instantly proud: OHII to William Hammerstein, April 22, 1943, "New Box," OHII LOC.

73 "What was the third act of this play": OHII OH, Columbia, p. 25.

74 After lunch at one: Fordin, *Getting to Know Him*, p. 210.

75 Dick and Oscar then hit upon the notion: Hammerstein, *Lyrics*, p. 15.

76 On his trusty yellow pad: OHII undated sketches, "Oklahoma! Materials" Box, OHII LOC.

76 Years later, someone would ask Rodgers: Wilk, *OK!*, p. 84.

77 Even as Oscar began collaborating: Meryle Secrest, *Stephen Sondheim: A Life* (New York: Vintage Books, 2011), p. 32.

77 For his part, Sondheim would acknowledge: Ibid., p. 37.

80 "So I did," Holm would recall: Holm OH, SMU.

80 The show was "too clean": Langner, *Magic Curtain*, p. 376.

80 "The entire show was a bald contrivance": Ethan Mordden, *Rodgers and Hammerstein* (New York: Harry N. Abrams, 1992), p. 24.

81 "Coming out of a clear blue sky": OHII eulogy for Helburn, Box 33, OHII LOC.

82 The Guild had decided to invest: Wilk, *OK!*, pp. 99–105.

83 "First, I informed him": Agnes de Mille, *Dance to the Piper* (Boston: Little, Brown, 1952), pp. 246–47.

84 In a later draft titled simply: OHII draft, "Oklahoma Materials" folder, OHII LOC.

84 She repeatedly asked Rodgers: Jeff Lunden OH of de Mille, provided to author.

84 "The first three days were absolutely crucial": Ibid.

85   Hammerstein was equally impressed: Hammerstein essay for *Dance*, Box 33, OHII LOC.

85   Rehearsals began on February 8: Irving telephone interview with author.

85   "It was like being in a cement mixer": Lunden OH of de Mille.

85   "You know, we had no real chorus kids": Garde OH, SMU.

86   That night, Betty Garde would remember: Ibid.

86   In her dressing room at the Shubert: Holm OH, SMU.

87   Greenstone would not only reap: Wilk, *OK!*, pp. 245–48.

87   Richard Rodgers interrupted: Fordin, *Getting to Know Him*, p. 198.

87   Still, Mamoulian would remember: Mamoulian OH, SMU.

87   Then a member of the ensemble: Wilk, *OK!*, p. 200.

88   Leonard Bernstein once described: *New York Times*, "Does Music Trump Story? More Answers to Your Broadway Questions," December 8, 2010.

88   The assertion was true enough: *New York Times*, "Eight Bars and a Pencil: Music Arranger Tells The Secrets of The Tunes You Hum," June 8, 1947.

88   But Bennett, a musical polymath: Robert Russell Bennett, *The Broadway Sound: The Autobiography and Selected Essays of Robert Russell Bennett*, ed. George J. Ferencz (Rochester, NY: University of Rochester Press, 1999), p. 2.

88   "Mother brings a beautiful baby": Ibid., p. 300.

89   An orchestrator's pay was good: Steven Suskin, *The Sound of Broadway Music: A Book of Orchestrators and Orchestrations* (New York: Oxford University Press, 2009), p. 31.

89   So he hopped a train for Boston: Ibid., pp. 190–91.

89   "But I certainly could hear it!": Wilk, *OK!*, p. 223. (Note: Blackton's original name was Jacob Schwartzdorf; he changed it shortly after *Oklahoma!* opened.)

89   Still, Oscar was cautiously optimistic: OHII to William Hammerstein, undated, Box 6 of 9, OHII LOC.

90   Among the options floated: Wilk, *OK!*, p. 196.

90   Betty Garde would insist: Garde OH, SMU.

90   The word had already been reproduced: Wilk, *OK!*, p. 205.

90   "I don't know what to do": Fordin, *Getting to Know Him*, p. 201.

91   "'Stop making love to Rodgers'": Lunden OH of de Mille.

92   The critics were just as effusive: Green, *Fact Book*, p. 514.

92   "No, thanks, Jules": Richard Rodgers, *Musical Stages*, p. 226.

92   "Shall we sneak off to someplace quiet": Ibid.

92   "No, legs, no jokes, no chance": RR to Walter Winchell, June 27, 1961, RR NYPL.

93   The first five shows alone: Wilk, *OK!*, pp. 232–33.

93   When Oscar's tenant farmer, Peter Moen: Fordin, *Getting to Know Him*, p. 203.

93   At one point in the run, Armina Marshall: Langner, *Magic Curtain*, p. 377.

93   By May, Helburn and Langner: Correspondence, Box 5 of 9, OHII LOC.

93   By 1949, a year after the Broadway run ended: Correspondence, Box 6 of 9, OHII LOC.

93   Press reports noted: Harry Ruby to OHII, Box 5 of 9, OHII LOC.

94   When Celeste Holm was cast: Holm OH, SMU.

94   And indeed, at every performance: Wilk, *OK!*, p. 237.

94   The theater historian Ethan Mordden: Mordden, *Rodgers and Hammer-stein*, p. 45.

94   In the succinct summation of the theater historian Max Wilk: Wilk, *OK!*, p. 262.

94   "I'd had a pretty crummy night": John Hersey to RR, December 14, 1979, RR NYPL.

4: BUSTIN' OUT

96   "I am suddenly a much cleverer man": OHII to William Hammerstein, April 12, 1943, "New Box," OHII LOC.

96   "Of course the red carpet was rolled out": OHII to William Hammerstein, July 14, 1943, Box 6 of 9, OHII LOC.

96   "Dick and I don't want": OHII to William Hammerstein, May 2, 1943, Box 6 of 9, OHII LOC.

97   For his part, Rodgers would recall: Richard Rodgers, *Musical Stages*, p. 235.

97   Shortly after *Oklahoma!* opened: Ibid., p. 234; OHII to William Hammerstein, April 22, 1943, "New Box," OHII LOC.

98   By Sunday, his white blood count: Marmorstein, *Ship Without a Sail*, pp. 428–31.

98   "To those of us in the hospital": Richard Rodgers, *Musical Stages*, p. 231.

99   Without confiding his plans to anyone: Fordin, *Getting to Know Him*, pp. 179–81.

100   Finally, that November: Ibid., pp. 181ff., 204ff.

100   He wrote to his son Bill: OHII to William Hammerstein, October 13, 1943, Box 6 of 9, OHII LOC.

101   "Bravo!" wrote the *Herald Tribune*: Green, *Fact Book*, p. 501.

101   That Christmas, Oscar took out an ad: Photostat of ad, Box 3, OHII LOC.

102   "I thought it was quite the opposite": Michaelis interview with OHII, New York, circa 1959-60, available in reference libraries, for eg. https://www.jstor.org/stable/25602279, p. 94.

103   "He had paid us a lot of money": Richard Rodgers, *Musical Stages*, p. 237.

104   Oscar himself was under no illusions: OHII to William Perlberg, June 4, 1945, Box 4 of 9, OHII, LOC.

104   "Nice, I believe, would be the word for it": Green, *Fact Book*, p. 548.

105   "Is it possible for someone to hit you": Ferenc Molnár, *Liliom: A Legend in Seven Scenes and a Prologue* (New York: Boni and Liveright, 1921), p. 137.

105   John Mason Brown summed up: Secrest, *Somewhere for Me*, p. 273.

106   "And I studied that": Michaelis interview with OHII, p. 80.

106   Finally Rodgers lit upon the idea: Richard Rodgers, *Musical Stages*, p. 238.

106   "I began to see an attractive ensemble": *New York Times*, "Turns on a Carousel: An Account of Adventures in Setting the Play 'Liliom' to Music," April 15, 1945.

106   After a meeting with Dick and Oscar: Theresa Helburn to R&H, December 17, 1943, R&H office files.

107   By the next month, Helburn was advising: Ibid.

108   "There will be no dialogue or lyric": OHII to William Hammerstein, August 15, 1944, "New Box," OHII LOC.

108 By the time of the producers' story conferences: Theresa Helburn memo, December 17, 1943, R&H office files.
108 "Yes, I would," Julie replies: Molnár, *Liliom*, p. 32.
108 Oscar's first stab at a lyric: Fordin, *Getting to Know Him*, p. 225.
109 Stephen Sondheim would call: Ethan Mordden, *Beautiful Mornin': The Broadway Musical in the 1940s* (New York: Oxford University Press, 1999), p. 87.
109 The scene ends as it did: Richard Rodgers and Oscar Hammerstein, *Six Plays by Rodgers and Hammerstein* (New York: Modern Library, 1953), p. 111.
110 Oscar's portrait of Victorian New England: Lillian Ross, "Enchanted Evening," *New Yorker*, April 7, 2008.
110 So exhaustive were her labors: Playbill.com, September 19, 2011, http://www.playbill.com/article/getting-to-know-her-meet-alice-hammerstein-mathias-oscars-daughter-com-182717.
110 But consider her careful précis: Robert P. Tristam Coffin, *Mainstays of Maine* (New York: Macmillan, 1945), pp. 119–22; see also Alice Hammerstein notes, *Carousel* Green Box, OHII LOC.
112 After a backers' audition: OHII exchange with Gerald Loeb, Box 2 of 9, OHII LOC.
113 "What you say about sheep": Fordin, *Getting to Know Him*, p. 228.
113 Rodgers and Hammerstein themselves tangled: Theresa Helburn to OHII and reply, circa October 5, 1944, R&H office files.
114 At the end of Clayton's next audition: Clayton OH, SMU.
115 "There is our Liliom!": Langner, *Magic Curtain*, p. 391.
115 From the outset: Theresa Helburn to R&H, December 17, 1943, R&H office files.
115 Raitt would never forget: Raitt OH, SMU.
115 "It was not the anxiety to have a happy ending": Michaelis interview with OHII, p. 81.
116 "I tell you," she remembered years later: Johnson to Ted Chapin, *R&H News*, July 1, 2003, http://www.r http://www.rnh.com/news/588/CHRISTINE-JOHNSON-RECALLS-HER-RIDE-ON-CAROUSEL-by-Ted-Chapin.nh.com/news/588/CHRISTINE-JOHNSON-RECALLS-HER-RIDE-ON-CAROUSEL-by-Ted-Chapin.
116 When Ferenc Molnár showed up: Richard Rodgers, *Musical Stages*, p. 241.
117 "Apparently, certain kinds of fur": Secrest, *Stephen Sondheim*, p. 53.
117 "The staff repaired": Agnes de Mille, *And Promenade Home* (Boston: Little, Brown, 1958), p. 243.
117 "We veterans are": *Boston Post*, March 25, 1945.
117 In the second act, he had discarded: OHII script draft, *Carousel* Green Box, OHII LOC.
118 But there wasn't enough time: OHII red leather scrapbook, *Carousel*, OHII LOC.
118 "We gotta get God out of the parlor": *New York Times*, "Carousel: Surviving to Become a Classic," April 7, 1996.
118 Mamoulian proposed adding: Mamoulian OH, SMU.
118 Agnes de Mille, for one: de Mille, *And Promenade Home*, p. 238.
119 "Now I can write you": Richard Rodgers, *Musical Stages*, p. 242.

119   He managed to drag himself: Ibid., p. 243.
119   The session went badly: Langner, *Magic Curtain*, p. 392.
119   After the show, Molnár approached: Richard Rodgers, *Musical Stages*, p. 243.
120   The reviews were rapturous: Green, *Fact Book*, pp. 535–37.
120   The original production would run: Ibid., p. 537.
120   Jan Clayton would recall: Clayton OH, SMU.
120   "I think it's more emotional": RR OH, CU, p. 264.

5: SO FAR

121   "Many of the old managers died broke": RR in *New York World-Telegram & Sun*, September 3, 1952.
121   The partners were ably abetted: *New York Times*, August 8, 1970.
122   A private and practical man: Howard Reinheimer Jr., telephone interview with author, February 2017.
122   "Business, business, all the time business": Don Walker, *Men of Notes* (Pittsburgh: Dorrance, 2013), p. 86.
122   But Rodgers's daughter Mary: Mary Rodgers OH, SMU.
123   Music copyrights typically lodged: OHII to William Hammerstein, April 22, 1943, "New Box," OHII LOC.
123   "This is all pretty complicated," Oscar told Bill: Ibid.
123   "More than anything, these recordings": Philip Furia, *Irving Berlin: A Life in Song* (New York: Schirmer Books, 1998), p. 217.
124   "We were anxious to keep active": Richard Rodgers, *Musical Stages*, p. 235.
125   "For as long as I could remember": John Van Druten, quoted in Joseph E. Mersand, ed., *Three Comedies of American Family Life* (New York: Washington Square Press, 1961), p. 8.
127   "A show about a dame who knows": Charlotte Greenspan, *Pick Yourself Up: Dorothy Fields and the American Musical* (New York: Oxford University Press, 2010), p. 152.
127   "So Herbert said to me": Wilk, *They're Playing Our Song*, p. 366.
127   "I asked Dorothy to give me time": Ethel Merman, *Merman: An Autobiography* (New York: Simon & Schuster, 1978), p. 139.
127   Dick and Oscar set out to woo him: Laurence Bergreen, *As Thousands Cheer: The Life of Irving Berlin* (New York: Viking, 1990), p. 448.
128   Logan had even studied briefly: Joshua Logan, *Josh: My Up and Down, In and Out Life* (New York: Delacorte Press, 1976), p. 51.
128   In a call with Rodgers: Ibid., p. 219.
129   Dorothy Rodgers was forced to reply: Mary Ellin Berlin Barrett interview with author, 2015.
129   Berlin was an inveterate worrywart: Mary Ellin Barrett, *Irving Berlin: A Daughter's Memoir* (New York: Simon & Schuster, 1994), p. 235.
130   In the end, Berlin turned out: Jeffrey Magee, *Irving Berlin's American Musical Theater* (New York: Oxford University Press, 2012), p. 243.
130   Years later, when asked: Ted Chapin e-mail to author.
130   "I would say Irving Berlin": Barrett, *Irving Berlin*, p. 239.
130   Berlin also proved: Logan, *Josh*, p. 225.

131   It opened at the Imperial Theatre: Brian Kellow, *Ethel Merman* (New York: Viking, 2007), p. 112.

132   "I don't think I had ever seen dogged pride": Logan, *Josh*, p. 231.

133   As if this frantic pace of producing were not enough: Christina Klein, *Cold War Orientalism: Asia in the Middlebrow Imagination, 1945–1961* (Berkeley: University of California Press, 2003), pp. 179–87.

134   Dick Rodgers was just as busy: Richard Rodgers, *Musical Stages*, p. 250.

135   There would be no walls, no windows: Rodgers and Hammerstein, *Six Plays*, p. 185.

136   When their ship docked: Fordin, *Getting to Know Him*, p. 250.

136   Typically, Rodgers immediately sat down: William G. Hyland, *Richard Rodgers* (New Haven, CT: Yale University Press, 1998), p. 167.

136   Years later, Oscar would describe: Michaelis interview with OHII, p. 90.

136   "I always felt his songs came out": Frederick Nolan, *The Sound of Their Music: The Story of Rodgers and Hammerstein* (New York: Applause Theatre & Cinema Books, 2002), p. 170.

139   "That's not the play you've written": Fordin, *Getting to Know Him*, p. 254.

139   Still, Mielziner was a genius: Ibid., p. 253; Mordden, *Rodgers and Hammerstein*, p. 97.

139   All this spectacle sent the budget: Secrest, *Somewhere for Me,* p. 283.

140   That August, a reporter for *Cue*: OHII red leather *Allegro* scrapbook, OHII LOC.

140   "It was a seminal influence": Secrest, *Stephen Sondheim*, pp. 53–56.

140   So Hammerstein took on direction: Fordin, *Getting to Know Him*, p. 254.

140   "It was not a satisfactory solution": Richard Rodgers, *Musical Stages*, p. 251.

140   The opening night of the New Haven tryout: Nolan, *The Sound of Their Music*, p. 172.

141   Luckily, the Shubert Theatre in New Haven: Richard Rodgers, *Musical Stages*, p. 252.

141   "Need I tell you, the audience": Nolan, *The Sound of Their Music*, p. 172; Secrest, *Stephen Sondheim*, p. 55.

141   Even with the opening night mishaps: Joshua Logan to OHII, September 4 and September 6, 1947, Box 24, JLL LOC.

142   And the reaction of the Boston critics: OHII red leather *Allegro* scrapbook, OHII LOC.

143   "like a wet firecracker": Mordden, *Rodgers and Hammerstein*, p. 99.

143   The New York critics were just as divided: OHII red leather *Allegro* scrapbook, OHII LOC.

143   "In *Allegro*, he was writing about the conflict": Stephen Sondheim, liner notes for *Allegro* studio cast album (First Complete Recording), Masterworks Broadway, 2009.

143   The *New Republic* archly observed: OHII red leather *Allegro* scrapbook, OHII LOC.

144   Rodgers's music came in for more than its share: Ibid.

144   Near the end of the run, the company dropped: Mordden, *Rodgers and Hammerstein*, p. 102.

144   A scaled-down, sixteen-city tour: Mary C. Henderson, *Mielziner: Master of Modern Stage Design* (New York: Back Stage Books, 2001), p. 160.

144   Cole Porter once remarked: Nolan, *The Sound of Their Music*, p. 172.
144   Josh Logan's take: Ibid., p. 171.
144   "I think it was too preachy": RR OH, Columbia, p. 282.
144   For his part, Hammerstein said: OHII OH, Columbia; Box A, OHII LOC.
145   "Of all the musicals I ever worked on": Richard Rodgers, *Musical Stages*, p. 253.
147   Normally the most unsentimental of men: Michaelis interview with OHII, p. 89.

6: ENCHANTED EVENING

147   "Josh, we're going to buy this son of a bitch!": Logan, *Josh*, p. 261.
147   "They'll want the whole goddamn thing": Ibid., p. 262.
147   "Did I owe someone money": Richard Rodgers, *Musical Stages*, p. 258.
147   Logan was the SOB in question: Logan, *Josh*, p. 266.
148   Hammerstein at first had trouble: Fordin, *Getting to Know Him*, p. 260.
148   In the end, Michener accepted: James A. Michener, *The World Is My Home: A Memoir* (New York: Random House, 1992), p. 291.
148   "Those fellows are so mad": Fordin, *Getting to Know Him*, p. 261.
149   "I wish I could tell you about the South Pacific": James A. Michener, *Tales of the South Pacific* (New York: Dial Press, 2014), p. 3.
149   "Lieutenant one bullshit goddam fool": Ibid., p. 209.
150   On a sheet of yellow legal paper: *South Pacific* Green Box, OHII LOC.
151   At an audition at Oscar and Dorothy's: Mary Martin, *My Heart Belongs* (New York: Quill, 1984), pp. 59–60.
152   Years later, Rodgers would recall: Richard Rodgers, *Musical Stages*, p. 260.
154   "Do we have to wait": Martin, *My Heart Belongs*, p. 160.
154   After some initial reluctance: *Business Week*, June 18, 1949.
155   "I suggested that he would probably run a laundry": Michener, *The World Is My Home*, p. 292.
155   He had written just twenty-six pages: *South Pacific* correspondence, Box 2, OHII LOC.
156   He offered to drive down to Doylestown: Logan, *Josh*, pp. 273–74.
156   "I realized that Oscar was throwing me": Ibid., p. 275.
156   But Logan was so excited: Ibid., p. 277.
156   "If this isn't the damnedest show": Laurence Maslon, *The South Pacific Companion* (New York: Fireside/Simon & Schuster, 2008), p. 116.
157   He was relieved to find that the only instrument: *New York Herald Tribune*, April 3, 1949.
157   "I spent a minute or so studying the words": Fordin, *Getting to Know Him*, p. 268.
157   In fact, the first three notes of the song: Amy Asch, ed., *The Complete Lyrics of Oscar Hammerstein II* (New York: Alfred A. Knopf, 2008), p. 338.
157   That in turn inspired Oscar: Fordin, *Getting to Know Him*, p. 268.
158   "They said I was balmy": Martin, *My Heart Belongs*, p. 162.
158   And because Martin could never get: Ibid., p. 173.
159   "I will never forget": Ibid., p. 163.

159 "She'll have to pay the price for her antecedents": Fordin, *Getting to Know Him*, pp. 183–84.

160 In the draft of the *South Pacific* script: Draft script, R&H office files.

160 *"You've got to be carefully taught!"*: Rodgers and Hammerstein, *Six Plays*, p. 346.

161 *"It will grow like a weed"*: Draft script, R&H office files.

161 "'I wish I'd said it first'": Logan, *Josh*, p. 278.

161 But the next day: Logan, *Josh*, p. 279; *South Pacific* Green Box, OHII LOC.

162 Logan was crushed: Logan, *Josh*, p. 280.

163 "The New York opening may be": Ibid., pp. 284–85.

163 For *South Pacific*, Rittmann would write: Logan OH, SMU.

163 "As her role in the shows increased": Susanna Krebs Drewry e-mail to author.

164 Rittmann's own account: Trude Rittmann interview by Nancy Reynolds, December 9, 1976, transcript call number *MGZMT 3-1187, Dance Oral History Project, Jerome Robbins Dance Division, NYPL.

164 "Dick looked me right in the eye": *Boston Globe*, "A Lifetime of Stories from Musical Theater," October 3, 1997.

164 "We used to stand in the wings and marvel": Don Fellows interview, CUNY *Theater Talk*, June 18, 1999, https://www.youtube.com/watch?v=5Sb0sJQ dalQ.

165 "No sooner would I adjust myself": Ezio Pinza, *Ezio Pinza, an Autobiography* (New York: Rinehart, 1958), p. 240.

165 Pinza himself acknowledged: Richard Rodgers, *Musical Stages*, p. 261.

165 "You can't have a really moving and believable romance": *Boston Herald*, March 14, 1949.

165 "Then I asked Trude": Logan, *Josh*, p. 286.

165 The movements were so complicated: Fellows, *Theater Talk*.

166 Logan sent the men: Ibid.

166 *"Talk about breakfus' coffee and toast"*: *South Pacific* Correspondence, Green Box 2, OHII LOC.

166 Logan took Betta St. John: Logan, *Josh*, p. 286.

167 *"Well, my friend"*: 92nd Street Y performance, "Lyrics and Lyricists: Getting to Know You, Rodgers and Hammerstein," April 6, 2014.

167 "That's awful!" Logan blurted out: Logan, *Josh*, p. 287.

168 *"Suddenly lucky"*: Asch, *Complete Lyrics*, p. 343.

168 *"Younger than springtime are you"*: Ibid., p. 340.

168 *"Now is the time"*: Ibid., p. 343.

169 "If Cable and Emile were going on a mission": Logan, *Josh*, p. 287.

169 After seeing an early run-through: Nedda Harrigan Logan memo, February 21, 1949, Box 124, JLL LOC.

169 "That's it," Dick said: Logan, *Josh*, p. 287.

169 *"I planned a lovely tomorrow"*: *South Pacific* Correspondence, Green Box, 2, OHII LOC.

169 *"I'll keep remembering kisses"*: Asch, *Complete Lyrics*, p. 342.

170 But from then on, Logan recalled: Logan, *Josh*, p. 289.

170 "I don't have one thousand": Michener, *The World Is My Home*, p. 294.

170 On March 5, Howard Reinheimer: Reinheimer memo to producers, *South Pacific* Correspondence, Green Box, OHII LOC.

170   DO YOU NEED A GOOD BARITONE?: Stephen Sondheim telegram to OHII, March 7, 1949, *South Pacific* Correspondence, Green Box, OHII LOC.

170   But Josh Logan, whose emotions could veer: Logan to OHII, March 7, 1949, Box C, OHII LOC.

171   His mood was not improved: Logan, *Josh*, p. 291.

171   Logan was somewhat reassured: Ibid., p. 293.

171   Rodgers himself was annoyed: William Stott with Jane Stott, *On Broadway: Performance Photographs by Fred Fehl* (Austin: University of Texas Press, 1978), p. 139.

172   "That night she tore the house apart": Ibid., p. 295.

172   There were a few other small changes: OHII to Essie Robson, March 9, 1949, *South Pacific* Correspondence, Green Box, OHII LOC.

172   Hammerstein was less sympathetic: Exchange with Thomas McWhorter, April 2 and April 11, *South Pacific* Correspondence, Green Box, OHII LOC.

173   Oscar happened to leave his overcoat: Pinza, *Ezio Pinza*, p. 243.

173   the critics offered raves all around: Steven Suskin, *Opening Night on Broadway: A Critical Quotebook of the Golden Era of the Musical Theatre, Oklahoma! (1943) to Fiddler on the Roof (1964)* (New York: Schirmer Books, 1990), pp. 639–43.

173   Helen Hayes wrote Oscar and Dorothy: Helen Hayes to OHII and DBH, April 11, 1949, *South Pacific*, Box 3, OHII LOC.

173   For his part, James Michener paraphrased: Stephen J. May, *Michener's South Pacific* (Gainesville: University Press of Florida, 2011), p. 111.

173   An advance sale of $500,000 quickly grew: *Business Week*, June 18, 1949.

174   Howard Reinheimer had set up: Ibid.

174   Each morning at seven o'clock: *New York Post*, June 7, 1949.

174   The demand was so intense: *New York Herald Tribune*, September 19, 1949.

175   In the end, Janet Blair: May, *Michener's South Pacific*, pp. 111–12.

175   The problem was so severe: OHII to Claudia Cassidy, August 1950, *South Pacific* Correspondence, Green Box, OHII LOC.

7: PARALLEL WIVES

177   Dorothy Rodgers had stumbled: Dorothy Rodgers, *My Favorite Things: A Personal Guide to Decorating and Entertaining* (New York: Atheneum, 1964), p. 4.

178   She would insist that this reputation: Dorothy Rodgers and Mary Rodgers, *A Word to Wives* (New York: Alfred A. Knopf, 1970), p. 197.

178   Her standard wedding present: Deborah Grace Winer, *On the Sunny Side of the Street: The Life and Lyrics of Dorothy Fields* (New York: Schirmer Books, 1997), p. 179.

179   "I always felt that I hadn't washed": Sheldon Harnick interview with author.

179   She was a collector: Fordin, *Getting to Know Him*, p. 144.

179   "Well, I don't care": Ibid., p. 215.

180   "It is a handsome, exciting room": Dorothy Rodgers, *My Favorite Things*, p. 47.

180   "They were perfectly civil": Mary Rodgers OH, SMU.

180   Stephen Sondheim was blunter: Sondheim e-mail to author, October 2015.

181 "But Rodgers and Hammerstein rejected it": Ewen, *Richard Rodgers*, p. 267.

181 As it happened, Cerf was dining: Helen M. Strauss, *A Talent for Luck: An Autobiography* (New York: Random House, 1979), pp. 254ff.

181 Strauss, citing Cerf's recommendation: Helen Strauss to RR, December 9, 1949, R&H office files.

181 "This is the book I mentioned": Liner notes by Ted Chapin, *The King and I*, 1992 studio cast recording, Philips.

182 "Can't talk now, Fanny": Sheridan Morley, *Gertrude Lawrence: A Biography* (New York: McGraw-Hill, 1981), p. 186.

182 Oscar, listening from the next room: Fordin, *Getting to Know Him*, p. 291.

182 "We were concerned": Richard Rodgers, *Musical Stages*, p. 270.

182 "That did it": Ibid.

182 So eager, by Helen Strauss's later account: Strauss, *A Talent for Luck*, p. 254.

183 On February 26, 1950: Fanny Holtzmann to OHII, Box 2 of 9, OHII LOC.

183 "Oh, she was a fey creature": John Green OH, SMU.

183 Her longtime chum: Barry Day, ed., *The Letters of Noel Coward* (New York: Alfred A. Knopf, 2007), pp. 204–6.

184 That was a message that resonated: Alfred Habegger, *Masked: The Life of Anna Leonowens, Schoolmistress at the Court of Siam* (Madison: University of Wisconsin Press, 2014), p. 360.

184 Logan turned them down: Logan, *Josh*, p. 307.

185 "I phoned Rex Harrison": RR to DFR, February 19, 1950, RR NYPL.

185 Rodgers fought Coward: Hyland, *Richard Rodgers*, p. 196.

186 "He scowled in our direction": Richard Rodgers, *Musical Stages*, p. 272.

186 His name was Yul Brynner: Jhan Robbins, *Yul Brynner: The Inscrutable King* (New York: Dodd, Mead, 1987), pp. 10–28.

187 "Here is a chance for more lusty comedy": Asch, *Complete Lyrics*, p. 350.

188 *"Shall I tell you what I think of you?"*: Rodgers and Hammerstein, *Six Plays*, p. 401.

188 By the fall, Oscar would be exchanging: Jo Mielziner to OHII, October 9, 1950, Box 2 of 3, OHII LOC.

188 "I hope my memo to you": Mielziner to OHII, October 16, 1950, Box 2 of 9, OHII LOC.

189 On December 5, Oscar wrote to Van Druten: OHII to John Van Druten, December 5, 1950, Box 2 of 3, OHII LOC.

191 Hammerstein was uncharacteristically proud: Logan, *Josh*, pp. 307–8.

191 Meantime, Rodgers was having troubles: RR to John Van Druten, November 28, 1950, Van Druten papers, NYPL.

192 But Rodgers set the lyric in four-four time: Mordden, *Rodgers and Hammerstein*, p. 141.

193 "I am completely pleased to do just the ballet": Jerome Robbins to OHII, November 11, 1950, Box 2 of 2, OHII LOC.

194 Robbins would hire Yuriko: Amanda Vaill, *Somewhere: The Life of Jerome Robbins* (New York: Broadway Books, 2006), p. 183.

194 But Rodgers suggested that the ballet: Richard Rodgers, *Musical Stages*, p. 274.

194 Rodgers sometimes chafed: Mordden, *Rodgers and Hammerstein*, p. 142.

195 "Having had plenty of experience": RR NYPL.

195   In January 1951, Reinheimer wrote: Reinheimer memo, Box 2 of 9, OHII LOC.

195   Helen Strauss passed along: Strauss to OHII, January 11, 1951, Box 2 of 9, OHII LOC.

195   This was a line of critique: OHII to Strauss, January 16, 1951, Box 2 of 3, OHII LOC.

195   "By its very nature, the story": Mordden, *Rodgers and Hammerstein*, p. 138.

196   At the next day's rehearsal: Richard Rodgers, *Musical Stages*, p. 272.

196   He was so thrilled: Logan to R&H, January 18, 1951, R&H office files.

197   The curtain rang down: "A Happy Tune: An Interview with Sandy Kennedy," *Lincoln Center Theater Review*, no. 65 (Spring 2015): 25–32.

197   The reaction of the New Haven critics: Amy Asch e-mail to author, April 22, 2017.

197   Robert Emmett Dolan was more sanguine: Robert Emmett Dolan to OHII, February 27, 1951, Box 2 of 3, OHII LOC.

198   She poured out her feelings: Gertrude Lawrence to RR, undated, RR NYPL.

199   Mary Martin, who claimed to have seen: Martin, *My Heart Belongs*, p. 122.

199   There is no record of his reply: Gertrude Lawrence to RR, undated, RR NYPL.

200   In Yul Brynner's words, the king: Yul Brynner OH, SMU.

202   "Dearest Occie," Lawrence wrote: Lawrence to OHII, undated, R&H office files.

203   "On the opening night she came on": Richard Stoddard Aldrich, *Gertrude Lawrence as Mrs. A.: An Intimate Biography of the Great Star* (New York: Greystone Press, 1954), p. 365.

203   Fanny Holtzmann, sitting next to Billy Rose: Edward O. Berkman, *The Lady and the Law: The Remarkable Story of Fanny Holtzmann* (Boston: Little, Brown, 1976), p. 344.

203   Howard Dietz, the lyricist and MGM publicist, was so excited: Dietz to OHII, undated, *King and I* Green Box, OHII LOC.

203   Oscar's old partner: Romberg to OHII, *King and I* Box 8, OHII LOC.

203   Dorothy Fields described: Ibid.

203   But as Oscar had feared: Green, *Fact Book*, pp. 581–84.

8: CATASTROPHIC SUCCESS

204   One such occasion was a two-part tribute: Ed Sullivan programs are archived in the Moving Image Research Center of the LOC, accessible digitally.

205   In 1951, Rodgers and Hammerstein would each earn: Fordin, *Getting to Know Him*, p. 304.

205   "I don't believe the firm": Bennett, *The Broadway Sound*, pp. 184–85.

205   Josh Logan once reported: Ted Chapin and Bruce Pomahac, conversations with author.

206   Rodgers once told the arranger Don Walker: Walker, *Men of Notes*, p. 219.

206   During the preparation of the text: OHII to Henry Simon, July 7, 1958, Box 3 of 9, OHII LOC.

207 The book's finished text: Richard Rodgers and Oscar Hammerstein II, *The Rodgers and Hammerstein Songbook* (New York: Simon & Schuster, 1968), pp. 180–81.

207 Dorothy Hammerstein told Stephen Sondheim: Sondheim e-mail to author.

207 On the other hand, Dorothy Rodgers: Nolan, *The Sound of Their Music*, p. 215.

207 When Rodgers learned: Secrest, *Somewhere for Me*, p. 307.

207 Their office secretary, Lillian Leff: Bennett, *The Broadway Sound*, p. 251.

208 "I am sorry that the lyrics": John Van Druten to OHII, December 1950, Box 2 of 3, OHII LOC.

209 "But the plot has a lot of hackneyed playwriting": Fordin, *Getting to Know Him*, p. 308.

209 The revival opened in New York: Green, *Fact Book*, pp. 223–24.

210 "For the difficult task of timing": Richard Rodgers, *Musical Stages*, p. 279.

210 In his memoir, Bennett would acknowledge: Bennett, *The Broadway Sound*, p. 210.

211 And from almost the opening night: Morris Jacobs memo to file, May 8, 1951, Box 2 of 9, OHII.

211 "Well as I know and mistrust": John Cornell to Morris Jacobs, October 3, 1953, RR NYPL.

211 Still, by the end of the Broadway run: Mordden, *Rodgers and Hammerstein*, p. 146.

212 "This is my official and documentary": OHII to Gertrude Lawrence, April 3, 1951; Lawrence to OHII, April 10, 1951, Box 2 of 3, OHII LOC.

212 "This is fanned into nothing by 3 o'clock": Lawrence to Van Druten, Van Druten papers, NYPL.

212 In April, Dick and Oscar asked Noël Coward: Day, ed., *Letters of Noël Coward*, p. 202.

213 Her friend Daphne du Maurier: Ibid., p. 206.

213 "Eight times a week": R&H to Lawrence, May 20, 1952, R&H office files.

213 Lawrence wrote Dorothy Hammerstein: Undated letter, Box 8, OHII LOC.

214 On Friday, September 5: Howard Reinheimer to Fanny Holtzmann, R&H office files.

214 Only after an autopsy: Morley, *Gertrude Lawrence*, pp. 197–98.

214 Oscar wrote a gently teasing tribute: *Town & Country*, June 1952, Box 33, OHII LOC.

215 "One of our aims was to avoid": Richard Rodgers, *Musical Stages*, p. 281.

215 He, too, told an interviewer: Nolan, *The Sound of Their Music*, p. 218.

215 Don Walker—not the stately Russell Bennett: Secrest, *Somewhere for Me*, p. 318.

216 "From the start we ought to have known": George Abbott OH, SMU.

216 Abbott hoped that when the action: Fordin, *Getting to Know Him*, p. 309.

217 "In some quarters we may be criticized": OHII to Van Druten, April 30, 1953, *King and I* Green Box, OHII LOC.

217 For his part, Rodgers would recall: Nolan, *The Sound of Their Music*, p. 222.

218 "To this day, if I sing it": Secrest, *Somewhere for Me*, pp. 318–19.

218 Throughout the rehearsal process: OHII undated notes, *Me and Juliet* Green Box 12, OHII.

218 *"A big black giant"*: Rodgers and Hammerstein, *Six Plays*, pp. 486–87.

219 Because Mielziner's sets were so cumbersome: Mordden, *Rodgers and Hammerstein*, p. 157.

219 Jimmy Hammerstein, who joined the company: Fordin, *Getting to Know Him*, p. 310.

220 The number proved prophetic: Green, *Fact Book*, p. 603.

220 Oscar's verdict was even more succinct: John Steele Gordon interview with author.

220 "The hell with them": Fordin, *Getting to Know Him*, p. 312.

221 "The gesture of hosting": Ibid., p. 313.

221 In 1950, as president of the Authors League: OHII affidavit of November 23, 1953, Box 8 of 9, OHII LOC.

221 Oscar told reporters he was surprised: Fordin, *Getting to Know Him*, p. 270.

221 Now, Hammerstein's outspoken advocacy: All information relating to OHII FBI file obtained by Joan Saltzman, September 6, 2010, FOIPA No. 1146557–000, 112 pages.

223 "It would be dishonest of me not to confess": OHII affidavit of November 23, 1953, Box 8, OHII LOC.

225 "The public tells us what it likes": Script for broadcast, November 23, 1953, Box 8 of 9, OHII LOC. Also reviewed entire broadcast at Paley Center, https://www.paleycenter.org/collection/item/?q=dinner+with+the+president&f=all&c=all&advanced=1&p=1&item=T77:0132.

225 In his own remarks, Eisenhower: http://www.presidency.ucsb.edu/ws/index.php?pid=9770.

226 What's more, Hammerstein was not thrilled: Nolan, *The Sound of Their Music*, p. 231.

227 In the spring of 1954: OHII souvenir program note on *Pipe Dream*, Box 8 of 9, OHII LOC.

227 "Whether we can get away with a factual house of prostitution": Fordin, *Getting to Know Him*, p. 323.

228 "I don't see how I can wedge her in": OHII to Steinbeck, July 26, 1955, Box 2 of 3, OHII.

228 "Doesn't that belting disturb you": Stott and Stott, *On Broadway*, p. 276.

229 "It isn't too early": Richard Rodgers, *Musical Stages*, p. 285.

229 "When he finally got cancer": Mary Rodgers interview in Maslon, *Richard Rodgers: The Sweetest Sounds*.

229 "Before that happened": Secrest, *Somewhere for Me*, p. 330.

229 "The next thing I knew": Richard Rodgers, *Musical Stages*, p. 286.

230 "I am delighted with *Pipe Dream*": Fordin, *Getting to Know Him*, p. 326.

230 *"Pipe Dream* became full of doilies": Secrest, *Somewhere for Me*, p. 327.

231 "like an off-duty visiting nurse": Fordin, *Getting to Know Him*, p. 326.

231 "One of the most serious criticisms": Ibid., p. 327.

231 The sole dirty joke: Ibid., p. 218.

232 Dick Rodgers was apparently aware: Secrest, *Somewhere for Me*, p. 268.

232 It isn't clear precisely when: Owen Shribman, telephone interview with author.

232 "contemplated calling a lawyer": Fordin, *Getting to Know Him*, p. 247.

232 Moss Hart detected a surprising lack of feeling: Moss Hart Diary, https://search.library.wisc.edu/catalog/999465334502121.

233 Steinbeck complained: Fordin, *Getting to Know Him*, p. 327.

233 "I have heard others describe": John Steinbeck to OHII, in John Steinbeck, *Steinbeck: A Life in Letters*, ed. Elaine Steinbeck and Robert Wallsten (New York: Penguin Books, 1989), pp. 516–17.

233 And when the show opened: Suskin, *Opening Night*, p. 554.

234 In a letter to the casting director: Steinbeck letter to John Fearnley, spring 1959, R&H office files.

234 "The guy has never been in a whorehouse": Fordin, *Getting to Know Him*, p. 328.

9: BEYOND BROADWAY

235 In the spring of 1954: Norton speech, March 31, 1954, Box 29, OHII LOC.

236 Hollywood's interest in *Oklahoma!*: Richard Rodgers, *Musical Stages*, p. 283.

237 Fred Zinnemann was less impressed: Zinnemann to OHII, September 30, 1953, Zinnemann papers, AMPAS.

238 Zinnemann was more impressed: Ibid.

238 But Hammerstein wrote: OHII to Joseph Schenck, October 22, 1953, Zinnemann papers, AMPAS.

239 "You and I seem to be standing": RR to OHII, Box 8 of 9, OHII LOC.

239 And Oscar, belying his reputation: OHII to Schenck, October 22, 1953, Zinnemann papers, AMPAS.

240 Jan Clayton asked Oscar: Clayton OH, SMU.

240 At virtually the same time: Shirley Jones, *Shirley Jones: A Memoir* (New York: Gallery Books, 2013), p. 46.

240 For Jones, it was a Cinderella story: Ibid., p. 42.

241 "Richard—boy, you sang it": Gene Nelson OH, SMU.

241 Zinnemann was acutely conscious: Zinnemann notes on final shooting script, June 1, 1954, Zinnemann papers, AMPAS.

241 That last desire proved: Fred Zinnemann, *A Life in the Movies: An Autobiography* (New York: Charles Scribner's Sons, 1992), p. 147.

241 Agnes de Mille had been hired: Richard Rodgers, *Musical Stages*, p. 285.

242 Rodgers himself tangled: RR memo to file, August 23, 1954, RR NYPL.

242 "Before anything appears on the screen": RR to Hornblow et al., October 29, 1954, Zinnemann papers, AMPAS.

242 That same week, George Skouras: Skouras to R&H, October 27, 1954, Zinnemann papers, AMPAS.

243 Total box-office receipts: Tally sheet, May 2, 1957, Arthur Hornblow papers, AMPAS.

243 Late in life, though: Richard Rodgers, *Musical Stages*, p. 285.

244 Fox's production chief Darryl Zanuck: Zanuck to OHII, May 12, 1955; OHII to Zanuck, May 17, 1955; Zanuck to OHII, May 20, 1955, Box 3 of 9, OHII LOC.

245 "tears rolling down his cheeks": Jones, *Shirley Jones: A Memoir*, pp. 82–83.

245   But the biggest problem: Geoffrey M. Shurlock to Frank McCarthy, June 27, 1955, Box 21, OHII LOC.

246   When the film opened: Green, *Fact Book*, p. 545.

246   Rittmann had a screen credit: Rittmann to sister Lotte Krebs, July 4, 1956; Susanna Krebs Drewry to author, May 13, 2017.

247   "The king dies because he has no will to live": Brynner OH, SMU.

247   The film opened: Green, *Fact Book*, p. 592.

247   But in an unhappy postscript: Mielziner settlement papers, R&H office files.

248   "I look at television a great deal": OHII speech, February 17, 1957, R&H office files, copy provided by Amy Asch.

248   He noted that it typically took him: Ibid.

248   Some of the early collaboration: OHII to RR, November 10, 1956, R&H office files.

249   "*I'm a sailor in the battle of Trafalgar*": *Cinderella* Green Box 4, Misc. Notes, OHII LOC.

250   Hammerstein initially named: OHII lyric sketches, *Cinderella* Green Box, OHII LOC.

250   They had nothing for her at the time: Mordden, *Rodgers and Hammerstein*, p. 152.

251   In later years, Julie Andrews: Julie Andrews, *Home: A Memoir of My Early Years* (New York: Hyperion, 2008), pp. 227ff.

251   It was all she could do: Ibid., p. 230.

252   "*If I weren't King*": Asch, *Complete Lyrics*, p. 384.

252   "At the stroke of 8, on Sunday night": Newspaper clip of CBS advertisement, *Cinderella* Green Box 4, Misc. Notes, OHII LOC.

253   "Apparently I picked up a bug": Secrest, *Somewhere for Me*, p. 334.

253   He thought it was best to forget: RR interview by Tony Thomas.

253   "I get a very peculiar feeling": Secrest, *Somewhere for Me*, p. 283.

254   In early 1957, Moss Hart: Ibid., p. 336.

254   "I began sleeping late": Richard Rodgers, *Musical Stages*, p. 293.

254   "He had ground to an absolute halt": Secrest, *Somewhere for Me*, p. 337.

254   "I voluntarily separated myself": Richard Rodgers, *Musical Stages*, p. 294.

254   In the mid-1950s, Payne Whitney: *New York Times*, "Letting Go of Payne Whitney" (Letter to Editor of *Times Magazine*), December 4, 1994.

255   "After a self-imposed exile": Richard Rodgers, *Musical Stages*, p. 294.

255   "You've piled mountaintop on mountaintop": Edna Ferber to RR, August 11, 1957, RR NYPL.

255   Moss Hart, himself a survivor: Moss Hart to RR, August 23, 1957, RR NYPL.

255   The most astute analysis: Clifton Fadiman to RR, undated, RR NYPL.

256   Rodgers wrote back: RR to Fadiman, October 10, 1957, RR NYPL.

257   "did not sound good at all": OHII to Logan, February 27, 1957, Box 4 of 9, OHII LOC.

257   Logan's first choice: Joshua Logan, *Movie Stars, Real People, and Me* (New York: Delacorte Press, 1978), p. 118.

257   "Mary and Dick are cool to us": OHII to RR, summer of 1957, undated, Box 3, OHII LOC.

257   Halliday was even colder: Mitzi Gaynor interview with author.

258 But from the beginning, Logan made a fatal mistake: Logan, *Movie Stars*, p. 124.

259 "This could be wonderful": OHII to Logan, Box 24, JLL LOC.

259 "Because," Darby explained: Ken Darby to RR, February 22, 1976, RR NYPL.

259 When the film opened: Green, *Fact Book*, pp. 576–77.

260 In later years, Rodgers would say: RR OH, Columbia, p. 304.

260 The film would make more money: Logan, *Movie Stars*, p. 129.

260 "I went over my personal income figures": OHII to RR, summer of 1957, Box 3, OHII LOC.

261 Oscar read the novel and liked it: Fordin, *Getting to Know Him*, p. 337.

261 "We have some score finished": RR to Arthur Hornblow, April 8, 1958, Hornblow papers, AMPAS.

262 "slight but adequate voice": Richard Rodgers, *Musical Stages*, p. 295.

262 Years later, Kelly himself: Kelly OH, SMU.

264 In mid-September, Dick wrote: Secrest, *Somewhere for Me*, p. 342.

264 "Think of the fun we're having": Nolan, *The Sound of Their Music*, p. 242.

264 Rodgers's progress reports to Dorothy: Secrest, *Somewhere for Me*, p. 343.

264 "Dick was always fast": Nolan, *The Sound of Their Music*, p. 242.

265 "Ta Doesn't Quite Make Up His Mind": Dan Dietz. *The Complete Book of 1950s Broadway Musicals* (Lanham, MD: Rowman & Littlefield, 2014), p. 331.

265 Critical reception was decidedly mixed: Green, *Fact Book*, p. 623.

265 But Kenneth Tynan: Ibid., p. 625.

266 "My only thought was to keep on": Richard Rodgers, *Musical Stages*, p. 296.

10: AUF WIEDERSEHEN

268 "They came back," Rodgers would recall: Richard Rodgers, *Musical Stages*, p. 299.

269 Maria was said to have loved the show: Max Wilk, *The Making of The Sound of Music* (New York: Routledge, 2007), p. 7.

269 In another account: Ronald L. Davis, *Mary Martin: Broadway Legend* (Norman: University of Oklahoma Press, 2008), p. 208.

270 And as a gesture of goodwill: Wilk, *The Making of The Sound of Music*, p. 9.

270 "an audience must go away": Ibid., p. 13.

270 Now Lindsay and Crouse sketched: Nolan, *The Sound of Their Music*, p. 246.

271 "She was bouncy, enthusiastic": Martin, *My Heart Belongs*, p. 245.

271 Sister Gregory's advice: David Kaufman, *Some Enchanted Evenings: The Glittering Life and Times of Mary Martin* (New York: St. Martin's Press, 2016), pp. 196–97.

272 As work on the show progressed: Sister Gregory to Hallidays, http://blogs.loc.gov/music/2013/01/sister-gregory-duffy-an-asset-to-the-abbey-and-the-theater-2.

272 Robert Emmett Dolan warned: Dolan to OHII, April 2, 1958, OHII LOC.

273 "As time goes on, Halliday is going": Timothy Crouse telephone interview with author.

273   Howard Reinheimer warned them: Reinheimer to R&H, February 6, 1959, *Sound of Music* Box 1, OHII LOC.

273   Oscar told his son Jimmy: Fordin, *Getting to Know Him*, p. 345.

273   "The four guys loved the material": Timothy Crouse e-mail to author, September 23, 2016.

275   *"To laugh like a brook"*: Asch, *Complete Lyrics*, p. 395.

275   By early May, Hammerstein was working: OHII sketches, *Sound of Music* Box 1, OHII LOC.

276   "You ask after the relationship": Rittmann to Lotte Krebs, October 31, 1959; Susanna Drewry to author.

276   Meantime, Sister Gregory was weighing in: http://blogs.loc.gov/music/2013/01/sister-gregory-duffy-an-asset-to-the-abbey-and-the-theater-2/.

278   "This makes it a song with a reason": Mark Horowitz e-mail to author, May 22, 2017.

279   "Given my lack of familiarity": Richard Rodgers, *Musical Stages*, p. 301.

279   Sister Gregory enthusiastically approved: Gregory to Hallidays, September 24, 1959, http://blogs.loc.gov/music/2013/01/sister-gregory-duffy-an-asset-to-the-abbey-and-the-theater-2/.

279   But it's at least possible: de Mille monograph, Rittmann cover letter, R&H office files.

280   By midsummer, it was Maria von Trapp's turn: Richard Halliday to R&H et al., July 31, 1959, *Sound of Music* Green Box, OHII LOC; Sister Gregory to Hallidays, August 4, 1959, http://blogs.loc.gov/music/2013/01/sister-gregory-duffy-an-asset-to-the-abbey-and-the-theater-2/.

281   From the beginning, the decision had been made: Kaufman, *Some Enchanted Evenings*, p. 197.

281   Eventually they saw Theodore Bikel: Bikel OH, SMU.

282   Bikel was sent to the society hairdresser: Kaufman, *Some Enchanted Evenings*, p. 199.

282   Casting the seven children: Ibid.

282   Martin not only learned how to cross herself: Nolan, *The Sound of Their Music*, p. 249.

282   "I think this will be the 46th time": OHII to Harry Ruby, September 1, 1959, Box 4 of 9, OHII LOC.

282   On September 16, he went for a checkup: Fordin, *Getting to Know Him*, p. 350.

283   "Dear Oscar: We are sixty": Howard Lindsay and Russel Crouse to OHII, September 17, 1959, *Sound of Music* Box 1, OHII LOC.

283   "Don't look at it now": Fordin, *Getting to Know Him*, p. 351.

284   Years later, Mary Martin would recall: Martin, *My Heart Belongs*, p. 239.

284   It was also a workout: Davis, *Mary Martin*, p. 213.

284   Halliday put a pedometer: Martin, *My Heart Belongs*, p. 249.

284   Martin was also receiving steady reassurance: Sister Gregory to Martin, September 17, 1959, http://blogs.loc.gov/music/2013/01/sister-gregory-duffy-an-asset-to-the-abbey-and-the-theater-2/.

285   The Boston opening was Tuesday: Kaufman, *Some Enchanted Evenings*, p. 202.

285   He sat in a box with Dorothy: Wilk, *The Making of The Sound of Music*, p. 43.

285   Oscar set to work on the lyrics: OHII sketch, undated, R&H office files.

286   "I love that Edelweiss": Secrest, *Somewhere for Me*, pp. 348–49.

286   In Boston, Rodgers finally let Halliday have it: Ibid., p. 350.

286   The New York opening: Wilk, *The Making of The Sound of Music*, p. 38.

287   And Kenneth Tynan's verdict: Green, *Fact Book*, p. 635.

287   The Hammersteins attended the opening: Wilk, *The Making of The Sound of Music*, p. 39.

288   "As in all your other shared creations": Max Schuster to R&H, November 28, 1959, RR NYPL.

288   Taken together, those record sales: Laurence Maslon, *The Sound of Music Companion* (New York: Simon & Schuster, 2007), p. 88.

289   After all, what movie: Wilk, *The Making of The Sound of Music*, pp. 54–56.

289   "God damnit!" he shouted: Kaufman, *Some Enchanted Evenings*, p. 202.

289   When a young Jon Voight joined: Jon Voight conversation with author, 2017 *Vanity Fair* Oscar party.

289   "How are you going to buck a nun?": Kellow, *Ethel Merman*, p. 188.

290   "It is increasingly apparent that we have something": RR to OHII, December 18, 1959, Box 4 of 9, OHII LOC.

290   Oscar had big ambitions for the casting: OHII, Notes on *Allegro* TV, Box A, OH LOC.

290   "I realize that right now": OHII to RR, April 7, 1960, Box 6 of 9, OHII LOC.

291   "This is the accepted age of retirement": Fordin, *Getting to Know Him*, p. 355.

291   "Goddamnit!" he burst out: Ibid., pp. 357–58.

291   One day that summer: Ibid., p. 358.

292   As late as July: Robert C. Kitchen to OHII, June 21, 1960; OHII reply, July 6, 1960, OHII LOC, Mark Horowitz e-mail to author.

292   "I understand this perfectly well": RR to Jerome Whyte, August 15, 1960, R&H office files, copy from Amy Asch copy.

292   On Oscar's last office visit: Benjamin Kean condolence letter to DBH, Box 7, OHII LOC.

293   As the days wore on, Oscar lay: Fordin, *Getting to Know Him*, p. 359.

293   "No man can work as long as Oscar did": Funeral file, OHII LOC.

293   Condolence letters flooded in: Letters from Hart, Ferber, and de Mille, X Box 7, OHII LOC.

294   "The guy is falling apart": Secrest, *Somewhere for Me*, p. 355.

294   Mutual friends confided: Edwin H. Knopf to RR, September 3 1960, RR NYPL.

294   With uncanny acuity, Sister Gregory: Sister Gregory to RR, August 24, 1960, RR NYPL.

295   Indeed, Dick's letters: RR to S. N. Behrman, September 6, 1960, RR NYPL.

295   "I suppose patience is a lesson": RR to Jan Clayton, September 6, 1960, RR NYPL.

295   "I am permanently grieved": Nolan, *The Sound of Their Music*, p. 266.

11: WALKING ALONE

296   "It was all very placid": Fordin, *Getting to Know Him*, pp. 343–45.
297   "I don't think we need a psychologist": RR to Edna Ferber, September 6, 1960, RR NYPL.
297   "Under the circumstances": Richard Rodgers, *Musical Stages*, p. 306.
297   "She would not represent a cause": Ibid., p. 307.
298   That was a debatable proposition: Diahann Carroll, *Diahann: An Autobiography* (Boston: Little, Brown, 1986), p. 114.
299   Rodgers's own take: Richard Rodgers, *Musical Stages*, p. 308.
299   "Thurgood Marshall is wildly enthusiastic": RR to Daniel Melnick, October 9, 1961, RR NYPL.
300   "It only confirmed that he accomplished": Carroll, *Diahann*, p. 113.
301   "It was just an obvious thing to do": Maslon, *The Sound of Music Companion*, p. 89.
301   "No musical with swastikas": Wilk, *The Making of The Sound of Music*, p. 61.
301   "The characters were more clearly defined": Saul Chaplin, *The Golden Age of Movie Musicals and Me* (Norman: University of Oklahoma Press, 1994), p. 209.
302   Chaplin agreed to try: Ibid., p. 218.
302   "Suddenly everything made sense": Julie Andrews e-mail to author, 2017.
302   "'That's our girl'": Maslon, *The Sound of Music Companion*, p. 92.
303   "Everyone on the film was unified": Andrews e-mail to author.
305   At first, Sondheim would remember: Secrest, *Stephen Sondheim*, p. 175.
305   "The more we worked on the show": Richard Rodgers, *Musical Stages*, pp. 318–19.
305   "Someday, when we see each other again": RR to Sister Gregory, April 30, 1965, RR NYPL.
306   he had warm words: RR to Dave Brubeck, January 24, 1966, RR NYPL.
306   In a similar letter: RR to Burt Bacharach, April 14, 1970, RR NYPL.
306   "I simply went back": Richard Rodgers, *Musical Stages*, p. 321.
307   "which meant we were not only working with him": Nolan, *The Sound of Their Music*, p. 281.
307   "If you wanted to talk to the composer": Ibid., p. 282.
308   "I'm glad you're here": Richard Rodgers, *Musical Stages*, p. 323.
308   "This is a unique talent": RR to Stephen Sondheim, June 3, 1970, RR NYPL.
309   Rodgers complained to Liza Minnelli: Secrest, *Somewhere for Me*, p. 388.
309   It was a major achievement: Ibid., p. 389.
309   At first, Harnick assumed: Sheldon Harnick interview with author.
310   "I didn't just have a good time": RR to Michael Bennett, June 23, 1975, RR NYPL.
310   "When he'd go to get in his car": Florence Henderson interview with author.
311   Dorothy Rodgers vetoed that idea: Nolan, *The Sound of Their Music*, p. 294.
311   He would sit, his daughter Linda would recall: Secrest, *Somewhere for Me*, p. 400.
311   "Thirty-eight years ago": Agnes de Mille to RR, undated, RR NYPL.

312   "As I went up the aisle": *New York Times*, "Oklahoma! Returns to Broadway: Free as the Breeze," December 14, 1979.

312   "In spite of our differences": Stephen Sondheim to DFR, December 31, 1979, RR NYPL.

312   Shirley Verrett, the Metropolitan Opera mezzo-soprano: Secrest, *Somewhere for Me*, p. 363.

312   The presiding rabbi: Ibid., p. 401.

313   "I don't think anybody": Mary Rodgers interview for the PBS documentary *Richard Rodgers: The Sweetest Sounds*, Laurence Maslon transcript to author.

313   "Dear Mr. Rodgers": Terrell Dougan to RR, February 28, 1968; RR reply, March 4, 1968, RR NYPL.

EPILOGUE: BLOOM AND GROW FOREVER

314   Even as a twelve-year-old boy: Crouse e-mail to author, September 23, 2016.

315   Barbara Cook would recall: Barbara Cook telephone interview with author.

315   By 1967, the critic Martin Gottfried: Martin Gottfried, *A Theater Divided: The Postwar American Stage* (Boston: Little, Brown, 1969), pp. 177–80.

316   On the occasion of the fiftieth anniversary: *New York Times*, January 24, 1993.

317   Brooks Atkinson wrote: Henderson, *Mielziner*, p. 173.

319   "Hammerstein rarely has": Sondheim, *Finishing the Hat*, p. 37.

320   "They thought big": Andrews e-mail to author.

BIBLIOGRAPHY

Aldrich, Richard Stoddard. *Gertrude Lawrence as Mrs. A.: An Intimate Biography of the Great Star*. New York: Greystone Press, 1954.

Andrews, Julie. *Home: A Memoir of My Early Years*. New York: Hyperion, 2008.

Asch, Amy, ed. *The Complete Lyrics of Oscar Hammerstein II*. New York: Alfred A. Knopf, 2008.

Atkinson, Brooks. *Broadway*. London: Cassell, 1971.

Ballard, Kaye. *How I Lost 10 Pounds in 53 Years: A Memoir*. New York: Back Stage Books, 2006.

Barrett, Mary Ellin. *Irving Berlin: A Daughter's Memoir*. New York: Simon & Schuster, 1994.

Bennett, Robert Russell. *The Broadway Sound: The Autobiography and Selected Essays of Robert Russell Bennett*. Edited by George J. Ferencz. Rochester, NY: University of Rochester Press, 1999.

Bergreen, Laurence. *As Thousands Cheer: The Life of Irving Berlin*. New York: Viking, 1990.

Berkman, Edward O. *The Lady and the Law: The Remarkable Story of Fanny Holtzmann*. Boston: Little, Brown, 1976.

Bikel, Theodore. *Theo: An Autobiography*. Madison: University of Wisconsin Press, 2014.

Block, Geoffrey. *Enchanted Evenings: The Broadway Musical from Show Boat to Sondheim*. New York: Oxford University Press, 1997.

———. *Richard Rodgers*. New Haven, CT: Yale University Press, 2003.

———, ed. *The Richard Rodgers Reader*. New York: Oxford University Press, 2002.

Boardman, Gerald. *American Musical Theatre: A Chronicle*. New York: Oxford University Press, 1978.

Braunlich, Phyllis Cole. *Haunted by Home: The Life and Letters of Lynn Riggs*. Norman: University of Oklahoma Press, 1988.

Bray, Christopher. *Sean Connery: A Biography*. New York: Pegasus Books, 2011.

Brynner, Rock. *Yul: The Man Who Would Be King*. New York: Simon & Schuster, 1989.

Carroll, Diahann. *Diahann: An Autobiography*. Boston: Little, Brown, 1986.

———. *The Legs Are the Last to Go: Aging, Acting, Marrying & Other Things I Learned the Hard Way*. New York: Amistad, 2008.

Carter, Tim. *Oklahoma!: The Making of an American Musical*. New Haven, CT: Yale University Press, 2007.

Chaplin, Saul. *The Golden Age of Movie Musicals and Me*. Norman: University of Oklahoma Press, 1994.

Chase, Ilka. *The Care and Feeding of Friends*. Garden City, NY: Doubleday, 1973.

Chotzinoff, Samuel. *A Little Nightmusic*. New York: Harper & Row, 1964.

Citron, Stephen. *The Wordsmiths: Oscar Hammerstein II and Alan Jay Lerner*. New York: Oxford University Press, 1995.

Coffin, Robert P. Tristam. *Mainstays of Maine*. New York: Macmillan, 1945.

Davis, Ronald L. *Mary Martin: Broadway Legend*. Norman: University of Oklahoma Press, 2008.

Day, Barry, ed. *The Letters of Noël Coward*. New York: Alfred A. Knopf, 2007.

Decker, Todd. *Who Should Sing Ol' Man River: The Lives of an American Song*. New York: Oxford University Press, 2015.

de Mille, Agnes. *Dance to the Piper*. Boston: Little, Brown, 1952.

———. *And Promenade Home*. Boston: Little, Brown, 1958.

Dietz, Dan. *The Complete Book of 1940s Broadway Musicals*. Lanham, MD: Rowman & Littlefield, 2015.

———. *The Complete Book of 1950s Broadway Musicals*. Lanham, MD: Rowman & Littlefield, 2014.

Dietz, Howard. *Dancing in the Dark*. New York: Quadrangle, 1974.

Ewen, David. *Richard Rodgers*. New York: Henry Holt, 1957.

Ferber, Edna. *A Kind of Magic*. Garden City, NY: Doubleday, 1963.

———. *A Peculiar Treasure*. New York: Doubleday, Doran, 1939.

———. *Show Boat*. Garden City, NY: Doubleday, Page, 1926.

Feuer, Cy, with Ken Gross. *I Got the Show Right Here: The Amazing, True Story of How an Obscure Brooklyn Horn Player Became the Last Great Broadway Showman*. New York: Simon & Schuster, 2003.

Fordin, Hugh. *Getting to Know Him: A Biography of Oscar Hammerstein II*. New York: Random House, 1977.

Furia, Philip. *Irving Berlin: A Life in Song*. New York: Schirmer Books, 1998.

Gordon, John Steele. "Rodgers & Hammerstein, Inc." *American Heritage*, September/October 1990.

Gordon, Max. *Max Gordon Presents*. New York: Bernard Geis Associates, 1963.

Gottfried, Marvin. *A Theater Divided: The Postwar American Stage*. Boston: Little, Brown, 1969.

Green, Stanley, ed. *Rodgers and Hammerstein Fact Book: A Record of Their Works Together and with Other Collaborators*. New York: Lynn Farnol Group, 1980.

Greenspan, Charlotte. *Pick Yourself Up: Dorothy Fields and the American Musical*. New York: Oxford University Press, 2010.

Habegger, Alfred. *Masked: The Life of Anna Leonowens, Schoolmistress at the Court of Siam*. Madison: University of Wisconsin Press, 2014.

Hagman, Larry. *Hello Darlin': Tall (and Absolutely True) Tales About My Life*. New York: Simon & Schuster, 2001.

Hammerstein, Oscar 2d. *Carmen Jones*. New York: Alfred A. Knopf, 1945.

———. *Lyrics*. Milwaukee: Hal Leonard Books, 1985.

Hanff, Helen. *Underfoot in Show Business*. Boston: Little, Brown, 1980.

Heggen, Thomas, and Joshua Logan. *Mister Roberts*. Annapolis, MD: Naval Institute Press, 1992. [Novel]

———. *Mister Roberts: A Play*. New York: Random House, 1948.

Helburn, Theresa. *A Wayward Quest*. Boston: Little, Brown, 1960.

Henderson, Florence. *Life Is Not a Stage: From Broadway Baby to a Lovely Lady and Beyond*. New York: Center Street, 2011.

Henderson, Mary C. *Mielziner: Master of Modern Stage Design*. New York: Back Stage Books, 2001.

Hischak, Thomas S. *The Rodgers and Hammerstein Encyclopedia*. Westport, CT: Greenwood Press, 2007.

Horowitz, Mark Eden. *Sondheim on Music: Minor Details and Major Decisions*. Lanham, MD: Scarecrow Press, 2010.

Hyland, William G. *Richard Rodgers*. New Haven, CT: Yale University Press, 1998.

Jablonski, Edward. *Irving Berlin: American Troubadour*. New York: Henry Holt, 1999.

Jones, Shirley. *Shirley Jones: A Memoir*. New York: Gallery Books, 2013.

Jowitt, Deborah. *Jerome Robbins: His Life, His Theater, His Dance*. New York: Simon & Schuster, 2004.

Kaufman, David. *Some Enchanted Evenings: The Glittering Life and Times of Mary Martin*. New York: St. Martin's Press, 2016.

Keel, Howard. *Only Make Believe: My Life in Show Business*. Fort Lee, NJ: Barricade Books, 2005.

Kellow, Brian. *Ethel Merman*. New York: Viking, 2007.

Klein, Christina. *Cold War Orientalism: Asia in the Middlebrow Imagination, 1945–1961*. Berkeley: University of California Press, 2003.

Knapp, Raymond, Mitchell Morris, and Stacy Wolf, eds. *The Oxford Handbook of the American Musical*. New York: Oxford University Press, 2011.

Krasna, Norman. *John Loves Mary: Comedy in Three Acts*. New York: Dramatists Play Service, 1974.

Kreuger, Miles. *Show Boat: The Story of a Classic American Musical*. New York: Oxford University Press, 1977.

Landon, Margaret. *Anna and the King of Siam*. New York: HarperCollins, 1997.

Langner, Lawrence. *The Magic Curtain*. New York: E. P. Dutton, 1951.

Laurents, Arthur. *Original Story By: A Memoir of Broadway and Hollywood*. New York: Applause Theatre Books, 2000.

Lawrence, Gertrude. *A Star Danced*. Garden City, NY: Doubleday, Doran, 1945.

Leachman, Cloris. *Cloris: My Autobiography*. New York: Kensington Books, 2009.

Lee, C. Y. *The Flower Drum Song*. New York: Penguin Books, 2002.

Leonowens, Anna. *The English Governess at the Siamese Court, Being Recollections of Six Years in the Royal Palace at Bangkok*. ReadaClassic.com, 2010.

Lewis, David H. *Flower Drum Songs: The Story of Two Musicals.* Jefferson, NC: McFarland, 2006.

Logan, Joshua. *Josh: My Up and Down, In and Out Life.* New York: Delacorte Press, 1976.

———. *Movie Stars, Real People, and Me.* New York: Delacorte Press, 1978.

Loos, Anita. *Happy Birthday: A Play in Two Acts.* New York: Samuel French, 1947.

Lovensheimer, Jim. *South Pacific: Paradise Rewritten.* New York: Oxford University Press, 2010.

MacRae, Sheila. *Hollywood Mother of the Year: Sheila MacRae's Own Story.* New York: Birch Lane Press, 1992.

Magee, Jeffrey. *Irving Berlin's American Musical Theater.* New York: Oxford University Press, 2012.

Mandelbaum, Ken. *Not Since Carrie: Forty Years of Broadway Musical Flops.* New York: St. Martin's Press, 1991.

Marmorstein, Gary. *A Ship Without a Sail: The Life of Lorenz Hart.* New York: Simon & Schuster, 2012.

Martin, Mary. *My Heart Belongs.* New York: Quill, 1984.

Marx, Samuel, and Jan Clayton. *Rodgers & Hart: Bewitched, Bothered, and Bedeviled.* New York: G. P. Putnam's Sons, 1976.

Maslon, Laurence. *The Sound of Music Companion.* New York: Simon & Schuster, 2007.

———. *The South Pacific Companion.* New York: Fireside/Simon & Schuster, 2008.

Mast, Gerald. *Can't Help Singin'.* Woodstock, NY: Overlook Press, 1987.

May, Stephen J. *Michener's South Pacific.* Gainesville: University Press of Florida, 2011.

Merman, Ethel. *Merman: An Autobiography.* New York: Simon & Schuster, 1978.

Mersand, Joseph E., ed. *Three Comedies of American Family Life.* New York: Washington Square Press, 1961.

Michener, James A. *Tales of the South Pacific.* New York: Dial Press, 2014.

———. *The World Is My Home: A Memoir.* New York: Random House, 1992.

Mielziner, Jo. *Designing for the Theatre: A Memoir and a Portfolio.* New York: Bramhall House, 1965.

Miller, Scott. *Deconstructing Harold Hill: An Insider's Guide to Musical Theatre.* Portsmouth, NH: Heinemann, 2000.

Molnár, Ferenc. *Liliom: A Legend in Seven Scenes and a Prologue.* New York: Boni and Liveright, 1921.

Monush, Barry. *The Sound of Music FAQ: All That's Left to Know About Maria, the Von Trapps and Our Favorite Things.* Milwaukee: Applause Theatre & Cinema Books, 2015.

Mordden, Ethan. *Beautiful Mornin': The Broadway Musical in the 1940s.* New York: Oxford University Press, 1999.

———. *On Sondheim: An Opinionated Guide.* New York: Oxford University Press, 2016.

———. *Rodgers and Hammerstein.* New York: Harry N. Abrams, 1992.

Morley, Sheridan. *Gertrude Lawrence: A Biography.* New York: McGraw-Hill, 1981.

Nolan, Frederick. *Lorenz Hart: A Poet on Broadway.* New York: Oxford University Press, 1994.

————. *The Sound of Their Music: The Story of Rodgers and Hammerstein*. New York: Applause Theatre & Cinema Books, 2002.

Pinza, Ezio. *Ezio Pinza, an Autobiography*. New York: Rinehart, 1958.

Riggs, Lynn. *Green Grow the Lilacs*. New York: Samuel French, 1958.

Robbins, Jhan. *Yul Brynner: The Inscrutable King*. New York: Dodd, Mead, 1987.

Rodgers, Dorothy. *The House in My Head*. New York: Avenel Books, 1967.

————. *My Favorite Things: A Personal Guide to Decorating and Entertaining*. New York: Atheneum, 1964.

————. *A Personal Book*. New York: Harper & Row, 1977.

Rodgers, Dorothy, and Mary Rodgers. *A Word to the Wives*. New York: Alfred A. Knopf, 1970.

Rodgers, Richard. *Letters to Dorothy*. New York: New York Public Library, 1988.

————. *Musical Stages: An Autobiography*. New York: Random House, 1975.

Rodgers, Richard, and Oscar Hammerstein II. *Oklahoma!* Milwaukee: Applause Theatre & Cinema Books, 2010.

————. *Pipe Dream*. New York: Viking, 1956.

————. *The Rodgers and Hammerstein Songbook*. New York: Simon & Schuster, 1968.

————. *Six Plays by Rodgers and Hammerstein*. New York: Modern Library, 1953.

————. *South Pacific*. Milwaukee: Applause Theatre & Cinema Books, 2014.

Rodgers, Richard, Oscar Hammerstein II, and Douglas Carter Beane. *Cinderella*. Milwaukee: Applause Theatre & Cinema Books, 2014.

Rodgers, Richard, Oscar Hammerstein II, and Joseph Fields. *Flower Drum Song*. New York: Farrar, Straus and Cudahy, 1959.

Rodgers, Richard, Oscar Hammerstein II, Howard Lindsay, and Russel Crouse. *The Sound of Music*. Milwaukee: Applause Theatre & Cinema Books, 2010.

Santopietro, Tom. *The Sound of Music Story*. New York: St. Martin's Press, 2015.

Secrest, Meryle. *Somewhere for Me: A Biography of Richard Rodgers*. New York: Alfred A. Knopf, 2001.

————. *Stephen Sondheim: A Life*. New York: Vintage Books, 2011.

Sheehan, Vincent. *The Amazing Oscar Hammerstein: The Life and Exploits of an Impresario*. London: Weidenfeld and Nicolson, 1956.

Simpson, Paul. *A Brief Guide to The Sound of Music: 50 Years of the Legendary Musical and the Family Who Inspired It*. Philadelphia: Running Press, 2015.

Skouras, Thana. *The Tale of Rodgers and Hammerstein's South Pacific*. New York: Lehman, 1958.

Slide, Anthony, ed. *"It's the Pictures That Got Small": Charles Brackett on Billy Wilder and Hollywood's Golden Age*. New York: Columbia University Press, 2015.

Sondheim, Stephen. *Finishing the Hat: Collected Lyrics (1954–1981) with Attendant Comments, Principles, Heresies, Grudges, Whines and Anecdotes*. New York: Alfred A. Knopf, 2010.

Steinbeck, John. *Steinbeck: A Life in Letters*. Edited by Elaine Steinbeck and Robert Wallsten. New York: Penguin Books, 1989.

————. *Sweet Thursday*. New York: Bantam Books, 1976.

Stong, Phil. *State Fair*. New York: Literary Guild, 1932.

Stott, William, with Jane Stott. *On Broadway: Performance Photographs by Fred Fehl*. Austin: University of Texas Press, 1978.

Strauss, Helen M. *A Talent for Luck: An Autobiography*. New York: Random House, 1979.

Suskin, Steven. *Opening Night on Broadway: A Critical Quotebook of the Golden Era of the Musical Theatre, Oklahoma! (1943) to Fiddler on the Roof (1964)*. New York: Schirmer Books, 1990.

———. *The Sound of Broadway Music: A Book of Orchestrators and Orchestrations*. New York: Oxford University Press, 2009.

Taylor, Deems. *Some Enchanted Evenings: The Story of Rodgers and Hammerstein*. New York: Harper & Brothers, 1953.

Trapp, Maria Augusta. *The Story of the Trapp Family Singers*. New York: Scholastic Book Services, 1971.

Vaill, Amanda. *Somewhere: The Life of Jerome Robbins*. New York: Broadway Books, 2006.

Van Druten, John. *Playwright at Work*. New York. Harper & Brothers, 1953.

———. *The Widening Circle: A Personal Search*. New York: Charles Scribner's Sons, 1957.

Viertel, Jack. *The Secret Life of the American Musical: How Broadway Shows Are Built*. New York: Sarah Crichton Books, 2016.

Walker, Don. *Men of Notes*. Pittsburgh: Dorrance, 2013.

Wilder, Alec. *American Popular Song: The Great Innovators, 1900–1950*. New York: Oxford University Press, 1972.

Wilk, Max. *The Making of The Sound of Music*. New York: Routledge, 2007.

———. *OK!: The Story of Oklahoma!* New York: Applause Theater & Cinema Books, 2002.

———. *They're Playing Our Song: Conversations with America's Classic Songwriters*. Westport, CT: Easton Studio Press, 2008.

Winer, Deborah Grace. *On the Sunny Side of the Street: The Life and Lyrics of Dorothy Fields*. New York: Schirmer Books, 1997.

Zinnemann, Fred. *A Life in the Movies: An Autobiography*. New York: Charles Scribner's Sons, 1992.

Zinsser, William Knowlton. *Easy to Remember: The Great American Songwriters and Their Songs*. Jaffrey, NH: David R. Godine, 2001.

ACKNOWLEDGMENTS

This book was Dee Dee Myers's idea, and for it—and for so many other good ideas and good times—she has my everlasting love. She knows how much I care about this subject, and how long I have cared about it, and she had the good sense to propose that I write about it when I lacked the confidence to try. Book writing can be a lonely exercise, but Dee Dee and our children, Kate and Stephen—themselves avid fans of the musical theater—were always there at the end of the day. They're *Something Wonderful*, and the book is for them.

Paul Golob, executive editor at Henry Holt and Company, seconded Dee Dee's enthusiasm and made the book a reality, backed by Holt's publisher, Steve Rubin, and their strong editorial team. This is the third book I have written with Paul, and I can't imagine a better, more patient, more caring, or more diligent partner. As always, it was a pleasure to work with him.

My debt to Ted Chapin, president and chief creative officer of Rodgers and Hammerstein, is incalculable. From the start, he offered unstinting cooperation and unfettered access, while imposing no editorial control or conditions. He answered arcane queries at all hours and opened countless doors in the world of Dick and Oscar and the theater more broadly. I could not have written the book without him, and I record my thanks here with the greatest warmth. Ted's assistant, Nicole Harman, and his former R&H colleagues Bert Fink and Bruce Pomahac were also helpful beyond measure. Bert has been *the* go-to source for information about Rodgers and Hammerstein over a professional working friendship that has now spanned more than twenty years, while Bruce generously conducted a four-hour master class in the mechanics of Rodgers's music that was a highlight of my research and the best part of a fine Wisconsin summer day. My in-laws, Steve and Judy Myers, let Bruce and me borrow their piano—just one of the many things I've had to thank them for over these twenty-plus years.

Once again, my old friend Karen Avrich contributed peerless fact-checking and backstopping, while my lawyer Bob Barnett ably handled the practicalities of the contract. The bosses at my day jobs—John Harris and Carrie Budoff Brown at *Politico*, and Graydon Carter and Cullen Murphy at *Vanity Fair*—indulged this project with a generosity above and beyond any reasonable measure, and Cullen read the manuscript with his usual keen eye and wise heart. Melissa Goldstein unearthed the compelling photographs that help bring Dick and Oscar to life in these pages.

I owe particular thanks to a new friend, Joan Saltzman, a recovering Philadelphia lawyer and playwright, who is an expert on all things Hammerstein. Joan shared Oscar Hammerstein's official FBI file, which she had obtained through a Freedom of Information request, and she also hunted in vain for the passport files of both Rodgers and Hammerstein. Her research, and her infectious enthusiasm, enriched my work. Timothy Crouse shared excerpts from his father's diary from the production of *The Sound of Music* and also read parts of my manuscript, offering valuable advice and saving me from inelegant errors. Amy Asch, the editor of *The Complete Lyrics of Oscar Hammerstein II*, was a valued research resource, as was her mentor, the great musical theater historian Robert Kimball, the only man I know who is an equal authority on the 1964 Civil Rights Act and *Annie Get Your Gun*. Mana Allen, a third-generation member in good standing of the Broadway tribe, went out of her way to help research the papers of Trude Rittmann and generously opened other doors at the New York Public Library's theater, dance, and photo collections at Lincoln Center. The theater historian Laurence Maslon, an expert on *South Pacific* and *The Sound of Music*, shared original interviews for the script of his and Roger Sherman's American Masters PBS documentary, *Richard Rodgers: The Sweetest Sounds*, along with his time and a tour of the Tisch School of the Arts at New York University, where he teaches. NPR's Jeff Lunden likewise unstintingly shared interview tapes from his compelling radio documentaries on Rodgers and Hammerstein and their work.

The Library of Congress is a national treasure—and so is Mark Eden Horowitz, a senior music specialist in its Music Division and the keeper of its priceless archives of the Great American Songbook. Mark and his colleagues, especially Caitlin Miller, provided invaluable guidance and support in my repeated forays through the Hammerstein papers, and both also read parts of the manuscript. At the New York Public Library's Lincoln Center branch, Annemarie van Roessel, assistant curator at the Billy Rose Theatre Division, gave me a detailed *tour d'horizon* of its Richard Rodgers archive and other holdings, while Cassie Mey of the Jerome Robbins Dance Division granted permission to quote from an oral history of Trude Rittmann, and Jeremy Megraw, photograph librarian in the Rose Division, was a generous guide to its images. I am grateful to Terre Heydari, operations manager at the DeGolyer Library of Southern Methodist University, for assistance in securing permission to quote from the revealing oral histories that Professor Ronald Davis conducted over many years with Broadway and Hollywood luminaries—and to Professor Davis for compiling them in the first place. Special thanks to Patricia Ward Kelly for permission to quote from the interview with her late husband, Gene Kelly. At the Margaret Herrick Library of the Academy of Motion Picture Arts and Sciences in Beverly Hills, Jenny Romero cheerfully helped access the Davis oral histories, as well as the papers of Fred Zinnemann, Arthur Hornblow Jr., and others. Martin Gostanian at the Paley Center for Media in Beverly Hills was a cheerful guide to recordings of some of Rodgers and Hammerstein's many television appearances.

Dame Julie Andrews, and her manager Steve Sauer, took time to answer e-mail queries, even though she was at work on her own memoir covering some of the same material, and I can attest that her kindness and graciousness are, indeed, "practically perfect, in every way." Mary Ellin Berlin Barrett, André Bishop, John Steele Gordon, Sheldon Harnick, Frank Rich, Jonathan Schwartz, and Claudette Sutherland all generously answered questions by phone or in person, and Stephen Sondheim offered revealing insights in several e-mail exchanges. Will Hammerstein gave me a moving tour of his grandfather's Highland Farm. The late Barbara Cook, Florence Henderson, and George S. Irving, who were, before their deaths, among the last living collaborators to have worked with Rodgers and Hammerstein firsthand, all gave lively and helpful telephone interviews, and I will treasure their memory. Owen Shribman shared memories of his mother, Temple Texas, and Howard Reinheimer Jr. did the same for his father. Gigi Reinheimer helped with family photos.

For permission to quote from the published works of Rodgers and Hammerstein I thank Rodgers and Hammerstein, a division of Concord Music, and for permission to quote from unpublished letters and other writings of Rodgers and Hammerstein I thank their heirs and literary executors, especially Adam Guettel. Similarly, for permission to quote other letters and unpublished writings, I thank John Brown and Catherine Collins (John Mason Brown); Tita Cahn (Sammy Cahn); Benn Clatworthy (Gertrude Lawrence); Susanna Krebs Drewry (Trude Rittmann); Anne Fadiman (Clifton Fadiman); Julie Gilbert (Edna Ferber); Dr. Catherine Carlisle Hart and Christopher Hart (Moss Hart); Brook Hersey (John Hersey); Christopher Knopf (Edwin H. Knopf); Tom and Harrigan Logan (Joshua Logan); Marcia Messing (Harold Messing); Jonathan Prude (Agnes de Mille); Elizabeth Winick Rubinstein (John Steinbeck); and Tim Zinnemann (Fred Zinnemann). Terrell Dougan allowed me to publish her touching letter to Richard Rodgers.

At Holt, I also owe thanks to the marketing and publicity mavens, Maggie Richards, Pat Eisemann, and Carolyn O'Keefe; the managing editor, Kenn Russell, who supervised the book's production; Muriel Jorgensen, the copy editor; Kelly S. Too, who designed the book; and Nicolette Seeback and Karen Horton, who created the jacket. Caroline Wray kept track of all the paper. Margo Feiden and Daria Enrich paved the way for use of the wonderful Al Hirschfeld lithograph.

There is a long shelf of worthy and well-researched books about Rodgers and Hammerstein and the Broadway musical, and many of them are cited in the bibliography. But two authors must be singled out: Steven Suskin, whose meticulously documented book on Broadway orchestrators, and pair of compilation volumes of opening night reviews, were a constant source of reliable data; and Ethan Mordden, whose studies of Rodgers and Hammerstein and the Broadway musical are authoritative, quirky, opinionated, and always alive. I owe both of them a great deal, as I also do Geoffrey Block, Hugh Fordin, Frederick Nolan, and Meryle Secrest—the pathbreaking biographers of Rodgers and Hammerstein, to whom all subsequent scholars are in debt.

Paige Andrews, Betsey Apple, Scott Berg, Tony Bill, Frank Clines, Tiki Davies, Janet Elder, Linda Greenhouse, Mark Halperin, Betsy Kolbert, Alison Mitchell, Adam Nagourney, Martin Nolan, Carol Phethean, David Sagal, Lee Satterfield and Patrick Steel, Allen Sviridoff, Jim Warren, Steve Weisman, Max Woodward, JoAnn Young, and the late Rosemary Clooney, George Furth, Marvin Hamlisch, and Eden Ross Lipson all helped along the way. I'm especially grateful to Andrea Stevens, Connie Rosenblum, Marty Gottlieb, and other former colleagues and editors at the *New York Times* for allowing me to moonlight from my career as a political reporter by writing about Broadway and Hollywood—and Rodgers and Hammerstein—from time to time. They could not have known it, but they were planting a seed, because that work gave me the chance to interview Mary Rodgers and James Hammerstein, for which I'll always be grateful.

When I was a boy, our house was filled with *Playbill*s and original Broadway cast albums. This was in no small part because my uncle Ralph Stanley Purdum had journeyed all the way from Macomb, Illinois, to 145 West 44th Street in Manhattan, where he plied his trade as an actor in plays, films, and commercials. In the early 1960s, my parents went to see him—and eight shows a week—bringing home the proof. How I wish I had queried him more when he uttered a sentence like: "When I was walking down Fifth Avenue with Van Johnson . . ." How I wish, also, that I had asked him more about his time paying the bills by working as Jules Glaenzer's assistant at Cartier, where his celebrity clients included Ellin Berlin and Grace Kelly. And how I wish I'd asked him about his out-of-town castmates, including Temple Texas.

The first professional musical I saw was a touring company of

Mame, starring Celeste Holm, in Chicago in 1968, when I was just eight years old and getting my first long dress pants. As we stood in the forecourt of the Shubert Theatre, I noticed the publicity pictures, and whined to my parents: "Oh, no! It's in black and white?" *Au contraire*, they assured me, it was live and in color, with real people on the stage. So it was, and from "Open a New Window" on I was hooked. For that and so much else, I have Connie and the late Jerry Purdum to thank. This book is for them, too.

PERMISSIONS ACKNOWLEDGMENTS

Grateful acknowledgment is made for the use of the following materials.

Excerpts from lyrics of:

Oklahoma! – Copyright © 1943 by Williamson Music Co.
"Oh, What a Beautiful Mornin'"
"People Will Say We're in Love"
"The Surrey with the Fringe on Top"
"Oklahoma"
"The Farmer and the Cowman"
"Lonely Room"
"I Cain't Say No"
"Many a New Day"
"Someone Will Teach You" (Early Draft)

Carmen Jones – Copyright © 1943 by Hammerstein Properties LLC.
"Dat's Love"

State Fair – Copyright © 1945 by Williamson Music Co.

"Western People Funny"
"Song of the King"
"Shall We Dance?"

Me and Juliet – Copyright © 1953 by Williamson Music Co.
"Opening of Me and Juliet"
"No Other Love"
"The Big Black Giant"
"Intermission Talk"

Pipe Dream – Copyright © 1955 by Williamson Music Co.
"All Kinds of People"
"Everybody's Got a Home but Me"
"The Happiest House on the Block"

Cinderella – Copyright © 1957 by Williamson Music Co.
"In My Own Little Corner"
"The Prince Is Giving a Ball"
"Impossible"

Flower Drum Song – Copyright © 1958 by Williamson Music Co.
"Chop Suey"
"I Am Going to Like It Here"

The Sound of Music – Copyright © 1959 by Williamson Music Co.
"The Sound of Music"
"Do-Re-Mi"
"My Favorite Things"
"Sixteen Going on Seventeen (Reprise)"
"So Long, Farewell"
"Edelweiss"

Excerpts from letters and writings of Richard Rodgers used by permission of the Estate of Richard Rodgers.

Excerpts from letters and writings of Oscar Hammerstein II used by permission of Hammerstein Properties LLC.

Excerpt from letter of Sammy Cahn used by permission of Tita Cahn.

Excerpts from letters of Agnes de Mille used by permission of Jonathan Prude.

Letter of Terrell Dougan used by permission of Terrell Dougan.

Excerpts from letters of Sister Gregory Duffy used by permission of Toni Harris.

Excerpt from letter of Clifton Fadiman used by permission of Anne Fadiman.

Excerpts from letters of Edna Ferber used by permission of Julie Gilbert.

Excerpts from letters of Moss Hart used by permission of Catherine and Christopher Hart.

Excerpt from letter of John Hersey used by permission of Brook Hersey.

Excerpt from letter of Edwin Knopf used by permission of Christopher Knopf.

Excerpt from letters of Gertrude Lawrence used by permission of Benn Clatworthy.

INDEX

Abbott, George, 61, 64, 87, 216–17, 250, 267
Academy Awards, 13, 38, 104, 126, 237, 244, 246, 303
Adams, Edie, 3–4, 239, 250
Adler, Buddy, 256, 259
Adler, Richard, 309
African Americans, 100, 134, 297–98, 317
Albert, Eddie, 239
Alda, Robert, 238
"Alexander's Ragtime Band," 129
All About Eve (film), 181, 254
Allegro, 134–46, 172, 215
    cast and creative team, 139–40
    critics on, 142–43
    failure of, 145, 148, 234
    finances and, 139, 143
    Hammerstein on, 121, 136, 144–45
    Logan on, 141–42, 144, 290
    opening night, 143–45
    Rodgers on, 144, 146
    Sondheim on, 141, 143
    South Pacific and, 168
    touring company, 144

    TV adaptation, 290
    written, 134–39
Allen, Elizabeth, 305
"All the Things You Are," 208
Allyson, June, 238
Alton, Robert, 216
Always You, 22–23, 26
American Ballet Caravan, 163
American Committee for the Protection of Foreign Born, 222
American Society of Composers, Authors and Publishers (ASCAP), 126–28, 134, 205
America's Sweetheart, 56
Anderson, Elaine, 66–67
Anderson, Maxwell, 235
André Charlot's Review of 1924, 32
Andrews, Dana, 103
Andrews, Julie, 3, 228, 239, 248, 251, 302–3, 320
Androcles and the Lion, 306
Anna and the King of Siam (film), 181–84, 187, 244. *See also The King and I*
Anna and the King of Siam (Landon novel), 180–84
Annie, 311

Annie Get Your Gun (Berlin), 136, 228
  Berlin writes lyrics and music,
    129–31
  conceived, 126–28
  critics on, 131
  Martin and, 151–52, 154, 269
  opening night, 207
  revivals, 306
  royalties and, 130
  success of, 131–32, 144
  touring company, 151–52, 154
  TV version, 267
"Annie McGinnis Pavlova," 19–20
Ann-Margret, 297
Anti-Defamation League of B'nai B'rith,
  224–25
anti-Semitism, 134
"Any Old Place with You," 44
Anyone Can Whistle, 304
Anything Goes, 270
"Anything You Can Do, I Can Do
  Better," 131
Appointment in Samarra (O'Hara), 61
Arlen, Harold, 48, 297
Arnaz, Desi, 60, 225
Arsenic and Old Lace (Kesselring), 308
"Art and Mass Media" (Hammerstein),
  248
Asian Americans, 159, 192, 196, 262,
  265
Astaire, Fred, 60
Atkinson, Brooks, 62, 66, 131, 143,
  173, 209, 220, 265, 287, 317
"Au Clair de la Lune," 150
"Auld Lang Syne," 176
Authors Guild, 134
Authors League, 221
"Auto Show Girl, The," 42
"Away from You," 310
Awe, Jim, 156
Axelrod, Herman, 19
Ayers, Lemuel, 78, 113
Ayres, Lew, 102

Babes in Arms, 59–60, 79
Bacall, Lauren, 312
Bacharach, Burt, 306
Bainter, Fay, 103
Baker, Belle, 51
Balanchine, George, 60, 163
"Bali Ha'i," 157–58

Ball, Lucille, 225
Ballard, Kaye, 3
Ballard, Lucinda, 9
Ball at the Savoy, 102
Ballet Russe de Monte Carlo, 82–83
Baltimore Sun, 120
Bancroft, Anne, 302
Barber of Seville, The (Rossini), 115
Barnes, Clive, 310
Barnes, Howard, 173
Battelle, Kenneth, 282
Battles, John, 140
Bayes, Nora, 24
Bean, Jack, 258
Beane, Douglas Carter, 253
Beethoven, Ludwig van, 88
Behrman, Sam, 295
Belmont, Alan H., 221–22
Bemelmans, Ludwig, 64
"Bench Scene, The," 109, 251
Bender, Milton, 63
Benét, Stephen Vincent, 134
Bennett, Michael, 310, 315
Bennett, Robert Russell, 87–89, 91,
  100, 113, 157, 162–64, 185, 205,
  207, 210, 215, 242
Benson, Sally, 184
Bergman, Ingrid, 106
Berlin, Irving, 48, 51, 94, 116, 121,
  128–32, 144, 152, 270, 306,
  318–19
Berlin, Mary Ellin, 129
Berman, Pandro, 179
Bernstein, Leonard, 7, 88
Best Foot Forward, 64, 124
Betsy, 51, 129
"Bewitched, Bothered and Bewildered,"
  62, 144
Bigley, Isabel, 216
Bigman, Rose, 92
Big Parade, The (film), 53
Bikel, Theodore, 281–82, 285–86,
  289
Billboard charts, 288, 303
Bishop, André, 317
Bizet, Georges, 98
blacklist, 221–23
Blackton, Jay, 85, 89, 130, 242
Blair, Janet, 175
Blanchard, Susan, 33, 226, 232
Blane, Ralph, 64

Blitzstein, Marc, 123
"Blue Room," 51
"Blue Skies," 51, 129
Blyden, Larry, 264
Bock, Jerry, 308
"Body and Soul," 183
Bolger, Ray, 60–61, 67, 238
Bolton, Guy, 25, 41
Boone, Pat, 290, 297
Boston Herald, 118, 142, 285
Boston Post, 117–18, 142, 172
Bowers, Dwight, 123
Boyer, Charles, 244
Boy Friend, The (Wilson), 228
"Boys and Girls Like You and Me," 87
Brackett, Charles, 247
Bradley, Bill, 12
Brahms, Johannes, 71
Brando, Marlon, 7, 125
Brazzi, Lydia, 258
Brazzi, Rossano, 257–58, 260, 304
Brice, Fanny, 24
Brill, Leighton, 18
British Royal National Theatre, 316–18
Brooks, Van Wyck, 255
Brown, John Mason, 105, 173
Brownell, Herbert, 225
Brubeck, Dave, 306
Bryant, Glenn, 100
Brynner, Yul, 7, 186–87, 197, 200, 204, 207, 211, 214, 246–47, 262, 310, 317
Buck, Pearl, 159, 293
Buloff, Joseph, 79
Burning Bright (Steinbeck), 208, 226
Burton, Richard, 237, 297, 300
Bus Stop (film), 256
BUtterfield 8 (O'Hara), 61
Buttons, Red, 262
By Jupiter, 67–68, 216
Byram, John, 31
Byron, George Gordon, Lord, 173

Cahn, Sammy, 206, 311–12
Caldwell, Erskine, 72–73
California Senate Subcommittee on Un-American Activities, 222
Call Me Madam, 270
Camelot, 304
Canby, Vincent, 317

Cannery Row (Steinbeck), 3, 226
"Can't Help Lovin' Dat Man," 29–30
Capote, Truman, 297
"Carefully Taught," 160–61, 172–73, 221
Carlisle, Kitty, 254
Carmen (Bizet), 98–99
Carmen Jones, 107, 258
   copyright, 100
   written, 98–103
Carmichael, Hoagy, 238
Carousel, 2, 7, 12, 251, 162, 169, 172, 196
   adaptation of *Liliom* proposed, 104–7
   cast and creative team, 113–15, 139
   critics on, 118, 120
   finances and, 112–14, 120, 137
   Hammerstein writes book and lyrics, 106–13, 125
   Molnár on, 116–17
   opening night, 119–20
   out-of-town tryouts, 117–19
   rehearsals, 119
   revivals, 315–19
   Rittman and, 163
   Rodgers on appeal of, 120
   Rodgers writes music, 107–8
   Sondheim on, 109
   South Pacific vs., 174
   touring company, 120
Carousel (film), 244–46, 256
   cast, 244–45
   rights, 244
"Carousel Waltz, The," 245
Carpenter, Constance, 197, 214
Carroll, Diahann, 63, 297–300, 304
Carson, Jack, 248
Cassidy, Claudia, 175
Catholic Charities, 224
"Cave, The" (Michener), 149–50, 155
CBS TV, 1–4, 248, 252, 267
Cerf, Bennett, 18, 178, 181
Chapin, Ted, 316, 318
Chaplin, Saul, 301–3
Chapman, John, 120, 143, 220
Chappell & Co., 68, 123–24
Charnin, Martin, 307, 310–11
Chase, Ilka, 4
Chee-Chee, 52
Chekhov, Michael, 186

Chevalier, Maurice, 57
Chicago Tribune, 175
"Childe Harold" (Byron), 173
Children of Dreams (film), 35
Chinese Lantern, The, 45
Ching, William, 140–41
Chocolate Soldier, The (Strauss), 40
"Chop Suey," 263
Chorus Line, A, 310
Christians, Mady, 125
Churchill, Winston, 293, 297
Cinderella
  Broadway production, 252–53, 318
  created for TV, 1–6, 248–52
  critics on, 5, 252
  interracial version, 252
  London production, 252
  original cast album, 2
  TV remake, 252
  written, 10–11, 249–52
CinemaScope 55, 241, 245, 259
Cinerama, 236–37
Civil Rights Congress, 222
civil rights movement, 298–99
Clark, Marguerite, 53
Clayton, Jan, 114, 120, 240, 295
Cleopatra (film), 300
Clift, Montgomery, 238
"Climb Ev'ry Mountain," 12, 274, 280,
  283–84
Clooney, Rosemary, 238, 262, 293
Clurman, Harold, 203, 228, 233
Cochran, Charles, 52–53
Cochrane, June, 46
"Cockeyed Optimist, A," 154
Cody, Buffalo Bill, 6, 17, 126
Coffin, Robert P. T., 111
Cohan, George M., 59
Cohen, Alexander, 310–11
Cohen, Harold, 183
Cohen, Irving, 122, 162
Cohn, Harry, 82
Colbert, Claudette, 287
Columbia Pictures, 36, 82
Columbia Records, 2, 100, 288
Columbia University, 8, 18–19, 41–42,
  45, 121, 212
  Law School, 19, 121
Comden, Betty, 91
"Come Home," 138, 141
Communist Party, 133, 220–24

Company, 308
Concord Bicycle Music, 319
*Connecticut Yankee in King Arthur's
  Court, A* (musical), 52, 97–98
  revival, 97–98
Connelly, Marc, 171
Connery, Sean, 7, 211
Cook, Barbara, 315
Cornell, John, 211–12
Cornell, Katharine, 287
Cousins, Norman, 134
Coward, Noël, 9, 183, 185, 212–13,
  293, 306
Cradle Will Rock, The, 123
Crain, Jeanne, 103
Crawford, Cheryl, 289
Crawford, Joan, 211, 293
Crichton, Judy, 232
Crist, Judith, 303
Crosby, Bing, 303
Crouse, Anna, 285, 287–88
Crouse, Lindsay, 195
Crouse, Russel "Buck," 55, 195, 268,
  270–73, 276, 283, 285, 287, 289,
  314–15
Crouse, Timothy, 55, 195, 273, 314–15
Crowther, Bosley, 243, 247
"Cuddle Up a Little Closer," 23
Cue, 140
Cullman, Howard, 171
Curtis Institute, 85
Cypher, Jon, 4, 5

Daffy Dill, 24
Damone, Vic, 238
Dance magazine, 85
"Dancing on the Ceiling," 55
Dandridge, Dorothy, 246
Danish Yankee at King Tut's Court, A,
  45
Darby, Ken, 259–60
Darling, Jean, 315
Da Silva, Howard, 79, 221
Davis, Bette, 254
Davis, Ronald, 269
Dawson, Mark, 216
Day, Doris, 238, 240, 257, 290, 302
Dean, James, 238
Dearest Enemy, 51
Decca Records, 123
Delibes, Léo, 151

Dell'Isola, Salvatore, 170
de Mille, Agnes, 194, 264, 280
   Allegro and, 139–40, 143
   Carousel and, 113, 117–19, 163
   death of Hammerstein and, 294
   Oklahoma! and, 82–85, 89, 91,
     241–42, 311
   on Rodgers, 312
DeMille, Cecil B., 82, 211
de Mille, William, 82
"Den of Iniquity," 62
Desert Song, The, 28, 32
Dewey, Thomas E., 224
Dexter, John, 305
Dickey, Annamary, 140
Die Trapp Familie (film), 267–68,
   270–71
Dietrich, Marlene, 287
Dietz, Howard, 18, 203, 265
Disney, Walt, 46, 302
Disneyland, 13
Dixon, Lee, 79
Do I Hear a Waltz?, 304–6
"Do I Love You Because You're
   Beautiful?," 10–11
"Doin' What Comes Naturally," 130
Dolan, Robert Emmett, 197, 272
Dole, Bob, 12
Donehue, Vincent J., 267–68, 282
Donen, Stanley, 301
"Don't Ever Leave Me," 34
"Don't Marry Me," 264
"Do-Re-Mi," 276, 280, 289–90, 303
Dorsey, Tommy, 103
Dougan, Terrell, 313
Drake, Alfred, 7, 79–80, 87, 185, 211
Dramatists Guild, 221
Drewry, Susanna, 163–64
Dreyfus, Louis, 123
Dreyfus, Max, 122–23
"Dry Rot" (Michener), 155
Dubin, Al, 206
Dulles, John Foster, 223
du Maurier, Daphne, 183, 213
Dunne, Irene, 125, 181–82
Durante, Jimmy, 59
Dvonch, Frederick, 199

Eastwood, Clint, 186
Ebsen, Buddy, 238
"Edelweiss," 12–13, 285–86

Ed Sullivan Show, The, 2
Eisenhower, Dwight D., 80, 222–23,
   225
Elizabeth II, Queen of England, 212
Emmy Awards, 13, 210, 297
Emperor Jones, The (O'Neill), 24
*English Governess at the Siamese
   Court, The* (Leonowens), 183–84
Ephron, Henry, 245–46
Ephron, Phoebe, 245–46
Erickson, Lief, 281
Etting, Ruth, 53
Evergreen, 55
Everybody Loves Me, 248
"Everybody's Got a Home but Me,"
   230–31
"Every Little Movement Has a
   Meaning All Its Own," 23
Ewen, David, 7, 181

Fadiman, Clifton, 255–56
Falkenburg, Jinx, 174
"Farmer and the Cowman, The," 82,
   91, 311
Fearnley, John, 117, 130, 186, 234, 238
Federal Bureau of Investigation (FBI),
   221–23, 225
Feiner, Ben, 53
"Fellow Needs a Girl, A," 137, 141
Fellows, Don, 164–66, 172–73
Ferber, Edna, 28–30, 53, 64, 255,
   293–94, 297
Ferrer, Jose, 293
Feuer, Cy, 226, 228, 230, 234, 311
Fiddler on the Roof, 226, 308
Fields, Dorothy, 126–27, 129–30, 179,
   203, 260, 319
Fields, Herbert, 51, 97, 126–27, 129,
   260
Fields, Joseph, 126, 260–61, 264
Fields, Lew, 44, 51, 126
Fields, W. C., 24
"Filles de Cadix, Les" (Delibes), 151
Finn, Myra. *See* Hammerstein, Myra
   Finn
Fiorello!, 287
Firefly, The, 23
Fisher, Eddie, 225
Fitelson, H. William, 270
Fleming, Renée, 12
Flower Drum Song (film), 265

Flower Drum Song, The (Lee novel), 260–61
Flower Drum Song (musical), 297
  Andrews on, 320
  ballet, 265
  cast and creative team, 261–62
  critics on, 265
  decision to create, 260–62
  finances and, 264–65
  Hammerstein writes book with Fields, 260–61
  Hwang revival, 265
  London production, 290
  lyrics, 263–64
  opening night, 265–66, 273
  out-of-town tryouts, 264–65
  rehearsals, 264
  rights, 260–61
  Rodgers writes score, 261, 263–65
  title, 273
  written, 268, 272
"Flower Garden of My Heart, The," 62
Flowering Peach, The (Odets), 307
Fly with Me, 45
"Fo' Dolla" (Michener), 147, 149, 151
Follies, 315
Fonda, Henry, 128, 146, 226
Fontanne, Lynn, 46
Forbes, Kathryn, 124–25
Fordin, Hugh, 33, 182, 296
Foster, Stephen, 12
France, 65–66
Freaky Friday (Mary Rodgers), 318
Free for All, 102
Friml, Rudolf, 6, 23, 26
Frissell, Toni, 282
Froman, Jane, 12, 225
From Here to Eternity (film), 237
Funny Thing Happened on the Way to the Forum, A, 304
Furs and Frills, 20–21
Furth, George, 308

Garde, Betty, 79, 85–86, 90
Gardner, Ava, 245
Garland, Judy, 244
Garrick Gaieties, The, 6, 46–47, 51, 206
Gaynor, Janet, 102, 273
Gaynor, Mitzi, 257–58, 260
"Gentleman Is a Dope, The," 140–41

Gentlemen Prefer Blondes (Loos novel), 132
Gentlemen Prefer Blondes (musical), 260
George VI, King of England, 212
Gershwin, George, 28, 48, 71, 78, 126, 183
Gershwin, Ira, 183, 319
"Getting to Know You," 2, 199, 203, 212, 224
Ghostley, Alice, 3–4, 27
Gibbs, Wolcott, 38, 62–63
Gilbert and Sullivan, 11–12
Girl Friend, The, 51
Gish, Lillian, 312
"Git Along, You Little Doggies!," 66
Glaenzer, Jules, 92, 112
Glass Menagerie, The (film), 181
Glenn, Frank, 284
Goldwyn, Samuel, 58, 97, 244
Gone with the Wind (film), 303
Gone with the Wind (Mitchell novel), 122
Gordon, John Steele, 179
Gordon, Max, 38, 82, 87, 100, 248
Gottfried, Martin, 315
Gould, Jack, 5
Goulet, Robert, 317
Graham, Martha, 194
Grahame, Gloria, 239
Grammy Awards, 13
"Grand Night for Singing, A," 103
Granger, Farley, 211
Great Gatsby, The (Fitzgerald), 6
Green, Adolph, 91
Green, Johnny, 16, 183, 293
Green, Stanley, 310
Greene, Graham, 208
Green Grow the Lilacs (Riggs), 65–69, 106, 108. *See also Oklahoma!*
  Hart and, 68
  Helburn asks Rodgers to turn into musical, 67–68
  rights, 82, 148
  Rodgers asks Hammerstein to collaborate on adapting, 68–73, 81–82, 99
Greenstone, Al, 87
Greenwood, Charlotte, 79, 239–40
Gregory, Sister, 271–72, 274, 276–77, 279–81, 284, 294–95, 305

"Guadalcanal March," 210
Guardsman, The (Molnár), 46
Guettel, Adam, 319
Guthrie, Woody, 133
Guys and Dolls (film), 244
Guys and Dolls (musical), 216, 226, 281
Gypsy, 287–89
Gypsy Jim, 25

"Habanera," 99
Hagman, Larry, 7, 211, 281
Hall, Juanita, 162, 166–67, 258, 262
Hallelujah, I'm a Bum (film), 108
Halliday, Richard, 7, 151–52, 154, 257–58, 268–70, 272–73, 277, 279–80, 284, 286, 288–89
Hamburger, Philip, 7, 31
Hamilton (Miranda), 6
Hamlet (Shakespeare), 194
Hammerstein, Alice (daughter), 25, 35, 101, 110–11, 180, 318–19
Hammerstein, Allie (mother), 16–17, 136
Hammerstein, Anna "Mousie" (stepmother), 18
Hammerstein, Arthur (uncle), 20, 22–23, 26, 124
Hammerstein, Dorothy Blanchard (second wife), 8, 38, 74, 135–36, 151, 180, 205, 221, 248, 274, 285, 290
    career of, 159, 177–79
    Carmen Jones and, 100
    Carousel and, 117, 119
    death of, 318
    Dorothy Rodgers and, 177–81
    King and I and, 180–82, 213
    marriage to Oscar, 32–34, 232–33
    Oklahoma and, 89–90
    on "Ol' Man River," 30
    Oscar's illness and death, 284, 290–94
    on relationship of Oscar and Rodgers, 207–8
    Rodgers's fiftieth birthday and, 214–15
    Sondheim and, 77
    Sound of Music and, 285
    South Pacific and, 156, 159, 164, 173
Hammerstein, James (son), 34, 77, 101,
159, 180, 208, 219, 264, 266, 273, 291, 316, 318
Hammerstein, Myra Finn (first wife), 20, 25, 27, 32–33, 35–37, 138
Hammerstein, Oscar, I (grandfather), 15–17, 22
Hammerstein, Oscar, II
    affairs and, 12, 232–33, 248
    Allegro and, 135–45, 290
    Andrews on, 320
    Annie Get Your Gun produced by, 126–32, 151
    awards, 34, 38, 104, 175, 203
    Bennett as orchestrator and, 87–89
    birth of, 15–16
    business acumen and, 2–3, 8–9, 12, 16, 18, 121–24
    Carmen Jones and, 98–102
    Carousel and, 106–19, 134
    Carousel filming and, 244–46
    childhood and early life in theater and, 15–22, 39, 41, 136–37
    children and, 12, 34–35, 77, 180
    Cinderella and, 1–5, 10–11, 248–52
    collaboration with Harbach, 23–28
    collaboration with Kern, 27–31, 35–38, 123, 137
    collaboration with Rodgers, begun with *Oklahoma!*, 6–7, 38, 64, 68–69
    collaboration with Rodgers, revived after *King and I*, 214–15
    collaboration with Romberg, 28, 32, 35, 137
    collaborative skill of, with Rodgers, 6–12
    death of, 291–96
    death of father and, 19
    death of Kern and, 128
    death of Lawrence and, 214
    death of mother and, 17–18
    decides on career in theater, 16
    de Mille and, 82–85
    depressions and, 8
    Desert Song with Harbach and Romberg and, 28, 32
    divorce from Myra and, 33–35, 37
    early failures of, 25
    early musical with Rodgers, *Up Stage and Down*, 42

Hammerstein, Oscar (*cont'd*)
"Edelweiss" as last lyric by, 286
education of, 8, 18–20
fame and, 235–36
FBI investigation of, 220
finances and, 80, 93, 101–2, 113–14, 147, 154, 170, 174–75, 195, 205, 234, 236, 260, 289
first lyrics by, for *Furs and Frills*, 20–21
first musical by, *Always You* with Stothart, 22–23
first play by, *The Light*, 21–22
Flower Drum Song and, 261–66, 290
Hamburger on, 7–8
Happy Birthday produced by, 132–33
Hart and, 18–19, 31, 44
health problems and, 263–64, 282–84, 286, 290–91
hit songs and, 37–38, 148
Hollywood and, 8, 35–38, 56
homes of, 25, 177
homes of, Doylestown farm, 38, 64, 71–72, 77, 98, 148, 156, 159, 291
homes of, Jamaica, 274, 289–90, 296
I Remember Mama produced by, 125
John Loves Mary produced by, 133
King and I and, 181–91, 195–97, 199–208, 211–14
King and I filming and, 243–44, 246–47
"Last Time I Saw Paris" written with Kern, 37–38
Lawrence and, 212–14
legacy and influence of, 2, 6–8, 12–13, 137, 314–20
Logan credit for *South Pacific* and, 171
on love and understanding, 177
lyric style of, 7–8, 24, 29–31, 71, 319–20
marriage to Dorothy Blanchard, 32–35, 164, 177, 179–80, 232–33, 292–93
marriage to Myra Finn, 20, 25, 32
Me and Juliet and, 215–20
meets Rodgers at Columbia Varsity Shows, 19, 42
memoir begun, 291
Michener share in *South Pacific* and, 170

Mielziner sues, 247
Music in the Air with Kern and, 36, 208–9
music publishing and, 122–23
New Moon with Romberg and, 35
Oklahoma! and, 68–76, 78–86, 89–93, 96–97, 134, 236
Oklahoma! filming and, 236–44
original books by, 137
performers and, 27
personality and appearance of, 9, 12, 15, 21, 231–32
Pipe Dream and, 226–28, 230–34
politics and, 9, 37, 133–34, 159, 184, 220–25
Porter on, 144
producing and, 124–25
racial prejudice theme and, 159–61, 172
recording contracts and, 123–24
Rodgers's fiftieth birthday party and, 214–15
Rodgers's relationship with, 16, 31, 39, 41, 203–8, 253, 255, 294–96
Rodgers's star billing over, 206–7
Rose-Marie with Harbach and, 26–27
Show Boat with Kern and, 6, 10, 28–31, 37, 90
Sondheim on, 18, 21, 29, 31, 77–78, 140, 143, 304, 308, 319–20
Sound of Music and, 268, 272–79, 282–83, 285, 287–90, 302
South Pacific and, 147–61, 164–68, 170–75, 184, 205, 210
South Pacific filming and, 256–60
State Fair film remake and, 102–4
Sunny River with Romberg and, 38
Sunny with Kern and Harbach and, 27–28
Sweet Adeline with Kern and, 34
television and, 248
television tribute to, 3, 240, 267
theatrical knowledge of, 6–7, 124
Three Sisters with Kern and, 36
Tickle Me with Harbach and, 23–24
Toast of the Town tribute to Rodgers and, 204
travels to Australia, 135–36
travels to England, 27, 32–33
travels to Paris, 27, 37–38, 65

on urban irony, 267
Variety ad and, 101–2
Very Warm for May with Kern and, 37
writing methods and routine of, 9, 23–28, 70–74
Hammerstein, Reginald (brother), 16–18, 126, 208
Hammerstein, William (son), 18, 25, 27, 35, 72, 90, 96, 100–101, 108, 123, 137, 180, 291, 311, 316, 318
Hammerstein, Willie (father), 16–19, 27
Hammond, John, 100
Haney, Carol, 262, 264–65
Hanff, Helene, 90
"Happiest House on the Block, The," 231
Happy Birthday (Loos), 132–33
"Happy Talk," 166
Happy Time, The, 298
Harbach, Otto, 23–24, 26–28
Harburg, E. Y., 30, 319
Harnick, Sheldon, 179, 308–9
Harrington, Donald Szantho, 293
Harrison, Ray, 140
Harrison, Rex, 181–82, 184–85, 225, 244
Hart, Dorothy, 98
Hart, Frieda, 43–44, 63
Hart, Lorenz, 6, 18–19, 30–31, 215, 220, 297, 319
    alcoholism and, 44, 48, 63, 67–68, 97–98, 124, 253
    background and personality of, 42–44, 47–48
    collaboration with Rodgers, 42–48, 51–64, 67–68, 103, 123, 206
    Connecticut Yankee and, 97–98
    death of, 97–98
    Dorothy Rodgers and, 55–56
    finances and, 52, 63
    Hammerstein on, 44
    Hollywood and, 56–59, 63
    homosexuality and, 44, 63
    jazz interpretations of, 306
    Liliom and, 105–6
    Love Me Tonight and, 78
    lyric style of, 43–44
    Oklahoma! and, 69, 91–92
    On Your Toes and, 60–61
    Pal Joey and, 61–63, 209

Rodgers on, 42–43
Rodgers's musical style and, 71
writing method and, 47–48, 51
Hart, Max, 43
Hart, Moss, 38, 59, 232, 254–55, 293
Hart, Theodore Van Wyck, 43, 98
Haver, June, 238
Hawkins, William, 143
Hawks, Nancy, 171
Hayes, Bill, 216–18
Hayes, Helen, 132–33, 173, 178, 225, 267, 287, 312
Haymes, Dick, 103
Hayward, Leland, 133, 146–48, 165, 171, 197, 268–70
Heart of the Matter, The (Greene), 208
Hecht, Ben, 178
Heggen, Thomas, 146, 156
Heidt, Joe, 90
Heine, Heinrich, 43
Helburn, Theresa, 46, 66–68, 78, 80–83, 86, 90, 93, 104–8, 113–14, 140
Hellman, Lillian, 125
"Hello, Young Lovers," 194, 196, 212
Hell's Angels (film), 56
Henderson, Amy, 123
Henderson, Florence, 7, 239–40, 310
Hepburn, Audrey, 302
Hepburn, Katharine, 257, 304
Herbert, Victor, 23, 41
"Here in My Arms," 47
Herman, William, 282
Hersey, John, 94–95
Heyward, Dorothy, 57
Heyward, DuBose, 57
High Noon (film), 237
Hiss, Alger, 222
Hitchcock, Alfred, 301
Hitler, Adolf, 37, 133, 223, 268
Holden, Stephen, 316
Holiday Inn (film), 94
Holliday, Judy, 91
Holloway, Sterling, 46
Hollywood, 8, 35–37, 63, 56–69, 63, 102–4, 236–37
    blacklist and, 221
Hollywood Anti-Nazi League, 37, 133, 223
Hollywood League for Democratic Action, 133

Holm, Celeste, 7, 79–80, 86, 94, 213
Holtzmann, David, 213
Holtzmann, Fanny, 181–83, 203, 213–14
Home, James, 19
"Home on the Range," 12
"Home Sweet Home," 72
Homolka, Oscar, 125
"Honey Bun," 158–59
Hong, Arabella, 262
Hoover, J. Edgar, 222, 225
Hornblow, Arthur, Jr., 237, 240, 242, 261
Horne, Marilyn, 246
Horowitz, Mark, 278
Hoschna, Karl, 23
Hotel Splendide (Bemelmans), 64
Hot Heiress, The (film), 56
House of Flowers, 297
House Un-American Activities Committee (HUAC), 221–22
Houston, Whitney, 252
"How Do You Solve a Problem Like Maria," 13, 276
Howdy Doody Show, 228
Hudson, Rock, 290
Hughes, Elinor, 118, 142, 285
Hughes, Howard, 56
Hunter, Jeffrey, 238
Hwang, David Henry, 265
Hyman, Harold, 18, 128, 135, 196–97, 293
Hytner, Nicholas, 316–17

"I Am Going to Like It Here," 263
Ibsen, Henrik, 45
"I Cain't Say No," 84, 86
"I Can't Give You Anything but Love," 126
"I Could Write a Book," 62
"I Do Not Know a Day I Did Not Love You," 307
I'd Rather Be Right, 59
"I Enjoy Being a Girl," 262
"If I Loved You," 108–9, 196
If I Were King, 45
"If I Weren't King," 251–52
"I Have Confidence," 302
"I Haven't Got a Worry in the World," 132
Imagem Music Group, 318–19

I Married an Angel, 60, 128
"I'm Gonna Wash That Man Right Outa My Hair," 158, 171–72
"Impossible," 250–51
Independent Citizens' Committee of the Arts, Sciences, and Professions, 133
"Indian Love Call," 151
Infants Relief Society, 42
Inge, William, 237
"In My Own Little Corner," 249
"Intermission Talk," 219–20
I Remember Mama (film), 125
I Remember Mama (musical), 11, 310–11
I Remember Mama (Van Druten play), 124–25, 185
Irving, George S., 11, 85
"Isn't It Kinda Fun," 103
"Isn't It Romantic?," 57
"It Might As Well Be Spring," 104
"It Takes All Kinds," 230
"I Whistle a Happy Tune," 2
"I Wish I Were in Love Again," 59

Jack Paar Show, The, 297
Jacobs, Lester, 37
Jacobs, Morris, 124
Jacobson, Henry, 32
Jacobson, Henry, Jr., 32, 231
Japanese Americans, 159, 262
Jazz à la Carte, 45
Jazz Singer, The (film), 35, 56
Jennings, Talbot, 184
Jimmie, 24
John Loves Mary, 133–34
Johnson, Bill, 228
Johnson, Christine, 116
Johnson, Van, 238
Joker Is Wild, The (film), 257
Jones, Shirley, 7, 238–41, 244–45
Jumbo, 59, 100
"June Is Bustin' Out All Over," 112

Kahn, Madeline, 307
Kapp, Jack, 123
Kaufman, George S., 38, 59, 121
Kaye, Danny, 307–8
Kazan, Elia, 106, 146, 186
Kean, Benjamin, 282–83, 292
Kelly, Gene, 61–62, 79, 262, 264, 301
Kennedy Center Honors, 310

Kenney, Ed, 262
Kenyon & Eckhardt, 2
Kern, Eva, 127
Kern, Jerome, 6, 9, 48, 88, 121, 126, 151, 320
  collaboration with Hammerstein, 27–31, 34–38, 123, 137
  death of, 127–28
  Green Grow the Lilacs and, 68
  Hart and, 44
  Rodgers and, 41
  Show Boat and, 28–31
Kerr, Deborah, 246
Kerr, John, 258
Kerr, Walter, 220, 234, 265, 287, 300, 312
Kikuchi, Yuriko, 194
Kiley, Richard, 298
Kilgallen, Dorothy, 232
King, Henry, 245
King and I, The, 2, 7, 287, 272
  Andrews on, 320
  ballet, 185, 193–94, 221
  cast and creative team, 182–87, 194–95, 207
  critics on, 197, 203
  decision to create, 180–84
  finances and, 185, 194–95, 211
  Hammerstein writes book and lyrics, 184, 187–91, 199–202, 207, 208
  Lawrence and, 182–84, 212–14
  Leonowens memoir and, 183–84
  Logan on, 196, 199
  London production, 237
  opening night, 202–3
  out-of-town tryouts, 196–99
  portrayal of Asia and, 316
  revivals, 306, 310, 317, 319
  Rodgers writes music, 187–88, 191–93, 199, 207–8
  success of, 203–4, 211–13
  Tony Awards and, 203
King and I, The (film), 244, 246–47, 256
  ballet music and, 246–47
  critics on, 247
Kingsberg, Malcolm, 242
Kirk, Lisa, 140–41
Kiss Me, Kate, 185, 209, 215, 228
Kitchen, Robert, 292
Knopf, Eddie, 294

Koch, Ed, 312
Kollek, Teddy, 312
Korean War, 224, 262
Kraft, Hy, 37, 221
Krasna, Norman, 133
Kresa, Helmy, 129
Kroll, Jack, 307

Ladd, D. M., 221–22
Lady Be Good (film), 38
"Lady Is a Tramp, The," 59–60
La La Land (film), 58
Lanchester, Elsa, 237
Landon, Margaret, 180–81, 184, 195
Lane, Burton, 304
Lang, Harold, 209
Lang, Walter, 104, 246
Langner, Lawrence, 46, 66–67, 80, 82–83, 86, 90, 93, 113, 119
Lasker, Albert, 174
Lasso, Orlando di, 280
"Last Time I Saw Paris, The," 38, 224, 251
Laurents, Arthur, 304–5
"Laurey Makes Up Her Mind," 83–84
Laurie, Piper, 238
Lawrence, Gertrude, 32, 181–85, 189, 196–99, 202–4, 211–14, 272
Layton, Joe, 289, 307
Lazar, Irving "Swifty," 289
Leachman, Cloris, 175
Leave It to Jane, 41
Leave It to Me, 78, 151
Leaves of Grass (Whitman), 293
Leavitt, Phillip, 42–44
Lee, Bill, 258
Lee, C. Y., 260–61
Lee, Gypsy Rose, 287
Lee, Peggy, 306
Leff, Lillian, 207–8
Lehman, Ernest, 301–2
Leigh, Janet, 53–54, 238
Lennon, John, 49
Leonowens, Anna, 183–84, 186
Lerner, Alan Jay, 3, 206, 228, 253, 304
Lester, Edwin, 152
Leuwerik, Ruth, 270
Levy, Jacob, 39–40
Levy, Newman, 206–7
Levy, Rachel, 39–40
Lido Lady, 54

Liebeneiner, Wolfgang, 270
Life magazine, 80, 143, 282
Life with Father (Lindsay and Crouse), 3, 270
Light, The, 22
Light in the Piazza, The (musical), 319
"Light in the Piazza, The" (Spencer story), 292, 319
Li'l Abner (musical), 3, 250
Liliom (film), 244
Liliom (Molnár), 105–7, 115. See also *Carousel*
Lillie, Beatrice, 32, 121
Lincoln Center Theater, 306, 317
Lindsay, Howard, 3, 251, 268, 270–73, 276, 281, 283, 287, 289, 293, 314
Lloyd Webber, Andrew, 318
Loeb, Gerald M., 112
Loesser, Frank, 226, 228, 281
Loewe, Frederick, 3, 98, 206, 253, 304
Logan, Joshua, 60, 128, 132–33, 205–6, 237, 262
  Allegro and, 141–42, 144, 290
  Annie Get Your Gun and, 128, 130–32, 151
  King and I and, 184, 191, 196, 199
  Pulitzer and, 175
  South Pacific and, 146–48, 154–58, 160–63, 165–73, 175, 184, 210–11, 256–60
Logan, Nedda, 146, 156, 169, 171, 258
Lombard, Carole, 122
London productions, 51–56, 175, 210–11, 228, 237, 288
"Lonely Goatherd, The," 280
Lonely Romeo, A, 44
"Lonely Room," 79
Long, William Ivey, 253
"Look for the Silver Lining," 27
Loos, Anita, 132–33
Los Angeles Civic Light Opera, 152
"Love Look Away," 264
"Lovely Night, A," 251
Love Me Tonight (film), 57–58, 78
"Lover Come Back to Me," 35
Lowell, Robert, 254
Luke, Key, 262
Lunt, Alfred, 46
Lute Song, 186–87
Lyon, Ben, 56

MacArthur, Douglas, 211, 224
MacDonald, Jeanette, 57
MacKenna, Kenneth, 146–47, 174
MacLaine, Shirley, 7, 220
MacRae, Gordon, 240, 244–45
Madame Butterfly (Puccini), 152
Magic of Todd-AO, The (film), 243
Magna Theatre Corporation, 237, 242
Mainstays of Maine (Coffin), 110–11
Main Street to Broadway (film), 206
"Make Believe," 10
Mama's Bank Account (Forbes), 124
Mamoulian, Rouben, 57–58, 78, 83, 85, 87, 113–14, 118, 244
Mandel, Frank, 24
"Manhattan," 46
"Man I Used to Be, The," 234
Mankiewicz, Herman, 18, 19
Mankiewicz, Joseph L., 181
Mantle, Burns, 38
"Many a New Day," 217
"March of Siamese Children, The," 207, 214
Marshall, Armina, 86, 93, 114, 119
Marshall, George C., 224
Marshall, Thurgood, 299
Martin, Ernest, 226, 228, 234
Martin, Hugh, 64
Martin, Mary, 207, 308
  Annie Get Your Gun and, 151–52, 267
  King and I and, 186, 199
  Oklahoma! and, 78
  Peter Pan and, 3, 267
  Sound of Music and, 7, 267–73, 281–84, 287–90
  South Pacific and, 7, 152–54, 156, 158–59, 163, 169–72, 175, 182, 199, 210–11, 257–58
  Tony Award, 289
Marvin, Lee, 238
Marx, Groucho, 9, 78
Marx, Harpo, 293
Mary Jane McKane, 25
Mary Poppins (film), 302–3
Masters of Melody (documentary), 47
Mayer, Louis B., 36
Mayes, Herbert, 287
McCall's magazine, 287
McCarten, John, 104, 260
McCartney, Paul, 49

McCormick, Myron, 158, 162, 175–76
McCracken, Joan, 217
McCrary, Tex, 174
McCullers, Carson, 228
McDonald, Audra, 317
McHugh, Jimmy, 126
McLeod, R. W. Scott, 223
McWhorter, Thomas, 172
Me and Juliet, 228, 237, 239–40
  cast and creative team, 215–17, 219
  critics on, 219–20, 225
  failure of, 253
  finances and, 215, 220
  Hammerstein on, 220
  opening night, 219–20
  written, 215–20
Meehan, Thomas, 311
Meet Me in St. Louis (film), 114
Melnick, Daniel, 229, 299
Melnick, Linda Rodgers. *See* Rodgers,
  Linda
Member of the Wedding (McCullers),
  228
Meredith, Burgess, 106
Merman, Ethel, 80, 126, 127, 131–32,
  134, 151, 225, 232, 287–89, 306,
  308
Merry Widow, The (Lehár), 26, 40, 306
Metro-Goldwyn-Mayer (MGM), 36,
  58, 82, 93, 114, 146–47, 174, 239,
  241
Metropolitan Opera, 16, 60, 116, 140,
  152, 228, 257, 312
Michener, James A., 147–52, 155, 157,
  159, 167, 173–74, 184, 262
  offered share of *South Pacific*, 170
Mielziner, Jo, 113, 117, 132, 139, 146,
  157, 162, 185, 188, 195, 215, 219,
  247, 258
Miller, Arthur, 235
Miller, Gilbert, 171
Miller, Marilyn, 27–28
Mineo, Sal, 7
Minnelli, Liza, 309
Miranda, Lin-Manuel, 6
Mister Roberts, 146–47, 156
Mitchell, Margaret, 121–22
Moen, Peter, 73, 93, 113
Molnár, Ferenc, 46, 105, 107–10,
  115–17, 119
Mongkut, King of Thailand, 180–81

Monroe, Marilyn, 186, 254
"Moon in My Window," 305
"Moon of My Delight," 52
Mordden, Ethan, 94
Morehouse, Ward, 120
Moreno, Rita, 246
"More Than Just a Friend," 297
Morris, William, 181
Morrow, Doretta, 196
Mortimer, Lee, 222
"Mountain Greenery," 51
Munson, Ona, 56
Musical Stages (Rodgers
  autobiography), 42, 45, 134, 145,
  220, 310
Music in the Air, 36, 128, 208–9
My Fair Lady, 3, 226, 228, 251,
  253
"My Favorite Things," 277–78, 280,
  304
My Favorite Things (Brubeck album),
  306
My Favorite Things (Dorothy Rodgers
  book), 179–80
"My Funny Valentine," 59
"My Heart Belongs to Daddy," 151
"My Heart Stood Still," 51–52
"My Time of Day," 281
"My Wife," 168

Nash, Ogden, 211
National Association for the
  Advancement of Colored People
  (NAACP), 224
National Committee to Win the Peace,
  222
National Negro Congress, 222
Native Americans, 131
Nazi Germany, 94, 269–70, 284–85
NBC TV, 3, 209, 267, 270, 306
Nelson, Gene, 239, 241
Nelson, Ralph, 4–5
New Haven Register, 87
Newman, Alfred, 246
Newman, Paul, 237–38
New Moon, The, 35
New Republic, 143, 203
Newsweek, 307–8
New Toys, 25
New York American, 31
New York Daily Mirror, 222

New York Daily News, 38, 92, 120, 143, 220

New Yorker, 7, 31, 37–38, 47–48, 61–63, 104, 173, 260, 265, 292

New York Evening World, 19, 27

New York Herald Tribune, 26, 31, 61, 92, 101, 141, 173, 220, 234, 259–60, 265, 287, 303

New York Post, 143, 173, 174, 287

New York State Federation of Women's Clubs, 94

New York Sun, 46

New York Times, 5, 23, 31, 62, 66, 68–69, 92, 120, 125, 131, 143, 148, 173, 203, 209, 243, 247, 265, 287, 300, 310, 312, 316–17

New York World-Telegram & Sun, 143, 252, 294

Nichols, Lewis, 120

Nietzsche, Friedrich, 100

Nimitz, Chester W., 80

Nimmo, James, 16–17

Nixon, Marni, 246

Nixon, Richard, 12, 210, 293

No, No, Nanette, 56

"No Other Love," 217–18

North by Northwest (film), 301

Norton, Elliot, 118, 142, 172, 233, 235, 285

No Strings, 298–300, 304, 306
  critics on, 300
  Tony Awards, 300
  written, 298–300

"No Way to Stop It," 280, 301

"Now Is the Time," 168

Nuyen, France, 258

Obama, Barack, 12

Odets, Clifford, 307

Of Thee I Sing, 175

Oh, Boy, 41

"Oh, What a Beautiful Mornin'," 2, 70–72, 91, 95, 242, 306

O'Hara, John, 61, 209

Oklahoma!, 2, 11, 13, 172, 185, 208, 217, 221, 226, 292
  ballet, 83–85, 89
  Bennett's orchestrations and, 88–89
  Carousel and, 110, 113
  cast and creative team, 78–86
  cast recording, 123–24

critics on, 87, 91–92, 316

de Mille and, 82–85

finances and, 80–82, 87, 92–93, 123–24

Hammerstein on, vs. *Show Boat*, 90

Hammerstein writes book and lyrics, 69–76

Hart bows out of, 68–69

Helburn proposes, 65–69

Hersey on, 94–95

opening night, 89–93

out-of-town tryouts, 86–89

Pulitzer Prize, 93, 175

revivals, 311–12, 318–19

revolutionary nature of, 6–7

rights and, 93, 236

Rodgers and Hammerstein agree to collaborate on, 68–69

Rodgers and Hammerstein writing method and, 69–72

Rodgers writes music, 76–77

South Pacific vs., 174

statehood idea and, 65, 81–82

Steinbeck on, 233

success of, 6, 89–97, 100, 106, 121, 124, 129, 134, 137

title, 90

touring company, 93, 114–15, 244

World War II and, 93–95

Oklahoma! (film), 262
  cast, 238–40, 243
  critics on, 243
  finances and, 239–40, 243
  Rodgers and Hammerstein produce, 236–44, 259

"Oklahoma" (song), 80–81, 87–89, 91

"Old Black Joe," 72

"Old Fashioned Wedding, An," 306

"Ol' Man River," 30, 72, 224

On a Clear Day You Can See Forever (Lerner & Lane), 304

Once Upon a Mattress (Mary Rodgers), 288

One Dam Thing After Another, 52

"One Foot, Other Foot," 137–38

O'Neill, Eugene, 24, 235

One Minute, Please, 42

"On the Sunny Side of the Street," 126

On the Town, 140

On the Waterfront (film), 239

On Your Toes, 6, 60–61

On Your Way, 19
"Operation Alligator" (Michener), 149,
    155, 258
"Ordinary Couple, An," 280, 302
Oregon Shakespeare Festival, 318
Osborn, Fairfield, 188
"Our Heroine" (Michener), 150,
    152
Our Town (Wilder), 135, 139, 143

Pajama Game, The, 262
Pal Joey, 6, 61–62, 209
Papp, Joseph, 4
Paramount Pictures, 36, 57, 236, 267,
    270
Peace Pirates, The, 19
Pearl Harbor, 38
Peggy-Ann, 51, 54
People's Songs, 133
"People Will Say We're in Love,"
    74–76, 87
Perlberg, William, 104
Peter Pan, 3, 267
Peters, Lauri, 289
Picnic (film), 256
Picnic (Inge play), 237
Pinza, Ezio, 152–54, 163–65, 171, 173,
    175, 182, 256–57
Pipe Dream
    critics on, 233–34
    failure of, 3, 234
    Steinbeck on, 234
    written, 226–31, 233–34, 241
Pittsburgh Post-Gazette, 183
Plummer, Christopher, 281, 302–3
Pomahac, Bruce, 50
Pop, 24
Porgy and Bess (musical), 78
Porgy (Heyward and Heyward play), 57
Porter, Cole, 30, 48, 78, 80, 88, 126,
    144, 151, 185, 270, 319
Potash, Shirley, 156
"Prelude to Ballet," 84
Prince, Harold, 173, 293, 308, 315
"Prince Is Giving a Ball, The," 249–50
Prude, Walter, 143
Puccini, Giacomo, 107, 152
Pulitzer Prize, 13, 93, 150, 175, 270
"Puzzlement, A," 189–90, 194, 197,
    211–12
Pygmalion (Shaw), 3

Queen O' Hearts, 24
Quinn, Anthony, 186

racial prejudice, 7, 29, 134, 147,
    151–52, 159–61, 172, 210, 262,
    298–300, 317
Radio Writers Guild, 221
Raitt, John, 7, 114–15, 267
Reagan, Ronald, 12, 133
"Real Nice Clambake, A," 111–12
Reinheimer, Howard, 32, 37, 121–22,
    148, 161–62, 170–71, 174–75,
    182, 195, 214, 223–24, 236, 273,
    275
"Remittance Man" (Michener), 150,
    155
Repairs Inc., 178–79
Republican Party, 222–23
Revuers, The, 91
Rex, 309–10
Reynolds, Debbie, 238
Riggs, Rollie Lynn, 65–66, 69–70,
    72–73, 76, 82, 148
Rio Rita, 32
Rittmann, Trude, 113, 162–67, 170,
    185, 194, 246–47, 276, 280
RKO, 36, 179
Robards, Jason, Jr., 238
Robbins, Jerome, 185, 193–94, 221,
    246
Roberts, Joan, 78, 80
Robeson, Essie, 172
Robeson, Paul, 133, 172
Robinson, Jackie, 160
Rockefeller, Nelson, 293
Rodeo (de Mille ballet), 83
Rodgers, Dorothy Belle Feiner (wife), 8,
    61, 264, 290, 309
    Berlin and, 129
    career of, 177–79
    Carousel and, 316–17
    children and, 56, 180
    death of, 318
    death of Richard and, 312
    Dorothy Hammerstein and, 177–81
    Hart and, 55–56, 58–59, 63–64, 98
    heart attack of, 308
    homes and, 69, 177
    I Remember Mama and, 125, 311
    King and I and, 180–81
    marriage to Richard, 53–56

Rodgers, Dorothy Belle Feiner (wife) (*cont'd*)
  Oklahoma and, 92
  publishes *My Favorite Things*, 179–80
  relationship of Rodgers and Hammerstein and, 207
  Richard's health problems and, 229, 253–55
Rodgers, Linda (daughter; *later* Melnick), 69, 76, 92, 180, 229, 254, 311, 319
Rodgers, Mamie Levy (mother), 39–40, 44
Rodgers, Mary (daughter), 56, 58, 69, 71, 76, 79, 92, 122, 125, 129, 173, 180, 229, 253, 288, 313, 316, 318–19
Rodgers, Morty (brother), 19, 40–42, 119, 229
Rodgers, Richard
  aging of, 264, 306–7, 310–11
  alcoholism and, 11–12, 253–54, 256, 305
  Allegro and, 135–36, 138, 140–41, 143–46
  Andrews on, 320
  Androcles and the Lion and, 306–7
  Annie Get Your Gun produced by, 126–32, 151
  autobiography *Musical Stages* and, 42, 45, 134, 145, 220, 310
  awards and, 104, 175, 203, 210, 300, 303, 310
  Bennett's orchestrations and, 87–89, 91, 210
  Berlin and, 128–31
  Bernstein on, 7
  birth of, 39
  Broadway debut *Lonely Romeo* with Hart and, 44–45
  business acumen and, 2–3, 8–9, 121–24
  Carousel and, 106–9, 113–20
  Carousel filming and, 244–46
  Carroll on, 299–300
  childhood and early life of, 8, 39–42
  on *Chorus Line*, 310
  Cinderella and, 1–5, 10–11, 248–53
  collaboration with Hammerstein, as conundrum, 8–9

collaboration with Hammerstein, begun with *Oklahoma*, 6–7, 38, 64, 67–72
collaboration with Hammerstein, revived after *King and I*, 214–15
collaboration with Harnick on *Rex*, 309–10
collaboration with Hart, 6, 42–48, 51–64, 67–68, 206
collaboration with Sondheim on *Do I Hear a Waltz?*, 304–6
collaborative skill of, with Hammerstein, 6–12
on commercial projects, 146
composing and work habits of, 9, 39, 76–77, 96, 319
composing method with Hammerstein and, 70–72
composing method with Hart and, 47–48
Connecticut Yankee revival with Hart and, 97–98
death of, 312–13
death of Hart and, 98
death of Hammerstein and, 291–92, 294–97
death of Lawrence and, 214
de Mille and, 82–85, 311–12
depressions and, 8, 11–12, 253–56, 260, 266
early collaboration with Hammerstein, *Up Stage and Down*, 42
early musical influences, 40–41
education of, 8, 45
Ewen on songwriting of, 7
on failure, 235
fame of, 235–36
fiftieth birthday party, 214–15
finances and, 9, 52, 63, 80, 93, 102, 113–14, 147, 154, 170, 174–75, 195, 205, 234, 236, 260, 289–90
first copyrighted song, 42
first meets Hammerstein at Columbia Varsity Show, 19
first musical, *One Minute Please*, 42
Flower Drum Song and, 261–66, 290
Garrick Gaieties with Hart and, 6, 45–47
Halliday and, 286

Hammerstein's political problems and, 221, 224–25
Hammerstein's relationship with, 16, 30–31, 203–8, 232, 296
Hammerstein vs., 308
Happy Birthday produced by, 132–33
on Hart's lyric writing, 30–31
health problems of, 40–41, 228–29, 233, 307, 309
Hersey on *Oklahoma!* and, 94–95
hit songs and, 148
Hollywood and, 8, 53, 56–59
homes of, 53, 69, 177–79, 254
I Remember Mama as last musical of, 11, 124–25, 310–12
jazz interpretations and, 306
King and I and, 181–88, 190–99, 202–8, 211–14
King and I filming and, 243–44, 246–47
Lawrence and, 196, 198–99, 213
legacy and influence of, 2, 6–8, 12–13, 314–20
Lerner and Loewe vs., 253
Logan's credit for *South Pacific* and, 161–62
London shows with Hart, 51–53
lyrics written by, 297–99, 307
marriage to Dorothy Feiner, 53–59, 177–80, 308, 311
Mary Rodgers on, 12, 313
Me and Juliet and, 215–20, 253
Mielziner sues, 247
musical style of, 48–50, 55, 71
music publishing and, 122–23
Music Theater of Lincoln Center led by, 306
No Strings with Taylor and, 298–300
Oklahoma! and, 65–69, 71, 75–88, 91–97, 99, 236, 311–12
Oklahoma! filming and, 236–44
On Your Toes with Hart and, 6, 60–61
Pal Joey with Hart and, 6, 61–63, 209
personality and appearance of, 9, 47–48, 207–8, 313
Pipe Dream and, 226–29, 233–34, 253
politics of, 9
Porter on, 144
producing and, 124–25

recording contracts and, 123–24
revivals and touring companies and, 315
Rittmann's arrangements and, 163–64, 194, 276
Sondheim and, 305, 308, 312
Sound of Music and, 268, 272–76, 279–81, 285–90, 308
Sound of Music filming and, 290, 300–303
South Pacific and, 147, 151–59, 161–62, 164–75, 205, 210
South Pacific filming and, 256–60
State Fair film remake and, 102–4, 297
success and, 45–47, 50–51, 93, 96–97
television tribute to, 3, 240, 267
theatrical knowledge of, 6, 124
Toast of the Town tribute and, 204–5
Two by Two and, 307–8
Victory at Sea score and, 209–10, 217
womanizing and, 12, 53, 54–55, 240, 307
Rodgers, Tily (aunt), 40
Rodgers, William Abraham (father), 25, 39–41
Rodgers and Hammerstein Fact Book, The, 206
Rodgers and Hammerstein firm, 50, 122–25, 309, 316, 318
  Annie Get Your Gun and, 126–32
  Happy Birthday and, 132–33
  I Remember Mama and, 124–25
  John Loves Mary and, 133
  sold, 318–19
  stops producing plays by others, 208
Rodgers and Hammerstein Pictures, 36–37
Rodgers and Hammerstein Songbook, The, 206–7
Rogers, Ginger, 312
Rogers, Will, 102–3
Romberg, Sigmund, 6, 28, 35, 122, 137, 203
Roosevelt, Eleanor, 98
Roosevelt, Franklin D., 59
Rose, Billy, 34, 59, 100, 141, 203, 208, 234
Rose-Marie, 26–27, 52
Rosenberg, Julius and Ethel, 222

Rowe, Clive, 316
Ruby, Harry, 282
Russell, Lillian, 43
Russell, Rosalind, 257
Ryan, Robert, 238

Salomon, Henry, 209–10
Sandburg, Carl, 23
Saratoga Trunk (Ferber), 64
Sardi, Vincent, Jr., 293
Sargeant, Winthrop, 50
Saroyan, William, 61, 79
Saturday Review, 134, 173
Savage, Archie, 172
Saxon, Luther, 100
Say It with Jazz, 45
Say Mama!, 45
Sayonara (film), 262
Schenck, Joseph, 237–39
Schrier, Morris, 171
Schubert, Franz, 79
Schumann, Robert, 71
Schuster, Max, 288
Schwartz, Jonathan, 319
Schwarzenegger, Arnold, 13
Screenwriters Guild, 221
Segal, Vivienne, 61, 97, 209
Selznick, David O., 18, 58
Selznick, Irene Mayer, 146
Selznick, Myron, 18
"Shall I Tell You What I Think of
     You?," 187–88
"Shall We Dance?," 200–201
Shamroy, Leon, 258–59
Sharaff, Irene, 185, 189, 194–95, 214,
     246
Shaw, George Bernard, 3, 45
Sher, Bartlett, 317
Sherwood, Robert E., 121
"Shine On, Harvest Moon," 24
Shipley, Ruth, 223
Short, Hassard, 100
Show Boat (Ferber novel), 28–30
Show Boat (film), 36
Show Boat (musical), 64, 90, 103, 162,
     175
   Oklahoma! and, 92
   revival, 127
   success of, 31, 137
   themes of, 6, 10, 28–31, 33, 37
Shribman, Joe, 232

Shribman, Owen, 232
Shriver, Maria, 13
Shubert brothers, 43, 82, 212
Sills, Beverly, 312
Simmons, Jean, 244
Simon, Henry, 206–7
Simon, Paul, 319
Simple Simon, 52–53, 55
Sinatra, Frank, 103, 237, 244–45, 257,
     312
"Sixteen Going on Seventeen," 283
Skin of Our Teeth, The (Wilder), 267
Skouras, George, 237, 239, 242–43
Skouras, Spyros, 289
Slaughter on Tenth Avenue (ballet),
     60–61
"Small House of Uncle Thomas, The,"
     194
Smith, Cecil, 144
Smith, Faye Elizabeth, 87
Smith, Muriel, 100, 258
Smith, Oliver, 240, 262
Snow White and the Seven Dwarfs, 53
Sobel, Ronald, 312
"So Far," 138
"Softly, as in a Morning Sunrise," 35
"Soliloquy," 115, 169, 196, 245
"So Long, Farewell," 279
"Some Enchanted Evening," 154,
     164–65, 171
"Someone to Watch over Me," 183
"Someone Will Teach You," 74–75
Something for the Boys, 80
"Something Good," 302
"Something Wonderful," 192–93
Sondheim, Herbert, 77
Sondheim, Janet Fox "Foxy", 77
Sondheim, Stephen, 18, 21, 29, 31, 159,
     170, 315
   Allegro and, 140–43
   on *Carousel*, 109, 117
   Company and, 308
   death of Hammerstein and, 291
   death of Rodgers and, 312
   Do I Hear a Waltz? and, 304–5
   Gypsy and, 287–88
   Hammerstein mentors, 77–78
   on Hammerstein and Rodgers, 207,
     296, 308
   on Hammerstein's lyrics, 319–20
   meets Harold Prince, 173

West Side Story and, 266
Song of the Flame, 28
"Song of the High Seas," 210
Sothern, Ann, 38
Sound of Music, The, 7, 12, 307
  cast and creative team, 281–82
  critics on, 285, 287–88
  film version vs., 301–2
  finances and, 286–90
  Hammerstein writes lyrics, 273–79,
    285–86
  Lindsay and Crouse write book,
    270–71, 273
  Maria von Trapp on, 280–81
  Martin and, 267–73
  opening night, 286–88
  original cast album, 288
  out-of-town tryouts, 284–86
  rehearsals, 282–84
  reputation of Rodgers and
    Hammerstein and, 314–15
  revivals, 318–19
  rights, 268–70
  Rodgers writes music, 273–76, 286
  Sister Gregory as advisor on, 271–72,
    276–77, 280–81
  success of, 288
  Timothy Crouse on, 314–15
  title, 271, 273, 275
  Tony Awards, 282, 289
Sound of Music, The (film) 280,
    300–303
  Academy Awards and, 303
  cast, 290, 302–3
  critics on, 303
  finances and, 289, 300–301, 303
  new songs for, 302
  script, 301–2
  soundtrack album, 303
  success of, 303
"Sound of Music, The" (song) 273–74,
    279, 302
South Pacific, 2, 7, 12, 239, 287
  awards, 175
  Bennett's orchestration and, 157, 163
  cast and creative team, 152–54,
    162–67, 182
  choreography, 165
  copyright, 162
  critics on, 172–73, 317
  as cultural phenomenon, 174–75

finances and, 3, 154, 162, 173–75
  Hammerstein writes book and lyrics,
    148–61, 166–67
  idea for, and Michener book, 146–47
  King and I and, 187, 195–96, 203
  Logan and, 155–56, 160–62, 165–67,
    170–71
  London production, 210–11, 217
  Martin and, 152–54, 271
  Michener offered share of, 170
  opening night, 173–75
  out-of-town tryouts, 165, 169–73
  portrayal of Southeast Asia and, 316
  racial theme and, 159–60, 320
  rehearsals and, 162–67
  revivals, 317, 319
  Rittman arrangements and, 162–67
  Rodgers writes music, 156–58
  Steinbeck on, 233
  success of, 173–77, 204–5
  touring company, 175, 217, 221,
    257–58
South Pacific (film)
  cast, 256–58
  critics on, 259–60
  finances and, 256, 260
  soundtrack album, 260
Spanish Civil War, 223
Spencer, Elizabeth, 292
Spencer, Natalie, 80
Springsteen, Bruce, 100
Stack, Robert, 238
Stanislavski, Konstantin, 128
Stanwyck, Barbara, 126–27
Star Is Born, A (film), 244
"Star-Spangled Banner, The," 12
State Department, 220, 223–24
"State Fair," 103–4
State Fair (film, 1945 remake)
  102–4, 224, 246
State Fair (film, 1961 remake), 290, 297
State of the Union, 270
Steele, Mary, 220
Steiger, Rod, 239
Stein, Jules, 179
Steinbeck, Elaine, 226
Steinbeck, John, 3, 208, 226–28,
    230–31, 233–34, 293
Stevens, Gary, 63
Stevens, George, 125
Stewart, James, 128

Stickney, Dorothy, 3, 5, 251
St. John, Betta, 162, 166–67
Stone, Peter, 307
Stoppard, Tom, 308
Storch, Larry, 262, 264
Story of the Trapp Family Singers, The (von Trapp), 269
Stothart, Herbert, 22, 24, 26, 28
"Stouthearted Men," 35
Stowe, Harriet Beecher, 194
Strasberg, Lee, 66
Strauss, Helen, 181–82, 195
Streetcar Named Desire, A (Williams), 146–47
Strindberg, August, 45
Stritch, Elaine, 209
Student Prince (Romberg), 28
Styne, Jule, 206
"Suddenly Lucky," 168, 199
Sullavan, Margaret, 128
Sullivan, Ed, 204–5, 234
Summertime (film), 257, 304
Sunny, 27–28
Sunny River, 38, 78, 96, 99, 101
Surrey Enterprises, 122
"Surrey with the Fringe on Top, The," 13, 76, 84, 91
Surtees, Robert, 241
Suzuki, Pat, 262
Swanson, Gloria, 211
Sweeney Todd (Sondheim), 315
Sweet Adeline, 34
"Sweetest Sounds, The," 298–99
Sweet Thursday (Steinbeck), 226–27, 234

Tabbert, William, 162
Tailor in the Chateau (Armont and Marchand), 57
Tales of the South Pacific (Michener), 184. See also *South Pacific*
    libretto adapted from, 147–53
    Pulitzer Prize, 150
Talmadge, Norma, 179
Tammany Hall, 43
Taubman, Howard, 300
Taylor, Deems, 209
Taylor, Elizabeth, 257, 300
Taylor, James, 319
Taylor, Samuel, 298
Tea and Sympathy (film), 258

Temple, Shirley, 78
Temple Bells, 45
"Ten Cents a Dance," 53
Ten Commandments, The (film), 211
Terris, Norma, 175
Texas, Temple, 232, 248, 262
"Thanksgiving Follies," 158
"That's For Me," 103
"That Terrific Rainbow," 62
Theatre Arts magazine, 144
Theatre Guild, 45–47, 57, 124
    Allegro and, 135–36
    Carousel and, 104–7, 113–15, 244
    Oklahoma! and, 66–69, 78–82, 85–87, 93, 100, 148, 236
"Theme of the Fast Carriers," 210
"There Is Nothin' Like a Dame," 2, 165
"There's Always Room for One More," 42
"There's No Business Like Show Business," 130, 132
"They Didn't Believe Me," 27
"They Say It's Wonderful," 130–31
This Is the Army (Berlin), 128–29
"This Nearly Was Mine," 169
Thomas, Danny, 238
Thompson, Jim, 194
Three Sisters, 36, 101
Tickle Me, 23–24
Time, 131, 143, 233, 246
Time of the Cuckoo, The (Laurents), 304
Time of Your Life, The (Saroyan), 61, 79
Tinney, Frank, 23–24
"Tired Businessman, The," 26
Toast of the Town (TV show), 204
Tobacco Road (Caldwell), 72–73
Todd, Michael, 80, 86–87, 127, 236–37
Todd-AO, 236–37, 241, 258–59
Together with Music (TV special), 267
"To Keep My Love Alive," 97
Tolson, Clyde, 222
"Tom and I," 189–91
Tone, Franchot, 66
Tony Awards, 13, 175, 203, 282, 289, 300, 319
Too Many Girls, 60
Tormé, Mel, 116–17
Town & Country magazine, 214
Tozzi, Giorgio, 257

Trapp Family Singers, 267–69, 301; *see also* von Trapp
Traubel, Helen, 228
"Tree in the Park, A," 51
"Trolley Song, The," 114
Truman, Harry S., 224
Twain, Mark, 52
20th Century Fox, 102–3, 181, 185, 195, 244–47, 256, 289, 300
"Twin Soliloquies," 152–54, 163
Two by Two
    critics on, 307–8
    written, 307–8, 310
Tyler, Judy, 228
Tynan, Kenneth, 265, 287

Ullmann, Liv, 311
Umeki, Miyoshi, 262, 264
Uncle Tom's Cabin (Stowe), 185, 194
"Under the Southern Cross," 210, 217
United American Spanish Aid Committee, 222
United Negro College Fund, 224
U.S. Navy, Distinguished Public Service Award, 210
U.S. Senate Subcommittee on Internal Security, 222
U.S. Supreme Court, 225
Universal Pictures, 290
University Players, 19, 128
Up Stage and Down, 42

Valentino, Rudolph, 28
Valiant Years, The (documentary), 297
Van Druten, John, 125, 185, 188–89, 191, 202–3, 208, 212, 217
Van Heusen, James, 206
Van Horne, Harriet, 252
Variety, 37, 101, 248, 287
Varsity Show, 8, 19–20, 41–43
"Venus," 43
Verrett, Shirley, 312
Very Good Eddie, 41
Very Warm for May, 37, 96, 101, 208
Veterans of the Abraham Lincoln Brigade, 223
Victory at Sea (documentary)
    awards, 210
    Rodgers score, 209–10, 217
Vidor, King, 53
Viennese Nights (film), 35

Vietnam War, 315–16
Voice of the Turtle, The (Van Druten), 125
Voight, Jon, 289
von Trapp, Georg von, 269
von Trapp, Maria Augusta von, 268–70, 280–82, 287, 293

Wagner, Richard, 209
Wagner, Robert F., 294
"Waiting," 197
"Wake Up, Little Theater," 217
Walker, Don, 113, 206, 215–16
Wallach, Eli, 238
Walston, Ray, 217, 258
"Waltz for a Ball," 249
Warner, Jack, 35, 56, 290
Warner Bros., 35, 56, 64, 181, 240, 244
War Production Board, 98
Warren, Harry, 206
Warren, Leslie, 252
Warrior's Husband, The (Thompson), 67
Wasner, Franz, 269
Wasserman, Herman, 71
Wasserman, Lew, 171
Watanabe, Eleanor "Doodie," 159
Watanabe, Jennifer Blanchard, 159
Watanabe, Jerry, 159
Watch on the Rhine (Hellman), 125
Watts, Richard, Jr., 143, 173
"Way You Look Tonight, The," 126
Weaver, Sylvester "Pat," 209
Weill, Kurt, 109
Weingart Institute, 18, 41
"We Kiss in a Shadow," 192
Welcome House agency, 159
"Western People Funny," 197–98
West Side Story (film), 301
West Side Story (musical), 266, 304
"What's the Use of Wondrin'?," 114
"When You're Driving Through the Moonlight," 251
"Where or When," 59
Where's Charley?, 226
White, Miles, 78
"White Christmas," 94, 130
"Who," 28
"Why, Why, Why," 197
Whyte, Jerry, 86, 292
Wickes, Mary, 311

Wilder, Alec, 48–49
Wilder, Billy, 173, 301
Wilder, Thornton, 134–35, 235, 267
Wildflower, 24
Wild Rose, The, 28
Wild West Show, 6, 17, 126
Wilk, Max, 94
William Morris Agency, 181
Williams, Emlyn, 171
Williams, Molly, 171
Williams, Tennessee, 146, 235
Williamson, Nicol, 310
Williamson Music, 122–23
Winchell, Walter, 92–93, 170, 232
Winkle Town, 46
Winnie the Pooh (film), 46
Winninger, Charls, 103
Winters, Shelley, 7
Wise, Robert, 301–2
Wizard of Oz, The (film), 61
Wodehouse, P. G., 41
"Wonderful Guy, A," 156, 169–72
Wonderful Town, 250, 260
Wood, Grant, 78, 192
Woodward, Joanne, 238
Woollcott, Alexander, 46
Words and Music, 53
World Federalist Movement, 134, 184, 224, 293
World of Suzie Wong, The (Osborn), 265

World War I, 21–22, 28, 155
World War II, 12, 69, 94, 103, 106, 119–20, 124–25, 133, 146, 148, 159, 174, 178, 184, 186, 194, 209, 221, 262, 268–69
Wright, Martha, 175
Writers Board for World Government, 134
Writers' War Board, 133, 159
Wyler, William, 301
Wynn, Ed, 52

Yellen, Sherman, 310
"Yesterday," 49
"You Are Never Away," 138, 141
"You Can't Get a Feller with a Gun," 129
You'd Be Surprised, 45
You'll Never Know, 45
"You'll Never Walk Alone," 2, 12, 115–17, 225
"Younger Than Springtime," 168
You're in Love, 20

Zanuck, Darryl, 102–3, 182, 185, 244–45, 301
Zanuck, Richard, 301
Ziegfeld, Florenz, 28, 31, 129
Ziegfeld Follies, 24
Zinnemann, Fred, 237–43, 245, 259
Zinsser, William, 49, 259–60